Japanese Morphophonemics

Linguistic Inquiry Monographs
Samuel Jay Keyser, general editor

Japanese Morphophonemics   Junko Ito and Armin Mester

Markedness and Word Structure

The MIT Press
Cambridge, Massachusetts
London, England

This book was set in Times New Roman on 3B2 by Asco Typesetters, Hong Kong, and was printed and bound in the United States of America.

Library of Congress Cataloging-in-Publication Data

Ito, Junko.
  Japanese morphophonemics : markedness and word structure / Junko Ito and Armin Mester.
    p.   cm. — (Linguistic inquiry monographs ; 41)
  Includes bibliographical references and index.
  ISBN 0-262-09036-8 (hc. : alk. paper) — ISBN 0-262-59023-9 (pbk. : alk. paper)
  1. Japanese language—Morphophonemics. 2. Japanese language—Phonology. I. Mester, Armin. II. Title. III. Series.
PL558.9.I76   2003
495.6′15—dc21   2003045909

10 9 8 7 6 5 4 3 2 1

Contents

Series Foreword

We are pleased to present the forty-first in the series *Linguistic Inquiry Monographs*. These monographs present new and original research beyond the scope of the article. We hope they will benefit our field by bringing to it perspectives that will stimulate further research and insight.

Originally published in limited edition, the *Linguistic Inquiry Monographs* are now more widely available. This change is due to the great interest engendered by the series and by the needs of a growing readership. The editors thank the readers for their support and welcome suggestions about future directions for the series.

Samuel Jay Keyser
for the Editorial Board

Acknowledgments

This research was partially supported by Faculty Senate grants from the University of California at Santa Cruz and by the National Science Foundation under grant SBR-9510868. The completion of the book was made possible by our year-long research sabbatical (spring 2001–winter 2002) in Kyoto, Japan, and at Kobe University, which was funded by a Japan Foundation fellowship to the first author and a research fellowship from the Japan Society for the Promotion of Science to the second author. (The authors' names appear in alphabetical order.) For making it possible for us to focus on this project during 2001–2002, we would like to thank our colleagues in the Department of Linguistics at UC Santa Cruz; and for guidance and support throughout this project, we are indebted to Professors Shosuke Haraguchi and Osamu Fujimura.

Part of this research was first presented at the 1996 Kobe Phonology Forum hosted by the Phonological Society of Japan (Ito and Mester 1996a) and at the 1996 Western Conference on Linguistics (WECOL) at UC Santa Cruz. Later presentational venues included colloquia at the universities of Tübingen, Marburg, and Stuttgart, Rutgers University, Tsukuba University, Indiana University, and Advanced Telecommunications Research Institute International (ATR; Kyoto, Japan); the Scandinavian Summer School in Phonology (Hvalfjorður, Iceland, 1997); the Berkeley Analogy Workshop (UC Berkeley, 1997); Landelijke Onderzoekschool Taalwetenschap (LOT; Utrecht, The Netherlands, 1998); North-eastern Linguistics Society 31 (NELS 31 Georgetown University, 2000); the International Conference on Phonology and Morphology (Hankuk University, Korea, 2001); the Optimality Theory Workshop (Meikai University, Urayasu, Japan, 2001); and the Linguistic Society of America/Deutsche Gesellschaft für Sprachwissenschaft (LSA/DGFS) Summer School in Linguistics (Düsseldorf, Germany, 2002). We are grateful to the audiences and participants at these presentations for helpful comments and suggestions.

For comments on an earlier written version of this book (Ito and Mester 1998), we wish to thank two anonymous reviewers as well as John Alderete, Erik Baković, Caroline Féry, René Kager, Haruo Kubozono, Kazutaka Kurisu, John McCarthy,

Jaye Padgett, Joe Pater, Alan Prince, Paul Smolensky, Philip Spaelti, Keiichiro Suzuki, Koichi Tateishi, Adam Ussishkin, Rachel Walker, and Moira Yip. For helpful and detailed comments on the final version, we are indebted to three anonymous reviewers and to Haruo Kubozono, Linda Lombardi, and Timothy Vance.

We benefited from many discussions in class lectures and informal research group meetings at UC Santa Cruz, and we are grateful to our colleague Jaye Padgett, to our students and research visitors, and to the Santa Cruz phonology community for extensive advice and constructive criticism. During our sabbatical year 2001–2002, the free-spirited monthly meetings of the Phonological Association in Kansai afforded us many an opportunity to settle data questions and test ideas in discussions with our fellow PAIKers, including Haruka Fukazawa, Itsue Kawagoe, Mafuyu Kitahara, Haruo Kubozono, Kazutaka Kurisu, Harold Kusters, Francis Matsui, Akio Nasu, Kohei Nishimura, Philip Spaelti, Shin'ichi Tanaka, Isao Ueda, Noriko Yamane, Yuko Yoshida, and Hideki Zamma (with apologies to those whose names we may have left out).

Last, but not least, thanks to Haruo Kubozono for crucial support in planning our research sabbaticals in Japan and for many informal research meetings on issues relating to the material dealt with here. We are indebted to him for granting us much of his precious time and for sharing with us his understanding of Japanese accentology and of many other aspects of Japanese phonology and phonetics.

Two people left us as we were engaged in this research, Anna Hüske and Shizue Ito. We dedicate this work to their memory.

Chapter 1

Introduction

つれづれなるままに、日くらし、
硯にむかひて、心に移りゆくよしなし事を、
そこはかとなく書きつくれば、
あやしうこそものぐるほしけれ。

—吉田兼好「徒然草」

What a strange, demented feeling it gives me
when I realize I have spent whole days before this inkstone,
with nothing better to do, jotting down at random
whatever nonsensical thoughts have entered my head.

—Kenko, *Tsurezuregusa*

The sound pattern of Japanese, with its characteristic pitch accent system and rich segmental alternations, has provided important evidence at crucial points throughout the development of modern phonological theory. To take a few examples, Bloch 1950 and Martin 1952 were milestones in the development of structuralist phonemics, McCawley 1968 marked a high point in classical generative phonology, and the comprehensive treatment in Haraguchi 1977 of the pitch accent systems found in Japanese dialects was instrumental in establishing nonlinear phonology as the mainstream framework.

The last decade has seen the rise of Optimality Theory (OT), a new conception of a generative grammar, and especially of its phonological component, that is built directly on the often conflicting demands of different grammatical principles and incorporates a specific kind of optimization as the means of resolving such conflicts. Inaugurated in Prince and Smolensky 1993 (see Kager 1999 for a textbook introduction, and McCarthy 2002b for an overview and key references), OT is a constraint-based theory minimizing the role of the phonological derivation. The burden of explanation is instead shifted to strictly output-based markedness constraints, working in tandem with a class of input-output (and other) faithfulness constraints. For a given input, an OT grammar selects, as the output, the best among a large field of conceivable alternative candidates. In response to the highly conflicting nature of phonological constraints, an OT grammar imposes a strict rank order of importance on the total set of constraints. Unlike traditional generative grammars, whose output is a form that passes all constraints, in selecting a winning candidate OT does not require perfection (i.e., no violations whatsoever—an impossibility in a world of multiply conflicting demands), but optimality (i.e., minimization of violations).

Since the fundamental shift of perspective connected with OT casts a fresh light on many of the processes, alternations, and generalizations about sound patterns that are the traditional subject matter of phonology, it seems appropriate to submit central issues of Japanese phonology to renewed scrutiny. Within traditional Japanese philology—from the classic work of Moto'ori Norinaga in the eighteenth century to the work of the first Western scholar to make a lasting contribution, Benjamin Lyman (1894)—the distribution of voiced and voiceless consonants, as well as alternations involving the two classes, such as the morphophonemic process inserting a distinctive obstruent voicing mark at the juncture of compounds, has always occupied center stage. It also figures prominently in the earliest studies in modern phonology (see Martin 1952), and interest has continued in the generative era (e.g., McCawley 1968; Otsu 1980; Ito and Mester 1986; Mester and Ito 1989). Here we revisit this class of phenomena in a comprehensive way from an OT-based perspective, with the goal of advancing understanding of Japanese phonology and, at the same time, of the theoretical framework itself, as it is brought to bear on a substantive class of facts and generalizations.

The central analytical thread of this book is thus the interweaving of descriptive and theoretical issues surrounding the voicing phonology of Japanese. In pursuing both well-known and less-explored issues in this area, we hope that an OT approach not only provides new solutions to old puzzles, but also raises interesting new questions for both descriptive and theoretical research.

1.1 The Phonology of Voicing in Japanese: Alternations and Distributional Patterns

Three core issues surround obstruent voicing in Japanese, and they arise in different domains of increasing size: (1) morphemes (the restriction against multiple obstruent voicing in native Japanese morphemes), (2) simplex compounds (the morphophonemic voicing process at compound junctures), and (3) long compounds (voicing patterns in embedded compounds). Two subsidiary issues concern differences that arise through (4) diachronic changes and (5) lexical stratification. We briefly explicate these here, noting the chapter(s) in which the discussion primarily takes place.

1. The native morpheme structure restriction limits obstruent voicing to one occurrence per morpheme. Thus, *kita* (no voiced obstruents) as well as *kaze* and *gake* (one

voiced obstruent) are licit (and existing) native morphemes ('north', 'wind', and 'cliff', respectively), but strings like *gaze* and *gage* are not. Primary analysis of the morpheme structure restriction is found in chapter 2, but the restriction plays a role throughout the book.

2. The compound voicing process *rendaku* affects the second member in a compound, requiring its initial segment to be voiced. Thus, *kami* 'paper' voices in the compound *hari gami* 'poster paper'. When *rendaku* interacts with the morpheme structure restriction just described, the voicing alternation is blocked, as in *kita kaze* 'north wind' (**kita-gaze*) (this restriction on *rendaku* voicing is traditionally known as *Lyman's Law*). The basic analysis is presented in chapter 4, with important extensions in chapter 7.

3. In longer compounds, *rendaku* voicing may apply iteratively, affecting all non-initial members, such as *samasi* 'awaken' and *tokee* 'clock' in *me-zamasi-dokee* 'alarm clock, lit. eye-opening clock'. What is important here is the internal structure of the compound. In left-branching compounds, those that can be thought of as being gradually built up by adding a simplex word at the end (e.g., **me**, *me*-**zamasi**, *me-zamasi*-**dokee**), voicing applies to all noninitial members. However, when a simplex word is added at the beginning (**hasi**, **huna**-*basi*, **nisi**-*huna-basi* 'western boat-bridge'), the situation is different. Whenever a compound contains another compound as a noninitial member, the embedded compound does not accept *rendaku* voicing on its initial segment. Given the complexity of the phenomena involved, all ingredients of the analysis need to be in place before the special behavior of such long compounds can be taken up; they are therefore discussed in the last chapter of the book, chapter 8.

These three interrelated topics constitute the descriptive core of the book. Two other topics, diachronic variation and lexical stratification, are more loosely connected, but they interact with the first three in crucial ways.

4. Evidence from Old Japanese (known as the *strong version of Lyman's Law*), viewed together with the situation in the modern language, casts further light on the scope and domain of voicing dissimilation. Chapter 5 offers a principled account of the hitherto unexplained differences between the workings of Lyman's Law voicing dissimilation in Modern and Old Japanese. Some remaining analytical issues are taken up in chapter 7.

5. The voicing pattern in Japanese affects mostly native forms, and also has both systematic and idiosyncratic exceptions (as is typical of morphophonemic processes in general). This issue is taken up in chapter 2 for the morpheme structure restriction and in chapter 4 for compound voicing. Chapter 6 presents a systematic overview and analysis of the phonological lexicon in Japanese as it relates to voicing and stratification.

Beyond voicing, issues treated with some degree of analysis include dissimilative degemination (section 3.1.2), deaccentuation (section 3.2), and the establishment of accentual domains (section 8.4.2). Beyond Japanese, topics discussed in some detail include Sanskrit aspiration (sections 2.1 and 2.2) and reduplication (section 3.3.4), Latin degemination (section 3.1.1) and lateral dissimilation (section 3.3.3), and Dutch and German coda devoicing (sections 2.2.2 and 8.4.1).

1.2   Overview of Theoretical Issues

The theoretical issues involved in formal analysis of the voicing interactions outlined above, and the attendant complexities, are necessarily multifaceted. We will have occasion to explore in depth some of the major issues in current OT, and to touch on several less central—yet important—aspects of phonological theory.

Although the issues are interconnected and intersect at many points, they can be broadly categorized as primarily dealing with one of the three components of an OT grammar: markedness, faithfulness, and the interface between phonology and other parts of grammar.

1.2.1   Markedness Thresholds

Throughout this book, we give serious (and formal) attention to conjoined markedness constraints, including self-conjoined markedness constraints. In chapter 2, we lay the theoretical groundwork by presenting the theory of local constraint conjunction, starting with Smolensky's (1993, 1995, 1997) work and extending the details of the proposal in certain directions. In particular, we argue for a markedness-based conception of the Obligatory Contour Principle (OCP). Partially building on previous work (Ito and Mester 1996a, 1998; Alderete 1997; Suzuki 1998), we show how an OT conception of phonology makes it possible to understand the OCP as *multiply violated markedness*. Rather than being an irreducible principle affecting representations, it emerges as a natural by-product of simple run-of-the-mill phonological markedness constraints and the fundamental OT notion of multiple violations.

The core ideas are these: (i) OCP effects obtain when a *given marked type of structure* is present *more than once*, (ii) multiple violations of the same markedness constraint clustered in the same local domain do not simply add up, but interact more strongly, so that a double violation is worse than the sum of two individual violations, and (iii) this notion of violation enhancement can be formally expressed by means of *self-conjunction of constraints*.

Besides applying in cases previously analyzed as OCP effects (such as the morpheme-internal dissimilation of aspirates in Sanskrit), self-conjoined constraints have uses in other areas, such as degemination and deaccentuation. We explore a novel use of self-conjunction in chapter 8, where a violation of a self-conjoined interface constraint anchoring morphological to prosodic categories accounts for the complex behavior of compounds differing in their internal constituent structure. A different type of conjoined constraint, involving a sequential markedness constraint and a faithfulness constraint and penalizing devoicing in a voiced environment, plays an important role in chapter 7.

A central challenge for constraint conjunction theory is to find a general principle assigning each conjunction its proper local domain, and this question receives an additional twist in the case of self-conjunctions. In chapter 5, we make a specific proposal and show that it provides the key, together with a proper understanding of phonological and morphological domains, for a principled understanding of the development of voicing dissimilation patterns in the historical phonology of Japanese.

1.2.2 Varieties of Faithfulness

While markedness constraints are traditional elements of phonological theory, faithfulness constraints are the central innovation of OT. The specific conception of an input-output accounting system encoded in these constraints is the theory's strength (and also its Achilles' heel, as skeptics have not failed to notice; see, e.g., Chomsky 1995). Not surprisingly, to a significant extent the development of OT has been the development of its faithfulness component, with "containment theory" giving way to "correspondence theory," and with further extensions such as "output-output constraints," "positional faithfulness," "sympathy," and even "antifaithfulness," which are all localized within the faithfulness component (for references, too numerous to be included here, see Kager 1999 and McCarthy 2002b). We will have occasion to touch on many of these issues in varying degrees of detail, and two of them, lexically stratified faithfulness and symmetric/asymmetric faithfulness constraints, are the focus of chapters 6 and 7, respectively.

Pursuing what it means in OT for a phonological restriction to be limited to a particular lexical stratum (e.g., native words vs. loanwords), in chapter 6 we draw some general conclusions regarding the way the faithfulness component gives rise to such variation within the lexicon. The basic idea is to use the resources of correspondence theory (McCarthy and Prince 1995) to make faithfulness constraints and constraint families (such as IDENT) specific to particular lexical strata. We show that stratum-specific input-output faithfulness constraints are not only descriptively able to account for the multilayered organization of a language's lexicon, but also successful in capturing higher-level implicational relations between nativization processes, thus deriving the existence of a core-periphery structure in the lexicon from basic tenets of OT.

In chapter 7, we take up a more formally oriented question regarding the basic symmetry or asymmetry of faithfulness constraint families such as IDENT, as it relates to a specific issue in the phonology of voicing in Japanese (compensatory devoicing). Comparing various approaches (faithfulness conjunction, special/general faithfulness, markedness-enhanced faithfulness), we discuss and elaborate on previous arguments relating to the issues of "majority rule" and harmonic completeness. A recurring theme in the book is the overlap found in markedness-based approaches and faithfulness-based approaches, ranging from those involving base-reduplicant correspondence in Sanskrit (section 3.3.4) to output-output correspondence in complex compounds in Japanese (section 8.1.2). We examine the pros and cons of positional faithfulness and its positional markedness counterpart for prosodic word-initial position in Japanese (section 8.3.2). We also extensively discuss and compare approaches to coda devoicing, a prime case of both positional (onset) faithfulness and positional (coda) markedness (section 2.2.2), giving some evidence in favor of the latter (section 8.4.1).

1.2.3   Exponence and Anchoring

A proper understanding of morphophonemic phenomena requires access to their phonological content as well as to their grammatical (morphological and syntactic) properties and constituency. In traditional descriptions of such processes, a mixture of phonological and grammatical predicates are used to capture the phenomena, such as phonological voicing at certain types of grammatical/morphological junctures (compound junctures, junctures of nonbranching morphological constituents, etc.).

In output-oriented OT, the existence of a phonological exponent realizing a morphological element is enforced by the constraint REALIZE-MORPHEME, which, as we argue in chapter 4, plays a crucial role in the Japanese compound-voicing phenomena. The basic idea is to do equal justice to the formal-morphological and the substantive-phonological sides of things by dividing the labor between morphology and phonology. Placement of the feature-sized linking morpheme at certain compound junctures is the responsibility of morphology, its surface realization that of phonology.

Also important in this regard are the constraints involved in mapping grammatical structure to phonological constituent structure. Along with economy-driven structure assignment, these interface constraints, requiring the anchoring of grammatical edges to appropriate prosodic edges, are vital prerequisites for the proper analysis of complex compound structures discussed in chapter 8.

1.3   Notation and Romanization

In this section, we present background material regarding the way we transliterate Japanese examples in this book and how they are pronounced. For those unfamiliar with the language, the comparison charts with International Phonetic Alphabet (IPA) equivalents will simultaneously provide a brief introduction to the automatic allophonic processes of Japanese. For phonetic details, see Vance 1987; for phonological and morphophonemic arguments, see McCawley 1968 and Ito and Mester 1995b.

For the purposes of this study, with its focus on morphophonemic processes, an IPA-based phonetic transcription would be counterproductive since a host of irrelevant and distracting allophonic details would obscure the basic patterns under discussion. For this reason, and in order to not stray too far from the standards accepted in Japan and elsewhere, it is convenient to employ a transliteration based on phonemic principles.

Our usage largely follows the Kunrei system of romanization (with some modifications; see below), defined as ISO-3602 (1989-09-0) by the International Organization for Standardization.[1] As indicated below, the Kunrei romanization differs in several points from the Hepburn romanization, which is overtly based on English orthography, linguistically unsystematic, and less suitable for our purposes.[2] For words and names that are well established in English, however, we will use their familiar spelling in the text (i.e., ⟨Tokyo⟩ instead of ⟨tookyoo⟩, ⟨Kunrei⟩ instead of ⟨Kunree⟩, etc.).

1.3.1 Vowels

Standard Japanese has a five-vowel system, with a phonemic length contrast. Vowel length is indicated by doubling the vowel symbol.

(1) *Short and long vowels*

Romanization		IPA equivalent	
a	aa	a	aː
e	ee	ɛ	ɛː
i	ii	i	iː
o	oo	ɔ	ɔː
u	uu	u	uː

• The high back vowel [u] is commonly described as unrounded and often transcribed as [ɯ].

• In the ISO and Kunrei systems, long vowels are diacritically marked by ˆ (*gakkô* 'school', etc.), except for the long mid front vowel [ɛː], which is rendered as ⟨ei⟩ (*sensei* 'teacher', etc.). In the interest of a simple and at the same time uniform transcription, we instead use orthographic gemination (*gakkoo, sensee,* etc.) and distinguish tautosyllabic long vowels from heterosyllabic vowel-vowel sequences by ⟨'⟩ (*satooya* 'sugar shop' vs. *sato'oya* 'foster parent', etc.).

1.3.2 Consonants
All consonants, except for glides, are either plain or palatal(ized).

(2) *Plain consonants*

		Romanization					IPA equivalent				
Obstruents	Voiceless	p	t	s	k	h	p	t	s	k	h
	Voiced	b	d	z	g		b	d	d͡z/z	g	
Sonorants	Nasal	m	n				m	n			
	Nonnasal	w	r	y			w	ɾ	j		

• [d͡z] and [z] do not contrast in the modern language, and both are romanized as ⟨z⟩. The fricative [z] is usually found intervocalically, the affricate [d͡z] elsewhere.

(3) *Palatalized consonants*

		Romanization					IPA equivalent				
Obstruents	Voiceless	py	ty	sy	ky	hy	pʲ	t͡ʃ	ʃ	kʲ	ç
	Voiced	by		zy	gy		bʲ	d͡ʒ/ʒ		gʲ	
Sonorants	Nasal	my	ny				mʲ	ɲ			
	Nonnasal		ry					ɾʲ			

• The affricate/fricative contrast [t͡ʃ]/[ʃ] is neutralized for their voiced counterparts; that is, both correspond to a single phoneme romanized as ⟨zy⟩. Like the corresponding plain consonant in (2), the latter is described as always affricated in careful pronunciation ([d͡ʒ]), and sometimes deaffricated to [ʒ] intervocalically.
• For most speakers, [t͡ʃ], [ʃ], [ʒ] are more accurately transcribed as prepalatal [t͡ɕ], [ɕ], [ʑ].
• Hepburn romanization resorts to English orthographic practice (⟨ch⟩, ⟨sh⟩, ⟨j⟩ for ⟨ty⟩, ⟨sy⟩, ⟨zy⟩) in these cases.

1.3.3 Coda Consonants
There are only two kinds of codas in Japanese, obstruent codas and nasal codas. The former exist only as first parts of geminates and are indicated as double consonants (4). The latter fall into two types, nasal glides (5a) and nasal stops followed by homorganic stops (5b), both of which are romanized as ⟨n⟩.

(4) *Coda obstruents*

Romanization	IPA equivalent	Example	
pp	pː	toppuu	'sudden wind'
ppy	pʲː	happyoo	'announcement'
tt	tː	batta	'grasshopper'
tty	t͡ʃː	pittyaa	'pitcher'
ss	sː	hossori	'thinly'

Romanization	IPA equivalent	Example	
ssy	ʃː	hassya	'departure'
kk	kː	makka	'shining red'
kky .	kʲː	takkyuu	'table tennis'

· Voiced geminates are found in the foreign vocabulary only, as in *baggu*, *beddo*, *bazzi* (often nativized with voiceless geminates).

· Double [h] is found in foreign names, approximating voiceless velar fricatives (e.g., *bahha* 'Bach' and *gohho* 'van Gogh').

(5) *Coda nasals*

    a. ⟨n⟩ in coda position not followed by a stop (oral or nasal) stands for a nasal glide [N] without consonantal place of articulation (see Trigo 1988).

Romanization	IPA equivalent	Example	
n	N	hon	'book, true'
nw	Nw	honwari	'main (sumo) match'
ny	Nj	honya	'bookstore'
ns	Ns	honsai	'main wife'
nsy	Nʃ	honsya	'main company'
nh	Nh	yonhon	'four pieces'

    b. ⟨n⟩ in coda position followed by a stop (oral or nasal) stands for a nasal consonant homorganic to the following consonant.

Romanization	IPA equivalent	Example	
np	mp	honpoo	'basic salary'
nb	mb	honbun	'main text'
nm	mm	honmono	'real thing'
nt	nt	honten	'main branch'
nd	nd	hondai	'main issue'
nn	nn	honnen	'current year'
nt	nt͡s	kantuu	'pass through'
nz	nd͡z	honzuri	'final printing'
nty	ɲt͡ʃ	hontyoosi	'normal key'
nzy	ɲd͡ʒ	kanzya	'patients'
nk	ŋk	honkyoku	'head office'
ng	ŋg	hongoku	'own country'

• In juncturally ambiguous segment combinations, the marker ⟨'⟩ is used for purposes of disambiguation, indicating syllabifications deviating from normal coda-onset assignment.

Romanization	IPA equivalent	Gloss
ani	a.ni	'brother'
an'i	aɴ.i	'easy, easy-going'
kanyuu	kaɴ.juu	'persuade, canvass'
kannyuu	kan.nʲuu	'sinking, caving in'
ka'nyuu	ka.nʲuu	'join, become a member'

1.3.4 Automatic Allophonic Alternations

Automatic allophonic alternations are not indicated in the Kunrei romanization (just as aspiration of syllable-initial consonants, for instance, has no place in phonemic transcriptions of English).

(6) *Palatalization before [i]*

	Romanization	IPA equivalent
Accompanied by	si	ʃi
place shift	zi	ʒi
	ti	t͡ʃi
	ni	ɲi
	hi	çi
No change in	pi	pʲi
major place	gi	gʲi
	etc.	etc.

• Anterior coronals before [i] in recent loans, such as [tʲi], [dʲi], are indicated by diacritic ⟨'⟩ (e.g., *d'innaa paat'ii* 'dinner party').

(7) *Changes before [u]*

	Romanization	IPA equivalent
Affrication	tu	t͡su
Labialization	hu	ɸu

• In the foreign stratum, [t͡s] and [ɸ] are found in positions before vowels other than [u] (e.g., *tsaito* 'Zeit', *faito* 'fight', *firumu* 'film').
• Hepburn romanization employs ⟨ts⟩ and ⟨f⟩ even where they are positional variants of /t/ and /h/, with ⟨tsu⟩, ⟨fu⟩ for ⟨tu⟩, ⟨hu⟩.

1.3.5 Morphophonemic Voiced/Voiceless Pairings
A list of the nonobvious voiced/voiceless pairings is given for coronals in (8) and for labials in (9), with examples of morphophonemic voicing alternations.

(8) *Coronal fricatives and affricates*

Romanization	IPA equivalent	Example	
si	ʃi	sika	'deer'
zi	ʒi/d͡ʒi	ko-zika	'child-deer, fawn'
ti	t͡ʃi	tikara	'strength'
zi	ʒi/d͡ʒi	baka-zikara	'fool's strength'
sy	ʃ	syasin	'picture'
zy	ʒ/d͡ʒ	kao-zyasin	'face-photo, portrait'
ty	t͡ʃ	tyawan	'cup'
zy	ʒ/d͡ʒ	yunomi-zyawan	'drinking cup'
su	su	susi	'sushi'
zu	zu/d͡zu	maki-zusi	'rolled sushi'
tu	t͡su	tuki	'moon'
zu	zu/d͡zu	mika-zuki	'crescent moon'

(9) *[h]~[p]~[b] series*

Romanization	IPA equivalent	Example	
ho	ho	ni-hon	'two (long) objects'
po	po	ip-pon	'one (long) object'
bo	bo	san-bon	'three (long) objects'
hi	çi	ni-hiki	'two animals'
pi	pi	ip-piki	'one animal'
bi	bi	san-biki	'three animals'
hu	ɸu	ni-hun	'two minutes'
pu	pu	ip-pun	'one minute'
bu	bu	san-pun	'three minutes'

Chapter 2

Obligatory Contour Principle
Effects and Markedness
Thresholds

A well-known restriction on morphemes in Sanskrit, an ancient Indo-European language of India, limits the number of aspirated consonants to one. Thus, there are monoaspirate CVC$^\mathrm{ɦ}$ (1a) and C$^\mathrm{ɦ}$VC (1b) roots, but no diaspirate *C$^\mathrm{ɦ}$VC$^\mathrm{ɦ}$ (1c) roots.[1]

(1) *Grassmann's Law in Sanskrit as an OCP effect on the aspiration tier*

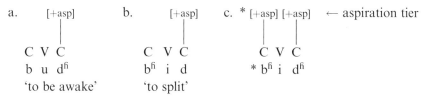

This restriction is often referred to as *Grassmann's Law*, with reference to the sound change that gave rise to it, deaspirating the first of two successive aspirates in a certain domain. The effects of this change separate the members of the Indo-Iranian subfamily (as well as Greek, where a similar change took place) from the rest of the Indo-European language family. In the synchronic phonology of Sanskrit, the ban against diaspirate roots is connected to the "aspiration throwback" alternation found with roots of the form CVC$^\mathrm{ɦ}$ (1a) when their root-final aspirate devoices in some context and becomes unable to maintain the voiced aspiration feature. The feature then appears instead on the initial consonant (schematically, /bud$^\mathrm{ɦ}$ . . . / → [b$^\mathrm{ɦ}$ut . . .]). The effects even extend into reduplication, resulting in the deaspiration of all reduplicated aspirates.[2]

Grassmann's Law is a simple instance of a crosslinguistically richly attested type of dissimilative restriction targeting the repeated occurrence of specific features or groups of features, including aspiration, egressive and ingressive airstream mechanisms, consonantal place of articulation, and so on (see Clements and Hume 1995 for an overview and references). How should phonology express the fact that (1c) is ruled out as a Sanskrit root, while (1a) and (1b) are admitted? And how can it do so in a systematic way that brings out the connections between this case and the many similar patterns of dissimilation found crosslinguistically? The classical autosegmentalist program is virtually built on the idea that all such questions are, in the final analysis, questions of representation. This exclusive focus on phonological representation as the medium of explanation (see McCarthy 1988 for a clear statement of the autosegmentalist credo) is its strength, from a formal point of view, but also its major weakness and limitation, as we will show.

In the autosegmentalist conception, (1c) is ruled out because it violates a constraint on representations. Two identical specifications—here, "[+aspirated] [+aspirated]"—are adjacent on the aspiration tier within the domain of the root. This violates the Obligatory Contour Principle (OCP), which is formulated in (2).

(2) *Autosegmental Obligatory Contour Principle*

Adjacent identical elements are prohibited on an autosegmental tier.

More generally, the autosegmental OCP bans representations of the schematic form (3), where identical feature specifications occur in two locations within some domain (such as "root"). Crucially, X_2 and X_4 are each linked to a separate [αF] specification, and the intervening X_3 bears no specification for [F]. What the autosegmental OCP encourages, to avoid the repeated occurrence of [αF], is either dissimilation of one or the other bearer of [αF], as in (3a), where X_4 has switched its value for F (resulting in a "contour" for this feature), or multiple linking of a single [αF] specification (3b).[3] While whole-scale segment deletion as in (3c) is sporadically found as an alternative to dissimilation,[4] still other kinds of repair, such as inserting a [−αF] buffer specification (3d) to break the tier adjacency of the two [αF] segments, are formally easy to conceive but rarely if ever found (see Archangeli 1986 on Nyangumarda vowels as a possible example).

(3) *OCP violation*

[αF]   [αF]   ← [F] tier

X_1 X_2 X_3 X_4 X_5

Repair by

a. Dissimilation   b. Fusion

[−αF] [αF]   [αF]

X_1 X_2 X_3 X_4 X_5 X_1 X_2 X_3 X_4 X_5

c. Deletion   d. Insertion

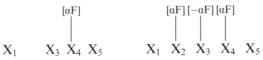

[αF]   [αF] [−αF] [αF]

X_1 X_3 X_4 X_5 X_1 X_2 X_3 X_4 X_5

The autosegmental representation incorporates a distinction between two kinds of adjacency in phonology (for discussion, see Archangeli and Pulleyblank 1987; Myers 1987; Odden 1994):

- segment adjacency (of the X slots in (3)), and
- tier adjacency (of the two [αF] specifications in (3) on the [F] tier).

Tier adjacency is the central concept in classical autosegmental theory, with its overarching goal of reducing apparent action-at-a-distance to local interaction. As long as nothing intervenes on the [F] tier, two identical [F] specifications in some domain count as adjacent, no matter how many X slots intervene between their bearers. It is in this way that the autosegmental OCP allows a locality-preserving representation of seemingly distant dissimilation processes involving features of nonadjacent segments, such as the [αF] specifications in (3).

For the autosegmental explanation of the Grassmann's Law effect in (1c) to succeed, it must be ensured that the two specifications involved "see" each other; in other words, it is imperative that the intervening segments not be specified for the feature [aspirated]. Underspecification is therefore a crucial prerequisite of such analyses, and representations such as (4) must not appear at the stage of the derivation where OCP-triggered dissimilation takes place.

(4) *Full specification for [asp]*

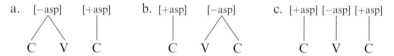

The need to rule out fully specified representations such as (4) leads to an essentially privative mode of representation, where only marked properties are indicated at the relevant stage, while their unmarked counterparts are left unrepresented.[5] Besides ensuring the transparency of "irrelevant" (qua later-inserted) intervening specifications, underspecification has the benefit of correctly predicting a broad typological generalization. Dissimilation predominantly affects marked (qua always-specified), not unmarked (qua as-yet-unspecified), values of features. In the case at hand, as in many similar ones, this allows two unaspirated stops to co-occur within a Sanskrit root, as in *pitár* 'father' with unaspirated [p] and [t]. The OCP restriction, while stated for the feature [aspirated] in general, is de facto limited to [+aspirated] elements. More generally, OCP-driven dissimilation targets marked features only, and this prediction obtains as long as application of the OCP is restricted to the featurally sparse early stages of the derivation, where underspecification is enforced on the relevant tiers. Correspondingly, the OCP is usually taken to have been "turned off" by the time representations are fully specified; otherwise, dissimilations affecting marked and unmarked values alike (voiced and voiceless, glottalized and nonglottalized, etc.) are predicted, a situation usually not found in natural languages.

The Sanskrit example illustrates two important points about the autosegmental OCP and its tier-based view of dissimilation. First, it crucially presupposes a derivation with separate stages that differ in degree of specification. Second, its basic mode of explanation is representational locality—the literal adjacency of the dissimilating pair of feature specifications on an autosegmental tier. To turn this vision into a workable theory, a host of additional assumptions are necessary about phonological representations and the specification of features. The simplicity of the statement of the autosegmental OCP itself obscures the less desirable details of the representational assumptions, which do not come cost-free. They include feature-geometric separation of feature groups,[6] very specific legislation about what to keep underspecified and until when, with carefully calibrated default mechanisms filling in features and feature values at specific points in the derivation,[7] not to mention still further ramifications of the representationalist approach, such as segregating the phonological content of each morpheme onto a separate tier.[8] Parts of this theoretical framework enjoyed independent support and led to interesting new discoveries, but others were less successful in this respect. Many of the subtheories (such as the various versions of underspecification theory) were fraught with problems and conflicts of their own, and the internal consistency of the overall edifice remained elusive.

Pursuing a new approach to dissimilation within OT, in this chapter we develop a model directly driven by markedness (section 2.1), formally implemented by means of constraint conjunction (section 2.2). On the empirical side, we begin our study of the morphophonemics of voicing in Japanese by looking closely at, and developing a formal OT analysis of, the morpheme structure restriction that limits obstruent voicing in native morphemes to a single occurrence (section 2.3).

2.1 Toward a New Understanding of Obligatory Contour Principle Effects

2.1.1 Dissimilation and Markedness

There is little question that dissimilation of identicals is to a significant extent grounded in markedness. Thus, the fact that voiced aspirates are in some cases limited to one occurrence per domain cannot be unrelated to the fact that such segments present phonetic difficulties. Plain voiceless consonants do not present similar difficulties and are therefore rarely, if ever, subject to such co-occurrence restrictions. If pure identity avoidance were the driving force behind dissimilation, irrespective of all markedness factors, such contrasting behavior would make no sense.

The autosegmental tier-based OCP attempts to give formal expression to this basic typological generalization, but it captures the grounding in markedness indirectly, namely, by means of underspecification. All feature specifications except for marked ones are absent at the relevant stage of the derivation (see the earlier discussion). It is natural to ask whether there is a more direct and more principled way of grounding dissimilation in markedness. The question receives additional urgency in OT since here a crucial prerequisite of the traditional conception has fallen by the wayside. The existence of an early underspecified stage of the derivation is hard to secure in a framework whose central tenet ("richness of the base") holds that inputs are free, not subject to any constraints (such as obligatory absence of all redundant or even all predictable specifications), and which has shifted the burden of explanation away from the derivation and sequence of operations of traditional linguistic theory to parallelist devices. Various hybrid conceptions are possible and conceivably have some merit,[9] but it is difficult to see how they could restore underspecificationism to its previous role.

The central claim in this chapter is that OCP effects like Grassmann's Law in Sanskrit are not connected to markedness in a roundabout way, through representation and underspecification, but instead are directly explained by the markedness constraints themselves, once the constraints and their interactive patterns, including local self-interactions, are properly understood. The basis of explanation is plain segmental markedness constraints like those in (5), which are neither new nor specific to OT. In some form or another, virtually every model of phonology makes crucial appeal to these central markedness factors, which are grounded in the physiological, acoustic, and perceptual properties of speech. In OT phonology, markedness constraints are cognitive representations of these factors within the grammar, making them computable within the overall system of interacting and competing constraints.

(5) *Segmental markedness constraints*

    a. *[+asp, +cons, −son, −cont]   "No aspirated plosives."
    b. *[+asp]   "No aspirated segments."
    c. *[+glot, +cons]   "No implosive or ejective consonants."
    d. *[+nas, −cons]   "No nasalized vowels or glides."
    e. *[+voi, −son]   "No voiced obstruents."
    f. *[V, −back, −high, +round]   "No nonhigh front rounded vowels."

Constraint (5a), while ruling out [+aspirated] (or [+spread glottis]) plosives, admits [h, ɦ]. It holds for phonological representations in languages such as Polish and Lardil that lack distinctively aspirated segments ([pʰ], [tʰ], etc);[10] it is violated in Hindi and Korean, where such segments exist and systematically contrast with unaspirated obstruents. Constraint (5b), a stricter version of the aspiration ban, is obeyed in languages such as French that lack aspirated segments altogether (i.e., including [h]) and is violated in most other languages, including Finnish and Arabic. Constraint (5c) rules out supralaryngeally articulated [+glottalized] (or "[+constricted glottis]") segments. It is observed in Italian, a language without ejectives ([kʔ], [tʔ], etc.) or implosives ([ɓ], [ɗ], etc.); it is violated, for example, in Navajo. Constraint (5d) holds in Indonesian and Quechua, languages without distinctive nasal vowels ([ã], [ĩ], etc.), and is violated in Portuguese and Dakota. Constraint (5e) is observed in Yokuts, which lacks voiced obstruents ([b], [d], [z], etc.), and is violated in Yoruba and English. Constraint (5f) holds in Albanian and Mandarin Chinese, which do not possess nonhigh front rounded vowels ([ø], [œ]), and is violated in Finnish and French.

The formulations in (5) make use of a conservative set of binary distinctive features, in the tradition of Jakobson 1939 and subsequent work. While any specific choice carries implications, we hope that, mutatis mutandis, privative and other conceptions can be substituted. Our formulations are not intended to advocate any particular theory of the features in terms of which markedness constraints should be expressed, but leave things open with respect to many questions—such as the specific distinctive feature system chosen, whether or not a richer set of phonetic properties should be accessible to direct phonological control (see Steriade 1995a and related work), or, at the other end of the spectrum, whether more abstract components constitute a superior set of elements for phonological analysis (e.g., Harris 1994). The important point is that, in some form or other, statements like those in (5) are essential ingredients of any viable framework for phonological analysis that has been proposed. The general form of these statements, cast in the form of constraints, is given in (6), where *feature combination* includes any nonempty set of feature specifications, from singleton sets to multimember combinations.

(6) No-φ: "The feature combination φ is prohibited, where φ = [αF₁, ..., αF_n], the F_i are distinctive features, and α, β ∈ {+, −}."

This chapter investigates to what extent OCP violations can be understood not as being due to some specific constraint on representations, but simply as local crossings of a markedness threshold. The idea is best illustrated by taking up the Sanskrit example, this time without any presumption that values for the feature [aspirated] need to remain unspecified wherever they are predictable (e.g., in vowels).

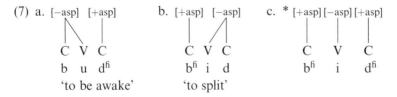

In containing a single aspirate, (7a) and (7b) each violate the markedness constraint (5b) once. On the other hand, in containing two aspirates, (7c) violates the markedness constraint (5b) twice, and the two violations are clustered in the same root. This fact alone stamps their co-occurrence as local, and there is no direct need for the symbolic representations of the two laryngeal aspiration gestures to be adjacent on a tier. In (7), the two [+aspirated] specifications are in fact not adjacent, but separated by [−aspirated].[11]

Many of the dissimilation phenomena traditionally characterized as OCP effects involve nothing beyond the repeated occurrence, in a small domain, of elements sharing identical specifications. This opens up an interesting and in some respects radical perspective. The finely articulated geometrical representations of feature structure, configured so as to make the dissimilating properties literally adjacent on some tier(s), might be unnecessary representational baggage, carried over without critical scrutiny from an earlier theory and analysis whose tenets and assumptions are meanwhile eroded.

2.1.2 Markedness Thresholds

In the line of explanation just sketched, the Sanskrit aspiration example involves asserting the existence of a critical threshold of markedness admitting, within a given domain (here, "morpheme"), one [+aspirated] segment (7a,b), but not two (7c). This kind of approach makes use only of what phonological theory is already known to possess, in anyone's understanding: markedness constraints and a set of domains (morphological and prosodic). In this respect, it has an immediate advantage of simplicity and directness over many actual or conceivable alternatives that require extra assumptions, and it commands our attention for this reason alone. And while it remains to be seen whether the simple markedness threshold idea can cover all the phenomena that the autosegmental and underspecificationist OCP has been called upon to explain, the basic model is surprisingly successful in accounting for a significant class of cases.[12]

The intuitive idea of a markedness threshold can be formally developed as follows. A candidate root with a single aspirate violates the markedness constraint No-C^h once. This is acceptable and indeed preferred to deaspiration; that is, No-C^h is ranked lower than the antagonistic feature faithfulness constraint IDENT, which militates against any changes in aspiration properties (8).

(8) F: IDENT

      M: No-C^h

A candidate root with two aspirates, on the other hand, violates No-C^h twice, triggering a violation of an enhanced markedness constraint M$^+$ as in (9) (more on this below). M$^+$ ranks above faithfulness, which makes it impossible for potential diaspirate roots like [b^{h}id^h] to ever reach the surface. Deaspiration of one of the aspirates will always be preferred.

(9) *Basic model of OCP dissimilation (preliminary version)*

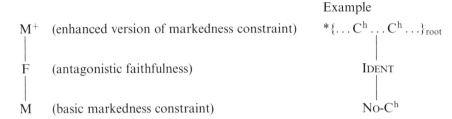

In this model, assessing co-occurrence restrictions involving identical features such as aspiration and similar OCP effects is a matter of computing markedness within a domain, a task an OT grammar is fully equipped to handle. It thus no longer necessitates (and motivates) a mode of representation where the identical features are adjacent on an autosegmental tier. To the extent that no other obvious benefit flows from a continued commitment to the goal of reducing all cases of co-occurrence restrictions to some kind of representational adjacency of specifications,[13] it is an advantage of the markedness threshold approach that it depends neither on specific geometrical models of feature structure nor on particular assumptions about the underspecification of unmarked or redundant feature values. It is rather an output condition on fully specified phonological representations such as (7c), which shows no adjacent [+aspirated] specifications since the intervening sonorants carry their [−aspirated] specifications.

The gist of our proposal, expressed in a preliminary way in (9) by the distinction between M^+ and M, is that the combined weight of two *φ-marks clustering within a given local domain such as a root (violations of a markedness constraint against the structure φ) exceeds that of the sum of two individual *φ-marks penalizing violations that are not locally clustered. This distinction is, we claim, one of the central sources of dissimilatory phenomena like Grassmann's Law in Sanskrit. As pointed out earlier, it is reasonable to leave open the possibility that additional factors are at work in specific cases of dissimilation, calling for an expansion of the approach. What commands attention is the remarkable fact that the simple markedness threshold model in (9) is fully capable of dealing with a significant range of cases without additional machinery.

2.2 Local Constraint Conjunction

Our next step is to probe the nature of the threshold constraint M^+, especially its relation to the basic markedness constraint M and its ranking with respect to it. What is needed is a formal expression of the intuitive idea that M^+ is in some way an "enhanced version" of M. The diagram in (9) illustrates the minimal route of direct stipulation, placing a whole new series $\{M^+\}$ of matching (while formally unrelated) enhanced markedness constraints next to the basic series $\{M\}$ of elementary markedness constraints. Stipulations of this kind hold little interest, however, and one would hope to be able to do better within a theory equipped with a minimum amount of deductive structure. What is needed is a general method of projecting $\{M^+\}$ on the basis of $\{M\}$. Many such methods are in principle possible, and they are well worth exploring, given how little is known at present about the internal structure of the constraint set that OT grammars are built on.

Building on our own earlier work as well as that of others (Ito and Mester 1996a, 1998; Alderete 1997; Suzuki 1998), we will here cast our model in terms of constraint conjunction (as first developed by Smolensky (1993, 1995, 1997)). Conceived of as an operation in Universal Grammar (UG), this is perhaps the most well established method within current OT for deriving complex constraints by combining basic constraints.[14] Anticipating our main result, we will formally interpret a double violation of a constraint C in some domain δ as constituting, in addition, a violation of a separate and higher-ranking constraint $C^2{}_\delta = C\&_\delta C$, the so-called local self-conjunction of C in domain δ. Postponing discussion of further issues, ramifications, and problems until chapter 3, we start by introducing the essentials of constraint conjunction theory and by showing how it gives formal expression to markedness thresholds. We then develop a detailed case study of an OCP-type co-occurrence restriction involving obstruent voicing in Japanese (section 2.3).

2.2.1 Defining Local Conjunction

OT phonology is based on a set $Con = \{C_1, C_2, \ldots, C_n\}$ of constraints that are taken to be universal, either in virtue of being innate, or in virtue of being projected uniformly across the species on the basis of more fundamental factors (the choice is not relevant to present concerns, and current knowledge offers little to resolve the issue). What matters is that Con is shared by all grammars and forms the basis of OT ranking and computation; it is in this sense that UG contains the set Con. Following Prince and Smolensky (1993), further structure defined on the set is generally assumed to be part of UG: constraints are grouped into constraint families, rankings within certain families are taken to be predictable on the basis of substantive factors and hence fixed, and so on. The theory of constraint conjunction asserts that in addition to these specific structures and relations, UG contains a general operation of *local conjunction* defined on the set Con. This operation introduces a new way in which individual grammars can differ, over and above the ranking they impose on the set of basic constraints—namely, in making use of combined constraints.

Combined constraints are produced by local conjunction of basic UG constraints (or, if recursive application is allowed, of other combined constraints). They allow grammars to capture a type of constraint interaction that is attested in the phonologies of natural languages but cannot be obtained in a theory exclusively built on direct strict domination. Consider a grammar where two constraints, C_1 and C_2 (whose relative ranking is immaterial), are both dominated by a third constraint A, as in (10).

(10) A
      |
      $\{C_1, C_2\}$

Under the regime of direct strict domination, a candidate violating both C_1 and C_2 but fulfilling A is more harmonic than a candidate violating only A, even though the former has two violations and the latter only one. As depicted in (11) in tableau form, under no circumstances can any number of violations of lower-ranking constraints "gang up" against even a single violation of one higher-ranking constraint.

(11) *The strictness of strict domination*

	A	C_1	C_2
▶ candidate$_1$		*	*
candidate$_2$	*!		

This is the celebrated strictness of strict domination, whose empirical and conceptual merits are laid out in Prince and Smolensky 1993, the foundational work on OT, and in the subsequent literature. Given (10), it is unavoidable that candidate$_1$, with two violation marks ($*C_1$, $*C_2$), wins over candidate$_2$, with only one violation mark ($*A$).

However, two types of considerations give reason to pause. First, it is a natural idea to give the constraint set *Con* internal structure, beyond that of a bare set of basic constraints $\{C_1, C_2, \ldots, C_n\}$. In particular, there is need for a systematic way of forming complex constraints out of simple ones, beyond the "harmonic alignment" mechanism introduced by Prince and Smolensky (1993) in the context of their analysis of Berber syllabification. Having a way of forming complex constraints out of simple ones keeps constraints from proliferating without proper analysis of their relations. It also imposes a useful network of derivational relations on the set of constraints that can be used to find a general way of predicting invariant ranking relationships (we will return to this point later with a concrete example). Once constraint combinations of some form are admitted, such as a combination of C_1 and C_2 in (10), the question arises whether anything of a general nature can be said about the ranking of such constraint combinations. As we will show, this has consequences for the spirit, if not the letter, of strict domination.

A second type of consideration, of a more directly empirical nature and in principle independent of the first, concerns the strict domination principle itself. It turns out that it sometimes overshoots the mark, by removing from the competition precisely the candidate that emerges as the correct output in the real world. The problem can be localized in a particular type of situation (we will study a concrete example below) where, even though violations of A are still fatal when compared with violations of C_1 and C_2 individually, a simultaneous violation of C_1 and C_2 within a local domain δ (the "worst-of-the-worst" case) weighs more heavily than a violation of A.

Local constraint conjunction is a way of achieving the desired result while continuing to observe the letter of strict domination. The idea is to turn the "worst-of-the-worst" case into a new constraint by itself, which can then be ranked separately in individual grammars. Restating Smolensky's proposal (see Smolensky 1995, 1997) for our purposes, we define a general operation of local constraint conjunction in (12).[15] It is an operation on the constraint set provided by UG that individual grammars make use of to form composite constraints.

(12) *Definition of local conjunction*

Let C_1, C_2 be constraints and δ be a (phonological or morphological) domain (segment, syllable, foot, prosodic word, ...; root, stem, morphological word, ...). Local conjunction is an operation "&" mapping the triplet (C_1, C_2, δ) into the locally conjoined constraint denoted by $C_1 \&_\delta C_2$ (equivalently, $[_\delta\ C_1 \& C_2]$), the δ-local conjunction of C_1 and C_2.

The open parameter δ in the conjunction scheme $C_1 \&_\delta C_2$ is to be filled by elements from the hierarchy of domains, as indicated.[16] Next we assign an interpretation to a locally conjoined constraint by fixing its mode of evaluation. The violation marks that a candidate receives for $C_1 \&_\delta C_2$ are directly determined by the violation marks that it receives for C_1 and C_2 individually, as formulated in (13) and illustrated in (14) in tableau format.

(13) *Evaluation of local conjunctions*

The local conjunction $C_1 \&_\delta C_2$ is violated by a candidate if and only if it has accrued a pair of violations marks ($*C_1$, $*C_2$) for C_1 and C_2 in some domain δ. For $C_1 \&_\delta C_1$, the special case of self-conjunction with $C_1 = C_2$, this implies that a candidate receives a violation mark for each pair of violation marks ($*C_1$, $*C_1$) it has accrued for C_1 in domain δ.

(14) a. *Conjunction of C_1 and C_2*

	$C_1\&C_2$	A	C_1	C_2
▶ candidate$_1$			*	*
candidate$_2$	*!	*		

b. *Self-conjunction of C*

	C&C (=C^2)	A	C
candidate$_1$	*!		**
▶ candidate$_2$		*	

The broadly defined outline of local conjunction theory in (12) and (13) admits a huge number of conjoined constraints, only a small subset of which will turn out to play a role in grammar, and many of which are unwanted. In our view, the task of distinguishing between "reasonable," "plausible," "expected" conjunctions and "unreasonable," "implausible," "unexpected" conjunctions cannot be relegated to the syntax of conjunction, which simply provides a system for expressing derived constraints. The distinction is an issue of phonological substance and phonetic groundedness, not one of formalization.

Nonetheless, one point of a slightly formal nature, sometimes overlooked by both practitioners and critics of conjunction, needs to be addressed. It concerns the fact that there are two slightly different versions of constraint conjunction theory. The *Platonist* version (adopted in Ito and Mester 1998; see Baković 2000 for further development) views the operation "&" as literally *part of UG*, in the sense that all local conjunctions are members of the universal constraint set to begin with. Conjunction extends the universal basic constraint set *Con* to a larger universal constraint set *Con*$_{UG}$. On the alternative *activationist* view, the operation "&" is a *mechanism made available by UG* to individual grammars as a means of extending, on a language-specific basis, the constraint set *Con* to a larger constraint set *Con*$_G$. On this approach, which we adopt here (and which seems akin to the line taken in Smolensky's work), constraint conjunction is a formal operation in constraint algebra that makes available a huge (in fact, infinite) class of conjoined constraints, only a finite (and actually rather small) subset of which become part of particular grammars.

The Platonist and the activationist versions of the theory, even though not easy to tease apart empirically, embody significant conceptual differences that are worth exploring. Provided constraint conjunction is a recursive operation, the Platonist approach, where all conjunctions exist in all grammars, implies that *Con*$_{UG}$ is infinite, a result with significant formal consequences for the learnability of OT grammars that is in any case not in the spirit of computational parsimony. While we are confident that ways could be found to overcome problems in this area (especially since the infinite set *Con*$_{UG}$ has a finite basis and a clearly defined structure), it is reasonable to ask whether there is any direct argument necessitating this kind of infinity.

On the other hand, while stipulating that conjunction is nonrecursive would remove the troublesome infinity, it seems an arbitrary move otherwise foreign to the theory of grammatical competence, as opposed to the study of performance (see Chomsky 1965 for relevant discussion and examples). Practical work with conjunctions in actual phonological analyses has also taught us that, once conjoined constraints are made use of at all, the need quickly arises to recombine a given conjunction with a further constraint (see Ito and Mester 2003 for many cases of this type).

These considerations, then, leave the Platonist conception of constraint conjunction in something of a dilemma. An independent problem with the notion that all conjunctions are present in all grammars, irrespective of the infinity and recursiveness issues, is that it potentially undermines otherwise desirable ranking generalizations concerning conjoined constraints (see section 3.3).

The activationist version of constraint conjunction theory avoids these problems since conjunctions enter individual grammars as individual constraints—by individual acts of activation, so to speak, not en masse. On the other hand, it still makes a large set of constraints in principle available to all grammars, contributing little in terms of formal restrictiveness. As noted above, we anticipate that the real answer to questions of restrictiveness lies elsewhere. There are substantive reasons why certain complex constraints expressed as conjunctions play a role in grammar and others do not, and it is the task of phonology and phonetics to explore all the underlying factors.[17]

In (14), we take formal note of our activationist version of constraint conjunction theory.

(15) *Role of local conjunction in grammars*

> A grammar G can expand the basic constraint set *Con* inherited from Universal Grammar to a superset $Con_G = Con \cup \{C_1 \& C_2\}$, for $C_1, C_2 \in Con$. Expansion is potentially recursive, so that Con_G can in turn be expanded to a superset $Con_{G'}$ by adding $C_3 \& C_4$ to Con_G, for $C_3, C_4 \in Con_G$, and so on.

As pointed out by Smolensky (1997), it can be assumed, without loss of generality, that conjunctions always outrank their constituents, as in (16).

(16) *Ranking (universal) of local conjunctions*

$$C_1 \&_\delta C_2$$
$$|$$
$$\{C_1, C_2\}$$

$C_1 \&_\delta C_2$ has tangible effects only when some other constraint is ranked *between* the conjoined constraint and the individual constraints C_1 and C_2, as in (17). Otherwise, the violation marks incurred for the derived constraint serve only as redundant (but harmless) reminders of the fact that the individual constraints are violated.

(17) $C_1 \&_\delta C_2$

Thus, $C_1 \&_\delta C_2$ is *potentially active* when there is some constraint A ranked between the conjoined constraint and at least one of the two basic constraints, C_1 or C_2.

2.2.2 Exemplification: Coda Devoicing

To illustrate the new type of explanation that local constraint conjunction makes possible within OT, we take up the case of coda devoicing well known from languages such as Dutch and German.[18] Some examples from German (after Vennemann 1972) appear in (18). For example, syllable-initial [d] in the genitive form [.ra:.dəs.] alternates with syllable-final [t] in the nominative [.rat.] and in the diminutive [.rɛ:t.çən.].[19]

(18) *German coda devoicing*

.ra:.dəs.	.ra:t.	.rɛ:t.çən.	'wheel (genitive, nominative, diminutive)'
.bʏn.də.	.bʊnt.	.bʏnt.nɪs.	'union (plural, singular); alliance'
.li:.bə.	.li:p.	.li:p.lɪç.	'dear (attributive, predicative); lovely'
.ta:.gə.	.ta:k.	.tɛ:k.lɪç.	'day (plural, singular); daily'
.mo.ti:.və.	.mo.ti:f.	.mo.ti:fs.	'motive (plural, singular, genitive)'
.le:.zən.	.li:s.	.le:s.bar.	'read (infinitive, imperative); readable'

The direction of the process (voiced to voiceless) is clear from the existence of nonalternating voiceless segments, which remain consistently voiceless regardless of syllable position (19).

(19) *Nonalternating (voiceless) forms*

.ra:.təs.	.ra:t.	'council (genitive, nominative)'
.ti:.fə.	.ti:f.	'deep (attributive, predicative)'
.a:.sən.	.a:s.	'(they, (s)he) ate'

The two basic constraints involved are the syllable structure constraint No-Coda (20) and the segmental markedness constraint No-D against voiced obstruents (21).[20]

(20) No-Coda: *C]$_\sigma$ "Consonants are disallowed syllable-finally."

(21) No-D: *[+voi, −son]   "Voiced obstruents are prohibited."

The crucial step in the analysis is pictured in (22). Given No-CODA and No-D, local constraint conjunction derives a new constraint No-CODA&$_\delta$No-D. This composite constraint militates against structures that simultaneously constitute syllable coda consonants and voiced obstruents.

(22) No-CODA&$_\delta$No-D   (composite constraint)

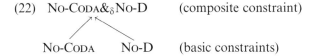

      No-CODA   No-D   (basic constraints)

The constraint-conjunctive analysis of coda devoicing in (22) gives formal expression to a very simple idea: voiced obstruents are marked elements, and syllable codas are marked positions. The phonology of German permits both, insisting on faithful parsing of the input. What is ruled out, however, is a voiced obstruent as a coda, or more generally, the marked in a marked position, a prototypical example of positional markedness. Here input voicing yields to the combined power of two markedness constraints. The domain δ in (22) is therefore the segment. It is segments that violate the ban against voiced obstruents (21) and the ban against consonants with coda roles (20).

The factor that makes actual devoicing possible, and at the same time limits it to codas, is the faithfulness ranking in (23), where IDENT (here militating against changes in the voicing feature) crucially intervenes between the conjoined constraint No-CODA&$_\delta$No-D and the simple feature markedness constraint No-D.

(23) No-CODA&$_\delta$No-D

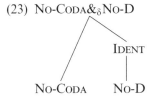

As tableau (24) shows, this ensemble of constraints results in coda devoicing (24a) but not in onset devoicing (24b).

(24) a. lieb *'dear (predicate)'*

/li:b/	No-CODA&$_\delta$No-D	IDENT	No-D	No-CODA
.li:b.	*!		*	*
▶ .li:p.		*		*

b. liebe *'dear (attributive)'*

/li:bə/	No-Coda&$_\delta$No-D	Ident	No-D	No-Coda
▶ .li:.bə.			*	
.li:.pə.		*!		

Another potential surface candidate for the input /li:b/ (24a) is [li:], which removes the coda voicing problem by eliminating the unloved coda altogether. As illustrated in the more detailed tableau (25) for the input /bʊnd/, such candidates lose because the higher-ranking constraint Max prohibits segment deletion (25).[21] The tableau also shows the nonoptimality of devoicing outside of coda position, as in candidate (25d), where the obstruent in the onset is devoiced.

(25) Bund *'union'*

/bʊnd/	Max	No-Coda&$_\delta$No-D	Ident	No-D	No-Coda
a. .bʊn.	*!			*	*
b. .bʊnd.		*!		**	**
c. ▶ .bʊnt.			*	*	**
d. .pʊnt.			**!		**

One might ask in what ways the constraint-conjunctive analysis is superior to simply positing a coda condition ruling out voiced obstruents in the coda. Instead of the conjoined constraint, why not have a coda condition like (26)?

(26) *Coda condition*

    *C]$_\sigma$

     |

[+voi, −son]

From the perspective of the general theory, conditions like (26) fall squarely into the theory of coda conditions first proposed by Ito (1986) as an alternative to the rule-based conceptions of Steriade (1982) and Levin (1985). Descriptively speaking, it is doubtless true that (26) can be substituted for the conjoined constraint, but this does not render the two equivalent: (26) places a new constraint against voiced obstruents in codas alongside (i) an existing constraint against codas and (ii) an existing constraint against voiced obstruents, without relating them in any way. It therefore fails at a very elementary level of theoretical analysis. While constraint conjunction increases the expressive power of the theory, it does so in a limited way that embodies important restrictions. For example, it is well known that, in contrast to the rich set of coda conditions, few conditions are imposed on onset consonants (beyond the usual sonority-based constraints). But stated as in (27), an onset condition prohibiting voiced obstruents in the onset is just as simple as the coda condition in (26).

(27) *Onset condition*

Could there be some kind of metatheory that would tell us that there are coda conditions but no onset conditions? Conceivably—but in a sense, we already have such a metatheory in the simple fact that there is a basic markedness constraint against the presence of codas (No-CoDA militates against codas), but none against the presence of onsets (ONSET militates for onsets). The missing piece is a deductive connection to these basic phonological principles, and this is what constraint conjunction supplies. It is easy to see that no onset condition parallel to (27) can be constructed through conjoining (with δ = segment) the constraint ONSET(*[$_\sigma$ V]) and No-D. A voiced obstruent in onset position does not violate the constraint ONSET; hence, it does not violate the conjoined constraint either.[22]

2.2.3 Markedness Thresholds as Self-Conjoined Constraints

With local constraint conjunction (12) in hand as an operation building new constraints by combining existing ones, we can turn the informal concept of markedness thresholds into a formally workable theory. The central premise is that the "Obligatory Contour Principle" is by itself neither a constraint nor a formal universal in phonological theory. The culprit in OCP-type dissimilations is not the adjacency of identical feature specifications on a tier, but the multiple presence of a marked type of structure within some domain. "Multiple presence" here results in more than the standard OT calculation of multiple violations of one constraint. Multiple violations of the markedness constraint do not simply add up, but interact with each other, so that a double violation within a given domain is worse than the sum of two individual violations.

We now have a systematic means of formalizing this idea, namely, the local conjunction of a constraint with itself. As the idea was defined in (17), a candidate violates the self-conjunction of constraint C with itself, C&$_\delta$C (C$^2_\delta$ for short), if it accrues two or more violation marks for C in domain δ. Self-conjoining the basic

markedness constraint No-φ yields the composite constraint No-φ²$_δ$ that prohibits
the co-occurrence of the structure φ with itself in domain δ. For the markedness
constraints in (28), self-conjoined counterparts are given in (29).[23]

(28) *Basic markedness constraints*

    a. No-C^h "No aspirated consonants."
    b. No-D   "No voiced obstruents."
    c. No-HL   "No falling tones."

(29) *Self-conjoined markedness constraints*

    a. No-C^h&$_δ$No-C^h = No-C$^{h2}{}_δ$ "No two aspirated consonants in domain δ."
    b. No-D&$_δ$No-D   = No-D²$_δ$ "No two voiced obstruents in domain δ."
    c. No-HL&$_δ$No-HL = No-HL²$_δ$ "No two falling tones in domain δ."

As with all conjoined constraints, the force of a self-conjoined constraint No-φ²
reveals itself only when some other constraint C intervenes in the ranking between
the composite constraint No-φ² and the corresponding simplex constraint No-φ, as
indicated in (30).[24] When this ranking scenario obtains, dissimilation of elements
that are identical in terms of φ is observed ("OCP effects").[25]

(30) No-φ²

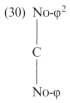

The most basic configuration of this kind obtains when the intervening constraint is a
faithfulness constraint relevant for the feature specification φ, as in (31). To avoid
unnecessary clutter in our analyses, we will in general make use of undifferentiated
IDENT for feature faithfulness, adding further distinctions in terms of specific features
and the like only when required by the facts under discussion.

    Setting the local domain δ for "morpheme" (indicated by *m* in (31)) gives rise to
OCP effects in morpheme structure (see McCarthy 1986, 208–219, for a taxonomy of
such effects).

(31) No-φ²$_m$

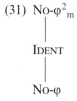

Returning to the example from Sanskrit in (1), let us consider the force of the constraints No-C^h (28a) and No-C^{h2} (29a). Substituting aspiration for the variable φ in (31), we obtain (32).

(32) No-C^{h2}$_m$

IDENT

No-C^h

This ranking amounts to a "morpheme structure constraint" against the co-occurrence of aspirates in Sanskrit. As illustrated in (33), hypothetical underlying diaspirate morphemes are not allowed to surface with their two aspirates intact since faithful diaspirate candidates like (33a) always lose on the highest-ranked self-conjoined constraint No-C^{h2}$_m$ to more harmonic deaspirating candidates (33b,c). The diaspirate candidate is thus harmonically bounded by other candidates, in the sense of Prince and Smolensky 1993, 176–178. On the other hand, across-the-board deaspiration (33d) is not called for. The ranking of the faithfulness constraint IDENT above the basic markedness constraint No-C^h ensures that some monoaspirate candidate, either (33b) or (33c), will win over (33d).

(33) *Morpheme-structural deaspiration effect*

/b^{h}id^h/ (hypothetical)	No-C^{h2}$_m$	IDENT	No-C^h
a. b^{h}id^h	*!		**
b. ▶ bid^h		*	*
c. ▶ b^{h}id		*	*
d. bid		**!	

Other constraints will determine the choice between (33b) and (33c) (e.g., provided other factors do not interfere, positional faithfulness will prefer (33c) to (33b)). The important point here is not the identity of the actual winner,[26] but the identity of the assured loser: diaspirate candidates such as (33a) will never emerge victorious. In this way, (33) derives the effects of a traditional OCP-based morpheme structure condition on the aspiration tier, and it does so without any specific assumptions about representations, underspecification, or privativeness of features.

In (33), the domain parameter δ is set for "morpheme," not for the larger domain "word."[27] This predicts that the limitation to one aspirate should hold only inside morphemes, not for a polymorphemic stem or word. This is indeed the case. The language shows an abundance of words with two aspirates, such as [dʱanibʱjaːm] 'rich (instrumental dual)', where root and suffix each contribute one aspirate.

2.3 The Japanese Voicing Restriction

A significant number of segmental markedness constraints give rise to OCP effects through self-conjunctive enhancement, along the general lines seen in the Sanskrit example above. We now turn to an instance involving the constraint against voiced obstruents, No-D, that is of central importance within the morphophonemic system of Japanese.[28] The native stratum of the lexicon is subject to a restriction limiting morphemes to a single voiced obstruent, an instance of the self-conjoined constraint No-D^2 with a morpheme domain. This morpheme-structural restriction limiting the contrastive use of obstruent voicing is clearly related to the compound voicing restriction known as Lyman's Law. In response to this duplication of a constraint on underlying representations by a separate restriction on derived voicing,[29] we earlier proposed an analysis that reduces both to the same principle, namely, the auto-segmental OCP operating on an underspecified voicing tier (see Ito and Mester 1986).[30] Focusing here on the co-occurrence restriction in morphemes, we develop an analysis that we will extend to the compound voicing aspects in chapter 4, providing a unitary analysis for the two related groups of phenomena.

2.3.1 Distribution of Obstruent Voicing in Native Morphemes

We illustrate the morpheme-internal restriction with native roots and affixes gleaned from a cursory survey of standard dictionaries. While our data set is far from exhaustive, it is detailed enough to represent the situation adequately. As shown in (34), obstruent voicing is clearly contrastive in Yamato morphemes of the form CV (C = obstruent).

(34) *CV forms (hyphens indicate bound status)*

[−son, −voi]	-ka	ki	ku	ke	ko
	Q	'tree'	'phrase'	'hair'	'child'
[−son, +voi]	-ga				
	NOM				
[−son, −voi]	-sa	-si	su	se	-soo
	AN	CONT	'vinegar'	'back'	AE
[−son, +voi]		-zi	-zu	-ze	-zo
		'road'	NEG	SP	SP
[−son, −voi]	ta	ti	-tu	te	to
	'rice field'	'blood'	COUNT	'hand'	'door'
[−son, +voi]	-da			-de	doo
	COP			INST	'how'

[−son, −voi]	ha	hi	hu	he	hoo
	'tooth'	'fire'	'two'	'fart'	'cheek'
[−son, +voi]	-ba			-be	
	COND			PERS	

Q = question marker; AN = adjective nominalizer (e.g., *aka-sa* 'redness'); CONT = continuative marker; AE = adjective ending; NOM = nominative marker; NEG = negation marker; SP = sentence particle indicating advice, warning (e.g., *abunai-ze/zo* 'mind you, it's dangerous'); COUNT = counter suffix (e.g., *hito-tu* 'one piece'); COP = copula marker; INST = instrumental marker; COND = conditional marker; PERS = 'persons and clan engaged in a certain occupation' (e.g., *katari-be* 'family of professional reciters').

While obstruent voicing is clearly distinctive in (34), there are a significant number of empty cells where no existing lexical item beginning with a voiced obstruent matches the voiceless form. The contrast, which appears more pronounced than what would be expected by way of accidental lexical gaps and the general markedness bias toward the voiceless series, has its roots in the sound pattern of Old Japanese (the language of the Nara period, eighth century A.D.). Old Japanese (see Unger 1975, 8; Frellesvig 1995, 65–68; section 8.3.2 below) possessed a voiced obstruent series contrasting with a voiceless one, but banned the former from word-initial position. Consequently, roots—as potentially word-initial morphemes—never showed voiced obstruents initially, whereas many suffixes began with such segments (i.e., this was not a restriction on morphemes per se). Over the centuries, a number of changes, such as loss of word-initial vowels (*ide-ru, idas-u > de-ru, das-u* 'go out', 'put out', etc.), undermined the distributional ban and gave rise to many forms beginning with voiced obstruents. Even so, the restriction is still manifested nowadays as an underrepresentation of voiced obstruents in root-initial position.

With this caveat, the synchronic diagnosis regarding (34) must be that obstruent voicing is fully distinctive. This becomes even more obvious in situations where word-initial position is not at issue, such as the VCV forms in (35), where (near-)minimal pairs are easily found.

(35) *VCV forms*

C [−son, −voi]	asi	asa	ase	usi
	'leg'	'morning'	'sweat'	'cow'
C [−son, +voi]	azi	aza	aze	uzi
	'taste'	'bruise'	'levee'	'worm'

C [−son, −voi]	ut-(u)	oto-(ru)	aka	oko-(ru)
	'shoot'	'be inferior'	'red'	'be angry at'
C [−son, +voi]	ude	odo-(ru)	age	ogo-(ru)
	'arm'	'to dance'	'fried tofu'	'to treat s.o.'

Against the background of this overall free distribution of obstruent voicing in monoconsonantal forms, we turn to biconsonantal morphemes of the form $C_1VC_2(V)$. (36) is a co-occurrence table with examples instantiating the existing combinations of voiced and voiceless obstruents in position C_1 (listed vertically) with voiced and voiceless obstruents in position C_2 (listed horizontally).[31]

(36) *CVC(V) forms*

		C_2 [−son, −voi]			C_2 [−son, +voi]			
		k	s	t	g	z	d	b
C_1 [−son, −voi]	k	kak-u 'write'	kusa 'grass'	kuti 'mouth'	kago 'basket'	kaze 'wind'	kado 'corner'	kubi 'neck'
	s	-sika 'only'	sas-u 'pierce'	sato 'village'	sugi 'cedar'	suzu 'bell'	sode 'sleeve'	soba 'near'
	t	tako 'octopus'	tas-u 'add'	tate 'shield'	toge 'thorn'	tozi- 'close'	tada 'free'	tabi 'journey'
	h	huka- 'deep'	hasi 'bridge'	hito 'person'	hige 'beard'	hiza 'knee'	hada 'skin'	hebi 'snake'
C_1 [−son, +voi]	g	gake 'cliff'		geta 'clogs'				
	z	zako 'small fish'		-zutu 'each'				
	d	-dake 'only'	das-u 'take out'	date 'dandy'				
	b	bake- 'disguise'	-besi 'must'	buta 'pig'				

As in (34), the historical absence of voiced obstruents from word-initial position has some lingering effects, but these are overshadowed by a much more important categorical effect: the complete absence of forms in the bottom right quadrant of (36), where morphemes with two voiced obstruents would appear.

The pattern becomes even more striking when we turn to triconsonantal morphemes of the form $C_1VC_2VC_3(V)$ and study the co-occurrence of voiced obstruents in positions C_1/C_3, to determine whether the dissimilative influence of obstruent voicing persists at a distance, that is, across an intervening C_2 consonant (which can be either a sonorant or a voiceless obstruent). The question is of interest in connection with the results of Frisch, Broe, and Pierrehumbert (1995), who found that the morpheme-structural place dissimilation effects in Arabic roots are significantly weaker at a distance (i.e., in C_1/C_3 combinations as opposed to C_1/C_2 combinations). In (37), sonorant consonants are included in the overall pattern (D = voiced obstruent and C = voiceless consonant or (voiced) sonorant consonant).

(37) *Triconsonantal forms*

CCC	kakasi	kakato	kasuka	katana	kataki	tasuke	tatami	hotoke
	'scarecrow'	'heel'	'faintly'	'sword'	'enemy'	'help'	'straw mat'	'buddha'
CCD	husag-	karada	kasegi	hakob-	manab-	wasabi	tokage	hituzi
	'block'	'body'	'earning'	'carry'	'learn'	'horseradish'	'lizard'	'sheep'
CDC	huzake	hadaka	kabuto	kazas-	kegas-	maguro	kagami	kuzira
	'joke'	'naked'	'helmet'	'hold up'	'stain'	'tuna'	'mirror'	'whale'
DCC	-bakari	donar-	damas-	damar-	-gotoki	-darake	bokas-	gasatu
	'only'	'shout'	'deceive'	'be silent'	'as such'	'be full of'	'shade'	'rude'

CDD	
DCD	
DDC	
DDD	

As can be judged from the lack of entries in the last four rows in (37), there are no triconsonantal morphemes with more than one voiced obstruent, irrespective of position: CDD, DCD, DDC, and DDD forms are all entirely absent.[32]

Given the data in (36) and (37), the basic morpheme-structural ban against co-occurrence of voiced obstruents cannot be in doubt, even if sporadic exceptions are found (see chapter 6 for further discussion).[33] The lists in (36) and (37) also show (i) that the restriction on multiple voicing concerns only obstruents (i.e., obstruent voicing can freely co-occur with sonorant voicing) and (ii) that there is no corresponding constraint against multiple voiceless obstruents. Nor is there a constraint against multiple (voiced) sonorant consonants, as witnessed by morphemes such as *nama* 'raw', *mura* 'village', *yane* 'roof', *wara* 'straw', and *yoru* 'night'.

The restriction against multiple voiced obstruents is illustrated in (38) from a different angle, by focusing directly on the contrastive resources of the lexicon. Three sets of minimal pairs are shown instantiating all combinations of voiced/voiceless obstruents, with the exception of double voicing.

(38) a.

−voi	+voi	−voi	+voi		b.	−voi	+voi	+voi	+voi
−son	+son	−son	+son			−son	+son	−son	+son
|	|	|	|			|	|	|	|
C	V	C	V			C	V	C	V
k	a	k	i			k	a	g	i
h	u	t	a			h	u	d	a
k	a	k	e			k	a	g	e
t	o	k	-u			t	o	g	-u

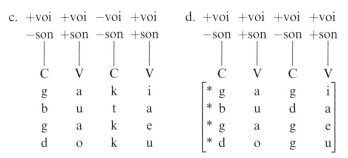

c. +voi +voi −voi +voi   d. +voi +voi +voi +voi
    −son +son −son +son   −son +son −son +son
     | | | | | | | |
     C   V   C   V   C   V   C   V
     g   a   k   i   * g   a   g   i
     b   u   t   a   * b   u   d   a
     g   a   k   e   * g   a   g   e
     d   o   k   u   * d   o   g   u

Glosses
a. 'persimmon', 'lid', 'betting', 'solve'
b. 'key', 'label', 'shadow', 'sharpen'
c. 'kid', 'pig', 'cliff', 'poison'
d. —

2.3.2 The Obligatory Contour Principle Effect on Obstruent Voicing

Starting with the obvious, the fact that obstruent voicing is contrastive in Japanese (special contextual effects aside) means that the faithfulness constraint IDENT against changes in feature specifications (here, voicing) must dominate the markedness constraint No-D (39).[34]

(39) *Contrastive voicing*

IDENT
|
No-D

This ensures that underlying voiced obstruents, as in *huda* 'sign' and *gake* 'cliff', are faithfully preserved in the output (40). If No-D dominated IDENT, all input voicing in obstruents would disappear (e.g., by devoicing), a situation encountered in languages lacking a voicing contrast in obstruents, such as Hawaiian and Yokuts.

(40) huda *'sign'*

/huda/	IDENT	No-D
▶ huda		*
huta	*!	

Even though the effects of the basic No-D constraint are thus severely curtailed by higher-ranking IDENT, the tables in (36)–(37) showing the highly significant absence of morphemes with two voiced obstruents demonstrate the dominant influence of a more specialized obstruent voicing constraint No-D^2_δ with δ = morpheme, henceforth referred to as $No\text{-}D^2_m$ (41).

(41) No-D^2_m (= $\text{No-D}\&_m\text{No-D}$): "No two voiced obstruents per morpheme
domain."

The general model of dissimilation that we have shown at work in Sanskrit aspiration (see (31)–(32)) accounts for the Japanese case in a straightforward way. The OCP effect results from the constraint ranking in (42), where No-D^2_m dominates IDENT, crucially curtailing the power of feature faithfulness to preserve input voicing contrasts in obstruents beyond one contrast (i.e., beyond one incidence of obstruent voicing). Additional obstruents will appear with neutralized voicing (i.e., voiceless).

(42) No-D^2_m
$\qquad$| $\Big\}$ effect of interaction: avoidance of multiple obstruent voicing
$\quad$IDENT
$\qquad$| $\Big\}$ effect of interaction: preservation of voicing specifications otherwise
$\quad$NO-D

The morpheme-structural OCP effect exerted by the markedness-dominated upper section of the hierarchy in (42) is illustrated in tableau (43) with a hypothetical doubly voiced input.

(43)

/gage/ (hypothetical)	No-D^2_m	IDENT	NO-D
a. gage	*!		**
b. ▶ kage		*	*
c. ▶ gake		*	*
d. kake		**!	

As in the Sanskrit case (see (33)), it is immaterial whether (43b) or (43c) (or, indeed, some third candidate) emerges as the overall winner as long as multiply voiced forms such as *gage (43a) have no chance to be selected as outputs, always being bested by some other candidate. On the other hand, a single instance of obstruent voicing within a morpheme, as in (44), survives intact because of the faithfulness-dominated lower section of the hierarchy in (42).

(44) gake *'cliff'*

/gake/		No-D^2_m	Ident	No-D
a.	gage	*!	*	**
b.	kage		*!*	*
c. ▶	gake			*
d.	kake		*!	

By interacting with other elements of the phonology of Japanese, this basic constraint system regulating obstruent voicing gives rise to extended morphophonemic dissimilation effects that will occupy us in chapter 4.

2.3.3 Distribution of Obstruent Voicing in Nonnative Strata

As it stands, the analysis in (42) predicts a restricted distribution of obstruent voicing throughout the phonological lexicon of Japanese. In assessing the implications of this prediction, we are directly confronted with the fact that the lexicon of a natural language is usually divided into several layers or strata, with slightly different phonological (and other linguistic) properties. The lexicon of Japanese is no exception.

The traditionally recognized subdivisions within the Japanese vocabulary, familiar from both the linguistic literature (including Martin 1952 and McCawley 1968) and standard lexicographic works such as the *Koozien* 広辞苑 (Shinmura 1983), are given in (45).

(45) *Traditionally recognized strata in the Japanese lexicon*

Yamato	**Sino-Japanese**	**Foreign**	**Ideophonic**
native morphemes (*wa-go* 和語)	centuries-old loans from Chinese, mainly used in compounds (*kan-go* 漢語)	more recent loans from Western languages, mostly from English (*gairai-go* 外来語)	extensive system of sound-symbolic expressions including sound- and manner-based items (*gisee-go* 擬声語 and *gitai-go* 擬態語)

A theoretical model of this kind of lexicon-internal structure using stratally indexed faithfulness as its central concept is developed in Ito and Mester 1999a (see also the references cited there). In chapter 6, which is devoted to matters of the lexicon, we will show that for a detailed linguistic analysis the traditional distinctions in (45) are often not fine enough, but they are useful guidelines as far as they go.

The voicing restriction holds for the native stratum of the vocabulary; all examples given in the previous section stem from this part of the lexicon. It is also observed, quasi-vacuously, by Sino-Japanese morphemes, which are subject to even more stringent requirements.[35] They can have at most two syllables, and the second syllable of disyllables can only consist of a voiceless coronal or velar obstruent followed by [i] or [u] (schematically: CV{t/s/k}V). Given these strictures, a Sino-Japanese morpheme clearly could never accommodate two voiced obstruents.

At the other end of the spectrum, given the role and purpose of ideophonic expressions,[36] it would be surprising (even though not entirely inconceivable) to find them limited to a single instance of obstruent voicing. As shown in (46), the voicing restriction is indeed not obeyed in a significant number of such items (data from Nasu 1999).

(46) *Double obstruent voicing in ideophonic morphemes*

gaba-	'too large'	daba-	'loose, watery'	zaba-	'washing, splashing'
gabu-	'gulping'	dabo-	'loose, big'	zabu-	'splashing'
gebo-	'belching'	dabu-	'baggy, be	zuba-	'boldly, frankly'
gebu-	'belching'		loose'	zubo-	'piercing, sinking'
giza-	'indented,	debu-	'fatty, plump'	zubu-	'go through, sink
	notched'	dobo-	'splashing'		into'
gobo-	'bubbling'	dobu-	'mud splash'		
guda-	'lamenting'				
guzu-	'slowly,				
	lazily'				

Nasu (1999) makes the important observation that almost all of these forms with two voiced obstruents have [b] as their second consonant (see Hamano 2000 for a study of the same phenomenon from a historical perspective). This casts an interesting light on the markedness of nonlinked [p] (i.e., [p] outside of geminates and assimilated clusters) even in Japanese ideophones and shows, moreover, that the voicing restriction might still not be completely inert here. Informally speaking, multiple voiced obstruents mostly occur through a "replacement" of internal single [p] by [b].

The voicing restriction is also not observed in Western loans, as shown by the examples in (47)–(49), whose language of origin is English, unless noted otherwise (*F* = French, *G* = German, *I* = Italian, *P* = Portuguese).

(47) *Western loans, 2σ*

baado	'bird'	boogu	'vogue'	gaido	'guide'
baddo	'bad'	buroodo	'broad'	geezi	'gauge'
bazzi	'badge'	buzaa	'buzzer'	gongu	'gong'
bebii	'baby'	daabii	'derby'	guddo	'good'
beddo	'bed'	daibaa	'diver'	gyaggu	'gag'
biibaa	'beaver'	debyuu	'début' (F)	gyangu	'gang'
bingo	'bingo'	deddo	'dead'	gyazaa	'gather'
biza	'visa'	deezii	'daisy'	zigu	'jig'
bodii	'body'	dezain	'design'	ziinzu	'jeans'
bombe	'Bombe' (G)	doggu	'dog'	zyaazii	'jersey'
bondo	'bond'	gaaden	'garden'	zyazu	'jazz'
boodaa	'border'	gaado	'guard'	zyobu	'job'
boodo	'board'	gaaze	'Gaze' (G)		

(48) *Western loans, 3σ*

bagetto	'baguette' (F)	debaggu	'debug'
bagina	'vagina'	debiru	'devil'
baraado	'Ballade' (G)	dekadan	'décadent' (F)
baruzi	'bulge'	dezaato	'dessert'
bibaatye	'vivace' (I)	dibaidaa	'divider'
bibiddo	'vivid'	diizeru	'Diesel' (G)
bideo	'video'	doguma	'dogma'
bigguban	'big bang'	gabotto	'gavotte' (I)
bindongu	'Bindung' (G)	gareezi	'garage'
binegaa	'vinegar'	gerende	'Gelände' (G)
bizitaa	'visitor'	goburan	'gobelines' (F)
biidoro	'vidro' (P)	googeru	'goggle'
boirudo	'boiled'	gooruden	'golden'
boorudo	'bold'	guraidaa	'glider'
buraboo	'bravo'	guraindaa	'grinder'
buraindo	'blind'	gurando	'grand'
burando	'brand'	guraundo	'ground'
burazaa	'brother'	gureedo	'grade'
bureedo	'blade'	gyabazin	'gabardine'
buroodo	'broad'	gyamburu	'gamble'
buruzon	'blouson' (F)	kaadigan	'cardigan'
dabingu	'dubbing'	kuroozu	'closed' (shop)
daburu	'double'	moogeezi	'mortgage'

randebuu   'rendez-vous' (F)   saiboogu   'cyborg'
robii'ingu   'lobbying'   zebura   'zebra'
rozzingu   'lodging'   zigoro   'gigolo'

(49) *Western loans, 4σ⁺*

bagabondo   'vagabond'   demagoogu   'Demagoge' (G)
biggubando   'big band'   gebaruto   'Gewalt' (G)
bizinesu   'business'   goburetto   'goblet'
birudingu   'building'   guroobaru   'global'
boodobiru   'vaudeville' (F)   ziguzagu   'zigzag'
burudoggu   'bulldog'   rezidento   'resident'
burudoozaa   'bulldozer'   riborubaa   'revolver'
dezitaru   'digital'   sabuzyekuto 'subject'

A quick glance at the data in (47)–(49), which include examples like *dibaidaa* 'divider' and *bagabondo* 'vagabond', is sufficient to dispel any notion that a restriction against co-occurrence of voiced obstruents could be at work in the foreign vocabulary. Rather, the distribution here simply reflects the conditions found in the donor languages. The four minimally contrasting items in (50) illustrate the full use the loan vocabulary makes of the contrastive resources of obstruent voicing. (50) should be compared with (38), where the gap in (38d) is a reminder of the drastic limitations that the OCP effect on voicing entails for the contrastiveness of obstruent voicing in native morphemes.

(50)

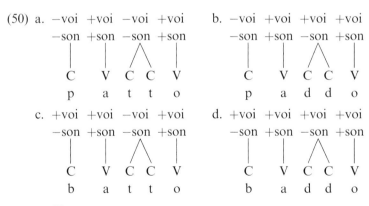

Glosses
a. 'putt'
b. 'pad'
c. 'bat'
d. 'bad'

The modern Japanese language as a whole, therefore, possesses morphemes with two or more voiced obstruents. Whereas the distribution of obstruent voicing is grammatically constrained in native morphemes, ruling out multiple obstruent voicing, it is grammatically free in ideophones and in loan morphemes (lexically fixed for each item, of course).

In assessing the general situation, it seems reasonable to set aside the subsystem of ideophonic items. While such items are usually shaped so as to broadly conform to the rules and restrictions holding in the language they inhabit, crosslinguistically they commonly violate specific segmental and prosodic restrictions. Within phonology, recognition of their special status goes back at least to Grimm 1822, where systematic note is taken of their special behavior with respect to otherwise valid sound laws. For the case at hand, the fact that they can contain multiple voiced obstruents (although still with limitations, as pointed out above) has no major implications for the overall system.

The loanword facts, on the other hand, command serious attention: such massive violations of some co-occurrence restriction within part of the common vocabulary must have repercussions within the whole system. At this point, we can in principle draw two different conclusions from the fact that loanwords are exempt from the voicing restriction that native items conform to.

In the first view, grammatical restrictions are generalizations about sets of data. They are valid in the synchronic grammar only to the extent that they are true generalizations holding over the total corpus of data available to the speaker. Thus, for speakers of English, the inclusion in their vocabulary of loanwords like *tsunami* or *tsetse fly* establishes /ts/ as a bona fide affricate phoneme or onset cluster in their grammar alongside /tʃ/; it is of little relevance that [ts] onsets are not otherwise encountered. For Japanese, the mere presence of items with double voicing within the same lexicon precludes, for the corpus-focused analyst, any possibility of a voicing restriction in the synchronic grammar. Instead, the limitation evidenced by native items is predicted to be synchronically opaque for contemporary speakers, a strictly historical fact, with the additional prediction that it should not be found to have other grammatical consequences and systematic reflexes within the synchronic language system. All that remains, in this view, is a curious accidental gap in the distribution of obstruent voicing.

A contrasting approach focuses not on the static corpus of language data, but on the grammar as a cognitive object, as it dynamically unfolds and develops through the activity of the speaker/hearer. Here restrictions can play an active role in the synchronic system even if they do not hold for the totality of the data. Learners do not confront the corpus of language data as a monolithic mass, with all generalizations being either true or false for all available facts. Rather, they impose a cognitive structure on this corpus, using their developing grammar and its constraint ranking as a guideline. This involves, among other things, a structured lexicon, with sets of lexical items that show systematically differing behavior with respect to certain markedness constraints and that share a significant number of properties. In this grammar-oriented approach, the voicing restriction may well be an active principle in the grammar of Modern Japanese—within a stratified lexicon, where it is limited to native (and Sino-Japanese) items and does not concern more peripheral elements of the lexicon. The fact that one group of morphemes is held to laxer standards of well-formedness is a common crosslinguistic observation that any theory of phonology must come to terms with, in this view: taking them to automatically falsify otherwise valid restrictions on a sound pattern precludes developing an adequate model of a speaker's phonological competence. Taking up the earlier example, the fact that many speakers of English can pronounce loanwords like *tsunami* or *tsetse fly* with initial [ts] does not automatically mean that /ts/ has become a full-fledged affricate phoneme or onset cluster in their grammar.

In the theory of lexical stratification we developed in earlier work (Ito and Mester 1995a, 1999a, 2001a), the constraint ranking responsible for the voicing restriction is active within the grammar of Japanese, but it is restricted to the core lexicon because the faithfulness constraint that intervenes between No-D and No-D^2_m is restricted in this way. In peripheral areas, No-D^2_m is counteracted by higher-ranking antagonistic faithfulness.

As diametrically opposed as these two approaches are (see Ito and Mester 2001a and chapter 6 below for further discussion of issues involved), at this point in our exploration of the morphophonemics of Japanese, which of them we adopt is of little immediate consequence. They agree on a central point, namely, that there exists a stage of the language, be it past or present, where the voicing restriction is a grammatical fact,[37] and little else is ultimately relevant for the theoretical issues dealt with in this chapter. The decision between the two options will in some form come down to determining whether there are other indications that the restriction is still "alive," "active," "productive" in the current language. In chapter 4, we will present strong evidence to this effect, making the second alternative the only tenable analysis and thereby supporting its underlying premises.[38] Before turning to this evidence, we investigate some of the empirical evidence showing that the new model of dissimilation is superior to the autosegmental tier-adjacency OCP (sections 3.1 and 3.2), and we investigate the status of self-conjoined constraints in the grammar and their contribution to the analysis of dissimilation (section 3.3).

Chapter 3

Extended Obligatory Contour Principle Effects and Further Issues

In this chapter, we present evidence that the strictly markedness-based theory of OCP effects developed so far constitutes an advance over the traditional OCP. Continuing to focus on the phonology of Japanese, with a brief excursus into Latin and Amharic, we will turn to patterns of dissimilative degemination and deaccentuation. As we will show, the phenomena in question fall through the cracks of the traditional autosegmental and representation-focused account but find a natural place in the new conception, thus providing direct empirical evidence for it.

A basic difference between the two theories concerns the range of phonological properties they are expected to apply to. Many of the insights of modern phonology rest on a well-motivated separation between "melody" (segmental features) and "prosody" (prosodic and rhythmic organization), as schematically illustrated in (1). The autosegmental OCP is, by its very definition, focused exclusively on elements located on autosegmental tiers (i.e., below the horizontal line in (1))—the various segmental features and feature bundles expressing laryngeal, manner, and place properties and also tonal contours. It is thus intrinsically dissociated from the part of the representation devoted to prosodic constituency, and for a good reason: elements expressing syntagmatic grouping and organization do not occupy tiers where a dissimilation principle could meaningfully apply. Even though analysts have occasionally tried to weaken this clear dichotomy for descriptive purposes, it remains true that it makes little sense to apply some extended version of the autosegmental OCP directly to prosodic and rhythmic structure. After all, a syllable (σ) does not seem to repel, by its mere presence, other syllables in its vicinity, and neither does a unit of moraic weight (μ) exert, all by itself, the kind of dissimilating effect on another μ found with consonantal place, aspiration, glottalization, or obstruent voicing. This is one aspect of the fundamental difference between units of phonological constituency and elements representing articulatory gestures.

This basic limitation of the traditional OCP to nonprosodic properties, while in general well founded, has one unfortunate consequence. Some phenomena whose characteristics bear a striking resemblance to featural OCP effects, such as length

(1) *Prosodic structure and melodic structure*

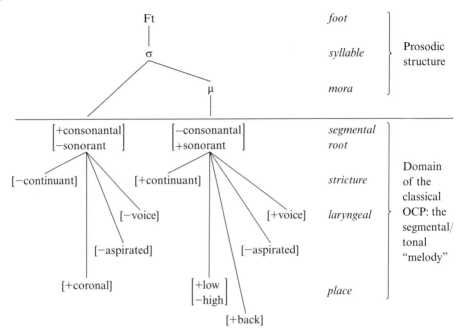

dissimilation, cannot be brought under the same rubric since the properties involved are represented in the prosodic section of phonological representation. Therefore, it is of interest that the approach developed here, which is exclusively built on markedness principles without any additional representational baggage, does not come with a similar built-in limitation to featural properties. One could impose such a limitation from the outside, but it would constitute a separate stipulation, not a natural outgrowth of the basic theory. The unadorned model makes a straightforward prediction different from that of the autosegmental OCP. Any markedness constraint should in principle be able to project an enhanced (i.e., self-conjoined) version of itself that imposes a special penalty on multiple infringements within the same local domain. Consequently, dissimilation effects similar to featural dissimilation should be found with other marked phonological properties, including prosodic properties such as length (vs. shortness) of vowels and consonants. Constraints dealing with them should be able to occupy the position of No-X in (2).[1]

(2) $\text{No-X}^2{}_\delta$

3.1   Geminate Dissimilation

Relevant examples are indeed not hard to find, and they include cases that were left
by the wayside as unsolved problems for the traditional feature- and tier-based OCP.
Here we discuss three cases involving dissimilative degemination, in Latin, Japanese,
and Amharic.

3.1.1   Lex Mamilla in Latin

The first case, well known from traditional historical linguistics, concerns *lex mamilla*
(named after a prototypical example) in the historical phonology of Latin. As shown
in (3), when the diminutive suffix /-ill-/ is added to a root that itself contains a geminate (e.g., /mamm + illa/), the root geminate is simplified (resulting in [mamilla]).

(3) Lex mamilla *effects*

mamma	'breast'	mamilla	diminutive	*mammilla
offa	'morsel'	ofella	id.	*offella
sakkus	'sack'	sakellus	id.	*sakkellus

An example where dissimilative degemination affects a morphologically derived
geminate is given in (4), a verb-prefix combination built on the root /mitt-/ 'to send'
and the prefix /ob-/.

(4) *Degemination of a "derived geminate"*

  ob- 'aside'   o-mitto: 'lay aside'   *om-mitto:

Of interest is the fact that underlying prefix-final /b/ disappears here without a
trace before a verb root with a geminate. Deletion of the prefix-final [b] in preconsonantal position is normal, but it is otherwise accompanied by compensatory
gemination of the root-initial consonant: /ob-kupo:/ → [ok-kupo:] 'to take posses-
sion', /ob-kido:/ → [ok-kido:] 'to fall down', /ob-fero:/ → [of-fero:] 'to place before,
to offer', and so on. In derivational parlance, this suggests the route /ob-mitto:/
→ /om-mitto:/ → [o-mitto:].

   The basic analysis of this type of geminate dissimilation appeals to both the simple
and the self-conjoined versions of the constraint No-Geminate (5).

(5) *No-Geminate*

The opposing faithfulness factor is the weight preservation constraint IDENT-R[μ] (6), which requires correspondence to be weight preserving. In other words, *n*-moraic elements need *n*-moraic correspondents.

(6) IDENT-R[μ]: "Let *weight(α)* be the moraic value of α and *R* any correspondence relation. Then xRx′ implies that *weight*(x) = *weight*(x′)."

IDENT-IO[μ] (IDENT[μ], for short) crucially intervenes between the simple and the enhanced version of NO-GEMINATE (NO-GEM), as in (7). The latter constraint's locality domain is obviously larger than "morpheme"; we will set it here as "stem."

(7)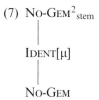

The tableau in (8) illustrates this analysis.

(8) mamilla *'breast (diminutive)'*

/mamm-i-lla/	NO-GEM²ₛₜₑₘ	IDENT[μ]	NO-GEM
mammilla	*!		**
▶ mamilla		*	*
mamila		**!	

Further issues arise when we ask why, instead of the leftmost geminate, degemination does not affect the suffixal (rightmost) geminate, which would result in the selection of **mammila*. The bias in favor of the suffixal geminate in the output might be due either to a direct directional bias (e.g., expressed as ALIGN-R(μ, PRWD)), to a preference for penultimate stress, or, more likely, to an IDENT-HEAD[μ] constraint (with the standard assumption that the category-determining diminutive suffix is the morphological head; see Revithiadou 1999 for general discussion regarding FAITH-HEAD effects). Everything else being equal, the position of IDENT-HEAD[μ] in the ranking is irrelevant—the correct output is chosen as long as it is present somewhere in the hierarchy (indicated in tableau (9) by a column separation).[2]

(9) mamilla *'breast (diminutive)'*

/mamm-i-lla/	NO-GEM²ₛₜₑₘ	IDENT[μ]	NO-GEM	IDENT-HEAD[μ]
mammilla	*!		**	
▶ mamilla		*	*	
mammila		*	*	*!
mamila		**!		*

Alderete (1997) provides examples where a similar kind of shortening affects long vowels in adjacent syllables.[3]

3.1.2 Geminate Simplification in Japanese

A constraint configuration virtually identical to the one in Latin characterizes the phonology of Japanese loanwords, where it results in widespread geminate dissimilation. The crucial background generalization about the adaptation of loanwords from English in Japanese (see Iwai 1989; Wade 1996; Katayama 1998; and other studies cited in these works) is that plosives following lax vowels in the source word are in general rendered as geminates. The law of adaptation is not based on orthography (i.e., the double or single spelling of the consonant in English); rather, it performs a prosodic mapping of coda consonants (after short nuclei) and ambisyllabics into their closest correspondents, within the limits of the much more tightly restricted syllable canon of Japanese. The effects are illustrated in (10).[4]

(10) *Gemination in Japanese loanwords as a strategy to preserve (partial) coda status*

ku**kk**ii	'cookie'	ho**tt**o	'hot coffee'
wa**kk**usu	'wax'	be**dd**o	'bed'
zi**pp**aa	'zipper'	u**dd**o	'wood'
a**pp**uru	'apple'	mo**bb**u	'mob'
pura**tt**ohoomu	'platform'	ba**gg**u	'bag'
pi**tt**yaa	'pitcher'	ba**zz**i	'badge'

This rule of adaptive gemination in loans is systematically broken, however, when it would result in an output with two geminates. In such cases, as shown by the contrasting examples in the two columns of (11), the first plosive appears as a singleton and not as a geminate, even though it follows a lax vowel in the English source word.[5]

(11) *Nongemination when there is another geminate later in the word*

C/____ ... C_iC_i		C_iC_i/elsewhere	
poketto[6]	'pocket'	pikkoro	'piccolo'
piketto	'picket'	sutakkaato	'staccato'
tiketto	'ticket'	zukkiini	'zucchini'
zyaketto	'jacket'	rokkufooru	'Roquefort'
moketto	'moquette'	sakkarin	'saccharin'
pikunikku	'picnic'	hikkorii	'hickory'
pipetto	'pipette'	appurike	'appliqué'
papetto	'puppet'	kappuringu	'coupling'
ketyappu	'ketchup'	batterii	'battery'

Our analysis in (12) and (13) (see Katayama 1998 for further details) represents source word consonants that are gemination candidates as moraic in the input, and expresses the directional bias leading to anticipatory degemination by means of the alignment constraint ALIGN-R(μ/c,ω). The latter assigns a violation mark for any mora separating a consonantal mora (μ/c) from the right edge of the prosodic word (ω) containing it.[7]

(12) pikkoro *'piccolo'*

/pik$_\mu$oro/	No-Gem$^2_{stem}$	Ident[μ]	No-Gem	Align-R(μ/c,ω)
▶ pikkoro			*	**
pikoro		*!		

(13) poketto *'pocket'*

/pok$_\mu$et$_\mu$o/	No-Gem$^2_{stem}$	Ident[μ]	No-Gem	Align-R(μ/c,ω)
pokketto	*!		**	***/*
▶ poketto		*	*	*
pokketo		*	*	**!
poketo		**!		

3.1.3 Templatic Degemination in Amharic

An additional twist occurs in situations where segmental identity is added as a further condition for degemination. Such a case is found in Amharic, a Semitic lan-

guage spoken in Ethiopia that is rich in geminates. Every Amharic consonant except
[ʔ] and [h] occurs in both a geminated and a nongeminated form, and words with
as many as five geminates are found: for example, Leslau (1997, 405) cites [lämmən-
nättäma**mm**änə**bb**ät] 'to the one in whom we have confidence'. Against this background of general tolerance toward co-occurring geminates, it is interesting to find a
particular kind of geminate dissimilation within the templatic system of verbs. Here
we are dealing with an alternation between two template shapes in (14): template 1
with gemination of both the second and third radical consonants, and template 2
with gemination of the third radical consonant only. The alternation is found in two
places in the verbal paradigm: in the intensive action of type A of the composite
verbs (14a) and in the attenuated action of type B verbs (14b).

(14) *Templatic degemination in Amharic*

$C_1VC_2C_2VC_3C_3$ (template 1) $C_1VC_2VC_3C_3$ (template 2)

  a. kəffətt (adärrägä)   'open completely   wədədd (alä)   (gloss missing)
                       and suddenly'
  b. läzzäbb (alä)   'be somewhat   läṭäṭṭ (alä)   'stretch somewhat'
                       soft'

Leslau (1997, 416) states the condition on the use of the "degeminating" template 2:
"The identity of the last two radicals brings about the dissimilation of gemination
and, as a result, the 2nd radical is not geminated."

The Amharic type of geminate dissimilation is especially suited to illustrate the
flexibility of the constraint-conjunctive formalization of our markedness-based conception of the OCP. Its central elements are segment-specific antigemination constraints, that is, conjunctions of the constraint No-Gem with specific markedness
constraints against individual segments, such as [ṭ] in (14b). No-Gem and {No-C},
where C is a variable over individual types of consonants and the braces indicate a
family of constraints, conjoin within the local domain of a segment (here understood
as a segmental structure containing a single root node, i.e., including geminates). As
shown in (15), No-Gem&$_{seg}${No-C} is itself dominated by Ident[μ], so a single cluster
such as [ṭṭ] does not activate the constraint.

(15) (No-Gem&$_{seg}${No-C})$^2_{stem}$

    |

  Ident[μ]

    |

  No-Gem&$_{seg}${No-C}

On the other hand, the stem-domain self-conjunction of NO-GEM&$_{seg}${NO-C} (i.e., [NO-GEM&$_{seg}${NO-C}]&$_{stem}$[NO-GEM&$_{seg}${NO-C}], or (NO-GEM&$_{seg}${NO-C})$^2_{stem}$ for short) dominates IDENT[μ], leading to degemination in situations where two [ṭṭ] clusters would otherwise arise within the same verbal stem.[8]

(16)

/lätt$_μ$ätt$_μ$/	(NO-GEM&$_{seg}${NO-C})$^2_{stem}$	IDENT[μ]	NO-GEM&$_{seg}${NO-C}	NO-GEM
lätt$_μ$ätt$_μ$	*!(ṭṭ … ṭṭ)		*(ṭṭ) *(ṭṭ)	**
▶ läṭätt$_μ$		*	*(ṭṭ)	*
läṭäṭ		**!		
/läzz$_μ$äbb$_μ$/				
▶ läzz$_μ$äbb$_μ$			*(zz) *(bb)	**
läzäbb$_μ$		*!	*(bb)	*
läzäb		*!*		

The analyses presented in this section highlight a significant advantage of the markedness-based approach to the dissimilation of (partially) identical structures within OT over the traditional OCP, namely, its ability to subsume dissimilation of prosodic properties without special extensions and assumptions about the geometry of phonological representations, which are unlikely to receive much independent support.[9]

3.2 Deaccentuation as Tonal Simplification

A different context where the markedness-based approach has advantages are cases where the dissimilating properties are in principle accessible to the classical OCP since they are represented on autosegmental tiers, but where achieving the necessary literal adjacency of identical specifications on a tier requires otherwise problematic assumptions about representations that the new approach is free of. Taking tonal features as an example, the point can be illustrated with a deaccentuation process in Japanese.[10] As is well known, the Japanese pitch accent consists of a steep fall in fundamental frequency (F0) that can be formally represented as a tonal HL contour linked to a single prosodic position (see Pierrehumbert and Beckman 1988, 121–126, for further analysis, and for discussion of the differences between the accentual HL unit and other sequences of H and L on the tonal tier). Roughly speaking, a prosodic word starts out on H until an accentual HL fall is reached, after which it continues on L. As a result, unaccented words have high pitch throughout, and in accented words, the preaccentual portion is high and the postaccentual portion is low. An additional twist concerns unaccented initial moras, which are low under specific conditions (see Pierrehumbert and Beckman 1988 for details). The basic pattern is illustrated in (17) with schematic F0 contours depicting the distinctive tonal fall. The examples are copula phrases consisting of a trisyllabic noun with the (unaccented) copula *da*. Since nouns can carry a lexical HL accent on any syllable (or on no syllable), there are overall four distinct accentual patterns.[11]

(17)

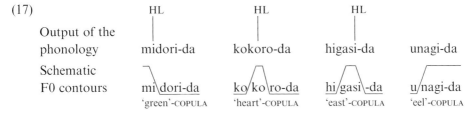

	HL	HL	HL	
Output of the phonology	midori-da	kokoro-da	higasi-da	unagi-da
Schematic F0 contours	mi\dori-da	ko/ko\ro-da	hi/gasi\-da	u/nagi-da
	'green'-COPULA	'heart'-COPULA	'east'-COPULA	'eel'-COPULA

Prosodic words are accentually culminative, permitting at most one accentual HL fall. Building on a basic No-HL constraint against falling tonal contours, we can identify the constraint ruling out more than one pitch accent per word as its enhanced (self-conjoined) version No-HL^2_ω, prohibiting the co-occurrence of the falling HL tone within the domain of the prosodic word (ω), and we have the by now familiar constraint ranking scheme in (18).[12]

(18) No-HL^2_ω

    IDENT

    No-HL

The morpheme-structural implications of this subhierarchy are indicated in (19). While a single HL associated with a morpheme is protected by faithfulness (19a), only one of the two HL melodies associated to a hypothetical doubly accented input form would survive (19b).

(19) a.

HL /midori/ 'green'	No-HL^2_ω	IDENT	No-HL
HL ▶ midori			*
midori		*!	

b.

HL HL /madora/ (hypothetical)	No-HL$^2_\omega$	Ident	No-HL
HL HL madora	*!		**
HL ▶ madora		*	*
HL ▶ madora		*	*
madora		**!	

The self-conjoined markedness constraint indexed to the domain of the prosodic word does the work of the accentual OCP constraint assumed by Kubozono (1995) and Tanaka (2001b), among others. These researchers argue that basic compounding in Japanese results in single prosodic words (see also section 5.2.2), and they attribute the deaccentuation of the first compound member to this OCP-type constraint.

(20) pe^{HL}rusya + ne^{HL}ko   → perusyane^{HL}ko   'Persian cat'
    sya^{HL}kai + se^{HL}edo   → syakaise^{HL}edo   'social system'
    ya^{HL}mato + nade^{HL}siko → yamatonade^{HL}siko   'Yamato woman'
    na^{HL}ma + tama^{HL}go → namata^{HL}mago   'raw egg'
    a^{HL}isu + koohi^{HL}i → aisuko^{HL}ohii   'iced coffee'

Owing to NONFINALITY constraints against accent on final syllables and feet (see Kubozono 1995 and Tanaka 2001b for details and analysis), the position of the accentual fall in the second compound member is not always identical to its position in the corresponding simplex word. What is important here is that the resulting compound word has only a single accentual fall, because of the high-ranking self-conjoined markedness constraint No-HL$^2_\omega$.[13]

We will return in chapter 8 to the accentual properties of compounds, in connection with correlations between compound voicing patterns and accentual behavior, and we will show that the deaccentuation of first compound members represents a kind of prosodic subordination that goes beyond the OCP. Here we take up some of the accentual patterns arising in the inflectional paradigms of verbs, where dissimilative deaccentuation is perhaps more clearly involved.

Unlike in the nominal forms seen above, where not only the presence versus absence but also the position of accent is distinctive (see Kitahara 2001 for an interesting study of its contrastive role), in verbal and adjectival forms only accentedness versus unaccentedness is distinctive, whereas the location of any given accent within the adjective or verb is predictable by general rules (see McCawley 1977 for a clear statement of the generalizations).[14] Illustrative forms are given in (21).

(21) *Verbal roots*

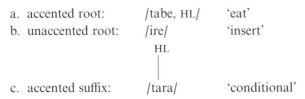

  a. accented root: /tabe, HL/ 'eat'
  b. unaccented root: /ire/   'insert'

  c. accented suffix: /tara/ 'conditional'

Verbal roots are either accented (i.e., have one underlying falling tone), as in (21a), or unaccented (have no underlying tone), as in (21b). The accent of recessive suffixes, such as the conditional suffix in (21c), appears only when combined with unaccented verb stems (*ire-ta*^{HL}*ra*) and deletes after accented verb stems (*ta*^{HL}*be-tara*), as shown in (22).

(22)

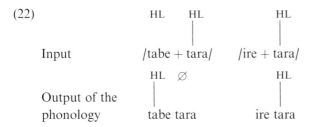

  Input   /tabe + tara/ /ire + tara/

  Output of the
  phonology   tabe tara ire tara

The accentually faithful candidate in (23) loses because of high-ranking No-HL$^2_\omega$. In addition to tonal dissimilation, this example involves a root faithfulness constraint, a type of positional faithfulness constraint (Beckman 1997), ranked somewhere in the hierarchy that, all other things being equal, selects the root-faithful candidate (23b) over the suffix-faithful candidate (23c).

(23) *Accented root + accented suffix*

HL HL | | /tabe + tara/	No-HL²_ω	IDENT	No-HL	IDENT-ROOT
a. HL HL | | tabe tara	*!		**	
b. ▶ HL | tabe tara		*	*	
c. HL | tabe tara		*	*	*!
d. tabe tara		**!		*

With an unaccented root (24), the underlying suffix tone survives because IDENT is ranked higher than the tonal markedness constraint No-HL.[15]

(24) *Unaccented root + accented suffix*

HL $\mid$ /ire + tara/	No-HL$^2_\omega$	IDENT	NO-HL	IDENT-ROOT
a. ▶ HL $\mid$ ire tara			*	
b. ire tara		*!		
c. HL HL $\mid$ $\mid$ ire tara	*!	*	**	*
d. HL $\mid$ ire tara		**!	*	*

This analysis, which makes crucial use of a markedness-based conception of OCP effects, has several advantages over a classical OCP approach.

First, the constraint No-HL^2 ruling out multiple complex (falling) tones requires no specific assumptions about the representation of the accent beyond the uncontroversial point that it involves a drastic fall in pitch. The fall is represented as an HL contour, following the successful and well-supported approach to tone and intonation representing pitch contours phonologically as sequences of level tones linked to a single prosodic position that has become standard since the mid-1970s.

This is significant because, from the perspective of the classical autosegmental OCP, as in the work of Leben (1973) and McCarthy (1986), a sequence "HLHL" on the tonal tier has no adjacent identical autosegments. To be able to invoke the autosegmental OCP to trigger deaccentuation, past analysts, including Poser (1984) and Pulleyblank (1986), needed to mark the accent by a single H tone rather than the contour HL, relying on later default rules to fill in the required L tone.

But representing the accent as H instead of HL, while crucial and apparently harmless from the point of view of the representation-based OCP, creates significant problems elsewhere, making it harder to capture the accent's phonetic characteristics.

This is shown by Pierrehumbert and Beckman (1988, 121–126), who argue that, whereas tonally sparsely specified phonological output representations play a central role in a successful phonetic account of Japanese pitch contours, the same is not true for the representation of the accent itself, which is best represented as HL, not as H.

To be able to invoke the representation-focused OCP with accents represented as HL, further melodic structure would have to be set up, which could then be scanned in the appropriate way. An obvious proposal is "[$_\tau$ HL] [$_\tau$ HL]," where τ is a tonal node, and where the sequence of identical tonal nodes τ counts as an illicit repetition. What remains to be determined, however, is whether there is any independent justification for extra melodic structure beyond its OCP-triggering role. In contrast, the strictly markedness-based account, while not incompatible with specific tonal geometries, makes no specific assumptions in this respect and can proceed on the basis of very simple representations.

Finally, there is an additional general consideration in favor of Pierrehumbert and Beckman's (1988) HL representation of accents and the present account of deaccentuation, which is ultimately based on the markedness constraint No-HL. It makes sense of the fundamental generalization that unaccentedness, rather than accentedness, is the default situation in Japanese (Akinaga 1960; Katayama 1995). Accented forms are marked simply in virtue of the fact that they violate the constraint No-HL ("No complex (falling) tone"). Note that it would not be possible to invoke the constraint No-H for this purpose since it is also violated in unaccented forms. What is marked about accented forms is the complex tone, the accentual fall, not high pitch by itself.

3.3 Further Issues in Constraint Conjunction

The remainder of this chapter deals with broader theoretical questions concerning the status of self-conjoined constraints in the grammar and their contribution to the analysis of dissimilation. The essence of our proposal is that the dissimilation of totally or partially identical elements traditionally accounted for by a specific principle, the OCP, can be reduced to a markedness threshold whose definition is simply the multiple violation of a markedness constraint. The formalization of this markedness threshold as self-conjunction is a separate matter. Here alternatives are conceivable and worth exploring, especially since self-conjunction stands apart from the general case of conjunction and might have some place in general phonological theory quite independent of the ultimate fate of the theory of local constraint conjunction. An inadequate alternative, we have argued, is the direct stipulation of markedness thresholds as completely unrelated constraints. Such a proposal, perhaps prompted by a mistaken notion that the fabrication of constraints is cost-free in OT, adds little in terms of theoretical substance, establishes no connections between clearly related constraints, and has no way of ruling out all kinds of unattested complex conditions. While we have also touched on the problematic aspects of the constraint-conjunctive approach, itself no innocent lamb in matters of descriptive power, it has the virtue of at least attempting to partially identify what kinds of complex constraints exist in OT: namely, only those that can be expressed as conjunctions of already existing constraints. This is a very natural restriction, and while the set of constraints it makes available is clearly still too large and needs to be narrowed down by other means, it compares favorably with the absence of any restriction whatsoever.[16]

Turning to the more circumscribed (and, as we have argued, independent) topic of the formal theory of self-conjunction, it is reasonable to ask whether there are any problems specifically connected with it. While in some respects self-conjunction might seem the most straightforward and most well-motivated type of conjunction (since there can be no doubt that the two conjuncts "have something to do with each other," which is a central cause of concern with respect to unrestricted conjunction), we will point to some issues that it raises.

3.3.1 Problems with Self-Conjoined Markedness

In dealing with featural dissimilation, Alderete (1997) proposes to replicate the place markedness subhierarchy (25) (Prince and Smolensky 1993) at the level of self-conjunction, as in (26).

(25) No-Lab, No-Dors
$$|$$
No-Cor

(26) No-Lab$^2_\delta$, No-Dors$^2_\delta$
$$|$$
No-Cor$^2_\delta$

While the argument that (26) allows a superior account of the inactivity of non-coronals in Tashlhiyt Berber dissimilation (and similar cases) is very convincing, the absence of any formal implicational link leading from (25) to (26) is a serious gap, however natural and expected the conclusion may be in itself. A theoretical result of Spaelti's (1997, 174–175) work on constraint conjunction is relevant in this context. Spaelti derives the preservation of ranking relations under self-conjunction (i.e., A ≫ B literally implies $A^2 \gg B^2$) from a more fundamental assumption, namely, the Universal Conjoined Constraint Ranking Hypothesis (UCCRH), stated here in (27).

(27) *Universal Conjoined Constraint Ranking Hypothesis (UCCRH, Spaelti 1997)*

If A dominates B, then the conjunction of A with Q dominates the conjunction of B with Q: $\forall ABQ \in Con$: IF $A \gg B$, THEN $A\&_\delta Q \gg B\&_\delta Q$.

This principle expresses the intuitively reasonable requirement that constraint conjunction always preserves ranking relations (assuming strict and total ranking): if A dominates B, conjunction with some other constraint Q cannot reverse this; that is, $B\&_\delta Q$ cannot dominate $A\&_\delta Q$. Given the UCCRH (27), Spaelti shows that ranking preservation for self-conjunction follows as a special case; that is, $A \gg B$ implies $A^2{}_\delta \gg B^2{}_\delta$. The proof is summarized in (28).

(28) *Ranking preservation*

    a. $A \gg B$ (by hypothesis)

    b. IF $A \gg B$, THEN   (UCCRH, (27))
        $A\&_\delta Q \gg B\&_\delta Q$

    c. $A\&_\delta Q \gg B\&_\delta Q$ (from (a) and (b))

    d. $A\&_\delta A \gg B\&_\delta A$ (from (c), by substituting A for Q)

    e. $A\&_\delta B \gg B\&_\delta B$ (from (c), by substituting B for Q)

    f. $A\&_\delta A \gg B\&_\delta B$; i.e.,   (from (d) and (e), by commutativity of "&" and
        $A^2{}_\delta \gg B^2{}_\delta$ transitivity of "$\gg$")

The result is ranking preservation under self-conjunction (29), which derives cases such as (26) as specific instances.

(29) IF $A \gg B$, THEN $A^2{}_\delta \gg B^2{}_\delta$

While (29) is a welcome result, the UCCRH (27) also uncovers further ranking properties of self-conjunctions that make them less than perfect expressions of the idea of OCP effects as enhanced markedness. As Kazutaka Kurisu and Adam Ussishkin (personal communications) have pointed out, given the UCCRH (27), the familiar markedness ranking NO-LAB $\gg$ NO-COR expressing the unmarked status of coronals (see Paradis and Prunet 1991) projects the ranking relations in (30).

(30) *UCCRH implications of NO-LAB $\gg$ NO-COR*

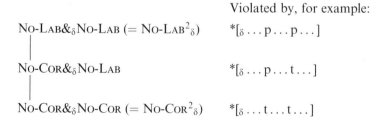

                                   Violated by, for example:

NO-LAB$\&_\delta$NO-LAB ($=$ NO-LAB$^2{}_\delta$)   *$[_\delta \ldots p \ldots p \ldots]$

NO-COR$\&_\delta$NO-LAB   *$[_\delta \ldots p \ldots t \ldots]$

NO-COR$\&_\delta$NO-COR ($=$ NO-COR$^2{}_\delta$)   *$[_\delta \ldots t \ldots t \ldots]$

Besides the ranking $\text{No-Lab}^2_\delta \gg \text{No-Cor}^2_\delta$, (30) contains the problematic ranking $\text{No-Cor}\&_\delta\text{No-Lab} \gg \text{No-Cor}^2_\delta$ declaring co-occurrence of a labial and a coronal a worse combination than an OCP-violating combination of two coronals—merely because labials are more marked than coronals. This kind of effect is unattested in any of the cases involving consonant co-occurrence restrictions in Semitic languages, and elsewhere.

As far as the formalization of local markedness thresholds as self-conjoined markedness is concerned, the Kurisu-Ussishkin conundrum illustrated in (30) creates a serious ranking problem under the Platonist interpretation of constraint conjunction theory (see section 2.2.1), where all conjunctions are automatically present in all grammars. In a legalistic sense, it does not affect the activationist version, which we have been assuming throughout, in the same way. Here the set of all conjunctions (infinite if conjunction is recursive) is not automatically part of all grammars; instead, as learners acquire the grammar of their language, they activate individual conjunctions on a case-by-case basis. Constraint conjunction is used as a formal tool expressing local interactions between violations of basic constraints, such as markedness thresholds, not as a theory providing all the reasons why it is those interactions that are crucial, and not others. Here the problematic ranking in (30) never becomes an issue as long as there is no reason to activate the constraint $\text{No-Lab}\&_\delta\text{No-Cor}$ in an individual grammar together with No-Cor^2_δ.

This answer remains somewhat shallow, however. It is left to some other part of the theory to explain why (certain) self-conjunctions are preferentially activated, and it remains true that wrong rankings are predicted within the network of universally possible conjunctions, even if they are not "downloaded" into individual grammars (and there is no guarantee that they never are). Overall, these considerations show that self-conjunction is not the ultimately ideal way of formalizing local markedness thresholds. The link it establishes to other conjunctions, while opening up interesting theoretical and empirical perspectives, is perhaps too close. The constraint-conjunctive formalization of enhanced markedness constraints takes them, intuitively speaking, not seriously enough: there is more to the repeated violation of No-Lab within a root than the violation of two markedness constraints that happen to be identical.

3.3.2 Dissimilation between Unmarked Elements

A different question regarding the formalization of the markedness threshold approach in terms of self-conjunction is this. If self-conjunction preserves ranking, as implied by the UCCRH (27), the approach seems to run into difficulties in cases where OCP dissimilation targets relatively unmarked elements while leaving relatively more marked elements undisturbed (i.e., the opposite of the situation in Tashlhiyt Berber, as analyzed in Alderete 1997). For example, in the northeast

Congo language Alur (Tucker 1969, 126), alveolar [t, d] and dental [t̪, d̪] coronal plosives exclude each other in roots.

(31) *Co-occurrence restrictions in Alur*

Well-formed roots	Ill-formed roots
t—t—	*t—t̪—
t̪—t̪—	*t̪—t—
d—d—	*d—d̪—
d̪—d̪—	*d̪—d—
t—d—	*t—d̪—
d—t—	*d̪—t—
t̪—d̪—	*t̪—d—
d̪—t̪—	*d—t̪—

Mester (1986, 27–32) analyzes this as an OCP effect on [coronal] in a geometric structure with further features (such as [distributed]) depending on [coronal], appealing to multiply linked (and hence OCP-safe) single-place specifications in case of total place identity. What is significant in the present context is that there is no indication that Alur shows OCP effects with labials and dorsals. Is this a case, then, where the OCP-as-markedness is faced with a ranking reversal such as the one in (32), contradicting both the specific claim in (26) and the general schema in (27)?

(32) a. NO-LAB, NO-DORS

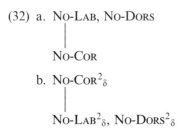

b. NO-COR$^2_\delta$

    NO-LAB$^2_\delta$, NO-DORS$^2_\delta$

(32b) is unlikely to provide the right answer. For cases like Alur, where coronal harmony plays a central role, every approach has to take into account the fact that, besides being unmarked, the coronal area is also highly populated, a variety of sub-places being occupied by segments of various manners. It differs in this respect from other places of articulation. What is ruled out is not just two coronals, but a combination of two placewise *different* coronals, each with a complex place specification. We anticipate, pending a more detailed investigation of such cases, that the markedness threshold approach can be extended along such lines without having to admit ranking reversals (which would achieve no more than a descriptive success). Further theoretical progress in this area might hinge on contrast-based notions explored in the work of Flemming (1995), Padgett (1997, 2003), Ní Chiosáin and Padgett (2001), and others.

3.3.3 Questions of Locality: Latin *l*-Dissimilation

Markedness thresholds, whether expressed as self-conjunctions or in some other way, militate against local clusterings of violation marks for one and the same markedness constraint. A crucial issue here is what counts as "local." The theory of locality and the theory of markedness are independent of each other, and it is to be expected that different aspects of locality play a role in markedness thresholds. What we have shown at work so far is *domain locality*, which will continue to occupy center stage in this book (see in particular chapter 5). Here two elements are neighbors in virtue of being contained in the same domain δ. Besides domain locality, phonology manifests the more basic kind of locality, namely, *adjacency*: two elements are neighbors in virtue of standing next to each other. A leading idea of autosegmental phonology (and its later developments, such as feature geometry (see Clements 1985) and related work) was the attempt to subsume all locality under some kind of adjacency. Domains such as the morpheme remained important, but for a research program seeking explanations chiefly in rich and finely articulated phonological representations, it was a natural step to geometrize even the locality relation holding between elements of the same morpheme (as in the Morpheme Tier Hypothesis of McCarthy 1986), in effect reducing it to adjacency.

In this chapter, we have outlined some of the problems and limitations of this theoretical framework in connection with the autosegmental OCP, and we have argued for an alternative conception based on phonological domains instead of representational adjacency that makes direct and exclusive use of markedness constraints.

It would be a fallacy to conclude from this, however, that adjacency has become superfluous in the new conception, having been entirely replaced by phonological domains. Given the fundamental role of the adjacency relation in phonology, this is a priori unlikely, and indeed it is not difficult to find OCP effects whose proper analysis requires adjacency as the essential locality factor, in a way not reducible to shared domains. The cases of length dissimilation between long vowels in adjacent syllables discussed by Alderete (1997) are potentially of this kind, pending a more detailed study of the phonologies of the languages involved.

Here we illustrate the continued role of adjacency, as well as more general questions of locality, with the perhaps most well-known case of liquid dissimilation: Latin *l*-dissimilation. The classical language has an adjective-forming suffix exemplified in (33) whose basic form is /-a:lis/ (preserved in English as /-al/—since most examples have direct counterparts in English, we have omitted glosses in this section as largely redundant).

(33) *Default variant* -a:lis

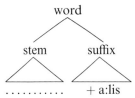

aktu-a:lis, ami:k-a:lis, du-a:lis, fi:n-a:lis, greg-a:lis, ho:r-a:lis, hospit-a:lis, ide-a:lis, karn-a:lis, kasu-a:lis, kaus-a:lis, kommu:n-a:lis, kri:mi:n-a:lis, kwie:t-a:lis, mamm-a:lis, mort-a:lis, naut-a:lis, origin-a:lis, prinkip-a:lis, ration-a:lis, soki-a:lis, usu-a:lis, verb-a:lis, vit-a:lis, etc.

When the base itself contains *l*, however, the lateral of the suffix changes into the rhotic *r*. This happens not only when the triggering *l* occupies the onset of the pre- ceding syllable (34a), but also when it stands at a greater distance (34b,c).

(34) *Dissimilation variant* -a:ris *after* l-*stems:* *[. . . l . . . l . . .]* → *[. . . l . . . r . . .]*

a. Onset [l] in adjacent syllables:

...[σ__ ...] [σ__ ...]...

angul-a:ris, ankill-a:ris, eksul-a:ris, insul-a:ris, kapill-a:ris, konsul-a:ris, puell-a:ris, pupill- a:ris, skol-a:ris, singul-a:ris, sol-a:ris, tabul- a:ris, etc.

b. Onset [l] in nonadjacent syllables:

...[σ__ ...]...[σ__ ...]...

auksili-a:ris, famili-a:ris, lakt-a:ris, lapid- a:ris, li:min-a:ris, li:ne-a:ris, lun-a:ris, milit- a:ris, pla:n-a:ris, salu:t-a:ris

c. Coda [l] in nonadjacent syllables:

...[σ ... __]...[σ__ ...]...

vulg-a:ris, pulment-a:ris

However, when *r* intervenes between stem-*l* and suffix-*l*, dissimilation of the latter to *r* is suppressed, and the suffix appears unchanged (35).

(35) *Blocking effect: no dissimilation to* r *after* l-*stems when* r *intervenes*

...l...r...l... ↛ *...l...r...r...

flor-a:lis, liber-a:lis, litor-a:lis, litter- a:lis, lustr-a:lis, plur-a:lis, etc.

On the other hand, a stem-*r* that does not intervene between the two *l*s does not prevent dissimilation (36).

(36) *Nonintervening stem-*r *does not block dissimilation*

*...r...l...l... → ...r...l...r...

agrikol-a:ris, kirkul-a:ris, partikul-a:ris, perpendikul-a:ris, re:gul-a:ris, etc.

Since the dissimilation process does not affect *l* in general in the classical language, but is virtually restricted to this one derivational suffix, it seems most adequate to analyze it as a case of phonologically controlled allomorphy. The suffix has two allomorphs, the default variant *-a:lis* and the special variant *-a:ris*, whose distribution is decided by general phonological constraints (see Mester 1994 for this kind of approach to phonologically conditioned allomorphy, and important further development in Tranel 1998; see also section 6.3.2 for a case in Japanese). We use A:LIS > A:RIS as a shorthand notation for the preference relation between the two allomorphs that appear in the input when the morpheme is inserted. Other formalizations are of course possible; the essential point is that adjectives end in *-a:ris* only when there is a dissimilation-triggering *l* in the stem (37).

(37) dua:lis

/{du} + {a:lis, a:ris}/	A:LIS > A:RIS
▶ dua:lis	
dua:ris	*!

We interpret the dissimilation constraint as No-L$^2_\omega$, taking the prosodic word (ω) as the relevant domain (see chapter 5 for further discussion of the issues involved in such cases). This constraint is dominated by all antagonistic faithfulness constraints (IDENT, etc.), and consequently it is in general inert in Latin phonology (cf. *Laelius* (name), *plaka:-bilis* 'easy to placate', *kla:v-ulus* 'nail (diminutive)', etc.). However, No-L$^2_\omega$ outranks the allomorph preference constraint A:LIS > A:RIS, leading to dissimilatory allomorph selection, as in (38).

(38) singula:ris

/{singul} + {a:lis, a:ris}/	No-L$^2_\omega$	A:LIS > A:RIS
singula:lis	*!	
▶ singula:ris		*

Regarding (35) *flor-a:lis*, *plu:ra:lis*, and so on, classical autosegmental analysis (see Steriade 1987) appeals to a [lateral] tier where only liquids receive a representation, and where they are specified as [+lateral] (laterals) and [−lateral] (rhotics). A rhotic *r* intervening between two *l*'s then means that the adjacency of the two [+lateral] specifications is broken by [−lateral]. There is no OCP violation, in this conception, and hence no dissimilation. This quintessentially autosegmental explanation cannot be directly replicated in strictly domain-based terms. After all, *flor-a:lis* shows two *l*'s in the domain of a word; the intervening *r* changes nothing about this fact.

Steriade (1995b) suggests an alternative to the tier adjacency analysis that at first glance seems to offer a way out: namely, *r*-dissimilation as a higher-ranking constraint blocking *l*-dissimilation. This suggestion enjoys independent support in Latin, where *r*-dissimilation is known to be a factor at least in the historical phonology, as shown by gaps in the application of rhotacism. Rhotacism is the process whereby intervocalic [s] changes into [r], as in *hono:s-is > hono:r-is* 'honor (genitive)' or *ama:-se > ama:-re* 'to love' (cf. *ama:-vis-se* 'to have loved'). In cases where rhotacism would place two rhotics in the same or adjacent syllables, it is blocked, as in *miser* 'poor' (**mirer*) or *kaesa:ries* 'dark head of hair' (**kaera:ries*).

Expanding the ranking by recruiting the constraint No-R$^2_\omega$, parallel to No-L$^2_\omega$, and adding it at the top of the hierarchy, the self-conjunction analysis can successfully deal with the *r*-intervention cases, as in (39).

(39) plu:ra:lis

/{plu:r} + {a:lis, a:ris}/	No-R$^2_\omega$	No-L$^2_\omega$	A:LIS > A:RIS
▶ plura:lis		*	
plura:ris	*!		*

Unfortunately, the dominant position of No-R$^2_\omega$ overshoots the mark and runs afoul of the facts in (36), where [...r...l...r...] within the prosodic word is wrongly excluded, as in (40).[17]

(40) re:gula:ris

/{re:gul} + {a:lis, a:ris}/	No-R$^2_\omega$	No-L$^2_\omega$	A:LIS > A:RIS
wrong winner ▶ re:gula:lis		*	
re:gula:ris	*!		*

In the face of such phenomena, it is possible that explanations more or less along classical autosegmental lines will need to be resuscitated as the ultimately correct ones. It is important to point out, though, that No-R$^2_\omega$ is probably too sweeping as an *r*-dissimilation imperative, quite independently of the problem illustrated in (40). Thus, in general rhotacism seems to be blocked when it would result in two *r*'s in adjacent syllables, not when it would result in two *r*'s anywhere within the prosodic word (the examples in (36) all fall into the adjacent-syllable category). This suggests, then, that the domain of No-R^2 should be restricted to adjacent syllables instead of the whole word, as in (41).

(41) a. plu:ra:lis

/{plu:r} + {a:lis, a:ris}/	No-R$^2_{\sigma\sigma}$	No-L$^2_{\omega}$	A:LIS > A:RIS
▶ plu:ra:lis		*	
plu:ra:ris	*!		*

b. re:gula:ris

/{re:gul} + {a:lis, a:ris}/	No-R$^2_{\sigma\sigma}$	No-L$^2_{\omega}$	A:LIS > A:RIS
re:gula:lis		*!	
▶ re:gula:ris			*

A cursory survey turned up only very few examples not falling into the adjacent-syllable category, including *Luperka:lis* 'belonging to the Lupercalia' (a festival devoted to the Lycean Pan, Lupercus) and *larva:lis* 'ghostly', both of which have the blocking *r* not in the syllable before *lis*, but in the preceding coda. The significance of these examples is not entirely clear—the first one derives from a name, and the second is attested only in post-Augustan Latin, when *l*-dissimilation had lost much of its force (see immediately below). If taken at face value, however, such forms argue that No-R$^2_{\sigma\sigma}$ is too limited in scope.

The last point leads to a last set of facts. It is well known that in post-Augustan Latin the variant *-a:lis* became more and more prevalent: *l*-dissimilation ceased to select the *r*-variant in later formations such as *kolle:gia:lis*, *filia:lis*, *glakia:lis*, *fluvia:lis*, *labia:lis*, and so on. Before concluding that *l*-dissimilation was entirely inert at this point, we must note that in all these forms the stem-*l* is separated by more than one syllable from the suffix-*l*. This raises the possibility that postclassically a weaker version No-L$^2_{\sigma\sigma}$ was still in force, requiring dissimilation in adjacent syllables. This is supported by the form *ve:la:ris* 'relating to a veil, curtain', first attested in the works of Plinius Maior (†79 A.D.), which still shows the dissimilated variant (hence English *velar* instead of **velal*).

Regarding the locality condition governing the markedness thresholds leading to OCP effects, we can draw from this short excursus into Latin phonology the general conclusion that, besides domain locality, direct adjacency relations continue to play an essential role. This points to an important issue that needs further thought and investigation, especially in light of recent work (Hansson 2001; Rose and Walker 2001) on the typology and formal analysis of long-distance agreement phenomena between consonants, namely, as a kind of syntagmatic consonant-to-consonant correspondence.

3.3.4 Reduplication: Motivating the Emergence of Unmarked Properties

In concluding this chapter, we turn to a group of processes that have a close affinity to traditional OCP effects in that they seem to involve a local markedness threshold that does not permit more than one occurrence of a given marked structure, but whose standard analysis in OT makes no use of this markedness factor and relies instead entirely on faithfulness.

It has commonly been observed that reduplicants are often simplified images of their bases. Not only are they partial copies; they also display reduced complexity in many other respects: onset clusters shrink to single consonants, mid vowels appear as high, tonal contours are flattened out, and so on. Steriade (1988) made the first systematic attempt to seize the common thread running through all these phenomena—the reversal to an unmarked state of affairs—and proposed an analysis that established a direct link to general markedness theory. Within OT, the phenomena in question were taken up under the rubric *emergence of the unmarked* in McCarthy and Prince 1994, 1995, where they were given a faithfulness treatment and served as a prime example of the distinction between base-reduplicant faithfulness and input-output faithfulness. The question to be explored here is whether local markedness thresholds can contribute anything to the explanation of these phenomena.

In order to illustrate concretely what is at stake, we return to the Sanskrit co-occurrence restriction on aspiration, which served as a preliminary illustration for the theory of self-conjunction (section 2.1.1). A well-known extension of the mono-aspirate rule beyond the domain of a single morpheme is the deaspiration found in reduplicated forms, illustrated by reduplicated perfects in (42).[18]

(42) *Deaspiration in Sanskrit reduplicated forms*

	Root	3sg. pres.	3sg. perf.	
a.	/bʱaj/	bʱajati	ba-bʱaːja	'divide'
b.	/cʱid/	cʱinatti	ci-cʱeːda	'cut'
c.	/ɦɾ/	ɦarati	ja-ɦaːra	'take'

The complex consisting of reduplicative prefix + base here shows quasi-monomorphemic behavior, different from all other derived environments. In line with the focus on representation as the main locus of explanation in autosegmentalist phonology, earlier approaches used facts such as those in (42) as crucial arguments for a reduplication-specific nonlinear mode of representation (see, e.g., Mester 1986,

241–247). In current OT, the standard approach to such deaspiration in reduplication invokes McCarthy and Prince's (1994, 1995) emergence-of-the-unmarked scheme, which can be implemented here through low-ranking IDENT-BR, leaving No-C^h sandwiched between input-output (IO) and base-reduplicant (BR) faithfulness; that is, IDENT-IO $\gg$ No-C^h $\gg$ IDENT-BR. Combining this with the ranking No-C$^{h2}_m$ $\gg$ IDENT-IO $\gg$ No-C^h established earlier (section 2.1.1) results in the overall ranking No-C$^{h2}_m$ $\gg$ IDENT-IO $\gg$ No-C^h $\gg$ IDENT-BR, as illustrated in (43).

(43) *Emergence-of-the-unmarked scheme*

/RED-b^{h}a:ja/	No-C$^{h2}_m$	IDENT-IO	No-C^h	IDENT-BR
a. b^{h}a-b^{h}a:ja			**!	
b. ▶ ba-b^{h}a:ja			*	*
c. b^{h}a-ba:ja		*!	*	*
d. ba-ba:ja		*!		

There is one aspect of this analysis, and of the theory it is embedded in, which seems to leave room for improvement. While the ranking in (43) copes with the facts, it ends up with two separate explanations for the two prongs of Sanskrit deaspiration: No-C$^{h2}_m$ $\gg$ IDENT-IO $\gg$ No-C^h takes care of the morpheme-structural one-aspirate limit (section 2.1.1), and IDENT-IO $\gg$ No-C^h $\gg$ IDENT-BR finishes things off by deaspirating all reduplicants. Besides the analysis-oriented question whether further unification is actually attainable in this specific case involving Sanskrit reduplication (known for its idiosyncrasies; see Whitney 1889), a more important general question arises regarding the factors that cause reduplicants to become unmarked in case after case (for many examples, see Steriade 1988; McCarthy and Prince 1994, 1995). The essence of reduplication is the repetition of material, resulting in the repeated instantiation of marked properties in a local domain. It is natural to suspect this to be one of the factors motivating a reversal to a less marked state in the reduplicant. In contrast, however, the standard correspondence-theoretic approach presents the emergence of unmarked properties in reduplicants as a context-free effect, attributed only to the fact that some BR faithfulness constraint happens to rank lower than its IO counterpart. As seen in (43), instead of capitalizing on the concrete phonological context provided by the base and focusing on the two violations of No-C^h in close proximity caused by faithful copying of aspirated consonants, the dissimilating influence of the base plays no role, and the phonological and morphological context is represented only at the metalevel, in the form of separate BR faithfulness.

In light of the approach pursued here, it is natural to hypothesize that at least one of the factors leading to the frequent loss of marked properties in reduplicants must be dissimilation with respect to the base. In this case, No-C$^{h2}_\delta$ should be crucially involved, for some domain δ, making it possible to explain the appearance of unmarked properties in reduplicants in a less abstract way that focuses directly on the tangible phonological properties of the forms concerned—that is, as markedness-driven dissimilation.[19] The issue is not whether FAITH-BR exists at all alongside FAITH-IO (which seems hardly in doubt), but how to find a theory that strikes the right balance between markedness- and faithfulness-based explanations, a task that must be left to future work.

Chapter 4

The Morphology and Phonology
of Compound Voicing

In OT, phonological processes arise out of the interaction of ranked and violable constraints. As the last chapter showed, this allows for a very simple and direct understanding of OCP effects, namely, as pure markedness effects. The dissimilation of elements standing in close proximity and sharing a marked property φ is reducible to the markedness constraint No-φ itself—in an enhanced version targeting locally clustered *φ-marks. As a case in point, the obstruent voicing restriction holding in native Japanese morphemes was shown to follow from the ranking in (1), with the faithfulness constraint crucially sandwiched between the basic markedness constraint and its enhanced version (recall that D stands for [+voi, −son], the natural class of voiced obstruents).

(1) *Core ranking for Japanese obstruent voicing established so far*

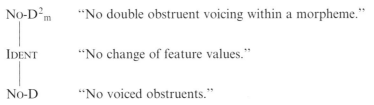

No-D^2_m "No double obstruent voicing within a morpheme."

Ident   "No change of feature values."

No-D   "No voiced obstruents."

It is often found that such static morpheme structure conditions are reflected in dynamic processes, such as morphophonemic alternations and their conditions, and Japanese provides a particularly clear instance of this kind of situation. In this chapter, we show how the effects of the basic constraint configuration in (1) reach beyond morpheme structure. They take on an active role in the phonology by interacting with the compound voicing alternation known as *rendaku* (連濁 'sequential voicing', from *ren* 連 'sequential' and *daku* 濁 'turbid, muddy (state)'), stated informally in (2).

(2) *Rendaku* ("sequential voicing"): "The initial segment of the second member of a compound is voiced."

After presenting the relevant facts and generalizations, we show that several rather intricate effects are correctly predicted once (1) is augmented as in (3) by the constraint REALIZE-MORPHEME (requiring here that the linking morpheme that is responsible for *rendaku* voicing be expressed in the output).

(3) *Expanded ranking for Japanese obstruent voicing*

$$\text{No-D}^2{}_m$$

REALIZE-M

IDENT

No-D

4.1 *Rendaku* as a Linking Morpheme

In a compound word C consisting of the two members m_1 and m_2, as schematically indicated in (4), *rendaku* affects the second member m_2, requiring its initial segment to be voiced.

(4) *Schematic compound structure*

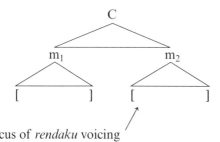

Here we here focus on simple compound structures that do not contain compounds as subconstituents. Recursive compound structures, in particular right-branching ones, have special properties that will be investigated in chapter 8.

4.1.1 The Empirical Scope of *Rendaku*

The central role of the compound voicing process in the lexicon of Japanese is illustrated in (5)–(8) (see also the larger collection of examples in the appendix). In (5), we show native monosyllabic roots of the form CV (C = voiceless consonant) undergoing the voicing process in second member position.

(5) *Monosyllabic undergoers (CV)*

C = k	ki	makura-gi	'pillow-wood, (railroad) crosstie'
		taki-gi	'burn-wood, firewood'
	ke	matu-ge	'eyebrow-hair, eyebrow'
		aka-ge	'red hair'
	ko	mai-go	'stray-child, missing child'
		huta-go	'two-child, twin'
C = s	su	awase-zu	'combine-vinegar, flavored vinegar'
		ume-zu	'plum vinegar'
	se	neko-ze	'cat-back, stoop, hunchback'
		uwa-ze	'above-back, height'
C = t	ta	ina-da	'rice-field, rice paddy'
		kakusi-da	'hide-field, hidden rice paddy (to avoid taxation)'
	ti	hana-zi	'nosebleed'
	te	kuma-de	'bear-hand, rake'
		su-de	'bare-hand, empty-handed'
	to	ami-do	'screen door'
		kuguri-do	'ducking-door, side door'
C = h	ha	ire-ba	'insert-tooth, dentures'
		musi-ba	'insect-tooth, decayed tooth'
	hi	tane-bi	'seed-fire, pilot light'
		mukae-bi	'welcome-fire, welcoming bonfire (for departed spirits)'
	he	iidasi-be	'say-start-fart; the one calling attention to a fart is the farter; the one who brings up a subject must be the first to act on it'

For disyllabic and trisyllabic forms, we show the segmental variety of the morphemes undergoing the process (see (6)–(7)). With a systematic exception to be discussed below, any consonantal segment of Japanese can occur in positions C_2 and C_3.[1]

(6) *Disyllabic undergoers (CVCV)*

a.

		C_2 = k, s, t [−son, −voi]		
C_1 = k	kaki	yoko-gaki	'horizontal-write, writing horizontally'	
	kasa	hi-gasa	'sun umbrella'	
	kutu	naga-gutu	'long-shoe, boots'	
C_1 = s	sake	ama-zake	'sweet-sake, sweet drink made from fermented rice'	
	sasi	kusi-zasi	'skewer-point, skewered'	
	sita	neko-zita	'cat-tongue, aversion to hot food'	

	C_2 = k, s, t [−son, −voi]		
C_1 = t	take	sao-dake	'pole-bamboo, bamboo pole'
	tosi	hebi-dosi	'snake-year, year of the snake'
	tati	sio-dati	'salt-abstaining, abstinence from salt and salty food'
C_1 = h	hako	gomi-bako	'waste-box, garbage can'
	hasi	huna-basi	'boat-bridge, pontoon bridge'
	hata	ido-bata	'well-side, place for housewives' gossip'

b.

	C_2 = n, m [+son, +nas]		
C_1 = k	kani	kabuto-gani	'helmet-crab, horseshoe crab'
	kama	aturyoku-gama	'pressure-pot, pressure cooker'
C_1 = s	sono	hana-zono	'flower garden'
	semi	natu-zemi	'summer cicada'
C_1 = t	tani	tanuki-dani	'badger valley'
	tama	ame-dama	'candy-ball, toffees'
C_1 = h	hone	se-bone	'back-bone, spine'
	home	beta-bome	'sticky-praise, exaggerated praise, flattery'

c.

	C_2 = r, y, w [+son, +approx]		
C_1 = k	kiri	yo-giri	'night-fog, night mist'
	kayo-i	zyuku-gayo-i	'school-commute, going to a prep school'
	kawa	tani-gawa	'valley-river, mountain stream'
C_1 = s	sara	hai-zara	'ash-dish, ashtray'
	saya	ne-zaya	'price-sheath, margin, spread (in prices)'
	siwa	ko-ziwa	'small-wrinkle, fine wrinkles'
C_1 = t	tori	umi-dori	'sea bird'
	tuyo-i	kokoro-zuyo-i	'heart-strong, feeling secure'
C_1 = h	hera	kutu-bera	'shoe-spatula, shoehorn'
	heya	aki-beya	'empty-room, available room (in a hotel)'

(7) *Trisyllabic undergoers (CVCVCV)*

a. | | C_2 and C_3 = [−son, −voi] | | |
|---|---|---|---|
| $C_1 = k$ | kakasi | nise-gakasi | 'false scarecrow' |
| | kakato | kinzoku-gakato | 'metal heels' |
| | kataki | koi-gataki | 'love-rival, rival in love' |
| $C_1 = s$ | sikake | iro-zikake | 'love-device, pretense of love' |
| | sitaku | tabi-zitaku[2] | 'trip-prepare, preparation for a trip' |
| | susuki | yama-zusuki | 'mountain-eulalia, mountain pampas grass' |
| $C_1 = t$ | tasuke | hito-dasuke | 'people-help, act of charity' |
| | tataki | hukuro-dataki | 'bag-hit, ganging up and giving a person a sound beating' |
| | tukusi | kokoro-zukusi | 'heart-render, heart effort, kindness' |
| $C_1 = h$ | hasika | syooni-basika | 'infant-measles, children's measles' |
| | hitasi | mizu-bitasi | 'water-soak, soaked in water, flooded' |
| | hotoke | iki-botoke | 'live-Buddha, living Buddha, incarnation of Buddha' |

b. | | C_2 or C_3 = [+son] | | |
|---|---|---|---|
| $C_1 = k$ | kawase | densin-gawase | 'telegraph-pay, telegraphic transfer/remittance' |
| | kokoro | otome-gokoro | 'maiden-heart, feelings of a girl' |
| | kusuri | nomi-gusuri | 'swallow-medicine, internal medicine' |
| $C_1 = s$ | sakana | yaki-zakana | 'burn-fish, broiled fish' |
| | samasi | me-zamasi | 'eye-open, eye-opener, alarm clock' |
| | sirusi | hata-zirusi | 'flag-mark, design on a flag, ensign' |
| $C_1 = t$ | tamasii | yamato-damasii | 'Yamato spirit' |
| | tatami | isi-datami | 'stone-tatami, stone pavement' |
| | tikara | baka-zikara | 'fool-strength, brute force' |
| $C_1 = h$ | hasira | kai-basira | 'shell-pillar, scallops' |
| | hayasi | matu-bayasi | 'pine forest' |
| | hanasi | ura-banasi | 'back-story, inside story' |

c. | C_2 and $C_3 = [+\text{son}]$

$C_1 = k$	konomi	onna-gonomi	'woman-liking, woman's favorites'
	koyomi	hana-goyomi	'flower calendar'
	kuruma	kaza-guruma	'wind-wheel, windmill'
$C_1 = s$	simari	to-zimari	'door-close, lockup'
	sirami	toko-zirami	'bed-louse, floor louse'
	sawari	hada-zawari	'skin-touch, feel'
$C_1 = t$	tamari	hi-damari	'sun-gather, sunny spot'
	tanomi	hito-danomi	'person-ask, reliance on others'
	tawara	kome-dawara	'rice-bag, straw rice bag'
$C_1 = h$	hanare	oya-banare	'parents-separate, independence from parents'
	harami	hidari-barami	'left-side-pregnant, male birth'
	hirame	sita-birame	'tongue-flatfish, sole'

Rendaku voicing on the second member is also a typical feature of reduplicated forms, as shown in (8).

(8) *Intensive/pluralizing reduplication*

a. k...-g...
---

kami	kami-gami	'god-god, gods'
kane	kane-gane	'before-before, since long ago'
karu	karu-garu	'light-light, lightly, thoughtlessly'
kasane	kasane-gasane	'repeat-repeat, repeatedly, doubly'
kata	kata-gata	'person-person, persons (honorific)'
ki	ki-gi	'tree-tree, trees'
kie	kie-gie	'vanish-vanish, vanishing'
kire	kire-gire	'cut-cut, pieces, scraps'
koe	koe-goe	'voice-voice, many voices'
koma	koma-goma	'fine-fine, minutely, in detail'
kori	kori-gori	'repent-repent, have enough of, learn by experience'
koto	koto-goto	'thing-thing, in everything, in every way'
kowa	kowa-gowa	'fear-fear, fearfully, timidly, cautiously'
kuma	kuma-guma	'corner-corner, nooks and corners'
kuni	kuni-guni	'country-country, countries'
kure	kure-gure	'repeat-repeat, repeatedly'
kuro	kuro-guro	'black-black, pitch black'
kuti	kuti-guti	'mouth-mouth, each entrance, every mouth, unanimously'

b. s...-z...

saki	saki-zaki	'far-far, in the distant future'
sama	sama-zama	'various-various, diverse, of all kinds'
same	same-zame	'sorrow-sorrow, sorrowfully, anguishedly'
samu	samu-zamu	'cold-cold, desolate, wintry'
sima	sima-zima	'island-island, islands'
simo	simo-zimo	'low-low, lower classes, common people'
sore	sore-zore	'that-that, each, respectively'
sue	sue-zue	'end-end, in the future'
suki	suki-zuki	'like-like, likes and dislikes, matter of taste'
sumi	sumi-zumi	'corner-corner, every nook and corner'

c. t...-d...

taka	taka-daka	'high-high, at most'
tika	tika-zika	'near-near, soon'
toki	toki-doki	'time-time, sometimes'
tokoro	tokoro-dokoro	'place-place, in various places'
tuki	tuki-zuki	'month-month, monthly'
tuku	tuku-zuku	'thorough-thorough, thoroughly, utterly'
tune	tune-zune	'usual-usual, always, usually'

d. h...-b...

hana	hana-bana	'flower-flower, many kinds of flowers'
hasi	hasi-basi	'edge-edge, all edges'
hi	hi-bi	'day-day, many days'
hie	hie-bie	'cold-cold, chilly'
hiro	hiro-biro	'wide-wide, extensive, spacious'
hisa	hisa-bisa	'long-long, long time, many days'
hito	hito-bito	'man-man, people'

Intensive/pluralizing reduplication (8) (see also (31)) must not be confused with the more well-known reduplicated mimetics (i.e., sound-symbolic expressions—see, e.g., Hamano 1986, 1998; Mester and Ito 1989), which never show *rendaku* voicing (e.g., *poko-poko, sara-sara, kata-kata*; not **poko-boko*, etc.). Besides the vast semantic and other combinatorial differences between the two, such as the impossibility of attaching the characteristic mimetic adverbial suffixes -*ri* and -*tto* (*poko-ri, pokko-ri, poko-tto*, etc.) to the morphemes in (8) (there are no **toki-ri, *tokki-ri, *toki-tto* alongside *toki-doki*, etc.), the accent patterns are fundamentally different. Intensive/pluralizing reduplications follow compound accentuation: their accent falls close to the internal boundary and is initial in the second member (e.g., *tokoro-dó̚koro*), often migrating to the last syllable of the first member if the second members is short (e.g., *kami⌐-gami*). In addition, many intensive/pluralizing forms are unaccented (e.g., *toki-doki*), just like ordinary compounds (as well as foreign loans) of exactly four light syllables. In mimetic reduplication, on the other hand, accent falls strictly on the first syllable of the first member (*to⌐ko-toko*, etc.). In this, they follow the default pattern of coordinative ("dvandva") compounds, which as a rule consist of two prosodic words, the first of which is accented, either bearing accent on its first syllable (*ip⌐pu-tasai* 'one husband–many wives, polygamy', *yo⌐ru-hiru* 'day and night', *ma⌐e-usiro* 'before and after', etc.) or preserving its noninitial accent (*yama⌐-kawa* 'mountain-river', following *yama⌐* 'mountain').[3]

The sheer wealth of compounds exhibiting *rendaku* can easily lead the analyst to overlook the basic fact that it is a genuinely lexical process, with all the special properties and idiosyncrasies that come with this status. In Ito and Mester 1986, the lexical nature of the process was explicitly captured in the framework of Lexical Phonology (Kiparsky 1982), and more or less equivalent statements can be found in most other works on the topic (see, e.g., Martin 1952; McCawley 1968; Otsu 1980; Vance 1987; Ohno 2000). *Rendaku* makes essential reference to vocabulary class and morphological structure and is by no means an automatic property of all compound structures.[4] We will focus here on the basic morphology and phonology of the process, noting only the basic background restriction that *rendaku* is (mostly) limited to native/nativized second members of (most types of) modifier-head compounds. In chapter 6, we will return to issues of vocabulary class, and the typology and proper analysis of exceptions.

4.1.2 Morphological Preliminaries

While most compounds in common use are simple concatenations of two morphemes, Japanese compounds are of course not in principle limited in this way. A category more inclusive than "morpheme" is therefore needed in order to characterize these compounds' immediate constituents. Besides recursivity—compounds embedded inside compounds—there are other sources of morphological complexity. For instance, when a compound's first or second member is a verb, it normally appears in its stem form, which consists of the root followed by appropriate stem-forming suffixes, as dictated by morphosyntactic factors. Examples appear in (9), where the additional elements are highlighted and curly braces "{ }" indicate morphological constituency.

(9) a.

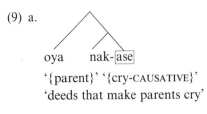

oya   nak-[ase]

'{parent}' '{cry-CAUSATIVE}'

'deeds that make parents cry'

b.

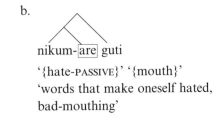

nikum-[are] guti

'{hate-PASSIVE}' '{mouth}'

'words that make oneself hated, bad-mouthing'

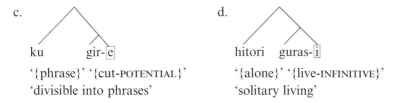

c.
ku   gir-[e]
'{phrase}' '{cut-POTENTIAL}'
'divisible into phrases'

d.
hitori   guras-[i]
'{alone}' '{live-INFINITIVE}'
'solitary living'

The suffixes that appear in this way in compounds are derivational, not inflectional. In terms of the "root-stem-word" hierarchy in (10), we can refer to them as *stem-forming* or *level I*, contrasting with *word-forming* or *level II* affixes.

(10) *Word structure*

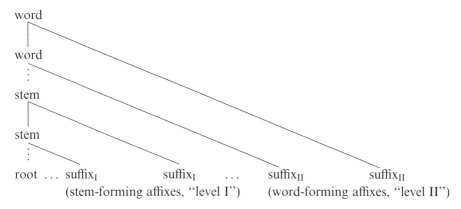

word

word
⋮
stem

stem
⋮
root ... suffix_I   suffix_I   ...   suffix_II   suffix_II
       (stem-forming affixes, "level I")   (word-forming affixes, "level II")

Following (10), the full morphological structure in (11) is assigned to a typical verb form with a derivational suffix and an inflectional ending.

(11) *Morphological structure of* tabesaseta *'{{eat-CAUSATIVE}-PAST}, made eat'*

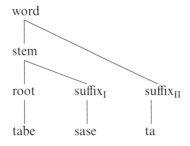

word

stem

root   suffix_I   suffix_II

tabe   sase   ta

The structures in (12) are assigned to the word compounds in (9a,b). For nominal elements such as *oya* 'parent', both root and stem are coextensive with the word.

(12) *Word compounding*

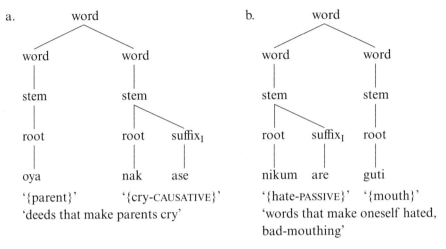

a.

```
                word
              /      \
          word        word
            |           |
          stem        stem
            |           |
          root       root   suffix_I
            |          |       |
          oya        nak     ase
       '{parent}'    '{cry-CAUSATIVE}'
       'deeds that make parents cry'
```

b.

```
                word
              /      \
          word        word
            |           |
          stem        stem
            |           |
       root  suffix_I   root
         |      |        |
       nikum   are      guti
     '{hate-PASSIVE}'  '{mouth}'
     'words that make oneself hated,
      bad-mouthing'
```

Crucially, we are dealing here with compounds whose members are independent words. There is a second type of compounding in Japanese, exemplified in (13), which directly concatenates roots (mostly of Sino-Japanese origin). Only word compounding, not root compounding, is the locus of *rendaku* voicing.[5]

(13) *Root compounding*

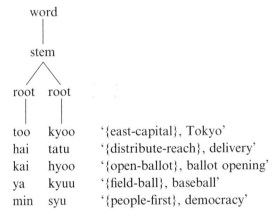

```
      word
        |
      stem
      /    \
   root   root
```

too	kyoo	'{east-capital}, Tokyo'
hai	tatu	'{distribute-reach}, delivery'
kai	hyoo	'{open-ballot}, ballot opening'
ya	kyuu	'{field-ball}, baseball'
min	syu	'{people-first}, democracy'

The distinction between two types of compounding is not a special quirk of Japanese, but has parallels in other languages, including English.[6] Thus, compounds such as *eight-legged* and *six-pack* are word compounds, where each member is an independent word, whereas *octo-pus* and *penta-gon* are root compounds consisting of bound elements. The combination charts (14) (for English) and (15) (for Japanese) illustrate the characteristics typical of such bound formations: noncompositionality (i.e., the meaning of the whole is only vaguely related to the meaning of its parts) and frequent unpredictable gaps.

(14) *(Latinate) English bound formations*

	-duce	-fect	-mit	-port	-pose	-vert
ad-	adduce	affect	admit			
de-	deduce	defect		deport	depose	
in-	induce	infect		import	impose	invert
per-		perfect	permit			pervert
re-	reduce		remit	report	repose	revert
sub-			submit	support	suppose	subvert

(15) *Sino-Japanese bound formations*

	zin	koku	syoku	sya	gaku	kai
bi	bizin		bisyoku		bigaku	
gai	gaizin	gaikoku	gaisyoku	gaisya		
ai	aizin	aikoku		aisya		
tai/dai		taikoku	taisyoku		daigaku	taikai
zen		zenkoku		zensya	zengaku	zenkai
syoo	syoozin	syookoku	syoosyoku		syoogaku	syookai
GLOSS	person	country	food	vehicle	learning	meeting
beauty	a beauty		epicurism		aesthetics	
outside	foreigner	abroad	dining out	imported cars		
love	lover	patriotism		own car		
large		great power	heavy eater		university	convention
all		national		all cars	all campus	all present
small	pedant	minor power	light eater		elementary school	minor faction

The general situation is that most root compounds are (semi)frozen and often noncompositional, while word compounds are productively formed and semantically transparent. As noted, here we will focus on word compounds, the locus of *rendaku* voicing, returning to Sino-Japanese root compounds in chapter 6.

4.1.3 The Formal Status of *Rendaku*

With these morphological preliminaries in place, we are in a position to address one of the most pressing questions for any account of the compound voicing phenomenon, as summarily characterized in (16) (essentially a repetition of (2), with the

additional qualification regarding the level of compounding): what is the status of
such a morphophonemic requirement in the grammar of a language?

(16) *Rendaku* ("sequential voicing"): "The initial segment of the second member of
      a word compound is voiced."

The formulation in (16) sounds like a crypto–OT constraint—but OT constraints
are held to be universal. Is it reasonable to offer (16) as an element of UG? The idea
is implausible from the start, since the phenomenon seems irreducibly language particular, and a voicing process of this kind in compounds does not represent a crosslinguistically recognizable process. As we show in more detail in section 4.1.5 and in
chapter 6, *rendaku* does not even hold true of all word compounds in Japanese.
Therefore, any claim that (16) represents some kind of universal requirement seems
hopeless.[7]

Granting this point, a conceivable position of retreat for a *rendaku*-as-constraint
approach is to declare (16) to be a language-particular constraint. While this constitutes a serious weakening of OT, which insists on the universality of all constraints, it
is not an altogether outlandish idea and can even claim a precedent (albeit one often
criticized) in Prince and Smolensky 1993 (in their analysis of the final-vowel truncation process in Lardil nominatives; see Kurisu 2001 and McCarthy 2002a for
different analyses of the Lardil case without language-particular constraints). But
contested precedents make weak arguments, and it turns out in any case that things
do not hinge on the general stigma of language-particular constraints, since (16) has
other problems over and above its nonuniversality.

This becomes clear once we inspect the formulation of (16) more closely. It is a
powerful amalgam of a morphological structural description ("the second member of
a word compound"), further narrowed down by a phonological localization ("the
initial segment of …") and coupled with a phonological structural change ("… is
voiced"). A central result of work in theoretical phonology over the last decades has
been to recognize that the first step toward explanation is to break such descriptions
down into their elementary parts. For this reason alone, the proper understanding
of *rendaku* voicing is to be sought not in a single highly specific constraint such as
(16), but in the combined action of several constraints, each general and well motivated, probably combined with a language-specific factor of a lexical nature. Even if
language-specific constraints were admitted, they would need to be limited in their
power, and this is where (16) fails, regardless of the ultimate answer to the question
of whether the constraints of OT grammars are all universal or whether some are
language-specific. A very different line of attack stays as far away as possible from
the messy details of the language-particular facts and approaches the task directly
from the universalist-typological side, focusing on crosslinguistically common pho-

nological processes, such as intervocalic voicing. Perhaps the operative factor leading to *rendaku* voicing can be directly identified with voicing assimilation?

There is a sense in which some kind of intervocalic voicing must be part of the overall explanation (see chapter 7), but as will become clear, it is only one ingredient in the overall synchronic analysis of the voicing process. An approach directly built on intervocalic voicing is attempted in Ito and Mester 1998, where agreement constraints against changes in glottal state play the decisive role. The analysis developed there turns out to be highly complex, requiring a whole supporting theory of sequential faithfulness to come close to the basic empirical facts, and is ultimately unable to account for the very limited distribution of this purported case of voicing assimilation. The main obstacle is the basic fact that Japanese otherwise shows little evidence for intervocalic voicing, and even among morphophonemic processes, *rendaku* voicing occupies an isolated position. It is thus not sufficient to restrict the process to derived environments (as some variety of "emergence of the unmarked"); rather, the context has to be narrowed all the way down to a single position, namely, the juncture between compound members. Further questions arise in view of the fact that even within its lexical field, compound voicing has many exceptions, both grammatically systematic and arbitrary ones (see section 4.1.5 and chapter 6, respectively). For these reasons, it remains to be seen whether the idea of directly subsuming *rendaku* voicing under some kind of voicing assimilation process can succeed as a serious and fully worked out analysis (i.e., beyond a vague appeal to a natural process that establishes no actual deductive relation).

4.1.4   Linking Morphemes in Japanese and Elsewhere

While it is often tempting, given the overall success of OT phonology, to launch a frontal attack on all analytical tasks by means of phonological constraints, the realization that (16) is not viable as a phonological constraint of any kind indirectly lends support to a very different approach to *rendaku* voicing (which is prefigured in Komatsu 1981, where the independence of *rendaku* voicing from its phonetic context is clearly recognized). Any proper understanding of morphophonemic phenomena needs to do full justice not just to their phonology, but also to their morphological side. Let us consider the possibility, then, that *rendaku* voicing literally represents a piece of morphology, that is, a morpheme by itself.[8] As such, it is introduced by the morphology and not by the phonology, and it occupies a definite linear position in the input representation.

Turning this into a concrete analysis, we posit, as part of the input, a feature-sized linking morpheme ℜ (17) consisting of the specification [+voiced]. It is natural to assume that ℜ acts as a prefix to the second member in word compounds, forming a constituent with it.

(17) Rendaku *as a morpheme*

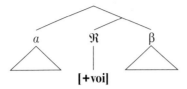

[+voi]

A concrete example appears in (18).

(18) yamatozakura *'Yamato cherry'* (Prunus yedoensis)

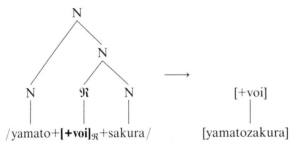

/yamato+**[+voi]**₉ᵣ+sakura/   [yamatozakura]

   Analyzed in this way, *rendaku* voicing joins many similar linking morphemes
found, for example, in a number of Germanic languages, where they are suffixed to
first members of compounds. This is illustrated in (19) with examples from German
showing so-called linking -*s*- (*Fugen-s*).

(19) *Linking morphemes in German compounds (f = feminine, m = masculine,*
      n = neuter)

		Compound with -*s*-		Genitive
a. der Tag, m.	'day'	Tag-**es**-zeitung	'daily newspaper'	des Tag-es
b. das Land, n.	'country'	Land-**es**-vorwahl	'country code'	des Land-es
c. die Liebe, f.	'love'	Liebe-**s**-brief	'love letter'	der Liebe(*s)
d. die Währung, f.	'currency'	Währung-**s**-union	'currency union'	der Währung(*s)
e. die Arbeit, f.	'work'	Arbeit-[**s**-ʃ]telle	'work-place, job'	der Arbeit(*s)
		Arbeit-[**s**-z]itzung	'work meeting'	

Similar to other linking elements (-*n*-, -*er*-, and -*e*-), the -*s*- in these examples represents a frozen case ending, the masculine/neuter genitive singular suffix. This is not
its synchronic role, however, since it appears not only with masculine and neuter
nouns (19a,b), but also with feminine nouns, where it has no legitimate basis as a
case suffix (19c,d).[9] The examples in (19e) show that there is in general no phonotactic or euphonic-segmental motivation for the appearance of -*s*-. We are dealing
with a genuine piece of "arbitrary" morphology. Historically speaking, many nouns

in first member position were marked with genitive case, and in many instances the case marker was -*s*. The morphological system then generalized this -*s* into a general linking element marking the first element of a compound.[10]

Similar linking elements in compounds[11] appear in other Germanic languages, such as Afrikaans, Danish, Dutch, Frisian, Icelandic, Norwegian, and Swedish— even English preserves a faint echo in isolated examples such as *spoke-s-man* and *mark-s-man*. Other Indo-European languages prominently featuring linking markers in compounds include Slavic languages such as Polish, Serbo-Croatian, and Russian (-*o*-, in Russian alternating with -*e*- after soft consonants); Greek (Ancient and Modern, usually -*o*-); Sanskrit; Persian; and Celtic languages, which show a linking effect (lenition) at the beginning of second members of compounds that is highly reminiscent of Japanese *rendaku*. Linking elements are equally common outside Indo-European, as shown by (among others) Tamil (Dravidian; see Aronoff 1998); Finnish (Finno-Ugric); Turkish (Altaic); Kabardian (Caucasian); Kusaiean, Taga-log, and Yapese (Austronesian); Thai (Tai); Cambodian (Austro-Asiatic); Zoque (Penutian); and Igbo and Yoruba (Niger-Congo). It can be concluded from this little survey that Japanese *rendaku*, understood as a linking morpheme ℜ (17), belongs to a crosslinguistically very common type of compound morphology.

4.1.5 Semantic Relations

In Japanese, ℜ is a feature of word compounds (12), not of root compounds (13). Since this is a morphological distinction without an immediate phonological ana-logue, it is already an indication that the distribution of the morpheme ℜ is mor-phologically determined, as expected for ordinary morphology. More importantly, even among word compounds the structural relation between the compound mem-bers has a crucial influence on the occurrence of *rendaku*. The basic rule is that only modifier-head compounds permit *rendaku* voicing. More precisely, two groups of compounds (both well represented in the lexicon) are systematically excluded from the process. The two types of nonundergoers are exemplified in (20) and (21), each time with minimally contrasting *rendaku*-undergoing compounds. First, dvandva (coordinate, double-headed) compounds (formations where neither part modifies the other, such as *te-asi* 'hands and feet, limbs') never show voicing (20).

(20) *Nonundergoers I: dvandva (coordinating) compounds*

	Coordinating compounds: no voicing		Ordinary (subordinating) compounds: voicing	
ko	oya-ko	'parent and child'	mai-go	'lost child'
ha	eda-ha	'branches and leaves'	waka-ba	'young leaves'
kaeri	yuki-kaeri	'coming and going'	hi-gaeri	'day-return, day trip'
kirai	suki-kirai	'likes and dislikes'	onna-girai	'woman-hater, misogynist'
ki	kusa-ki	'grass and tree, plants'	makura-gi	'pillow-wood, (railroad) crosstie'

Second, a particular subtype of modifier-head compounds—namely, those of the form OV, where *V* is a transitive verb stem and *O* a noun acting as its direct object (or theme argument)—generally resists voicing.[12]

(21) *Nonundergoers II: OV compounds versus other compounds*

OV compounds: no voicing		Other compounds: voicing	
sakana-turi	'fish-catching, catching fish'	iso-zuri	'beach-catching, fishing on a beach'
mono-hosi	'thing-dryer, frame for drying clothes'	kage-bosi	'shade-drying, drying in the shade'
zookin-kake	'dustcloth-hanger, place to hang dustcloths'	zookin-gake	'dustcloth-wiping, wiping with a dustcloth'
kami-sori	'hair-shaver, razor'	saka-zori	'reverse-shaving, shaving against the grain'

The unifying theme behind these two disparate classes of compounds is likely to be diachronic. The most plausible hypothesis about the historical origin of *rendaku* voicing (see Unger 1975) traces it to nasal-initial particles (mostly genitival *-no*, in other cases oblique *-ni*) suffixed to the first member of the compound. Vowel loss then led to postnasal voicing of following obstruents, and the eventual disappearance of the triggering nasal itself made the whole process morphophonemic. Schematically: [*onna-no*]-[*kokoro*] 'woman's heart' > [*onna-n*]-[*kokoro*] > [*onna-n*]-[**gokoro**] > [*onna*]-[*gokoro*]. This hypothesis receives strong support from the absence of *rendaku* voicing precisely in dvandvas (where neither *-no* nor *-ni* could possibly be affixed to the first member) and in NV compounds, where the N has the status of a direct object to V (here the appropriate particle would be *-o*, not *-no* or *-ni*).

This degree of sensitivity—not just to the overall type of the compound, but to fine details of its internal syntactic/thematic structure—provides a clue that *rendaku* is not an exclusively phonological phenomenon, but has a syntactic/morphological side that the analysis must not lose sight of. Overall, the *rendaku* morpheme $\mathfrak{R}$ is thus one instance of a well-represented type of morphological juncture marker, and an analysis like that in (17) is not at all unusual, when viewed from a crosslinguistic perspective.

4.2   The Phonology of Compound Voicing

With the linking morpheme and its substance, "[+voi]," supplied by syntax and morphology, the task of phonology is now no longer to account for the whole *rendaku* phenomenon; rather, it is the more modest one of determining how this substance is to be parsed, that is, how and when its voicing specification is realized. This division of labor between the syntactic/morphological and phonological sides of the grammar is a defining characteristic of morphophonemic processes in general. Analytically speaking, the overall result is simpler and more explanatory than an attempt to encapsulate all descriptive details in a single statement, such as the catch-all constraint in (16).

4.2.1   The Role of REALIZE-MORPHEME

Since what is at issue is not just whether some feature present in the input is realized in the output, but whether or not the morpheme $\mathfrak{R}$ receives any realization whatsoever in the output, it is reasonable to assume that the constraint REALIZE-MORPHEME (22) is crucially involved.

(22) REALIZE-M(ORPHEME): "Every morpheme in the input has a nonnull
       phonological exponent in the output."

Giving a precise and truly general definition of what is meant by the "phonological exponent" of a morpheme is a nontrivial task (see Kurisu 2001 for a theoretical and crosslinguistic study devoted to this and other issues connected with REALIZE-M, as well as for references to earlier work). For [+voi]$_{\mathfrak{R}}$, we simply assume here that having "a nonnull phonological exponent in the output" requires $\mathfrak{R}$'s [+voi] feature specification to be realized in an output segment.[13]

  For *rendaku* to take place at all, REALIZE-M must obviously dominate No-D, the simple markedness constraint against voiced obstruents (23).

(23) natuzora *'summer sky'*

/natu + ℜ + sora/	REALIZE-M	NO-D
▶ natu zora		*
natu sora	*!	

REALIZE-M also forces voicing faithfulness violations (24).

(24) akizora *'autumn sky'*

/aki + ℜ + sora/	REALIZE-M	IDENT
▶ aki zora		*
aki sora	*!	

Additional limitations on what constitutes a licit realization of ℜ follow from high-ranking uniformity and linearity requirements (see note 13). In order for the morphemic voicing to be distinctly recoverable, the realizing segment must not already correspond to a voiced segment in the input, and it must be adjacent.

The two dominated constraints IDENT and NO-D are ranked as required by contrastive voicing (25), giving the partial hierarchy in (26).

(25) mugi *'wheat'*

/mugi/	IDENT	NO-D
▶ mugi		*
muki	*!	

(26) REALIZE-M

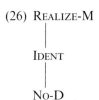

    IDENT

    NO-D

At this point, it is useful to recall the hierarchy from chapter 2, where the self-conjoined version of NO-D ranked higher than IDENT.

(27) No-D$^2{}_m$

IDENT

No-D

Combining the two partial hierarchies as in (28), we need to ask how the two highest-ranking constraints in (26) and (27), REALIZE-M and No-D$^2{}_m$, are ranked with respect to each other.

(28) REALIZE-M   No-D$^2{}_m$

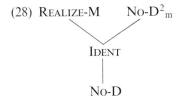

IDENT

No-D

We will show in section 4.2.3 that REALIZE-M is crucially dominated by No-D$^2{}_m$.

4.2.2 Lyman's Law in Compounds: Facts and Generalizations

On the phonological side of the *rendaku* process, there is a systematic phonological restriction on the kinds of forms that can show voicing. There is of course the large class of compounds whose second member begins with a (redundantly voiced) sonorant or a voiced obstruent and therefore cannot realize ℜ. But careful scrutiny of the internal consonantal makeup of the second members in *rendaku* compounds listed in section 4.1.1 reveals a systematic gap that is much more significant. The *rendaku* undergoers consist exclusively of voiceless obstruents and sonorants; there are no examples with internal voiced obstruents. This is no accident, and it recalls the morpheme-structural prohibition seen in chapter 2. With second members that contain a voiced obstruent, without exception *rendaku* voicing is absent (29), a strong OCP effect (in traditional parlance, *rendaku* voicing is "blocked by Lyman's Law").[14]

(29) *Prohibition against* rendaku *voicing ("Lyman's Law")*

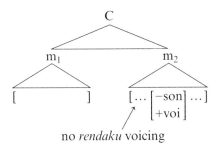

no *rendaku* voicing

The restriction is empirically documented in (30)–(33), a collection of compounds with native morphemes as second members that contain voiced obstruents in non-initial position (see also the larger collection of examples in the appendix). Most straightforward are cases where the blocking voiced obstruent C_2 is adjacent (modulo an intervening vowel) to C_1 in disyllabic words, as in (30) and (31).

(30) *Disyllables with [−son, +voi] as C_2*

	$C_2 = $ g, z, d, b		
$C_1 = $ k	kugi	ai-kugi	'matching-nail, double-pointed nail'
	kazu	kuti-kazu	'mouth-number, number of dependents'
	kado	hito-kado	'first-point, respectable'
	kubi	nama-kubi	'raw-head, freshly severed head'
$C_1 = $ s	sugi	ito-sugi	'thread-cedar, cypress'
	suzi	ie-suzi	'house-line, family lineage'
	sode	naga-sode	'long-sleeved'
	sabi	aka-sabi	'red rust'
$C_1 = $ t	tugi	hone-tugi	'bone-setting'
	tozi	kawa-tozi	'leather binding'
	tade	yanagi-tade	'willow smartweed'
	tubo	tya-tubo	'tea jar'
$C_1 = $ h	hugu	tora-hugu	'tiger globefish'
	hiza	tate-hiza	'stand-knee, sitting with one knee drawn up'
	hada	tori-hada	'bird-skin, gooseflesh, pimples'
	haba	kata-haba	'shoulder width (breadth)'

The reduplicated disyllables in (31) illustrate the strict nature of the restriction within a specific lexical field, namely, intensive/pluralizing reduplication. They should be contrasted with forms like *toki-doki* 'sometimes' and others listed earlier in (8), which show that voicing is otherwise a regular concomitant of this kind of reduplication.

(31) *Blocking of* rendaku *in reduplicated forms*

siba	siba-siba	'often-often, frequently'
sibu	sibu-sibu	'sour-sour, reluctantly'
tabi	tabi-tabi	'time-time, often, repeatedly'
tada	tada-tada	'just-just, simply'
tigire	tigire-tigire	'break-break, torn to pieces'
tobi	tobi-tobi	'jump-jump, skipping, alternately'
tubu	tubu-tubu	'grain-grain, beaded, pimpled'
tugi	tugi-tugi	'next-next, in succession, one by one'

The *rendaku*-blocking influence of voiced obstruents in C_2 position is also found in longer morphemes, as shown by the examples in (32).

(32) *Trisyllables with [−son, +voi] as C_2*

			$C_2 = g, z, d, b$
$C_1 = k$	kabuto	tetu-kabuto	'iron helmet'
	kudasi	hara-kudasi	'stomach-lowering, diarrhea'
	kuguri	inu-kuguri	'dog-pass, dog door'
	kuzure	yama-kuzure	'mountain-collapse, mountain slide, landslide'
$C_1 = s$	sabaki	mae-sabaki	'front-handle, maneuver at onset of sumo match'
	sizuka	mono-sizuka	'thing-quiet, serene, composed'
	sudare	tama-sudare	'bead screen'
	sugata	usiro-sugata	'back-figure, figure from behind, person's back'
$C_1 = t$	taguri	turu-taguri	'vine pulling'
	todoki	hu-todoki	'non-careful, rude, insolent'
	tubaki	yama-tubaki	'mountain camellia'
	tuzumi	sita-tuzumi	'tongue-drum, smacking one's lips'
$C_1 = h$	hagure	kui-hagure	'eat-go-astray, missing one's meal'
	hazure	miti-hazure	'road-miss, outskirts of town'
	hibari	kusa-hibari	'grass-lark, grass cricket, *Paratrigonidium bifasciatum*'
	hodoki	te-hodoki	'hand-untie, initiating, teaching'

Of particular significance are trisyllables with a voiced obstruent in C_3 position, which acts as a long-distance blocker even though it is separated from the morpheme-initial C_1 either by a sonorant (33a) or by a voiceless obstruent (33b) in C_2 position.[15]

(33) *Trisyllables with [−son, +voi] as C₃*

			C₃ = voiced obstruent		
a. C₂ = sonorant	m	tumugi	oosima-tumugi	'white pongee'
		kamado	seiyoo-kamado	'western-oven, Western kitchen range'
	n	sinogi	itizi-sinogi	'once-enduring, makeshift, temporary expedient'
		tunagi	zyuzu-tunagi	'rosary-link, tied in a row'
	r	kurage	denki-kurage	'electric jellyfish'
		sirabe	sita-sirabe	'under-investigation, preliminary inquiry'
	w	kawazu	ao-kawazu	'green frog'
		sawagi	oo-sawagi	'big-uproar, hubbub, racket'
b. C₂ = voiceless obstruent	k	tokage	ao-tokage	'green lizard'
		hakobi	hude-hakobi	'brush-carry, penmanship'
	s	kasegi	zikan-kasegi	'time-earn, holding out, stalling, putting off'
		susugi	kuti-susugi	'mouth rinse'
	t	kotoba	kaki-kotoba	'write-word, written language'
		tutuzi	yama-tutuzi	'mountain azalea'

The blocking effect of voiced obstruency is no less tangible at a distance, across an intervening C₂, than in adjacency (see section 2.3.1 for the parallel situation in morpheme structure). In view of the success of recent proposals arguing for strictly localist theories of assimilation (see, e.g., Gafos 1996; Ní Chiosáin and Padgett 2001; Walker 1998), where the domain of a feature can never be discontinuous, skipping a position, the existence of such patterns of dissimilation-at-a-distance (vs. the absence of the corresponding "assimilation-at-a-distance"—already neogrammarian typologies of sound changes contain examples of the former but hardly any of the latter) points to an asymmetry between assimilation and dissimilation, which were treated symmetrically in autosegmental tier-based models. The distinction makes intuitive sense, and since there is no question that other patterns of dissimilation are significantly weakened at a distance (cf., e.g., Frisch, Broe, and Pierrehumbert's (1995) findings for morpheme-structural place dissimilation in Arabic roots), it will be important for future work to determine which phonetic properties enter into long-distance dissimilation patterns and which do not.

Lists of contrasting pairs of compounds showing voicing and lack of voicing appear in (34)–(35).

(34) *Compounds showing voicing (indicated by v) and lack of voicing*

	aka-sabi	sabi	'red rust'
v	aka-zatoo	satoo	'brown sugar'
	ao-kawazu	kawazu	'green frog'
v	ao-gaeru	kaeru	'green frog'
	ao-tokage	tokage	'green lizard'
v	ao-datami	tatami	'green-tatami, new straw mat'
	hara-kudasi	kudasi	'stomach-lowering, diarrhea'
v	hara-gonasi	konasi	'stomach-manage, aid to digestion'
	hude-hakobi	hakobi	'brush-usage, penmanship'
v	hude-zukai	tukai	'brush-work, penmanship'
	itizi-sinogi	sinogi	'one-time-enduring, makeshift, temporary expedient'
v	itizi-barai	harai	'one-time payment'
	kui-hagure	hagure	'eat-miss, missing one's meal'
v	kui-daore	taore	'eat-fall, extravagance in food'
	kuti-kazu	kazu	'mouth-number, number of dependents'
v	kuti-guse	kuse	'mouth-habit, favorite phrase'
	kuti-susugi	susugi	'mouth rinse'
v	kuti-gitanai	kitanai	'mouth-filthy, foul-mouthed, abusive'
	naga-sode	sode	'long-sleeved'
v	naga-banasi	hanasi	'long talk'
	nama-kaziri	kaziri	'fresh-bite, superficial knowledge'
v	nama-gawaki	kawaki	'fresh-dry, half wet'
	oo-sawagi	sawagi	'great uproar'
v	oo-gakari	kakari	'large scale'
	sita-sirabe	sirabe	'down-investigate, preliminary inquiry'
v	sita-gokoro	kokoro	'down-heart, secret desire beneath the surface'
	tate-hiza	hiza	'stand-knee, sitting with one knee drawn up'
v	tate-bue	hue	'stand-flute, vertical flute'
	tya-tubo	tubo	'tea jar'
v	tya-dansu	tansu	'tea-drawers, cupboard'
	yama-kuzure	kuzure	'mountain-crumble, landslide'
v	yama-biraki	hiraki	'mountain-opening (for climbers)'

	zikan-kasegi	kasegi	'time-earning, holding out, stalling'
	zikan-tubusi	tubusi	'time-crushing, wasting time, spending time'
v	zikan-doori	toori	'time-exact, punctually'
	zyuzu-tunagi	tunagi	'rosary-link, tied in a row'
v	zyuzu-dama	tama	'rosary beads'

(35) *Reduplicated forms with similar meanings*

	siba	siba-siba	'often-often, usually, frequently'
v	tune	tune-zune	'usual-usual, always, usually'
	tabi	tabi-tabi	'time-time, often, repeatedly'
v	kasane	kasane-gasane	'repeat-repeat, repeatedly, doubly'
	tugi	tugi-tugi	'next-next, in succession, one by one'
v	tuki	tuki-zuki	'month-month, monthly'

Finally, (36) illustrates the restriction by contrasting undergoers and nonundergoers that all have *te*- 'hand' as first member.

(36) *Compounds with* te *'hand' as first member*

	kagami	te-kagami	'hand mirror'
v	kakari	te-gakari	'hand-hang, clue, track'
	kagi	te-kagi	'hand-key, hook'
v	kaki	te-gaki	'handwritten'
v	kakeru	te-gakeru	'hand-use, handle, deal with'
	kago	te-kago	'hand basket'
v	kata	te-gata	'hand-shape, note, bill, draft'
v	katai	te-gatai	'hand-firm, safe, reliable, of good reputation'
v	kami	te-gami	'hand-paper, letter'
	sage	te-sage	'hand basket'
	sabaki	te-sabaki	'hand-handle, handle skillfully'
v	sawari	te-zawari	'hand-touch, feel rough/soft to the touch'
v	sina	te-zina	'hand-item, jugglery, magic, tricks'
v	syaku	te-zyaku	'hand-pour, help oneself to sake'
	suzi	te-suzi	'hand-line, have a natural aptitude'
v	suri	te-zuri	'hand-printed'
v	sema	te-zema	'hand-narrow, small, narrow'
v	tasuke	te-dasuke	'hand-help, helping hand'
v	tate	te-date	'hand-stand, method'
v	tama	te-dama	'hand-ball, trifle with (a person)'
v	tika	te-zika	'hand-near, nearby, familiar'

	tigai	te-tigai	'hand-wrong, go wrong'
v	tukami	te-zukami	'hand-grasp, seize by hand, grasp'
v	tukuri	te-zukuri	'hand-make, handmade, homemade'
	tuzuki	te-tuzuki	'hand-continue, formalities, procedure, steps'
v	tumari	te-zumari	'hand-press, be pinched for money'
v	turi	te-zuri	'hand-fishing, hand-line fishing'
v	turu	te-zuru	'hand-string, connection'
v	tori	te-dori	'hand-take, real income, after-tax take-home pay'
v	tori	te-dori	'hand-capture, catch, seize'
v	hako	te-bako	'hand-box, box, case, casket'
	hazime	te-hazime	'hand-start, in the beginning'
	hazu	te-hazu	'hand-arrange, plan, arrangements'
v	hata	te-bata	'hand-flag, flag'
v	hana	te-bana	'hand-nose, blow (one's) nose with fingers'
v	hanasi	te-banasi	'hand-release, openly, without reserve'
v	hayai	te-bayai	'hand-fast, quickly, promptly'
v	hikae	te-bikae	'hand-keep, note(book), memorandum'
v	hiki	te-biki	'hand-guide, guidance, guidebook, introduction'
	hidoi	te-hidoi	'hand-bad, harshly, mercilessly'
v	hiroi	te-biroi	'hand-wide, extensive, large, spacious'
v	hukuro	te-bukuro	'hand-bag, gloves, mittens'
	huda	te-huda	'hand-sign, a hand (in cards)'

4.2.3   The Voicing Constraint Hierarchy

Taking up the analysis as it was left in (28) in section 4.2.1, tableau (37) shows how the multiple violation of the constraint No-D, which ranks below Realize-M and is normally overruled by it, triggers an additional violation of the self-conjoined voicing threshold constraint No-D^2_m. The latter ranks above Realize-M and forces its violation in the winning candidate.

(37) nagasode *'long-sleeved'*

/naga + $\Re$ + sode/	No-D^2_m	Realize-M	No-D
naga zode	*!		**
▶ naga sode		*	*

The hierarchy in (38), with four crucially ranked constraints, constitutes the core of the analysis of *rendaku* and Lyman's Law in Japanese.

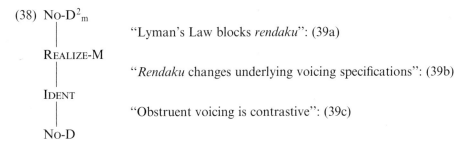

(38) No-D^2_m

           "Lyman's Law blocks *rendaku*": (39a)

  Realize-M

           "*Rendaku* changes underlying voicing specifications": (39b)

  Ident

           "Obstruent voicing is contrastive": (39c)

  No-D

For ease of reference, the important interactions are taken up one by one in (39).

(39) *Crucial rankings*

a.

/naga + ℜ + sode/	No-D^2_m	Realize-M	Ident	No-D
naga zode	*!		*	***
▶ naga sode		*		**

b.

/natsu + ℜ + sora/	No-D^2_m	Realize-M	Ident	No-D
▶ natsu zora			*	*
natsu sora		*!		

c.

/mugi/	No-D^2_m	Realize-M	Ident	No-D
▶ mugi				*
muki			*!	

The overall idea behind our analysis is that the *rendaku* phenomenon is best understood as the intersection of phonological and morphological generalizations. For the latter, we find significant parallels (mentioned in section 4.1.4) with linking morphemes in compounds in a host of languages. Since the typology of morphemes is independent of phonological properties—an aspect of *l'arbitraire du signe*—such juncture markers are not expected to constitute a natural class in phonological terms. And indeed, they include a phonologically heterogeneous class of elements such as segmental features (like voicing, continuancy, or sonorancy), segments identifiable with case markers (recall the German examples in (19)), suprasegmentals such as tone and stress (i.e., melodic elements and metrical structure), and gemination processes as in Malayalam (Mohanan 1986).

The picture of the analysis in (38)–(39) is still preliminary. It leaves many questions unanswered, such as why, instead of [naga sode], the winner in (39a) is not *[naga zote], violating IDENT but fulfilling REALIZE-M (see chapter 7, which focuses on the internal articulation of voicing faithfulness). Setting aside the self-conjoined constraint against multiple obstruent voicing, which expresses a familiar OCP-type requirement but whose details remain debatable, the other three constraints are well-motivated universal constraints of a fundamental character. The fact that the explanation hinges on the crucial ranking of all four constraints illustrates the explanatory power of this basic feature of OT architecture: while analyses limited to one level of crucial ranking between constraints often have straightforward translations into operations with settable parameters, a ranking depth of four points to a degree of interactivity that has no counterpart in the world of parameter setting.

4.3   Further Issues

4.3.1   Domain-Specific Faithfulness

Before turning to the issue of domains in chapter 5, we briefly take up a proposal by Fukazawa and Kitahara (2001), who recast the basic analysis developed so far by redistributing the tasks assigned to markedness and faithfulness in an interesting way, namely, by removing the domain restriction (i.e., to "morpheme") from the self-conjoined markedness constraint expressing the OCP requirement and by instead imposing a domain limitation on certain faithfulness constraints. The basic vision behind this proposal is interesting. Markedness should be domain-free, whereas faithfulness is independently known to have restrictions and limitations of various kinds. For the case at hand, this means that the constraint expressing the OCP requirement should not be limited to any domain but should have truly global reach, different from our No-D^2_m constraint or the classical OCP, which are limited to specific domains. Fukazawa and Kitahara implement this by means of a featural fusion account of *rendaku* and Lyman's Law that instead makes crucial use of domain-specific versions of the faithfulness constraint UNIFORMITY (banning many-to-one correspondence between input and output). Relying on winning outputs of a classical autosegmental form, with underspecified redundant [+voice] and multiple linking of [+voice] to obstruents across vowels, they interpret a form like *tabi bito* (from /tabi + ℜ + hito/ 'travel-person, traveler') as not violating the OCP within any domain, but rather showing featural fusion in the output, across the intervening vowel, of two separate [+voice] specifications in the input. This violates the word domain version of UNIFORMITY, but not the higher-ranking morpheme domain version (since the fusion is transmorphemic). On the other hand, such fusion (and hence the appearance of *rendaku* voicing) is ruled out tautomorphemically in a form like *nuri buda* (from /nuri + ℜ + huda/ 'lacquered lid') by the higher-ranking morpheme domain version of Uniformity.

While limiting domain specifications to faithfulness might in general be a worthwhile goal, the specific assumptions regarding underspecification and multiple linking are a liability of this alternative account.[16] More important, however, is another consideration. Any Uniformity-based approach to OCP effects encounters the basic problem that it relies on an IO faithfulness constraint to enforce what looks like a markedness imperative. The adoption of the principle of richness of the base entails that morpheme structure restrictions (e.g., on aspiration and obstruent voicing, as in Sanskrit and Japanese, respectively; see chapter 2) cannot exclusively follow from IO faithfulness constraints, but need a markedness-based explanation. For the case at hand, Uniformity-IO (which militates against fusion, but has nothing to say about input-given multiple linking) cannot rule out input representations with multiply linked obstruent voicing inside a morpheme, as in (40).

(40) [+voi]

g u d a

The multiple linking in (40), as an input-given representational property that is faithfully preserved in the output, is no faithfulness violation (in particular, no violation of morpheme-domain Uniformity-IO). Since it also does not violate any version of the OCP operating on autosegmental tiers, forms like /guda/ are predicted to constitute fully well formed Yamato morphemes—provided they are underlyingly represented as in (40), which is guaranteed to be a possible input by the principle of the richness of the base.

The upshot is that in its exclusive focus on the blocking of voicing in compounds (i.e., on the derivational side of the phenomenon), domain-bound IO faithfulness, coupled with an unlimited OCP, leaves the morpheme-structural side of this and other co-occurrence restrictions unaccounted for. One could consider supplementing it with a markedness version of Uniformity, as a second line of defense enforcing the morpheme-structural side of the OCP, but besides resurrecting the duplication problem, this would mean reintroducing the domain issue in another form.

4.3.2 Linking Morphemes as Emergent Morphology

Concluding this chapter, it is interesting to note that the theory of morpheme realization developed by Kurisu (2001) suggests an approach to *rendaku* that shifts even more of the analytical burden toward the constraint Realize-M than the one chosen here. Rather than positing voicing as an input property of the linking morpheme ℜ, Kurisu's approach leaves the latter without any phonological substance, relying instead on the faithfulness system to select obstruent voicing as the most harmonic (and in fact the only) realization of ℜ (as an "antifaithfulness" effect, but arising under the pressure of morpheme realization as the minimal violation of faithfulness, not by separate stipulation).

Potential evidence for the empty-ℜ analysis is provided by the idiosyncratic hiatus-breaker [s] restricted to compounds with *ame* 'rain' as their second element (41).[17]

(41) *Linking -s- in compounds with* ame *'rain'*[18]

haru-same	'spring rain, bean-jelly sticks'
aki-same	'autumn rain'
hi-same	'cold rain'
kiri-same	'misty rain, drizzle'
mura-same	'passing shower'

We need to ask here why the linking *-s-* itself is never voiced: why do forms like **haru-[z]ame* not exist? Under the empty-ℜ analysis, this makes immediate sense if the *-s-* itself counts as a realization of ℜ in this special case (e.g., by lexical stipulation). Since ℜ is already realized, standard minimization of constraint violations militates against a pointless violation of voicing faithfulness. For the analysis with a contentful morpheme ℜ, with voicing in the input, the situation is less clear. Why would the form with [z] not be selected, as the one where [+voi]$_\Re$ is realized?

This argument is not fully persuasive, however, given the availability of an alternative explanation, namely, that [+voi]$_\Re$ and [s]$_\Re$ simply constitute different allomorphs of the linking morpheme. If so, their competition is already resolved on morphological grounds; that is, the input for compounds like *haru-same* does not even contain [+voi]$_\Re$, and the question whether voicing is realized or not is moot.

We have not investigated the full consequences of this kind of empty-ℜ analysis for the faithfulness system, which would raise questions of ranking consistency and overall restrictiveness (see chapter 7 for some related discussion). Taking note of it as an interesting alternative, we here retain the more conservative assumption of a contentful ℜ morpheme.

Chapter 5
Morphological and Phonological Domains

A crucial element of the analysis developed so far is the high-ranking self-conjoined constraint No-D^2_m militating against co-occurrence of voiced obstruents. It is crucial here that the domain be fixed as "morpheme" and not as some other domain, be it "syllable," "prosodic word," or any of the other domains that are in principle available. Generally speaking, the domain of a conjoined constraint is either a prosodic or a morphological/syntactic category, as in (1).[1]

(1) *Hierarchies of domains*

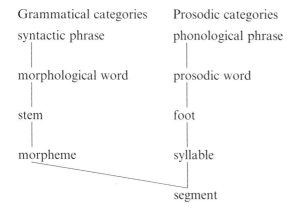

Grammatical categories	Prosodic categories
syntactic phrase	phonological phrase
morphological word	prosodic word
stem	foot
morpheme	syllable
	segment

But can any conjoined constraint in principle take any of these categories as its domain? Is the δ of No-φ^2_δ a free parameter, giving rise to a whole family of OCP requirements holding over various domains?

While conjunctions need domains, questions of excessive power immediately arise if any pairing of conjunctions and domains yields a valid conjoined constraint, and it becomes imperative to impose restrictions. Is the domain of evaluation of a conjoined constraint perhaps partially or even fully predictable from its elements, with no room left for parameterization? In investigating these questions, we will show that evidence from Old Japanese, combined with the situation in the modern language, provides crucial data for a theory of domains that interacts with OCP threshold constraints of the form No-$\varphi^2{}_\delta$.

5.1 Domain Issues

5.1.1 Minimal Shared Domains

Justifying a violation mark for a segmental markedness constraint such as No-Nasal-Vowel requires exhibiting only a small part of a candidate's representation, namely, the offending segment (but of course larger substrings will also suffice). On the other hand, justifying a violation mark for a constraint like No-Heavy-Syllable requires exhibiting a larger substring that corresponds to a whole syllable. Since the first constraint can be evaluated in any domain above and including the segment, whereas the second minimally requires inspecting syllable-sized substrings, the two constraints share all (and only) the domains above, and including, the syllable. The latter domain is minimal, in the sense that it does not dominate any other domain where both constraints can be evaluated. As we will show, the minimal shared domain of two constraints is a very useful concept, and we take note of it by providing a definition in (2).

(2) *Minimal shared domain (MSD)*

Let D(A) be the set of domains where constraint A can be evaluated, and D(B) the set of domains where constraint B can be evaluated. Then every member of the intersection of D(A) and D(B) that is minimal (i.e., does not dominate another member) is a *minimal shared domain* of A and B.

(2) allows for nonuniqueness since grammatical and prosodic domains (such as morphemes and syllables) do not stand in an inclusion relation. But in most practical cases, there is a single smallest domain, and we will tacitly assume a unique MSD unless indicated otherwise. A natural idea is to fix the domain δ of a conjoined constraint A&$_\delta$B as the MSD of the two constraints, as in (3) (see Hewitt and Crowhurst 1996 and Nathan 2001 for proposals expressing similar ideas).

(3) *Minimal Domain Principle (MDP)*

Let δ be a minimal domain shared by constraints A and B. Then their conjunction A&B has δ as a local domain.

To illustrate the MDP at work, let us return to a composite constraint familiar from chapter 2—namely, No-Coda&$_\delta$No-D, the constraint against voiced obstruent codas active in languages like Dutch and German. Determining the MSD requires determining the smallest domains where each of the constituent constraints can be individually evaluated (heuristically, "what they are constraints against"), with the fringe benefit of clarifying some aspects of constraint evaluation that are sometimes glossed over without much discussion. We interpret No-Coda as a constraint against segments that are (i) consonantal and (ii) syllable-final, and No-D as a constraint against segments that are (i) obstruents and (ii) voiced. We therefore have two constraints concerned with segments (in a certain role, of a certain type, etc.), and the MDP suggests "segment" as their MSD, and as the locality domain of the conjoined constraint.[2]

This is the correct result, and the restriction of the local interaction domain to "segment" turns out to be of some importance. Using examples from German for illustration, even though both *Neid* [naɪd] (4a) and *dein* [daɪn] (5a) incur a No-D violation and a No-Coda violation, only the former incurs a violation of the conjoined constraint, because it contains a segment that is both a voiced obstruent and in the offending coda position.

(4) Neid *'envy' (final devoicing)*

/naɪd/	No-Coda&$_{seg}$No-D	Ident	No-D	No-Coda
a. .naɪd.	*!		*	*
b. ▶ .naɪt.		*		*

(5) dein *'your' (no initial devoicing)*

/daɪn/	No-Coda&$_{seg}$No-D	Ident	No-D	No-Coda
a. ▶ .daɪn.			*	*
b. .taɪn.		*!		*

A domain higher in the hierarchy in (1) than "segment," be it prosodic (syllable, etc.) or grammatical (morpheme, etc.), is not just empirically incorrect for the conjunction No-Coda&No-D in German and Dutch—rather, no natural language appears to rely on the more global computation of markedness that such larger domains make possible. Thus, we find no instances of nonlocal compensation processes of the type "A voiced (or aspirated, etc.) obstruent onset is possible, but only if compensated for by the absence of a coda (and vice versa)." The markedness assessments are local and in a sense final (i.e., not relativized by a second-level accounting system).

In the same vein, Prince and Smolensky (1993) (along with many earlier researchers, such as Clements and Keyser (1982)) point out that the constraints Onset and No-Coda do not engage in compensatory interactions at the level of the syllable. No language has been reported to have the syllable canon {CV, CVC, V, *VC}—that is, a canon excluding onsetless syllables only when they are in addition marked by having a coda (the "worst-of-the-worst" case). This gap in the typology leads to a frequently raised question for constraint conjunction theory (which specializes in worst-of-the-worst scenarios): if ONSET and NO-CODA can be conjoined, doesn't their conjunction predict the existence precisely of the nonexistent system {CV, CVC, V, *VC}?

Everything here hinges on the domain of the conjoined constraint, and it is important to determine what the MDP actually entails. Prince and Smolensky (1993) make use of a syllable theory where *Onset* and *Coda* constitute labeled nodes that appear as such in phonological representations. Different from the conception that underlies this work (see below), their ONSET constraint literally outlaws syllable nodes that do not dominate an Onset node, just as their NO-CODA constraint rules out syllable nodes that dominate a Coda node. In this conception, the conjoined constraint's locality domain is therefore the syllable, as indicated in (6) (with subscripts added for clarity). ONSET$_{PS}$&$_\sigma$NO-CODA$_{PS}$ is violated by strings of the structure [$_\sigma$ VC], but fulfilled by [$_\sigma$ CVC], [$_\sigma$ V], and [$_\sigma$ CV].

(6) *ONSET$_{PS}$&$_\sigma$NO-CODA$_{PS}$*

    Local domain: syllable
    Violated by [$_\sigma$ VC]

Note, however, that this is a consequence of viewing the syllable as the MSD of the two constraints ONSET$_{PS}$ and NO-CODA$_{PS}$. In the rather different conception of syllabic representation that underlies this work (shared with much work antedating OT, as well as with many studies following Prince and Smolensky 1993), there are no nodes labeled *Onset* or *Coda*, and syllable constraints are viewed in segment-and-role terms. For example, as already noted in connection with the Dutch/German coda condition against voiced obstruents, the entity violating the constraint NO-CODA&$_{seg}$NO-D in (4) and (5) is viewed as a segment with a certain combination of properties, not as a syllable constituent with a certain internal structure.

This viewpoint casts new light on the ONSET–NO-CODA issue. The two familiar constraints are formally stated in (7), building on an earlier proposal in Ito 1989.

(7) a. ONSET: *X/[$_\sigma$[$_\mu$ __   "No syllable-initial moraic segments."
    b. NO-CODA: *C/   __]$_\sigma$ "No syllable-final consonantal segments."

Both are constraints against segments—of certain types, and with certain positional properties. The MDP therefore predicts the segment to be the domain of their conjunction, as in (8).

(8) *ONSET&$_{seg}$NO-CODA (on the basis of (7))*

    Local domain: segment
    Not violated by [$_\sigma$ VC]

It remains true that the form [$_\sigma$ VC] violates both ONSET (7a) and NO-CODA (7b) as individual constraints, the first by its initial (moraic) V and the second by its final C. But since the two offenses are committed in two different segments, there is no sense in which they trigger a violation of the conjoined constraint (8), whose domain is "segment."

Under the segment-and-role interpretation assumed here and throughout this book, the conjunction of the two constraints does not lead to a wrong typological prediction, and it poses no threat to constraint conjunction theory. What would constitute a violation of (8)? Good candidates, depending on their exact featural and phonetic characteristics, are syllabic consonants occurring without (separate) onsets, that is, structures of the form [$_\sigma$[$_\mu$ C]]. Here (8) does useful work since many languages that have syllabic consonants allow them only with consonantal onsets. This is the pattern found with English syllabic liquids and nasals, for instance, where forms like *bott*[l̩], *bott*[m̩], *butt*[n̩] are not matched by *[l̩]*bott*, *[m̩]*bott*, and *[n̩]*butt*.[3]

5.1.2 Domains for Self-Conjunctions

For a self-conjoined segmental constraint such as NO-D[2], determining the minimal domain shared by its subconstraints raises interesting issues (see also Nathan 2001 for discussion). The smallest domain where the simplex constraint NO-D can be evaluated is obviously the segment, but this does not carry over in a meaningful way to its self-conjunction—a single segment can incur only one NO-D violation, not two.[4] It is clear that a domain where different violations of NO-D can be expected to co-occur—that is, a meaningful dissimilation domain—is larger than a single segment.

Preserving the spirit of the MDP as we move up the hierarchy in search of suitable domains more inclusive than "segment," we face an ambiguity.[5] Segments are part of two separate families of structures, the prosodic hierarchy and the grammatical hierarchy (see (1)), whose constituents do not stand in inclusion relations with respect to each other. On the prosodic side, there are more and more inclusive phonological constituents. Here, according to the collective experience of past phonological work, the prosodic word stands out as a domain where certain properties are allowed to be instantiated only once (as shown, e.g., by processes of tonal dissimilation and pitch accent deletion operating at this level; see section 3.2). On the grammatical side, segments are the building blocks of linguistic signs, and thereby also stand in a relation with the grammatical hierarchy. Here the morpheme occupies a prominent position as a well-known dissimilation domain, as in the Sanskrit co-occurrence restriction on aspirates and many other comparable cases (see chapter 2).[6]

Our proposal capitalizes on this double affiliation of segments. In its strictest form (depicted in (9)), which we tentatively adopt here, it allows only one choice: whether the domain of the self-conjoined dissimilation constraint is grammatical/lexical in character (intuitively: directed toward linguistic signs as they are stored in the lexicon) or prosodic (intuitively: directly affecting prosodic constituents as they appear in the output).

(9) *Self-conjunction domains for dissimilation*

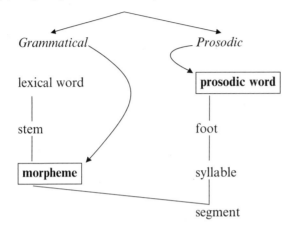

Once the basic type of domain is fixed as either grammatical/lexical or prosodic, there is no further freedom: "morpheme" and "prosodic word," respectively, are the preordained choices. All grammatical/lexical dissimilation is confined to the smallest linguistic sign, the morpheme; that is, the relevant self-conjoined markedness constraints come with the setting "δ = morpheme." The other type of dissimilation is genuinely prosodic in nature and holds of prosodic words; that is, the relevant self-conjoined constraints come with the setting "δ = prosodic word."

It is not clear to what extent prosodic constituents besides the prosodic word serve as actual domains of dissimilation. We are not aware of well-documented cases where a process enforcing the dissimilation of a (not prominence-related) property is limited to feet. "Syllable" looks like a more plausible domain, and candidate cases are not too hard to find. Consider, for example, the dissimilation pattern governing labial and dorsal (but not coronal) place in English words beginning with *s*C clusters, illustrated in (10). What is significant here is the absence of words like **spip*, **spib*, **skeck*, **skeg* versus the existence of *skip*, *speck*, and *stud*.

(10) s + *CVC-initial words in English*

C₁ \ C₂	Cor	Lab	Vel
Cor	stud	stab	stick
Lab	spit		speck
Vel	skit	skip	

However, Davis's (1991) study of this dissimilation pattern makes a strong case that it is in fact not syllable-bound, but holds for tautomorphemic consonants adjacent across a vowel, irrespective of syllabification. If this is indeed the case, it might point toward a larger generalization. Apart from directly prosodically triggered effects such as accent deletion and tonal dissimilation, most dissimilation processes are affairs of the lexicon. They take place in a domain that is stable (i.e., the morpheme), not in domains that rely on the context-dependent prosodic parsing of a string into syllables and feet.

In light of these considerations, while many ways of adding further options are readily conceivable, we will stay with the simple model providing only one lexical/grammatical and one prosodic domain (morpheme vs. prosodic word, respectively). Our main finding is, in a nutshell, that the voiced obstruent dissimilation pattern in connection with *rendaku* in Modern Japanese is lexical in nature, with the morpheme as its relevant domain. On the other hand, there is strong evidence that in Old Japanese, the corresponding process was phonologically governed and detectable in a more extended domain, namely, within the prosodic word as a whole.

5.2   The Domain of No-D^2

For the analysis of *rendaku*, the domain of the self-conjoined voicing constraint No-D^2 is critical because it is crucially not coextensive with the whole form under evaluation. *Rendaku* voicing is precluded by a voiced obstruent in the second member of the compound, but not by one in the first member, as the examples in (11) and (12) illustrate.

(11) *Voiced obstruent in second member of compound:* no rendaku *voicing in second member*

/huna + ℜ + tabi/ → huna‖tabi	[−v][+v]	'ship-journey, cruise'
/tora + ℜ + hugu/ → tora hugu		'tiger fugu (*Tetrodon rubripes*)'
/hito + ℜ + kage/ → hito kage		'person-shadow, shadow, figure'
/mati + ℜ + kado/ → mati kado		'street corner'

(12) *Voiced obstruent in first member of compound:* rendaku *voicing in second member*

/suzuri + ℜ + hako/ → suzuri‖bako	[+v] [+v]	'inkstone case'
/tabi + ℜ + hito/ → tabi bito		'travel-person, traveler'
/hada + ℜ + samui/ → hada zamui		'skin-cold, chilly'
/kage + ℜ + kuti/ → kage guti		'shadow-mouth, backbiting'

In traditional parlance (see the analysis in Ito and Mester 1986), Lyman's Law is an OCP effect on obstruent voicing within morphemes only (*huna-*dabi* but ✓ *tabi-bito*). Within the current theoretical framework, the locality domain of the self-conjoined voicing constraint No-D^2_δ is lexical, namely, δ = "morpheme." The formal analysis appears in (13) and (14).

(13) *Input voicing in second member:* huna tabi *'ship-journey, cruise'*

/huna + ℜ + ta**b**i/	No-D^2_m	REALIZE-M	No-D
a. huna **d**abi	*!		**
b. ▶ huna ta**b**i		*	*

(14) *Input voicing in first member:* tabi bito *'travel-person, traveler'*

/ta**b**i + ℜ + hito/	No-D^2_m	REALIZE-M	No-D
a. ▶ ta**b**i **b**ito			**
b. ta**b**i hito		*!	*

Both [ta**b**i **b**ito] (14a) and *[huna **d**abi] (13a) incur two violations of No-D. But in (14a) the two violations are spread out over the two morphemes that constitute the compound, whereas in (13a) they are clustered in (the exponent of) the second morpheme. Therefore, only (13a) incurs a violation of the self-conjoined morpheme domain constraint, whereas in (14a) neither the first member [ta**b**i] nor the second member [**b**ito] violates No-D^2_m.

This basic analysis of the morpheme-level dissimilation facts in Modern Japanese, which in its essentials is straightforward and paralleled by other cases, raises one question of general interest. Could things in principle have been different, as far as the size of the dissimilation domain is concerned? In particular, does UG allow for a variant form of Japanese that diverges by choosing (14b) as the winner instead of (14a)? This would mean transmorphemic blocking of voicing due to a stronger version of Lyman's Law—that is, one with a larger domain.

5.2.1   Extended Dissimilation Effects in Old Japanese

The history of Japanese answers these questions in the affirmative. As it turns out, at an earlier stage of the language *rendaku* voicing was in fact blocked beyond the domain of single morphemes. This is an important finding: it shows that any theory is incorrect which maintains, or implies, that "morpheme" is the only domain where self-conjoined segmental markedness constraints can trigger dissimilation. On the positive side, it lends support to the still quite restrictive binary-choice theory of locality domains proposed above, which allows for the phonological domain "prosodic word" as an option besides the lexical domain "morpheme."

For speakers of Japanese, the facts characterizing the transmorphemic "strong version of Lyman's Law" can most easily be approached from the perspective of the modern language, starting with an interesting observation about the failure of *rendaku* voicing to appear in names of a certain form. As in most other languages, names constitute an area of the lexicon rich in irregularities, with unpredictable and unusual readings of characters and other idiosyncrasies. Family names, which are usually lexicalized compounds, frequently show *rendaku* when the canonical conditions are met. Thus, *kita* 'north' and *kawa* 'river' yield the name *Kitagawa*, *kuro* 'black' and *ta* 'field' yield *Kuroda*, and so on. In names like *Kitakubo* (from *kita* 'north' + *kubo* 'hollow place'), we find the usual lack of voicing caused by the presence of the voiced obstruent *b* in the second member. Besides this expected Lyman-style blocking of *rendaku*, however, compound voicing is often absent in an idiosyncratic way, as shown by names like *Hosokawa* 'narrow river' (cf. *Kitagawa* above). Such idiosyncratic lack of *rendaku*, which is to a lesser extent also found in the general vocabulary and provides a strong argument for the inherently morphological character of *rendaku* (a voicing morpheme, as argued in chapter 4), is particularly characteristic of names. Sugito (1965) observes (see Sato 1988 for further corroboration) that such idiosyncratic lack of *rendaku* is especially frequent when the first part of the name contains a voiced obstruent. This results in characteristic distributional contrasts like those in (15), where the same morpheme /ta/ 'field' appears with [d] in (15a) *Ima + da* and *Yama + da* but with [t] in (15b) *Siba + ta* and *Kubo + ta*. The lack of *rendaku* voicing in (15b) is unexpected in terms of the usual Lyman scenario, since the voiced obstruent is located in the first (compound) member, where it should have no blocking effect (cf. the prototypical examples in (12)).

(15) *Extended Lyman effects in names:* /ta/ 'field' as [-ta] versus [-da]

    a. With *rendaku* voicing

       /ima + ℜ + ta/ → ima **d**a
       /yama + ℜ + ta/ → yama**d**a

    b. Without *rendaku* voicing

       /si**b**a + ℜ + ta/ → si**b**a **t**a   *si**b**a da
       /ku**b**o + ℜ + ta/ → ku**b**o **t**a   *ku**b**o da

Besides family names, there are a small number of other lexicalized compounds of the form /m$_1$ + ℜ + m$_2$/ exemplified in (16), where, for a given m$_2$, the lack of *rendaku* voicing appears to correlate with the presence of a voiced obstruent in m$_1$.

(16) *Extended Lyman effects in lexicalized compounds*

    a. With *rendaku* voicing

       /taki + ℜ + hi/   → taki **bi**   'firewood'

       /maru + ℜ + kanna/ → maru **ganna**   'round plane (tool)'

    b. Without *rendaku* voicing

       /tobi + ℜ + hi/   → to**bi hi**   'flying sparks'

       /mizo + ℜ + kanna/ → mi**zo kanna** 'groove plane'

Even though such extended Lyman effects are clearly not an active feature of Modern Japanese, their overall tendency is noteworthy. *Rendaku* is blocked when there is a voiced obstruent not later in the same morpheme, but earlier within the whole compound—prosodically speaking, within the same prosodic word. These sporadic and lexicalized effects of voiced obstruents in m_1 seen in (15) and (16) in Modern Japanese become more significant in the light of history, revealing themselves as contemporary relics of a much more pervasive pattern of dissimilation holding at an earlier stage.

Unger (1975, 8–9) (see also Vance 2002 for critical discussion) shows that a strong version of Lyman's Law was observed in Old Japanese, the language of the Nara period (eighth century A.D.), where "*rendaku* also did not take place if the first morpheme contained a voiced obstruent."[7] The finding is based on his exhaustive classification of all Old Japanese words attested in *manyoogana* (i.e., where voicing is phonetically interpretable) that contain two or more voiced obstruents (see Unger 1975, 12–15). The resulting list of 78 words (mostly long compounds), besides bearing out the usual Lyman generalization, significantly includes no unambiguous examples[8] that are parallel in structure to Modern Japanese *tabi-bito* (see (12))—that is, examples with an underlying voiced obstruent followed by a second morpheme-initial voiced obstruent that is derived by *rendaku*. Since *rendaku* is otherwise vigorously operative in Old Japanese compounds, this can only mean that they were subject to a stronger form of Lyman's Law encompassing the first member as well as the second.

Schematically speaking, voicing was suppressed not only in (17a), where the blocking segment occurs later in m_2, but also in (17b), where it occurs earlier in m_1. *D* abbreviates [+voi, −son], and the *rendaku*-derived voicing is indicated by boldface.

(17) a. m_1 m_2 b. m_1 m_2

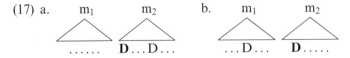

The Old Japanese pattern could be seen as a ban on voiced obstruents in successive syllables in a compound (*[$_\sigma$ D ...] [$_\sigma$ D ...]), that is, irrespective of their affiliation with the first or second member. While this would be a plausible interpretation of the facts and could easily be captured by means of self-conjunction (with adjacency serving as the locality condition), the actual restriction is stronger in the sense that there seems to be no absolute requirement that the blocking syllable in m_1 or m_2 be immediately adjacent to the potential *rendaku* target. While adjacency will often factually hold, given that many of the forms appearing as first members of compounds are mono- or disyllabic, the adjacency condition predicts, for example, that a trisyllabic morpheme as m_1 whose second consonant is a voiced obstruent should freely allow *rendaku* voicing at the beginning of m_2 since there is an intervening syllable (schematically, $/CVDCV + TVCV/ \rightarrow [CVDVCV-DVCV]$). This is not borne out by the facts. There are attested compounds with a trisyllabic medially voiced first member (such as *abura* 'oil') followed by an obstruent-initial second member, but none of them is written in a way unambiguously indicating *rendaku* voicing. This argues that the blocking effect does not require syllable adjacency and that Unger's (1975) generalization quoted above is the correct interpretation of the facts. The difference between Old and Modern Japanese is schematically summarized in (18).

(18) *Differences between Modern Japanese and Old Japanese*

Rendaku (yes/no)

	Modern Japanese	Old Japanese	Unattested
Voiced obstruent in m_1	yes	no	no
Voiced obstruent in m_2	no	no	yes

In the modern language, *rendaku* is blocked by a voiced obstruent in m_2, but not by a voiced obstruent in m_1 (see (11) and (12) for exemplification). But in Old Japanese, *rendaku* blockers are voiced obstruents either in m_2 or in m_1. The third logical pattern (also shown in (18)), in which *rendaku* would be blocked by a voiced obstruent on the left (i.e., in m_1) but not by one on the right (i.e., in m_2), is not attested, a point we return to below.

5.2.2   Diachronic Reranking of Constraints

To understand the difference in scope between the Old and Modern Japanese versions of Lyman's Law (including the latter's traces in certain lexical fields of Modern Japanese; see (15) and (16)), it turns out to be most fruitful to focus not on the linear precedence relations between the obstruents, but on higher-order prosodic constituency. Japanese compounds form a prosodic unit that carries at most one accent (for further discussion, see McCawley 1968, 1977; Poser 1984; Kubozono 1988, 1993; also chapter 8). The basic pattern, illustrated in (19), involves the systematic deletion (and not mere subordination) of any lexical accent in the first member of a compound. This makes Japanese compounds a classic example where the whole compound constitutes a single prosodic word (ω) in the phonological hierarchy. In this way, Japanese differs from many languages with stress accent (such as English; see Tanaka 2001a,b).

(19) *The basic accent pattern of compounds*

Input: m_1	Input: m_2	Output: ω	
/ya⌐mato/	/ta⌐masii/	[yamato da⌐masii]	'Yamato spirit'
/a⌐ka/	/mura⌐saki/	[aka mura⌐saki]	'reddish purple'
/natu⌐/	/mi⌐kan/	[natu mi⌐kan]	'summer mandarin, grapefruit'
/kurisu⌐masu/	/turi⌐i/	[kurisumasu turi⌐i]	'Christmas tree'
/pe⌐rusya/	/ne⌐ko/	[perusya ne⌐ko]	'Persian cat'
/na⌐ka/	/niwa/	[naka niwa]	'inner-garden, courtyard'
/mizu/	/hana/	[mizu bana]	'water-nose, running nose'

The schematic illustration in (20) focuses on the relevant prosodic and grammatical domains.

(20) *Hierarchical structure*

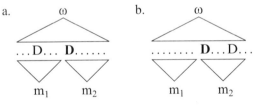

A ω-domain OCP violation is incurred when, in addition to the segment that realizes *rendaku* voicing, either m_1 or m_2 contains a voiced obstruent ((20a) and (20b))—the situation found in Old Japanese; but a morpheme domain violation is incurred when only m_2 contains an additional voiced obstruent—the situation found in Modern Japanese. In these terms, Unger's (1975) "strong version of Lyman's Law" is readily understood as being due to the activity of a constraint No-D^2_ω, indexed for the domain ω (= prosodic word) in Old Japanese. Since this activity manifests itself in preventing the realization of the voicing morpheme $\Re$, the crucial dominance relation is with respect to the constraint Realize-M, as seen in (21).

(21) *Old Japanese/Modern Japanese ranking difference (preliminary)*

    a. Old Japanese ranking   b. Modern Japanese ranking

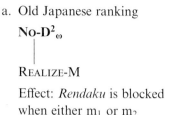

$$\text{No-D}^2_\omega$$
       |
   Realize-M

$$\text{No-D}^2_m$$
       |
   Realize-M

    Effect: *Rendaku* is blocked when either m_1 or m_2 contains a voiced obstruent.

    Effect: *Rendaku* is blocked only when m_2 contains a voiced obstruent.

While (21) still presents an incomplete picture, it is sufficient to derive the basic difference between the two stages of the language, as shown in (22) and (23).

(22) *Modern Japanese*

		No-D^2_m	Realize-M	No-D
/tabi + ℜ + hito/	► **tabi bito**			**
	tabi hito		*!	*
/huna + ℜ + tabi/	huna dabi	*!		**
	► **huna tabi**		*	*

(23) *Old Japanese (hypothetical forms paralleling Modern Japanese)*

		No-D$^2_\omega$	Realize-M	No-D
/tabi + ℜ + hito/	tabi bito	*!		**
	► **tabi hito**		*	*
/huna + ℜ + tabi/	huna dabi	*!		**
	► **huna tabi**		*	*

At first glance, the relevant change from (21a) to (21b) appears to be a change in parameter setting, the open parameter being the domain specification of a given self-conjoined constraint—here, from ω (prosodic word) to m (morpheme). More in the spirit of OT, however, is an alternative interpretation that views both the morpheme version and the prosodic word version of the constraint as existing in the grammars of both Old Japanese and Modern Japanese. The difference between the grammars is not a change in parameter setting, but a different position of $No\text{-}D^2_\omega$ in the hierarchy, as illustrated in (24).

(24) *Old Japanese/Modern Japanese ranking difference (final version)*

    a. Old Japanese   b. Modern Japanese
        constraint ranking   constraint ranking

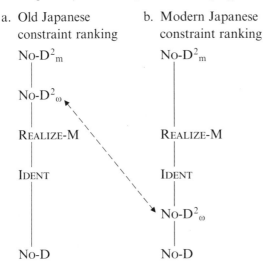

Under this view, the different domain versions exist in both grammars; *inapplicability* means just 'low ranking', not 'absence'; and the grammar change falls under the general rubric of reranking, where constraints appear to lose or gain in strength, rather than change their domain specifications.

In chapter 7, where we turn to a more detailed study of the way the faithfulness constraints on voicing interact with the rest of the phonology, we will show that the reranking interpretation in (24) is not only conceptually superior, but also demanded by the empirical facts. Another constraint turns out to intervene between $No\text{-}D^2_m$ and $No\text{-}D^2_\omega$ in Old Japanese, showing that $No\text{-}D^2_m$ is active and distinct from $No\text{-}D^2_\omega$. We are thus not dealing with a choice between one and the other, as in the parameter-setting scenarios of earlier frameworks.

5.2.3 Factorial Typology

Considering the factorial typology of the basic constraints involved in our analysis of Japanese morphophonemic voicing alternations, we note that intrinsically determined rankings lead to an important prediction. Consider the five conceivable *rendaku*-type voicing patterns modeled on Japanese in (25).

(25) *Conceivable* rendaku-*type voicing patterns*

Type	/kami + ℜ + tana/ 'divine shelf'	/nabe + ℜ + huta/ 'pot lid'	/nuri + ℜ + huda/ 'lacquered sign'	Characterization
(i)	[kami-dana]	[nabe-buta]	[nuri-buda]	voicing in all situations[9] (unattested, but possible)
(ii)	[kami-dana]	[nabe-buta]	[nuri-huda]	voicing unless m_2 contains D (= Modern Japanese)
(iii)	[kami-dana]	[nabe-huta]	[nuri-huda]	voicing unless m_1 or m_2 contains D (= Old Japanese)
(iv)	[kami-tana]	[nabe-huta]	[nuri-huda]	no voicing ever (= English, etc.)
(v)	[kami-dana]	[nabe-huta]	[nuri-buda]	voicing unless m_1 has D (unattested, impossible)

Modern Japanese falls under type (ii), and Old Japanese under type (iii). There is no reason to exclude type (i), *rendaku* voicing without Lyman effects, as a viable option (even though we know of no actual example of such a language or dialect), and type (iv) needs no discussion, since it is richly instantiated in most languages apart from Japanese. Type (v) is interesting in that it is very similar to type (ii), the only difference being that the exception clause refers to m_1 instead of m_2. Could there be a language with this kind of voicing pattern? Viewed in terms of the temporal order of the phonetic events, type (v) might look plausible as the "perseveratory" counterpart of the "anticipatory" blocking in type (ii). Nevertheless, there are good reasons to regard type (v) as impossible, as becomes clear once we lift our perspective beyond the one-dimensional temporal succession of phonetic events and study the hierarchical relations between grammatical and prosodic constituents.

Aside from real or at least conceivable cases of prosodic degeneracy, the phonological substance of morphemes is prosodified as parts of prosodic words. And apart from special cases of misalignment involving resyllabification across a word boundary and the like, elements that are affiliated with the same morpheme in general end up affiliated with the same prosodic word. Put differently, even though there is no formal containment relationship between prosodic words and (the exponents of) morphemes, as a matter of ordinary prosodic life, containment usually holds. In particular, this is true of all Japanese forms under discussion here. Factual ω-containment means that domain-indexed pairs of constraints such as No-D^2_m and No-D^2_ω are in a factual specific-general relationship. Any pair of voiced obstruents in a form triggering a violation of the former will trigger a violation of the latter, but not vice versa. This is shown in (26).

(26) *m-domain over ω-domain*

		No-D^2_m	No-D$^2_\omega$
/nabe + ℜ + huta/	{ }$_m$ { }$_m$ ▶ [nabe huta]$_\omega$		
	{ }$_m$ { }$_m$ [nabe buta]$_\omega$		*!
/nuri + ℜ + huda/	{ }$_m$ { }$_m$ ▶ [nuri huda]$_\omega$		
	{ }$_m$ { }$_m$ [nuri buda]$_\omega$	*!	*

Under factual ω-containment, the two constraints do not conflict; it will always (ceteris paribus) be worse to violate No-D^2_m than to violate No-D$^2_\omega$. Ranking No-D$^2_\omega$ above No-D^2_m as in (27) is ineffectual in the sense that the same winners are being selected as under the specific-over-general ranking (26).

(27) *ω-domain over m-domain*

		No-D$^2_\omega$	No-D^2_m
/nabe + ℜ + huta/	{ }$_m$ { }$_m$ ▶ [nabe huta]$_\omega$		
	{ }$_m$ { }$_m$ [nabe buta]$_\omega$	*!	
/nuri + ℜ + huda/	{ }$_m$ { }$_m$ ▶ [nuri huda]$_\omega$		
	{ }$_m$ { }$_m$ [nuri buda]$_\omega$	*!	*

In other words, the constraint system that we have developed predicts that *nuribuda* cannot win over *nurihuda* as long as *nabehuta* wins over *nabebuta*; that is, type (v) cannot exist. Under ω-containment conditions, and assuming Prince and Smolensky's (1993) strict ranking principle, the specific-over-general ranking in (28) is for all practical purposes intrinsic.

(28)

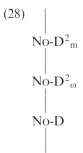

Given the ranking of these three constraints, there are four positions where the constraint REALIZE-M may be ranked, as shown in (29): (i) above $No\text{-}D^2_m$, (ii) between $No\text{-}D^2_m$ and $No\text{-}D^2_\omega$, (iii) between $No\text{-}D^2_\omega$ and $No\text{-}D$, and (iv) below $No\text{-}D$.

(29) *Different positions for* REALIZE-M

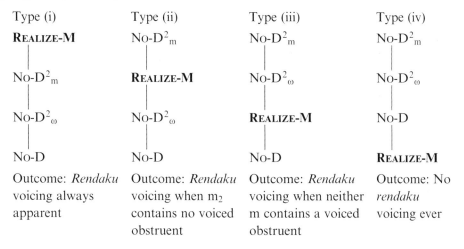

What kinds of languages do these partial grammars produce? The four resulting patterns are exactly parallel to those seen in (25). Types (ii) and (iii) are those posited for Modern Japanese and Old Japanese, respectively, and the other two, where REALIZE-M is either top-ranking (i) or bottom-ranking (iv), will produce systems with *rendaku* voicing everywhere and *rendaku* voicing nowhere, respectively. But there is no ranking position of REALIZE-M that produces type (v) in (25), in which a voiced obstruent in m_1, but not in m_2, blocks *rendaku* voicing (the underlying logic of the situation was discussed above in connection with (26) and (27)). This kind of predictive power shows the superiority of a theory that posits a family of constraints governing domains differing in inclusiveness. In a theory making use of conditions such as "voiced obstruent $\notin m_2$," no equivalent prediction can be made, since it remains purely accidental that the condition does not refer to m_1 instead. The same holds for an analysis working directly in terms of linear precedence relations, where it remains mysterious why a preceding voiced obstruent cannot be a *rendaku* blocker without a following voiced obstruent also being endowed with this power.

5.3 Further Issues

To conclude this chapter, let us take a last look at the typology of conceivable *rendaku*-type voicing patterns in (25). When we add another class of forms to the picture, exemplified by words like *naga-sode* 'long sleeved' with underlying voiced obstruents in m_1 and m_2, the question arises whether type (i), the across-the-board voicing pattern, actually splits into two, as indicated in (30): a true voicing-at-all-costs pattern (ia), and a variant (ib) that shies away from voicing just in the newly introduced double-voicing situation.

(30) *A further worst-of-the-worst interaction?*

Type	/kami + $\Re$ + tana/	/nabe + $\Re$ + huta/	/nuri + $\Re$ + huda/	/naga + $\Re$ + sode/	Characterization
(ia)	[kami-dana]	[nabe-buta]	[nuri-buda]	[naga-zode]	voicing at all costs
(ib)	[kami-dana]	[nabe-buta]	[nuri-buda]	[naga-sode]	voicing except between voiced obstruents

Since type (i) is so far unattested, questions about its further differentiation are somewhat hypothetical, and at present we do not know whether distributions with the subtlety shown by type (30ib) are actually encountered in natural languages. Let us assume, for the sake of the argument, that they exist—what kind of constraint configuration gives rise to them? Since we are dealing with a worst-of-the-worst interaction, the question is of some theoretical interest since the answer casts light on the power of conjunction—in particular, on the question of whether it is recursive. If recursive conjunction is permitted, one way of capturing the distinction between types (ia) and (ib) is as in (31) (a self-conjunction of No-$D^2{}_\omega$ would serve the same purpose, with slightly different predictions).

(31) *Recursive conjunction?*

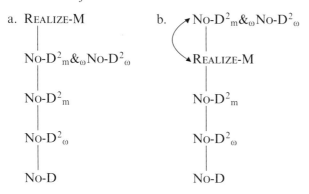

a. REALIZE-M

    No-D^2_m&$_\omega$No-D$^2_\omega$

    No-D^2_m

    No-D$^2_\omega$

    No-D

b. No-D^2_m&$_\omega$No-D$^2_\omega$

    REALIZE-M

    No-D^2_m

    No-D$^2_\omega$

    No-D

Illustrative tableaux appear in (32) and (33).

(32) *Type (ia): voicing at all costs*

		REALIZE-M	No-D^2_m&$_\omega$-No-D$^2_\omega$	No-D
/naga + ℜ + sode/	▶ **naga + zode**		*!	***
	naga + sode	*!		**

(33) *Type (ib): voicing except when both members have voiced obstruents*

		No-D^2_m&$_\omega$-No-D$^2_\omega$	REALIZE-M	No-D
/naga + ℜ + sode/	naga + zode	*!		***
	▶ **naga + sode**		*	**

A conjunction is violated only if both of its members are violated, and these violations are different. Thus, *naga zode* violates the conjunction No-D^2_m&$_\omega$No-D$^2_\omega$ because the pair (z, d) in the second morpheme violates No-D^2_m and the pair (g, z) violates No-D$^2_\omega$ in the whole prosodic word (and not, e.g., because the first pair violates both constraints). It is easy to see that recursive conjunction, if it is actually at work in grammars, has the capacity to give rise to rather complex patterns.

On the other hand, if interaction patterns such as voicing type (ib) (see (30) and (33)) are not a feature of natural languages, their absence would follow from the nonrecursivity of constraint conjunction (or minimally, from the unavailability of the type of recursion seen here).[10]

Chapter 6

Rules and Exceptions

Der Regel Güte daraus man erwägt,
dass sie auch mal 'ne Ausnahm' verträgt.

The quality of a rule is to be judged by
its ability to tolerate an occasional exception.

—Richard Wagner, *Die Meistersinger von Nürnberg*

In previous chapters, we have presented a detailed OT treatment of the compound voicing process of Japanese. While we attempted to do justice to the morphological side of the phenomenon—by anchoring *rendaku* voicing in a linking morpheme whose distribution is controlled by grammatical factors—the analysis focused chiefly on the phonological conditions of the process. Its systematic phonological blocking (Lyman's Law) due to a dissimilative restriction against multiple obstruent voicing was seen as a manifestation of a general feature of native Japanese morpheme structure. Applying the theory of OCP effects advanced earlier (chapter 2), we showed how such dissimilative tendencies can be made computable in a precise and explanatory way in OT phonology, interpreting them as self-conjunctions of markedness constraints operative in specific domains (chapter 4). Finally, appreciation of the marked difference between Old and Modern Japanese in the ability of compounds to undergo *rendaku* occasioned a sharpening of the theory of conjunction domains (chapter 5).

With this much of the phonology of *rendaku* in place, and reduced to principles of some generality, the reader might have come away with the impression that the process is a quasi-automatic feature of Japanese speech affecting any compound whatsoever. This is far from being the case, however, and although we have made distinctions in passing in earlier chapters, it is now time to take a realistic and more systematic look at the lexicon of the contemporary language, where second-member voicing is by no means an automatic accompaniment of compounding. *Rendaku* is sensitive to a synchronically active division of the Japanese lexicon into native (or Yamato) versus Sino-Japanese versus Foreign items, a division comparable to the distinction between native Germanic versus Romance/Latinate items in the lexicon of English.[1] Here *Sino-Japanese* conventionally refers to old loans from Chinese accumulated over centuries of borrowing, whereas *Foreign* denotes more recent loans, mostly from Western languages (and overwhelmingly from English).

We mentioned in chapter 4 that, special cases aside, *rendaku* voicing is restricted to native items, such as *kane* 'money' and *tana* 'shelf' in (1). It does not appear on nonnative morphemes, be they Sino-Japanese (such as *kin* 'gold, money' in (1a)) or Foreign (such as *keesu* 'case' in (1b)). This morpheme class distinction, synchronically arbitrary but nevertheless fully active and even (partially) encoded in the writing system, is at work in the contrasting behavior of pairs of morphemes as in (1), where the only reason why the forms on the right do not show voicing is that their second members are nonnative morphemes.[2]

(1) *Morpheme class (stratal) distinctions: undergoers versus nonundergoers*
    (Y = Yamato, S = Sino-Japanese, F = Foreign)

	Native morphemes: voicing		Nonnative morphemes: no voicing	
a.	kane (Y)	nise-gane	kin (S)	nise-kin
	'money'	'counterfeit money'	'money'	'counterfeit money'
b.	tana (Y)	garasu-dana	keesu (F)	garasu-keesu
	'shelf'	'glass shelf'	'case'	'glass case'

Rendaku affects only part of the lexicon, failing to apply in a host of both systematic and sporadic cases. In this respect, it is similar to many other morphophonemic processes that are sensitive to distinctions between vocabulary strata, and we will use it here as a window on the internal structure of the lexicon of a natural language, which is typically nonhomogeneous and shows considerable internal variation.

In this chapter, we show that the basic analysis of compound voicing developed to this point, which focuses on the general linguistic properties of the process and therefore abstracts away from real-world complications like those in (1), is not for that reason divorced from reality, but can be embedded in a realistic model of the Japanese lexicon. What is needed is a proper understanding of lexical stratification that allows the analyst to find a path through a multitude of generalizations, subgeneralizations, exceptions, exceptions to exceptions, and the like, and to penetrate to the large-scale organization lying behind it.[3]

6.1 Harmonic Completeness, Universal and Language-Specific

Upon closer inspection, the phonological lexicon of most languages studied in any degree of detail has turned out to be not a smooth and homogeneous whole, but a nonuniform, internally subdivided structure (see Ito and Mester 1995a,b, 1999a, 2001a for examples and references to earlier work)—hence the common experience that phonological processes and generalizations have systematic exceptions. Such processes and generalizations hold within a subdomain of the whole lexical space, but are violated in other areas such as onomatopoeia and unassimilated loanwords. Relevant examples can be found almost anywhere. For instance: (i) Postnasal stops in native Mazateco are never voiceless (in this, Mazateco is very similar to Japanese; see Ito, Mester, and Padgett 1995 and section 6.3 below), but such clusters are normal in Spanish loans such as [siento] '100'.[4] (ii) In native Chamorro (Chung 1983; see Kiparsky 1998 for a recent OT analysis), high and mid vowels do not contrast, but are in complementary distribution, with mid vowels occurring in stressed closed syllables, high vowels elsewhere. Height is contrastive, however, in the numerous loans from Spanish. (iii) Native Mohawk has no labial consonants, and stress in native words falls on the penultimate syllable. But loans from French have labials, and they are stressed on the final syllable (Postal 1968, 130). (iv) In Russian, velars are generally palatalized before front vowels (e.g., $k^j em$ 'who (instrumental singular)'), but unassimilated loans such as *kemping* show unpalatalized velars in this position (Padgett 2003).

6.1.1 Rule-Governed versus List-Based Behavior

There is reason to tread cautiously in this area, since we do not want to misinterpret every fossilized relic of a long-extinct alternation as active phonology. For example, the ablauting members among English irregular verbs (*sink, sank, sunk*, etc.), solidly native and of high frequency, exhibit patterns that can be traced back to a prehistoric stage where they had a clear phonological basis. Still, there is broad agreement among analysts that nowadays, the ablaut alternations in irregular English verbs constitute a closed system of listed allomorphs and are not part of active rule-governed phonology.[5] The mere fact that a process or condition was once active in a language does not mean it continues forever. But at the other extreme, most working phonologists do not automatically conclude from a handful of exceptions that a process does not constitute rule-governed behavior. What is at stake is rather the general typology of contrast between rule-governed and list-based linguistic behavior. The differences between productive derivation and lexical listing of variants are well known (see Pinker 1999 for an extended study of the numerous and fundamental differences, including grammatical, psycholinguistic, and neurological facts and processes, that separate rule-governed from list-based morphology, using English irregular morphology as a test case). Attempts to appeal directly to "analogy" (Ohno 2000) tend more to describe the problem than to solve it. After all, this notion itself is in serious need of explication—in modern understanding, in terms of a system of linguistic rules (see Kiparsky 1965 and subsequent work).

For Japanese *rendaku*, Fukuda and Fukuda (1994) conducted a psycholinguistic experiment designed to bear directly on this issue. On the one hand, if compound voicing constitutes a productive rule, it involves what the authors refer to as the implicit procedural memory of speakers, who should be able to apply the voicing rule to cases they have not yet encountered, such as infrequent or novel compounds. Developmentally impaired speakers who are otherwise known not to make use of implicit procedural memory should find it difficult to apply voicing in the latter cases. On the other hand, if compound voicing is simply a matter of lexically listed forms, implicit procedural memory should not be involved, and no significant difference between the two groups of speakers should arise. The results show typical characteristics of rule-based behavior. A word formation task involving three types of compounds (frequent, infrequent, and novel) was given to three groups of children: (i) six developmentally impaired children 8–12 years old, (ii) six age-matched nonimpaired children, and (iii) four younger nonimpaired children (who were hypothesized to have not yet fully acquired the operation of *rendaku*). For frequent compounds, there was no significant difference between any pairs of groups, but for both infrequent and novel compounds a clear difference emerged between group (i), the impaired speakers not making use of implicit procedural memory, and groups (ii) and (iii). As Fukuda and Fukuda (1994, 178) note, "The data indicate that the impaired children did not in fact voice most of the initial obstruents of the second member in nonfrequent and novel compounds, whereas the age-matched non-impaired children did voice the appropriate obstruents of all the compounds, and the younger non-impaired children voiced some initial obstruents of all the compounds."

Such findings leave little doubt that *rendaku* involves, not a memorized list, but implicit procedural memory of a morphophonemic rule. But this leaves us with a rule that holds over only part of the lexicon. Even though phonologists routinely assume nonuniformity of lexical structure, it merits closer attention, in particular when the dividing line does not separate clearly marginal material from the main body of the lexicon, but cuts through more central locations. Since stratal divisions of the lexicon are usually the result of extralinguistic factors, be they social, cultural, or political, they are a proper object for diachronic study. But they also have synchronic reality in that they pose a considerable challenge for language learners, who must come to terms with them even as they are figuring out the generalizations operative in the language in question.

The fact that learners acquire lexically partial generalizations with apparent ease shows that they must naturally fit into the basic organization of the grammar. An important clue regarding the relevant factors within a given language is provided by typological generalizations about the inventories of elements and structures admitted by different grammars.

6.1.2   Universal Implicational Hierarchies

Crosslinguistic research has uncovered a significant number of implicational hierarchies relating linguistic inventories. These markedness implications, holding with various degrees of strictness, are of the form, "If a language has β, it always/usually also has α, but not vice versa." In this situation, α is called *unmarked* in comparison with its *marked* counterpart β.

For example, Maddieson (1984) surveys the occurrence of voiceless stops in the inventories of a representative sample of 318 languages included in the UCLA Phonology Segment Inventory Database and observes that "an implicational hierarchy can be set up such that the presence of /p/ implies the strong likelihood of the presence of /k/, which similarly implies presence of /t/" (p. 35). We thus have the implications in (2a), the corresponding markedness order in (2b), and the corresponding universally fixed ranking of constraints in (2c).

(2)   *Inventory universals*

    a. p → k → t   "β → α" = "The presence of structure β implies the strong
                                 likelihood of the presence of structure α."

    b. [t] > [k] > [p]   "α > β" = "Structure α is less marked than structure β."

    c. *P ≫ *K ≫ *T   *β ≫ *α = "The constraint against structure β outranks
                                    the constraint against structure α."

Other universal markedness hierarchies involve vowels (e.g., [i] > [y], [y] > [ø]), laryngeal states of consonants (e.g., [k] > [g], [g] > [gʰ], [k] > [kʰ]), rhythmic feet (e.g., for quantity-sensitive trochees {('LL), ('H)} > ('HL) > ('LH) > ('L); Prince 1990), and many other structures.

In OT, such empirically established hierarchies are seen as the result of invariant rankings, as in (2c). The relevant constraints are members of constraint families whose internal ranking is universally fixed and cannot be changed in individual grammars (Prince and Smolensky 1993). The principle of strict ranking then entails that faithfulness constraints can intervene only in specific niches, as shown in (3).

(3)   a.   b.   c.

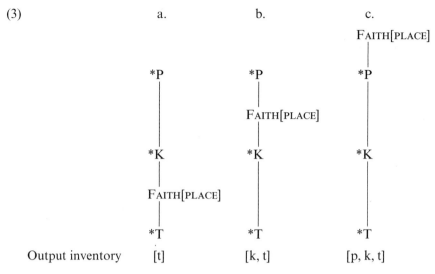

Output inventory   [t]   [k, t]   [p, k, t]

The output inventories have a characteristic subset structure: output inventory (3a) is a subset of (3b), and (3b) is a subset of (3c). This means that—as long as the assumptions underlying (3) are observed—there is no grammar that produces the system [p, t], which has a "hole" in containing the highly marked [p] while excluding the less marked [k]. Such systems are "harmonically incomplete" in the sense of (4) (see Prince and Smolensky 1993; Prince 1998).

(4) *Harmonic completeness*

Let α, β be elements or structures that can be compared with respect to markedness, with α being less marked than β. Then any system of linguistic structures S containing β must also contain α: If α > β and β ∈ S, then α ∈ S.

The idea of markedness, as developed in Prague School phonology (see in particular Trubetzkoy 1939), is virtually built on the finding that the output inventories of natural languages tend to be harmonically complete in the sense made more precise in (4). Recalcitrant gaps in individual cases notwithstanding (hence the careful wording "implies the strong likelihood" in the implicational universal from Maddieson 1984 quoted above), such as the well-known absence of [t] and [s] in the inventory of Hawaiian in the presence of [k], language inventories overwhelmingly obey Maddieson's implication $p \rightarrow k \rightarrow t$ (or equivalently, $\neg t \rightarrow \neg k \rightarrow \neg p$), and any theory needs to capture this broad typological generalization.

6.1.3 Language-Specific Implicational Hierarchies

The central finding of our previous work on the structure of the lexicon (see Ito and Mester 1999a and references cited there) is that a kind of harmonic completeness of inventory structure holds not only crosslinguistically, where it grows out of the interleaving of faithfulness with *universally fixed* markedness rankings, as in (3), but also within each individual grammar, where it emerges from the interaction of faithfulness with the *parochial* ranking of markedness constraints, as it is fixed for the language is question. Consider a schematic hierarchy $M_1 \gg \ldots \gg M_n$ of markedness constraints in a grammar, as in (5), and a faithfulness constraint FAITH-X concerned with input-output disparities with respect to some property X.

(5) $M_1 \gg M_2 \gg M_3 \gg M_4 \gg M_5 \gg M_6 \gg \ldots \gg M_n$

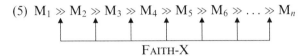

FAITH-X

The higher FAITH-X is ranked, the stronger its influence, the weaker the impact of M_i, and therefore the larger the output inventory of elements and structures admitted by the grammar. FAITH-X will of course not impinge on each and every lower-ranked M_i, but in an overall theory in which faithfulness constraints are independent from markedness constraints and highly symmetric, it will impinge on a substantial number of them.

The last point is worth emphasizing since it bears on the generality of faithfulness constraints. Increasingly fine-grained expansions of faithfulness, where markedness constraints are mirrored in a shadow world of individuated faithfulness constraints corresponding to them point by point, are rather problematic. Usually answering to perceived descriptive needs, such expansions of faithfulness are collectively detrimental to the overall theory since they undermine OT's basic markedness/faithfulness architecture, where phonological processes are not basic elements, but emerge from the interaction of conflicting and independent markedness and faithfulness constraints. The extreme situation, where each M_i is tied to its own F_i, constitutes in effect a revival of the "rule package" (structural description tied to a structural change) of traditional rule-based phonology, with "$SD_i + SC_i$" encoded as "$M_i \gg F_i$." In such a model, ranking relations are shallow and trivial, since F_i impinges on nothing besides its own M_i. For these reasons, among others, the general and symmetric character of faithfulness constraints is of particular importance in OT (see chapter 7 for further discussion in connection with voicing faithfulness).

As the basic set of faithfulness constraints is unfolded in its different correspondence-theoretic incarnations—for different classes of input items (roots vs. affixes: McCarthy and Prince 1995), different positions (prominent vs. nonprominent: Padgett 1995; Beckman 1997, 1998; Casali 1997; Lombardi 1999), and so on—an inventory subset structure emerges through different rankings of the individual constraints (FAITH-X-ROOT $\gg \ldots \gg$ FAITH-X-AFFIX, etc.). Other parts of the FAITH differentiation program seek to explain reduplicative identity, truncation, language game forms, and other output-output relations between basic forms and derived forms along similar lines (see, e.g., Benua 1995, 1997; McCarthy and Prince 1995; Ito, Kitagawa, and Mester 1996; Kenstowicz 1996, 1997; Burzio 1997; Ito and Mester 1997a; Steriade 1997; Kager 2000; and for a critical view, see Kiparsky 1998).

Elsewhere (Ito and Mester 1995a, 1999a), we argue that FAITH differentiation is also the key to the stratification of the lexicon ("loanwords" vs. "native vocabulary," etc.—also see Yip 1993; Davidson and Noyer 1997; Fukazawa 1998; Fukazawa, Kitahara, and Ota 1998; Pater 2000; Smolensky, Davidson, and Jusczyk 2000). An individual grammar fixes a particular markedness hierarchy, defining the overall setting for the language. Different sublexicons then arise because stratum-specific tokens of FAITH insert themselves in the hierarchy in different places. As schematically illustrated by the constraints F_a, F_b, F_c in (6), the overall lexicon has a subset structure of sublexicon inventories (i.e., a core-periphery organization), with $I_a \subset I_b \subset I_c$. The basic prediction is that each sublexicon should be harmonically complete with respect to the language-particular basic markedness hierarchy M_i.

(6) *Inventory subset structure*

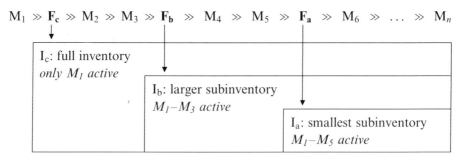

6.1.4 The FAITH Stratification Model

Before turning to the facts of Japanese, we illustrate the model here with a case that is interesting in its own right: the system of speech registers found in Jamaican Creole. This system is characterized by a remarkable series of nested subinventories like those in (6), each harmonically complete with respect to the basic markedness hierarchy. Building on the pioneering work of DeCamp (1971), Meade (1998) has uncovered an extensive system of lexical subsets and implications within the continuum of registers ranging from *basilect* to *acrolect* (the varieties of Jamaican Creole most/least distinct from British English, respectively; intermediate varieties are referred to as *mesolects*). Most Jamaican Creole speakers control several registers that are appropriate in different situations. The basic structure of this system is not different from sociolinguistic registers in other speech communities. What *is* significant is the number of levels and the subtlety of some of the distinctions involved. As

Meade (1998) shows in the work on which the analysis below is built, FAITH stratification is the key to understanding systems of this kind.

Two processes found in Jamaican Creole are sufficient to make our basic point: cluster simplification (e.g., [st]*ick* → [t]*ick*) and hardening of voiced interdentals (e.g., [ð]*at* → [d]*at*). The phrase *that stick* is pronounced as [dat tɪk] in the basilect (with both simplification and hardening) and as [ðat stɪk] in the acrolect (where neither process applies). Between these two is the mesolect pronunciation [dat stɪk] (with hardening but without simplification). However, there is no mesolect with the fourth logical possibility *[ðat tɪk] (with simplification but without hardening). There are thus only three distinct registers for *that stick*, and the summary in (7) reveals the subset relations {C, d, ...} ⊂ {C, d, CC, ...} ⊂ {C, d, CC, ð, ...}, where *C* and *CC* stand for simple and complex onset structures, respectively.

(7) *Registers for* that stick

/ðat stɪk/	Hardening (ð → d)	Simplification (CC → C)	Register
a. dat tɪk	yes	yes	basilect
b. dat stɪk	yes	no	mesolect
c. ðat stɪk	no	no	acrolect
d. *ðat tɪk	no	yes	(impossible register)

By ranking the two (descriptively named) markedness constraints involved as No-ð ≫ No-[CC, a grammar with differentiated FAITH constraints captures precisely this set of registers, as shown in (8) (after Meade 1998). In the basilect governed by lowest-ranking FAITH$_a$, the two markedness constraints outrank faithfulness, so the output is optimized with respect to markedness. Mesolect faithfulness FAITH$_b$ is sandwiched between the two markedness constraints, so the output fulfills the higher markedness constraint No-ð, but not the lower one, No-[CC. Acrolect faithfulness FAITH$_c$ ranks above both markedness constraints, forcing violations of both.

(8)

	← FAITH$_c$ (acrolect):	no hardening, no simplification	[ðat stɪk]
No-ð			
	← FAITH$_b$ (mesolect):	hardening, no simplification	[dat stɪk]
No-[CC			
	← FAITH$_a$ (basilect):	hardening, simplification	[dat tɪk]

The absence of a register with the mapping /ðat stɪk/ → [ðat tɪk] is straightfor-wardly explained: there are no more positions in the hierarchy where faithfulness can intervene. The indexed FAITH approach implies that all registers R must admit complex onsets if they admit the segment [ð] (i.e., ð ∈ R → [CC ∈ R), and this impli-cation follows from a central property of OT grammars: the total ranking of all constraints.[6]

6.1.5 Voicing in Japanese and Stratal Faithfulness

With these principles of lexical stratification in hand, let us now return to the *rendaku*-related phonology of Japanese and its effects throughout the lexicon of the language. Our goal is to test the hypothesis that stratum variation reduces to a kind of faithfulness variation—in other words, that the grammar accommodates vocabu-lary strata, with their attendant specific properties, by diversifying faithfulness con-straints and ranking them as appropriate. To see whether this model allows an illuminating and predictive approach to lexicon-internal variation, we will investigate how much of the variation regarding *rendaku* can be fruitfully interpreted in this way.

Besides the two high-ranking constraints related to voicing studied in preceding chapters—the multiple obstruent voicing ban No-D^2_m and REALIZE-MORPHEME (here insisting on the output realization of the linking morpheme $[+\text{voi}]_\Re$)—we will review the patterning of a third voicing-related constraint, NO-NC̥, which bans voiceless obstruents from postnasal position and gives rise to voicing alternations in Japanese.

The main focus now shifts to the input-output faithfulness constraint IDENT.[7] Seen from a distance at the level of basic phonological analysis, it appears as a monolithic unit; but seen up close in its actual operation in the lexicon, it reveals itself as con-sisting of a group of associated constraints that are all instances of one basic input-output faithfulness constraint, but that occupy subtly different positions in the markedness hierarchy.

As we will show in more detail later, investigation into the stratal restrictions of the three voicing-related constraints in Japanese leads to the divisions in the lexicon shown in (9).

(9)

Constraints	Strata				Effects
	Y	Sa	Sb	F	
No-D^2_m	yes	yes	yes	no	observes multiple obstruent voicing ban
REALIZE-M	yes	yes	no	no	realizes compound voicing morpheme
NO-NC̥	yes	no	no	no	observes postnasal voicing

The split among Y (Yamato), S (Sino-Japanese),[8] and F (Foreign) corresponds to the traditional distinction among *wago* (和語), *kango* (漢語), and *gairaigo* (外来語) and confirms its synchronic relevance. The classification in (9) is built on the overt behavior of contemporary speakers, not on the etymological origin of particular words. What matters is not the labels Y (Yamato), S (Sino-Japanese), and F (Foreign)—more neutral and less mnemonic terms could be chosen, and the synchronic groupings imposed by speakers by no means always coincide with etymology[9]—but the structure revealed by the distribution of *yes* and *no* in the cells of (9): (i) items observing No-NC̥ also observe REALIZE-M, but not vice versa; (ii) items observing REALIZE-M also observe No-D^2_m, but not vice versa; and (iii) items observing No-NC̥ also observe No-D^2_m (by transitivity), but not vice versa. As demonstrated for other constraints in Japanese and crosslinguistically in Ito and Mester 1999a, such patterns of hierarchical inclusion between areas of constraint activity in the phonological lexicon—a kind of harmonic completeness pattern, as explained earlier—are very common, indicating that a fundamental property of lexical constraint systems is at work.

In the rest of this chapter, we take up each constraint in turn, illustrating its stratal restrictions with relevant examples and providing analytical details.

6.2 No-D^2_m and Its Activity in the Lexicon

The multiple voicing constraint No-D^2_m holds for the Yamato vocabulary (see section 2.3) and the Sino-Japanese vocabulary: Y and S items do not contain more than one voiced obstruent.

(10) *Y morphemes: No-D^2_m is active*

tako	'octopus'	No Y morphemes such as	*dago
toge	'splinter'		*doge
geta	'clog'		*geda

(11) *S morphemes: No-D^2_m is active*[10]

getu	'month'	No S morphemes such as	*gezu
geki	'theater'		*gegi
doku	'poison'		*dogu
butu	'thing'		*buzu

On the other hand, F items (which are mostly Western loans) do not obey the multiple voicing restriction, as shown by the examples in (12) (see also the longer list in section 2.3).

(12) *F morphemes: No-D²ₘ is not active*

daburu   'double'
baggu   'bag'
bebii   'baby'
baabekyuu   'barbecue'

6.2.1 FAITH Stratification as Partial Deactivation of Markedness

In terms of stratal faithfulness, the fact that F items do not obey the multiple voicing restriction means that they are subject to a higher-ranking faithfulness constraint IDENT$_f$ that forces the realization of input-given multiple obstruents, overruling the ban expressed by No-D²$_m$.

(13) *High-ranking faithfulness IDENT$_f$ for F items*

IDENT$_f$

No-D²$_m$

IDENT

Since IDENT$_f$ dominates No-D²$_m$, voicing specifications for F inputs with multiple voiced obstruents are faithfully parsed, as shown in (14).

(14) *IDENT$_f$ in operation:* daburu *'double'*

/daburu/$_f$	IDENT$_f$	No-D²$_m$	. . .	IDENT
▶ daburu		*	. . .	
taburu	*!		. . .	*

The specific and high-ranking IDENT$_f$ marks violations in F items, as in (14), and the general (unindexed) and low-ranking IDENT marks violations for all items, whatever their stratum, as in (14) and (15).[11] The hypothetical multiply voiced item in (15) is subject only to the lower IDENT constraint; hence, its input voicing is not protected against No-D²$_m$ (other constraints will determine which segment is devoiced in the output, most likely resulting in initial devoicing for Y items and medial devoicing for S items).

(15) *Hypothetical input*

/dogu/$_{y/s}$	IDENT$_f$	No-D^2_m	...	IDENT
dogu		*!	...	
▶ doku			...	*
▶ togu			...	*

High-ranking stratal faithfulness ensures that the area of activity of the multiple voicing ban No-D^2_m in the phonological lexicon includes Y and S items and excludes F items. The behavior of F items with respect to this voicing constraint is thus a result of differentiated faithfulness, and not a restriction on the markedness constraint. In fact, markedness constraints are in every respect universal and cannot be indexed to a particular lexical class in some language (for justification, see Ito and Mester 1999a, 2002a).

In this model, systematic violations of constraints due to stratification, such as *daburu*, have in a sense been rationalized and brought into some kind of order, setting them apart from the usual notion of exceptions, with its implication of nonsystematicity and idiosyncrasy. In fact, nonsystematic exceptions have nothing to do with lexical stratification; if they did, we would end up with strata whose elements have nothing in common except that they violate a particular constraint, a patently absurd result.

FAITH stratification is not a theory of exceptions, but belongs in the context of the general M ≫ F ranking default holding for the initial state (Smolensky 1995) as well as for all subsequent stages of the developing grammar (Ito and Mester 1999a, 2002a; Prince and Tesar 1999). For the language learner, having a stratally indexed faithfulness constraint FAITH$_α$ is one way of maintaining a version of the low (default, dominated) position of faithfulness (in the present case, IDENT) relative to some markedness constraint M (here, No-D^2_m) in the face of counterevidence to M. This is only possible when the counterevidence turns out to be confined in a lexical area whose inhabitants have other things in common, so that there is an "α" to refer to. Consider a markedness constraint M that is active in the initial state (by general hypothesis) and has also been found to be active in fundamental parts of the language. Now the language learner encounters (and takes into consideration) anti-M data that also exist in the language. One option is to capitulate in the face of these anti-M data and to move directly from grammar (16a) to grammar (16c), deactivating M. Stratification means trying out option (16b), at the cost of setting up a stratum α. This move will only be economical if the items assembled in α have other properties in common—requiring indexation for other faithfulness constraints, combinatorial restrictions, and so on—that make it economical for the grammar to refer to them.

(16) *Partial versus complete deactivation of markedness*

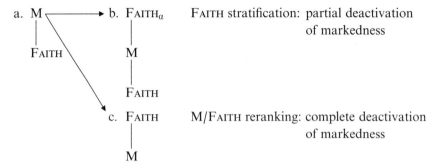

a. M ⟶ b. FAITH$_a$ FAITH stratification: partial deactivation
   | | of markedness
   FAITH   M
                |
                FAITH

          c. FAITH   M/FAITH reranking: complete deactivation
                | of markedness
                M

6.2.2 Negative and Positive Exceptions

Strata are linguistic generalizations, not collections of exceptions, and correspondingly FAITH stratification is not a way of making the unpredictable appear predictable and the unexpected expected, but a way of expressing a hierarchy of generalizations and subgeneralizations.

Where have all the exceptions gone, then? What would constitute a genuine exception in this model of lexical stratification—something not reined in by the system as it stands, including special faithfulness constraints such as IDENT$_f$? Inspecting the logic of the situation, we see that two possible types of exceptions remain: (i) items expected, given the rest of their behavior, to reside within the area where a constraint is effective (here, Y and S items) that still do not observe it (*negative exceptions*), and (ii) items expected, given the rest of their behavior, to reside outside the constraint area (here, F items) that in fact show evidence of its activity (*positive exceptions*).

A handful of well-known items fall in the first category, including *dango* 'dumpling', *budoo* 'grapes', and the compound *nawa-basigo* 'rope ladder' deriving from the input /nawa-hasigo/, where the second member displays *rendaku* voicing despite the resulting violation of the multiple voicing constraint. These forms, which are often regarded as Y items, constitute a well-known residue of recalcitrant data that any analysis must cope with. Regarding the first two examples, besides somehow listing them as pure exceptions that bypass (parts of) the constraint system, one needs to reckon with the possibility that they are fossilized or pseudocompounds consisting of two morphemes (i.e., /bu + doo/ and /dan + go/). The bimorphemic analysis is suggested by the usual way of writing these words in kanji, which uses two characters in each case (団子 /dan + ko/ 'group + offspring', 葡萄 /bu + doo/ 'grape + grape').[12]

The compound *nawa-basigo* 'rope ladder' is at first glance more problematic. Again a hidden bimorphemic analysis of the second member as /hasi + ko/ (see Haraguchi 2001) is not entirely out of the question, with *hasi* 'bridge' (written, however, with a different kanji) and *ko* 'offspring'. But this hardly improves matters. While it renders the co-occurrence of voiced obstruents in *basigo* heteromorphemic and therefore harmless, it also makes *nawa-basigo* a right-branching structure of the form [A[BC]]. It is well known (see Otsu 1980; Ito and Mester 1986; chapter 8 below) that right-branching compound structures resist the appearance of *rendaku* voicing, instead of facilitating it. In other words, whichever way one looks at this form, as simplex or as complex, *rendaku* voicing seems to have little going for it, leaving few options besides brute-force listing. However, the bimorphemic analysis contemplated by Haraguchi (2001) still holds promise, though in a somewhat different form: namely, by means of a correspondence relation between the problematic compound and the shorter substructure *nawa-basi* 'rope bridge', a compound in its own right, where *rendaku* is entirely unremarkable. A special output-output correspondence relation to this form (as a formal expression of a kind of bracketing paradox) is a possibility because it would supply a reason (somewhat akin to other bracketing paradoxes; see Spencer 1988) for the appearance of voicing in this form, instead of simply celebrating its exceptionality. Item-specific output-output relations are admittedly powerful devices, and further study is needed; but if such relations of analogy turn out to be crucial in such cases, considerations of restrictiveness cannot stop us from seeking explanations in the actual factors driving a speaker's behavior, instead of somewhere else.

As noted earlier, positive exceptions to the multiple voicing constraint also exist: namely, F items in which the constraint seems to be active. Nishimura (2001) has uncovered a novel and at first glance surprising generalization that is relevant in this context. It is well known that voiced obstruent geminates in foreign loans, which usually correspond to syllable-final voiced obstruents in the source language (e.g., *biggu* for 'big'; see Katayama 1998 and references cited there) and are excluded from the native inventory, are subject to sporadic devoicing in contemporary usage. Nishimura observes that such devoicing is more likely to occur in loanwords that contain a second voiced obstruent than in other cases (schematically, *baggu~bakku* 'bag' but *eggu~*ekku* 'egg'), and he accounts for this by positing a conjunction of the multiple obstruent voicing constraint No-D^2_m and No-Voiced-Geminate. His contribution casts an interesting light on issues relating to variation and lends support to the general approach taken here. If F items were simply exceptions to the markedness constraint No-D^2_m, or if No-D^2_m were itself restricted to non-F items, this sudden activity of the markedness constraint in an obscure corner of the foreign vocabulary would be surprising. But if markedness itself is never relativized to lexical classes, and foreign items are exempt through higher-ranking special faithfulness (Ident$_f$), it is not surprising that IDENT$_f$ itself can be trumped by an even higher-ranking conjoined version of the markedness constraint.

6.3   No-NÇ̥ and Its Activity in the Lexicon

The area of activity for postnasal voicing, informally stated in (17) (see Pater 1996 and references cited there for discussion of its formal status), includes Y items, but neither S nor F items.

(17) No-NÇ̥: "Sequences of the form   are excluded."

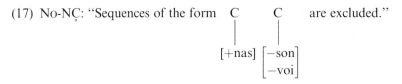

6.3.1   Distribution and Alternations

In the native vocabulary of Japanese, forms like *tompo* are impossible (18a) (Ito, Mester, and Padgett 1995), indicating that No-NÇ̥ is ranked above the faithfulness constraint. Complementing the distributional facts, a systematic voicing alternation (18b) affects every verbal suffix that occurs postnasally (such as the gerundial suffix /-te/: /yom-te/ → [yonde] 'read', cf. /mi-te/ → [mite] 'see'), indicating that No-NÇ̥ is firmly entrenched in the native phonological system (pace Rice 1997; see Ito, Mester, and Padgett 2001), actively forcing the creation of voiced obstruents through the ranking in (18).

(18) *No-NÇ̥* ≫ *IDENT (Y items: No-NÇ̥ is active)*

    a. tombo   'dragonfly'   *tompo
        kangae   'thought'   *kankae

    b. Cf. also alternations:

/yom + te/	→ [yonde]	'read'-GERUND	*yonte
/yom + ta/	→ [yonda]	'read'-PAST	*yonta
/yom + tara/	→ [yondara]	'read'-CONDITIONAL	*yontara
/yom + tari/	→ [yondari]	'read'-NONEXHAUSTIVE LISTING	*yontari

On the other hand, NÇ̥ clusters are very common in the nonnative strata. Sino-Japanese shows sporadic effects of postnasal voicing (see (28)), but the general situation is that both S items (19) (where "=" indicates root compounding; see chapter 4 and section 6.4.2) and F items (20) exhibit No-NÇ̥-violations, indicating that the faithfulness constraints for the nonnative strata are ranked above the postnasal voicing constraint.

(19) *IDENT$_s$ ≫ No-NC̥ (S items: No-NC̥ inactive)*

ken = ka   'quarrel'
gen = ki   'health(y)'
kan = koo   'sightseeing'
den = pa   'electric wave'
san = po   'walk'
sen = soo   'war'
kan = soo   'dry'
han = tai   'opposition'
han = too   'peninsula'

(20) *IDENT$_f$ ≫ No-NC̥ (F items: No-NC̥ inactive)*

panku   'puncture, flat tire'
torankiraizaa   'tranquilizer'
syanpuu   'shampoo'
konpyuutaa   'computer'
konsaato   'concert'
mansyon   'condominium'
sentaa   'center'
bentyaa   'venture (firm)'

The rankings in (18)–(20) are assembled into a single ranking in (21).

(21) {IDENT$_f$, IDENT$_s$}

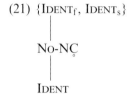

No-NC̥

IDENT

As shown in the previous section, the multiple voicing constraint No-D^2_m is itself sandwiched between IDENT$_f$ and undifferentiated IDENT, as in (22) (repeated from (13)), without a distinction between S items and Y items.

(22) IDENT$_f$

No-D^2_m

IDENT

Combining (21) with (22), we end up with the overall ranking in (23).

(23)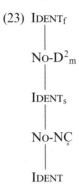
     IDENT$_f$

     No-D^2_m

     IDENT$_s$

     No-NÇ̥

     IDENT

While No-NÇ̥ is active on the native input in (24), higher-ranking faithfulness constraints protect the underlying voicelessness of the S and F inputs in (25) and (26).

(24) sinde *'die'-GERUND*

/sin-te/	IDENT$_f$	. . .	IDENT$_s$	No-NÇ̥	IDENT
sinte				*!	
▶ sinde					*

(25) kenka *'quarrel'*

/kenka/$_s$	IDENT$_f$	. . .	IDENT$_s$	No-NÇ̥	IDENT
▶ kenka				*	
kenga			*!		*

(26) sentaa *'center'*

/sentaa/$_f$	IDENT$_f$	. . .	IDENT$_s$	No-NÇ̥	IDENT
▶ sentaa				*	
sendaa	*!				*

6.3.2 Negative and Positive Exceptions: Syncope and Counter Phrases

As with the multiple voicing constraint, we find nonsystematic exceptions in connection with No-NÇ̥. First, there are a handful of often-cited negative exceptions—native forms with voiceless segments following nasals, such as the contraction *anta* familiar from colloquial speech as a syncopated version of the full form *anata* 'you' (see Rice 1997; Ito, Mester, and Padgett 2001). Like other situations where the results of syncope are structure-expanding in the sense that they exhibit a richer variety of consonant clusters than nonsyncopated forms,[13] the preservation of voiceless [t] in *anta* is a case where a higher-ranked output-output correspondence constraint provides a much-needed and precise explanation of the traditional idea that it is "by analogy" to the full form that such clusters become possible (recall the similar case in section 6.2.2).

More interesting are the positive exceptions ("overapplication") of postnasal voicing among S items, where a voiced allomorph sometimes appears postnasally, as in *kee-san* 'calculation' versus *an-zan* 'mental calculation' or *kan-zan* 'conversion', although this kind of voicing alternation is not the rule. The lexicalized character of postnasally voiced S allomorphs reveals itself most clearly in counter suffixes. Referring to multiples of certain types of objects (analogous to English expressions like **loaves** *of bread* or **heads** *of cabbage*), counter suffixes are a characteristic feature of Japanese. Most counters are S items and are suffixed to the S versions of numerals (e.g., *ni-hai* 'two cupfuls'). Many of these combinations are of high frequency, and since several S numerals end in a nasal (*san* '3', *yon* '4', *sen* '1,000', and *man* '10,000') and many S counters begin with voiceless obstruents, the situation depicted in (27) is not at all unusual. This is therefore an area where postnasal voicing has ample opportunity to show itself.

(27)

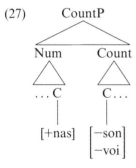

In (28), we have assembled a representative list of relevant counter phrases falling under the schema in (27). The list contains both frequent counters (e.g., *-hon*) and infrequent ones (e.g., *-kyaku*).[14]

(28) *Sporadic postnasal voicing in counter phrases*

Counter for		'3' san-	'4' yon-	'1,000' (is-)sen-	'10,000' (iti-)man-
blocks of tofu	/tyoo/	-tyoo	-tyoo	-tyoo	-tyoo
boats	/soo/	-soo	-soo	-soo	-soo
books	/satu/	-satu	-satu	-satu	-satu
chairs	/kyaku/	-kyaku	-kyaku	-kyaku	-kyaku
chapters	/syoo/	-syoo	-syoo	-syoo	-syoo
cups	/hai/	**-bai**	-hai	**-bai**	**-bai**
drops of liquid	/teki/	-teki	-teki	-teki	-teki
footwear	/soku/	**-zoku**	-soku	**-zoku**	**-zoku**
hanging scrolls	/huku/	-puku	-puku	-puku	-puku
houses	/ken/	**-gen**	-ken	-ken	-ken
lessons	/ka/	-ka	-ka	-ka	-ka
long objects	/hon/	**-bon**	-hon	**-bon**	**-bon**
pairs of objects	/tui/	-tui	-tui	-tui	-tui
pieces	/ko/	-ko	-ko	-ko	-ko
pieces of clothing	/tyaku/	-tyaku	-tyaku	-tyaku	-tyaku
poems	/syu/	-syu	-syu	-syu	-syu
points	/ten/	-ten	-ten	-ten	-ten
rolls of kimono material	/tan/	-tan	-tan	-tan	-tan
shots	/hatu/	-patu	-patu	-patu	-patu
small animals	/hiki/	**-biki**	-hiki	**-b/hiki**	**-b/hiki**
times	/hen/	**-ben**	-hen	**-ben**	**-ben**
times	/kai/[15]	-kai	-kai	-kai	-kai
volumes	/kan/	-kan	-kan	-kan	-kan
years of age	/sai/	-sai	-sai	-sai	-sai

It is obvious that postnasal voicing does not occur uniformly even within this narrowly circumscribed lexical field; rather, voiced and voiceless outcomes are scattered throughout the list. The numeral /san/ causes voicing in 6 out of 24 numeral-counter combinations, including combinations with some (but not all) of the frequent counters (such as /hon/) and with the relatively infrequent /soku/. On the other hand, /yon/ is allergic to voicing and never triggers it,[16] and /sen/ and /man/ range somewhere in between, causing voicing in a subset of the cases where /san/ does (with variation, as indicated).

The behavior of S vocabulary counter suffixes contrasts sharply with that of the verbal suffixes in the native Y system, where postnasal voicing is entirely uniform; and of course the grammar must account for this fundamental difference. The sporadic postnasal voicing in S items calls for a lexically based treatment, with a full listing of allomorphs and even of specific combinations, in contrast to the fully productive voicing alternation in Y items (see (18) and (24)). Using the constraint system to choose among lexically listed sets of allomorphs (cf. the Latin case analyzed in section 3.3.3; see also, e.g., Mester 1994; Tranel 1998, and references cited there), the analysis in (29) shows how No-NÇ is decisive in overruling the preference for the voiceless variant -*soku* of the counter suffix, parallel to the way it overrules the faithfulness constraint IDENT with Y items, as in (24). On the other hand, even though IDENT$_s$ outranks No-NÇ, it does not become active in cases like (29) since the output is faithful to one of the input allomorphs.

(29) sanzoku '*three pairs of shoes*'

/{san} + {soku, zoku}/$_s$	IDENT$_s$	No-NÇ	SOKU > ZOKU
sansoku		*!	
▶ sanzoku			*

While the two sides of the postnasal voicing phenomenon thus differ in scope, the analysis also captures its unified nature since sporadic postnasal voicing in S items is rooted in the same constraint, No-NÇ, as regular voicing in Y items. Since the constraint is part of UG, it is not at all surprising to see its influence reflected in the distribution of allomorphs, even where the alternation is not strictly predictable on phonological grounds.

6.3.3   Fitting the Pieces Together

Our investigation so far has resulted in (30), combining in a single hierarchy two stratal articulations of IDENT besides its unrestricted version and the two markedness constraints.

(30) IDENT$_f$

No-D^2_m

IDENT$_s$

No-NÇ

IDENT

This constraint ranking is responsible for a large part of the subset structure found in the Japanese phonological lexicon, as shown in (31) (which should be compared with the full picture given earlier in (9)).

(31)

	Y	S	F
No-D^2_m	yes	yes	no
No-NC̥	yes	no	no

The fact that S loans resemble both F loans (in violating No-NC̥) and native Y items (in observing No-D^2_m) is thus not just a quasi-sedimentary fact about the historical growth of the Japanese vocabulary through periods of cultural and economic exchange, military and political interactions, and the like; instead, it finds a place in the synchronic grammar acquired by contemporary learners of Japanese. Here, stratal faithfulness treats the items that vary along a number of dimensions related to voicing not as lists of unconnected exceptions, but as an integrated part of the overall voicing-related phonology of the language.

6.4   REALIZE-MORPHEME and the Distribution of *Rendaku* Voicing

Continuing to investigate what stratal faithfulness can contribute to the understanding of lexicon-internal variation, we turn to the constraint REALIZE-M(ORPHEME) that is responsible for appearance in the output of an exponent of the linking morpheme ℜ (which consists of the feature specification [+voi]).

6.4.1   F Items and Transitivity of Ranking

The relevant portion of the constraint hierarchy argued for in detail in chapter 4 is reproduced in (32).

(32) No-D^2_m

REALIZE-M

IDENT

Combining this ranking with the one in (22) results in (33).

(33)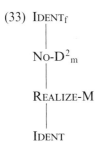

IDENT$_f$ is ranked above No-D^2$_m$ at the top of the constraint hierarchy, and, by transitivity, also dominates REALIZE-M. Consequently, the morpheme ℜ must go unparsed in the output for F items, as (34) illustrates.

(34) reesu kaaten *'lace curtain'*

/reesu$_f$ + ℜ + kaaten$_f$/	IDENT$_f$	No-D^2$_m$	. . .	REALIZE-M	. . .
reesu gaaten	*!		. . .		. . .
▶ reesu kaaten			. . .	*	. . .

The point here is not that ℜ is necessarily present in the input for all compounds, including the Japanese version of *lace curtain* (lexicon optimization alone suggests otherwise), but the richness-of-the-base-related reasoning that even if it is posited in the input, it has no effect on the output. The ranking No-D^2$_m$ ≫ REALIZE-M means that a high-ranking faithfulness constraint rendering the multiple voicing constraint inactive at the same time implies lack of *rendaku* voicing. The examples in (35) bear out this logic.

(35) *Compounds with F members: no* rendaku

tissyu peepaa	*tissyu beepaa	'tissue paper'
teeburu tenisu	*teeburu denisu	'table tennis'
paasonaru konpyuutaa	*paasonaru gonpyuutaa	'personal computer'
waado purosessaa	*waado burosessaa	'word processor'
huransu kussyon	*huransu gussyon	'French cushion', lit. 'France cushion'
reesu kaaten	*reesu gaaten	'lace curtain'

In other words, the constraint system embodies a principled explanation for the fact that items falling under IDENT$_f$ do not show *rendaku* voicing. It isn't simply an issue of appropriate inputs that would give rise to such outputs not happening to exist.

A second point is worth noting. If the stratal restrictions were stated separately for each constraint/process (here, postnasal voicing and *rendaku*), no implicational relation between the two would emerge. Here, the connection is established because (i) ranking relations are strict and transitive, and (ii) the restrictions are understood *not* as individual stratal restrictions on the markedness constraints themselves, but as separate faithfulness constraints for designated strata ranked at specific points in the hierachy.

6.4.2   S Items and Compounding

Recall from chapter 4 that there are two types of compounding in Japanese: word compounding (36a) and root compounding (36b).[17] The morpheme ℜ is a property of the former, linking two grammatical (morphological) words, that is, two independently occurring lexical items.

(36) *Structure of Japanese compounds*

   a. Word compounds   b. Root compounds

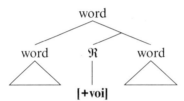   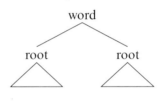

Root compounds are mostly composed of two S items. Given the absence of a linking morpheme in root compound structures (because of its syntactic-morphological classification as a *word* affix), the second member is not expected to show voicing (the notation "=" separating the S-root compound members in (37) follows McCawley 1968).

(37) *S-root compounds*

/kee = syoku/	keesyoku	*keezyoku	'light-eat, light meal, snack'
/syoku = si/	syokusi	*syokuzi	'eat-finger, forefinger, desire'
/si = hyoo/	sihyoo	*sibyoo	'finger-mark, index'
/hyoo = koo/	hyookoo	*hyoogoo	'mark-height, distance above sea level'
/koo = soku/	koosoku	*koozoku	'high-speed, rapid'
/soku = tatu/	sokutatu	*sokudatu	'speed-reach, express delivery'

The resulting root compounds themselves are of the morphological category "word" and therefore undergo further productive word compounding, with ℜ, as schematically illustrated in (38) and exemplified in (39).

(38)

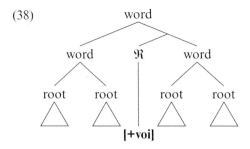

(39) /sin = bun + ℜ + hai = tatu/   sinbun haitatu   *sinbun baitatu   'newspaper delivery'
     /kyoo = to + ℜ + kan = koo/   kyooto kankoo   *kyooto gankoo   'Kyoto tourism'
     /nan = see + ℜ + syo = too/   nansee syotoo   *nansee zyotoo   'southwest islands'
     /se = dai + ℜ + koo = tai/   sedai kootai   *sedai gootai   'generation exchange'
     /kok = ka + ℜ + kee = satu/   kokka keesatu   *kokka geesatu   'national police'
     /sui = ri + ℜ + syoo = setu/   suiri syoosetu   *suiri zyoosetu   'detective novel'
     /tan = zyun + ℜ + hee = kin/   tanzyun heekin   *tanzyun beekin   'simple average'
     /ren = ritu + ℜ + see = ken/   renritu seeken   *renritu zeeken   'coalition government'
     /si = hoo + ℜ + si = ken/   sihoo siken   *sihoo ziken   'judicial exam'
     /bi = yoo + ℜ + tai = soo/   biyoo taisoo   *biyoo daisoo   'beauty exercise'

As these examples show, S items are similar to F items in that they also resist *rendaku* voicing in word compounds, although the two differ with respect to the multiple voicing ban (section 6.2). Avoidance of *rendaku* voicing but compliance with the multiple voicing ban are exactly the characteristics predicted to emerge when IDENT$_s$ is ranked below No-D^2_m but above REALIZE-M, as in (40).

(40) sinbun haitatu *'newspaper delivery'*

/sin = bun + ℜ + hai = tatu/	. . .	No-D^2_m	IDENT$_s$	REALIZE-M	. . .
▶ sinbun haitatu	. . .			*	. . .
sinbun baitatu	. . .		*!		. . .

Thus, root compounds consisting of S items do not show voicing for reasons of basic syntax and morphology: as a word affix, the linking morpheme cannot attach to roots. On the other hand, word compounds with two S items like those in (39) lack voicing for reasons of phonology: namely, high-ranking IDENT$_s$ dominating REALIZE-M. This seems to be the right division of labor between the two cases; and attempts to blur the boundary separating them—either by altering the grammatical structure of root compounds to make it possible to posit a linking morpheme, or by somehow preventing the linking morpheme's appearance in word compounds with S items—are likely to be misguided.

It is well known that S compounds do not all behave alike; there are very basic phonological differences between bimorphemic root compounds and larger word compounds involving the same class of morphemes.[18] It is perhaps the interplay of the grammatical and phonological factors they exhibit that has made it difficult to analyze them in the past. The distinction between roots and words is a valid and in fact fundamental morphological distinction that most affixes are in some way sensitive to. On the other hand, apart from the different stratal affiliations of the morphemes constituting them, there is no grammatical difference, morphological or syntactic, among the different kinds of word compounds, whether they are composed of S items, Y items, or F items or constitute hybrid formations involving various mixtures of these classes.

In our conception, relativization to strata is limited to faithfulness constraints; both the markedness constraints of phonology and the structural well-formedness constraints of syntactic and morphological theory remain free of any reference to vocabulary strata.

6.5   The Overall Structure of the Phonological Lexicon

The result of the preceding discussion is the by now familiar generalization that the linking morpheme $\mathfrak{R}$ can only be realized on Y items, not on F or S items. In terms of stratal faithfulness constraints, the ranking in (41) results.[19]

(41) IDENT_f

Collecting all relevant constraints in a single hierarchy results in (42), where the only ranking relation that still remains indeterminate is the one between REALIZE-M and NO-NC̥ (we will show later that REALIZE-M ≫ NO-NC̥ must hold).

(42)

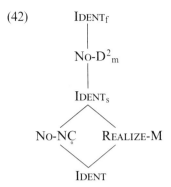

6.5.1 Hybrid Formations

Even though stratally homogeneous compounds are probably statistically most frequent, with both parts stemming from the same stratum, the words of a given stratum do not live in a cocoon. Rather, hybrid formations like those in (43), even though sometimes lamented by language mavens, are richly attested in contemporary Japanese, showing that compounding is in principle free and not stratum-bound.

(43) *Stratally uniform and hybrid compounds*

2nd member \ 1st member	-Y '-tidings' '-stories'	-S '-information' '-indicator'	-F '-drink' '-label'
Y- 'plum-' 'fake-'	ume dayori nise banasi	ume zyoohoo nise hyoozi	ume dorinku nise raberu
S- 'nutrition-' 'environment-'	eeyoo dayori kankyoo banasi	eeyoo zyoohoo kankyoo hyoozi	eeyoo dorinku kankyoo raberu
F- 'sports-' 'Internet-'	supootu dayori netto banasi	supootu zyoohoo netto hyoozi	supootu dorinku netto raberu

The class membership of the first member plays no role in the realization of the linking morpheme: whether the compound is Y+Y (/ume + tayori/ → *ume dayori*), S+Y (/kankyoo + hanasi/ → *kankyoo banasi*), or F+Y (/supootu + tayori/ → *supootu dayori*), all that matters is the Y status of the second member.[20]

In our analysis using differentiated stratal faithfulness, this is the expected result. Since only the second member violates faithfulness when realizing the voicing morpheme, the ranking of the faithfulness constraint regulating the first member (be it F, S, or Y) is of no consequence for *rendaku* voicing. Tableaux for compounds with members from different strata appear in (44)–(46). Y items are subject only to the general IDENT version, but F and S items are subject to both their specific stratal IDENT and the general IDENT.

(44) kisetu dayori *'season's greeting'*

/kisetu$_s$ + $\Re$ + tayori$_y$/	IDENT$_f$	NO-D^2_m	IDENT$_s$	REALIZE-M	IDENT
▶ kisetu dayori					*
kisetu tayori				*!	

(45) kankoo takusii *'sightseeing taxi'*

/kankoo$_s$ + $\Re$ + takusii$_f$/	IDENT$_f$	NO-D^2_m	IDENT$_s$	REALIZE-M	IDENT
kankoo dakusii	*!				*
▶ kankoo takusii				*	

(46) kari keeyaku *'provisional contract'*

/kari$_y$ + $\Re$ + keeyaku$_s$/	IDENT$_f$	NO-D^2_m	IDENT$_s$	REALIZE-M	IDENT
kari geeyaku			*!		*
▶ kari keeyaku				*	

6.5.2 Nonsystematic Exceptions

Besides being closely integrated into the structure of the Japanese lexicon through faithfulness to voicing and its stratal ramifications, *rendaku* shares another property with other lexical processes, namely, nonsystematic exceptions. There are two types of exceptions, one discussed here and one discussed in the next section.

First are the cases where the second member of the compound, even though it is native, does not undergo *rendaku*. These also come in two varieties (see also Ito and Mester 2001a, 25–26). On the one hand, there are a few morphemes that never show the alternation, such as *take* 'mushroom': *siitake, matutake, maitake, dokutake, benitake, tengutake,* and so on (denoting different varieties of mushrooms). In a thorough study of exceptions to *rendaku,* Rosen (2001) lists as members of this category *suso* 'cliff', *koi* 'love', *kasu* 'dregs', *tami* 'people', and *saki* 'tip'.

Besides this rather small group of consistent nonundergoers, there is a much larger group of sporadic nonundergoers. The most familiar example is provided by the names for the two Japanese syllabaries. The word /kana/ 'letter' shows voicing in *hiragana*, but remains unvoiced in *katakana*. In the face of such idiosyncratic exceptions, it is easy to overestimate the degree of irregularity and arbitrariness of the process. As emphasized by Haraguchi (2001), it would be very misleading to take the *katakana/hiragana* pair to represent the norm. While the contrast is certainly noteworthy, it is at least equally significant that every other compound with /kana/ in second position—in all, 23 entries in Iwanami 1992, a reverse lookup version of the *Koozien* (Shinmura 1983), the leading monolingual dictionary of Japanese—show uniform voicing: *irohagana, okurigana, hurigana, manyoogana, hentaigana, yomigana*, and so on (denoting various kinds of letters), as well as nonce formations such as *momizi-gana* 'kana symbols formed by autumn foliage'. This is where the generality of the pattern reveals itself, not in isolated examples. When the basic lexical conditions are met, voicing is the rule, lack of voicing is the exception. It is in this sense that *rendaku* is regular, not in the sense of being "exceptionless," which is probably a red herring in the case of most morphophonemic processes.[21]

6.5.3   Synchronic Stratum Membership ≠ Etymology

In a very different category of exceptions we find cases where *rendaku* has (etymologically speaking, at least) "overapplied" and affected items that came into the language as loans from Chinese or from Western languages, such as the examples in (47).

(47) *Nonnative* rendaku *undergoers I: Yamato look-alikes reclassified as Y items*

   a. From Portuguese

| karuta | iroha garuta | 'syllabary playing cards' |
| kappa | ama gappa | 'rain cape' |

   b. From Chinese

| kiku | no giku | 'wild chrysanthemum' |
| kasi | tya gasi | 'tea sweets' |

Noting that prototypical examples of this kind, such as *iroha garuta*, involve "native look-alikes" like *karuta* that are phonotactically indistinguishable from Y morphemes, Takayama (1999) analyzes them as having changed stratal membership.[22] In the present model, the change is simply a loss of indexation. "Yamato/native" needs no indexation but represents the default state of maximal unmarkedness. Besides the possibility of a shift to another indexation (see section 6.5.4), loss of indexation appears to be the most frequent change encountered.

Such divergences are an argument for (and not against) synchronic strata since they illustrate the well-known point that synchronic stratum membership, even though evidently rooted in the history of contact with other languages, is a matter of the synchronic grammar (i.e., is based on the productive generalizations of contemporary speakers) and will therefore almost by necessity often diverge from the "etymologically correct" classifications.[23]

6.5.4 Common Sino-Japanese

Besides such "native look-alikes," there is another group that realizes the linking morpheme, which consists of familiar everyday S words (all of them root compounds consisting of two elements: *ken-ka*, etc.). These items undergo *rendaku* as "positive exceptions," despite their Sino-Japanese origin.

(48) *Nonnative* rendaku *undergoers II: Sino-Japanese words in everyday use*

kenka	'quarrel'	oyako-genka	'parent-child quarrel'
tansu	'drawers'	yoohuku-dansu	'clothes-drawers, wardrobe'
suiryoo	'estimate'	ate-zuiryoo	'guesstimate'
kaisya	'company'	zidoosya-gaisya	'car company'
syasin	'photo'	kao-zyasin	'face-photo, portrait'
kesyoo	'makeup'	usu-gesyoo	'light makeup'
kisya	'train'	yo-gisya	'night train'
hootyoo	'carver'	deba-bootyoo	'pointed carver'
hyoosi	'rhythm'	te-byoosi	'hand-rhythm, beat time with the hands'
tyawan	'bowl'	yunomi-zyawan	'drinking-bowl, teacup'
toohu	'tofu'	yu-doohu	'hot tofu'
husoku	'lack'	ne-busoku	'sleep-deprived, lack of sleep'
hukin	'dustcloth'	dai-bukin	'table dustcloth'
kotatu	'footwarmer'	denki-gotatu	'electric footwarmer'

Takayama (1999) argues convincingly that these items constitute a separate substratum that we will call *Common Sino-Japanese* (*CS*). Such words tend to constitute nontechnical expressions of everyday life, as can be seen from the common use of the native honorific prefix *o-* instead of the S prefix *go-*: *o-syasin, o-kesyoo,* and so on.[24] These words continue to have non-Y phonotactics, such as NC-clusters, palatalized rhotics, and all the morphophonological alternations characteristic of S words (vowel~zero alternations, gemination, etc.; see Kurisu 2000 for a detailed OT analysis). Unlike cases such as the Portuguese loanword *karuta* in (47), which offer the learner no overt indication of being anything but native, the forms in (48) cannot be considered to have simply changed stratal membership.

The productivity of *rendaku* as it applies to CS items is well illustrated by an example like *kaisya* 'company' in (49), which realizes the linking morpheme without exception in all compounds where it appears as second member.

(49) *Compounds with* kaisya *'company' as second member*

booeki-gaisya	'trading ~'	kyoohan-gaisya	'cooperative sales ~'
booseki-gaisya	'spinning ~'	motikabu-gaisya	'holding ~'
denki-gaisya	'electric ~'	muhai-gaisya	'non–dividend paying ~'
doozoku-gaisya	'family-owned ~'	muzin-gaisya	'mutual aid or credit finance ~'
eeri-gaisya	'profit-making ~'	oya-gaisya	'parent ~'
gooben-gaisya	'joint venture ~'	seesan-gaisya	'liquidation ~'
goomee-gaisya	'unlimited partnership ~'	simai-gaisya	'affiliated ~'
goosi-gaisya	'limited partnership ~'	sinpan-gaisya	'credit ~'
hakkoo-gaisya	'issuing ~'	sintaku-gaisya	'trust ~'
hokan-gaisya	'safety-deposit ~'	sitauke-gaisya	'contract ~'
hoken-gaisya	'insurance ~'	sooko-gaisya	'warehousing ~'
hoomatu-gaisya	'short-lived ~'	syooken-gaisya	'securities ~'
kankee-gaisya	'affiliated ~'	syoozi-gaisya	'commercial ~'
kanren-gaisya	'associated ~'	takusii-gaisya	'taxi ~'
keeretu-gaisya	'affiliate ~'	unsoo-gaisya	'shipping ~'
kensetu-gaisya	'construction ~'	yakuhin-gaisya	'pharmaceutical ~'
ko-gaisya	'subsidiary ~'	yuugen-gaisya	'limited ~'
kookuu-gaisya	'airline ~'	yuuree-gaisya	'ghost/bogus ~'
koosee-gaisya	'~ needing reorganization'	zyutaku-gaisya	'trustee ~'

6.5.5   Toward a Synchronic Explication of the Subset Structure

How does this new class of CS words fit into the phonological lexicon? Recall the overall constraint hierarchy in (42), which left one ranking undetermined, namely, that between No-NC̥ and Realize-M. We now have the means to resolve the indeterminacy. For CS words, No-NC̥ is inactive (just as for other S words), but Realize-M is active, indicating that the ranking must be Realize-M ≫ Ident$_{cs}$ ≫ No-NC̥.

The final version of the hierarchy appears in (50), where the arrows indicate how stratal faithfulness is fully distributed over this section of the hierarchy.

(50)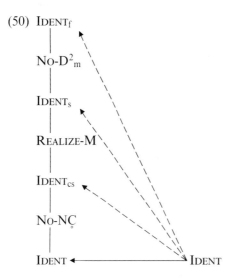

Given the position of the associated faithfulness constraint IDENT$_{cs}$ in the hierarchy, CS items are expected to obey the multiple voicing restriction and undergo *rendaku* (i.e., realize the voicing morpheme), but should be able to freely violate the postnasal voicing constraint No-NC̥. Tableau (51) illustrates some of these effects.

(51) *IDENT$_{cs}$ and the characteristics of Common Sino-Japanese words*

/oyako-kenka/	No-D^2_m	REALIZE-M	IDENT$_{cs}$	No-NC̥	No-D
▶ a. oyako-genka			*	*	*
b. oyako-kenka		*!		*	
c. oyako-kenga		*!	*		*
d. oyako-genga	*!		**		**

The highly ranked multiple voicing constraint No-D^2_m continues to cause Lyman's Law effects in CS forms. Takayama (1999) makes the important observation that *rendaku*-undergoing CS forms, which are root compounds consisting of two bound roots (see section 4.1.3), act like simplex morphemes in that none of them displays a medial voiced obstruent. Thus, *syuuzi* 'calligraphy', which takes the honorific prefix *o*- (*o-syuuzi*), does not voice (*nihon-syuuzi*, **nihon-zyuuzi* 'Japan Calligraphy (Association)'; also note *kami-syoozi*, **kami-zyoozi* 'paper sliding door', *arukooru tyuu-doku*, **arukooru zyuudoku* 'alcoholic poisoning', etc.).[25]

In a traditional approach whose conceptual toolbox is limited to "rules" and "exceptions," CS forms are doubly exceptional, in the sense that they are exceptions to the generalization that S items themselves are exceptions to *rendaku* voicing. It is clear that such characterizations shed little light on the actual situation and the underlying mechanisms. In the theory of stratified faithfulness, the existence of a *rendaku*-undergoing substratum with the constellation of properties seen in (48) is not an additional exotic fact, but comes as the last step toward a full distribution of faithfulness over the niches provided by a totally ranked hierarchy, as indicated in (50).

6.6   Concluding Remarks

Reviewing the main findings of this section and of the whole chapter, there is no question that *rendaku* has exceptions. While we would be missing the nature of morphophonemic processes if we immediately concluded from the existence of an exception that there is no rule, it is also ultimately not fruitful to retreat into the safe Galilean world of an idealized version of Japanese where compound voicing always proceeds as planned, postnasal voicing is an all-or-nothing affair, and so on, dismissing all counterexamples as distracting noise. In fact, the easily applied label of exception becomes counterproductive when it is interpreted as an invitation not to push analyses as far as they will go. As we have shown in the case of *rendaku*, as well as for obstruent voice dissimilation and postnasal voicing, taking on these processes in their actual complexity, including the patterning and lexical distribution of the various kinds of underapplication and overapplication, is a fruitful enterprise since it leads to a deeper understanding of the way phonology, as a formal system of ranked constraints, interacts with the lexicon.

This interaction is mediated through faithfulness constraints, and here the stratal diversification of faithfulness plays a crucial role. As we have argued elsewhere (see Ito and Mester 1995a,b, 1999a, 2001a), it provides the phonology with the means to fold the nonuniformities of a historically evolved stratified lexicon into a single coherent synchronic system. In OT, the total set of possible linguistic structures, a central part of human linguistic competence, forms a hierarchy of more and more inclusive sets of structures. Basic OT principles ensure that individual languages arise by carving out subsets from this vast set, always including the core. This is the essence of harmonic completeness (Prince and Smolensky 1993), and it is the intervention of faithfulness constraints at specific points in the overall ranking that is decisive. Focusing on the distribution of compound voicing within the Japanese lexicon, we have shown how distinctions between vocabulary strata also arise as effects of differentially ranked faithfulness. This idea, a natural outgrowth of current OT, captures crucial organizational properties of the lexicon akin to harmonic completeness. Crucially, stratal restrictions observed in the activity of constraints are not expressed as specific exclusion clauses of some kind, or as restrictions on the relevant constraints themselves, but are consequences of the different positioning of stratal faithfulness in the constraint hierarchy. The formal results are fully developed hierarchies like the one in (50), where stratal faithfulness is distributed over all steps of the hierarchy. By insisting on strict ranking and by limiting stratal indexation to faithfulness, the model captures the delicate balance between markedness and faithfulness effects that is the hallmark of lexicon-internal variation.

Chapter 7
Voicing Faithfulness

In phonology, markedness is a familiar concept, and markedness principles play a central role in most theoretical frameworks. Faithfulness, on the other hand, as a special element of grammar controlling the identity/divergence between the input to the phonology and its output, is an innovation of parallelist OT, with few precedents in traditional linguistics.[1] Genuine serialism perceives no need for a mechanism selecting the best output from among alternatives, weighing markedness and faithfulness factors—the output is simply what is left when the sequence of operations that make up the grammar stops applying to a given input. Optimization is no fundamental organizing principle of grammar; rather, it emerges out of the operations. Any observed limitations on input-output divergences are viewed as consequences of restrictions on what operations can do.

Seen through the eyes of a traditional serialist, therefore, the very idea of faithfulness as a component of grammar must appear ill conceived and out of place. But it is precisely the deep problems of serialist grammar, laid bare by the never-resolved issue of conspiracies, the existence of top-down effects in prosody inexplicable under bottom-up structure building, and the like, that led to a more and more pronounced shift of the locus of explanation in phonology away from rules and operations toward output constraints—and with this shift, the concept of faithfulness came to the forefront. The crucial step was taken in OT (Prince and Smolensky 1993), which locates all explanation in constraints and trivializes the role of operations. In *Gen*, (almost) anything goes, giving rise to a very inclusive candidate set—but input-output identity constraints keep track of every change, establishing faithfulness as a concept of grammar. It arises as a logical consequence of the formal liberation of "structural changes" from their "structural descriptions," which were bundled together in the conventional rule package. The interaction of the two, modeled in OT through ranking and minimal violation, gives rise to the linguistic processes found in language.

Given the radical novelty of faithfulness, it is hardly surprising that many questions about this aspect of OT are at present wide open. This chapter makes a small

contribution to the discussion by probing in some detail the nature of voicing faithfulness, insofar as it plays a role in the phonology of *rendaku*. We start out with a
hitherto unaddressed ranking paradox in our analysis as developed so far. Its resolution relies on a specific conception of voicing faithfulness (section 7.1), which we
then develop further and extend within faithfulness theory (section 7.2). A comparison and discussion of various theories of IDENT (section 7.3) forms the basis for a
superior solution built not exclusively on faithfulness, but on a local conjunction of
markedness and faithfulness (section 7.4).

7.1 A Voicing Asymmetry

The core of the phonology of compound voicing in Japanese, as developed so far, is
repeated in (1), with an informal description of the effects of the constraints as they
make their contributions within this system.

(1) *Basic ranking established so far*

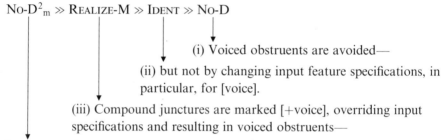

$$\text{NO-D}^2{}_m \gg \text{REALIZE-M} \gg \text{IDENT} \gg \text{NO-D}$$

(i) Voiced obstruents are avoided—

(ii) but not by changing input feature specifications, in
    particular, for [voice].

(iii) Compound junctures are marked [+voice], overriding input
    specifications and resulting in voiced obstruents—

(iv) except when this would place two such segments in a single morpheme
domain.

7.1.1 The Status of IDENT[VOI]
In light of the open questions about faithfulness mentioned above, perhaps the most
pressing issue to tackle now is what has so far been encapsulated as "IDENT."

(2) IDENT: "For segment S in representation X and its correspondent R(S) in a
    linguistically related representation Y, if S is [αF], then so is R(S)."

As stated in (2), IDENT penalizes changes in any feature specification, including
sonorancy, place of articulation, manner, laryngeal state, and so on. We have so far
not focused on the internal differentiation of IDENT, but it is clear that faithfulness
does not treat changes affecting all these different properties in the same way. For the
rendaku-related phonology, only changes in voicing values are at issue, and the relevant instantiation of IDENT is the one that is specific to voicing, as in (3).[2]

(3) IDENT[VOI]: "For segment S in representation X and its correspondent R(S) in a linguistically related representation Y, if S is [αvoi], then so is R(S)."

Focusing now on the input-output version of IDENT[VOI], further questions arise immediately. Is this constraint, as defined in (3), literally all there is to voicing faithfulness? Or is it a stand-in for a whole group of still more specific constraints? A first issue concerns the unadorned reference to [voi], irrespective of the type of segment involved. Is adding/removing voicing from sonorants literally the same (i.e., qua faithfulness—apart from the markedness of the resulting segments) as adding/ removing voicing from obstruents? The habit of referring to segmentally unspecified [+voi] is perhaps a legacy of underspecificationist phonology, where only contrastive voicing—largely identical to obstruent voicing—is marked in the input. In such a context, "[+voi]" was equivalent to "[+voi, −son]." With the foundations of under-specification theory eroded in OT, no such implications hold for input specifications. In the present context, it seems most reasonable to narrow the constraint down to IDENT[VOI]/OBS (4), which is specifically concerned with obstruent voicing.

(4) IDENT[VOI]/OBS: "For a [−son] segment S in representation X and its correspondent R(S) in a linguistically related representation Y, if S is [αvoi], then so is R(S)."

While (4) raises some questions of its own,[3] it seems more likely to lead to a sustainable theory than the attempt to keep IDENT[VOI] neutral in terms of major segment class by pursuing a pure markedness approach, ascribing all differences to the strong avoidance of devoiced sonorants. In this alternative view, the [+voi] of obstruents and of sonorants is treated in exactly the same way qua faithfulness; it is the undominated position[4] of the markedness constraint *[−voi, +son] against voiceless sonorants that is responsible for removing all candidates with devoiced sonorants from the competition. Both approaches have their merits, and we are not in a position to settle this rather fundamental choice at this point. Fortunately, the choice between the two approaches is not of central importance in the present context—either way, the upshot will be that the faithfulness constraint in question is, practically speaking, only concerned with obstruent voicing. For the sake of brevity and in order to avoid cluttering the tableaux, we will refer to the constraint as IDENT[VOI]; but we will understand and evaluate it as restricted to obstruent voicing, unless stated otherwise.

A more difficult question concerns the "[voi]" of IDENT[VOI]. Is the symmetry expressed here actually justified? Does devoicing the voiced always constitute just as serious a breach of faithfulness as voicing the voiceless? While a fully symmetric IDENT[VOI] has restrictiveness and conceptual parsimony on its side, it is not clear whether the resulting theory can successfully deal with the facts of actual phonological processes.

7.1.2 Voicing versus Devoicing

The analysis we have been developing up to this point gives strong indications that devoicing and voicing are indeed treated very differently in the phonological system of Japanese. The issue confronts us in the form of a ranking paradox involving symmetric IDENT[VOI] (4) that has so far not entered the picture because only a limited field of output candidates was considered in tableaux. As developed up to this point, the grammar makes a wrong prediction for all inputs of the form /T...D.../, with an internal voiced obstruent, when they fall in the scope of the linking morpheme ℜ. As shown in (5) for a compound with /sode/ 'sleeve', things go wrong once we include candidates that have changed input voicing elsewhere than at the beginning of the second member, the canonical location of *rendaku*.

(5) *A problem: unwanted devoicing in compensation for ℜ-realization (*nagasode *'long-sleeved')*

/naga + ℜ + sode/	No-D²ₘ	REALIZE-M	IDENT[VOI]	No-D
a. naga zode	*!		*	***
b. wrong winner ▶ naga zote			**	**
c. actual winner naga sode		*!		**
d. naka zote			***!	*
e. naka sode		*!	*	*
f. naka sote		*!	**	

The actual output is (5c) *naga-sode*, where the linking morpheme ℜ that is part of the input remains unrealized in the output, in violation of REALIZE-M. But the current grammar, propelled by the ranking REALIZE-M ≫ IDENT[VOI], encourages any number or kind of voicing changes as long as they lead to affix realization. It therefore selects the incorrect (5b) *naga-zote*, which complies with both No-D²ₘ and REALIZE-M, making up for the overt realization of the affix in the newly voiced [z] by a compensatory devoicing of the medial [d].

Reversing the ranking of REALIZE-M and IDENT[VOI], in an attempt to remove the devoicing candidate (5b) from the competition on faithfulness grounds alone, overshoots the mark by excluding all compound voicing. This is therefore a genuine ranking paradox. There are valid reasons to rank the constraints REALIZE-M ≫ IDENT[VOI], and there are also valid reasons to rank them the opposite way.

7.1.3 The Case of Old Japanese
We gain an important clue regarding the source of the problem by noting that the constraint system performs even worse with respect to the ranking variant holding in Old Japanese. The crucial difference between the two grammars (summarized in (6); see chapter 5 for detailed motivation) concerns the ranking of the constraint No-D^2_ω, which militates against the co-occurrence of voiced obstruents in the domain of a prosodic word (i.e., beyond the domain of a single morpheme). Unlike Modern Japanese, the grammar of Old Japanese ranks this constraint above REALIZE-M.

(6) *Old Japanese versus Modern Japanese constraint ranking*

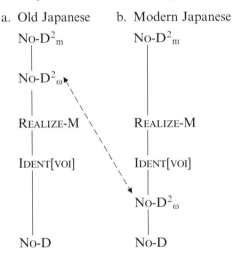

a. Old Japanese   b. Modern Japanese

Since REALIZE-M in turn dominates IDENT[VOI], transitivity of domination means that No-D^2_ω ≫ IDENT[VOI] also holds. This ranking poses a serious problem, however. Quite independent of *rendaku* voicing, it threatens any voiced obstruent in the first member of a compound with dissimilative devoicing, as shown in (7).

(7) *Threat of rampant devoicing in Old Japanese*

/naga + $\Re$ + sode/	No-D$^2_\omega$	Realize-M	Ident[voi]	No-D
a. [$_\omega$ naga zode]	*!		*	***
b. [$_\omega$ naga zote]	*!		**	**
c. actual output [$_\omega$ naga sode]	*!	*		**
d. wrong winner ► [$_\omega$ naka zote]			***	*
e. [$_\omega$ naka sode]		*!	*	*
f. [$_\omega$ naka sote]		*!	**	

Here the competition selects a candidate that is still further away from the actual output (7c) than the wrong winner in (5): namely, (7d) *naka-zote*, with three changes in obstruent voicing. This wrong winner, besides realizing $\Re$ in the newly voiced [z] and making up for it by devoicing the following [d] (just as in the problematic tableau (5) for Modern Japanese), then also devoices the medial [g] in the first morpheme. No such across-the-board devoicing of underlying voiced obstruents in compounds occurred in Old Japanese. Thus, Unger's (1975, 12–14) list of attested Old Japanese words with two or more voiced obstruents contains complex words such as *tabi-yadOri*, *yörödu-tabi*, and *ka-ga-nabëte*, as well as reduplications like *siba-siba* and *tubara-tubara*, which Unger characterizes as "words in which voiced obstruents occur in consecutive morphemes, but only medially after the first morpheme containing one."[5]

The correct Old Japanese form is therefore (7c) *naga-sode*, identical to the Modern Japanese form in preserving both of the input-voiced obstruents. Besides the unambiguous testimony of the Old Japanese facts, it is also questionable whether a derivation like /naga + $\Re$ + sode/ → [nakazote] is possible in any language. Such pervasive segmental changes at the compound level are probably ruled out by high-ranking output-output constraints tying bound occurrences of items to their free forms (see Ito and Mester 1997a).

7.2 Faithfulness Approaches to the Voicing Asymmetry

A standard answer in OT to problems such as the one described in section 7.1 is an elaboration of the faithfulness system. This section considers several such possibilities.

7.2.1   Self-Conjoined Faithfulness as a Nonviable Option

A natural initial reaction to the paradox is to focus on the number of voicing changes per domain. Perhaps two violations of IDENT[VOI] per morpheme domain are excluded, whereas one is allowed? To implement this, we can make use of self-conjoined IDENT[VOI]^2_m, ranking it above REALIZE-M as in (8).

(8) *Morpheme-domain self-conjunction of faithfulness (IDENT[VOI]^2_m)?*

/naga + ℜ + sode/	No-D^2_m	IDENT[VOI]^2_m	REALIZE-M	IDENT[VOI]	No-D
a. naga zode	*!			*	***
b. ▶ naga sode			*		**
c. naga zote		*!		**	**

While conjunctions of faithfulness constraints in the domain of a segment are familiar (see Kirchner 1996 and many subsequent studies), a conjunctive adding up of faithfulness violations in a morpheme, whether involving the same or different constraints, has no precedent elsewhere, to our knowledge.[6]

As it turns out, the putative solution by means of IDENT[VOI]^2_m in (8) dissolves empirically for the case of Old Japanese, once the full ranking and a more inclusive set of candidates are taken into consideration, as in (9). The problem is that there are still other unwanted but superior competitors with only one voicing change, namely, (9e) *naka-sode* and (9f) *naga-sote*. Only one IDENT[VOI] violation is involved in either case, and hence no higher-ranked self-conjoined IDENT[VOI]^2_m can rule these candidates out.

(9) *Nonviability of morpheme-domain faithfulness conjunctions (Old Japanese ranking)*

/naga + ℜ + sode/	No-D^2_m	No-D$^2_\omega$	IDENT[VOI]^2_m	REALIZE-M	IDENT[VOI]	No-D
a. naga zode	*!	*!			*	***
b. actual output naga sode		*!		*		**
c. naga zote			*!		**	**
d. naka zote			*!		***	*
e. wrong winner I ▶ naka sode				*	*	*
f. wrong winner II ▶ naga sote				*	*	*
g. naka sote				*	**!

Taking a second look at the unwanted winners in the previous tableaux, we find that they all share a simple property: underlyingly voiced segments have lost their voicing in the output. The proper generalization appears to lie not in the number of faithfulness violations, but in their direction: "voiceless → voiced" is allowed, but "voiced → voiceless" is not. As a matter of fact, it seems that no phonological alternation of any degree of generality in either Old or Modern Japanese phonology involves devoicing.[7]

7.2.2 Toward a Solution: Splitting IDENT[VOI]

A symmetric IDENT[VOI] making no distinction between the two values of the voicing feature is by itself unable to express this fundamental asymmetry. In Ito and Mester 1998, the issue did not arise because we assumed an asymmetric theory of IDENT, distinguishing [+F] and [−F] versions for every feature F. Ranked as in (10), such constraints make the necessary distinction.

(10) *Asymmetric IDENT[± VOI]*

/naga + $\Re$ + sode/	No-D^2_m	IDENT[+VOI]	REALIZE-M	IDENT[−VOI]
a. naga zode	*!			*
b. ▶ naga sode			*	
c. naga zote		*!		*

However, positing IDENT[±F] constitutes a drastic move in the direction of a much more powerful theory of feature faithfulness. Increased descriptive flexibility is bought at the price of a host of new ranking options, many of which are problematic (as we will show in section 7.3).

In preparation for more thoroughly comparing the theoretical alternatives in the rest of this chapter, where the ultimate solution will be seen not to lie in faithfulness alone, our first step here will be a more moderate increase in IDENT's access to feature structure. Besides the general constraint (11b) that applies, as before, to all segments (or rather, to all obstruents; see the remarks in connection with (4)), let us assume the existence of a special version (11a) for [+voi] obstruents.

(11) *Voicing faithfulness: Specific/General IDENT (S/G IDENT)*

a. IDENT[+VOI]/OBS (applies only to voiced obstruents)

   Given a [−son] segment S in representation X and its correspondent R(S) in a linguistically related representation Y, if S is [+voi], then so is R(S).

b. IDENT[VOI]/OBS (applies to all obstruents)

Given a [−son] segment S in representation X and its correspondent R(S) in a linguistically related representation Y, if S is [αvoi], then so is R(S).

With its specific/general structure, S/G IDENT fits well into the context of other well-established parts of faithfulness theory, such as positional faithfulness. The additional analytical flexibility it provides can be seen in the constraint hierarchy (12), where IDENT[+VOI] is ranked separately from general IDENT[VOI].

(12) *Differentiating IDENT[+VOI] and IDENT[VOI]*

No-D²$_m$

IDENT[+VOI]

REALIZE-M

IDENT[VOI]

No-D

Given this expanded conception of voicing faithfulness, compensatory devoicing (as in (5)) is correctly excluded as an option. In (13), the problematic internal devoicer (13c) is correctly ruled out by IDENT[+VOI], which dominates REALIZE-M. Devoicing of underlying voiced obstruents is therefore no longer a way to obey the OCP ban against the co-occurrence of voiced obstruents within a morpheme. Instead, the candidate (13b) without *rendaku* voicing is correctly selected.

(13) *IDENT[+VOI] ≫ REALIZE-M*

/naga + ℜ + sode/	No-D²$_m$	IDENT[+VOI]	REALIZE-M	IDENT[VOI]
a. naga zode	*!			*
b. ▶ naga sode			*	
c. naga zote		*!		**

While dominating REALIZE-M, IDENT[+VOI] remains itself under the domination of No-D²$_m$, ensuring that the morpheme structure effect banning multiple voiced obstruents still holds as before. Thus, a candidate like (14a), faithful to a (hypothetical) Lyman's Law–violating input, is occulted by candidates (14b) and (14c).

(14) $No\text{-}D^2{}_m \gg \textsc{Ident}[+\textsc{voi}]$

/maguda/ (hypothetical)	$\textsc{No-D}^2{}_m$	$\textsc{Ident}[+\textsc{voi}]$	$\textsc{Realize-M}$	$\textsc{Ident}[\textsc{voi}]$
a. maguda	*!			
b. ▶ maguta		*		*
c. ▶ makuda		*		*

For normal *rendaku*-voiced forms such as *naga-gutu* 'long-shoe, boots', the analysis is the same as before. Since general $\textsc{Ident}[\textsc{voi}]$ ranks below $\textsc{Realize-M}$, the candidate with compound voicing is selected.

(15) $\textsc{Realize-M} \gg \textsc{Ident}[\textsc{voi}]$

/naga + ℜ + kutu/	$\textsc{No-D}^2{}_m$	$\textsc{Ident}[+\textsc{voi}]$	$\textsc{Realize-M}$	$\textsc{Ident}[\textsc{voi}]$
a. naga kutu			*!	
b. ▶ naga gutu				*

Finally, the problem of rampant devoicing in Old Japanese seen in (7) disappears with the richer conception of voicing faithfulness, given the revised hierarchy (16).

(16) *Old Japanese versus Modern Japanese constraint ranking (revised)*

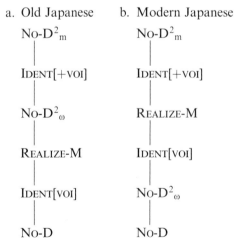

    a. Old Japanese   b. Modern Japanese

As before, the Old Japanese ranking relation $\textsc{No-D}^2{}_\omega \gg \textsc{Realize-M}$ results in extended blocking of *rendaku* voicing (i.e., by voiced obstruents in first members of compounds), and the ranking $\text{No-D}^2_m \gg \text{IDENT}[+\text{VOI}]$ means that hypothetical inputs such as /maguda/ in (14) meet the same fate in Old Japanese as in Modern Japanese, preventing morpheme-internal double obstruent voicing from ever arising. The crucial new feature is that the ranking $\text{IDENT}[+\text{VOI}] \gg \text{No-D}^2_\omega$ now forestalls any active devoicing within the prosodic word domain, as shown in (17).

(17) *No more excessive devoicing in Old Japanese (cf. (7))*

/naga + ℜ + sode/	No-D^2_m	$\text{IDENT}[+\text{VOI}]$	No-D^2_ω	REALIZE-M	IDENT[VOI]
a. [$_\omega$ naga zode]	*!		*		*
b. [$_\omega$ naga zote]		*!	*		**
c. ▶ [$_\omega$ naga sode]			*	*	
d. [$_\omega$ naka zote]		*!*			***
e. [$_\omega$ naka sode]		*!		*	*

All of this seems to show, then, that symmetric IDENT[VOI] is too weak as a theory of feature faithfulness since it is unable to assign different weights to voicing and devoicing as faithfulness violations. The latter can be accomplished by asymmetric versions of IDENT, including S/G IDENT with its specific constraint targeting [+voi] obstruents.

But things are not as clear-cut as they may appear. On the one hand, there is also the fully bivalent IDENT (see McCarthy and Prince 1995, based on work by Pater (1996)), which is routinely assumed in many studies, including our own earlier work (Ito and Mester 1998). Here, for every feature F, IDENT[+F] and IDENT[−F] are separate and individually rankable constraints. On the other hand, while symmetric IDENT has descriptive deficiencies, it also has advantages—as we will show, ones that cannot easily be brushed aside—over any version of asymmetric IDENT. It is therefore time to step back and ask how the various versions of IDENT differ and how they fit into the overall structure of OT.

7.2.3 Specific/General Faithfulness

The general approach taken so far has a characteristic architecture. The specific and high-ranking faithfulness constraint IDENT[+VOI] is complemented not by its polar opposite, the equally specific IDENT[−VOI], but by plain IDENT[VOI] applying indiscriminately to either value. In a broader perspective, we can envision an architecture for the faithfulness system where all partitioning of broad constraints into subconstraints follows this kind of structure, as in (18).

(18) *Specific/General doctrine of faithfulness partitioning*

Faithfulness constraints split along specific/general lines; that is, they sprout more specific subconstraints while preserving the general version.

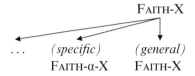

FAITH-X

... (*specific*)   (*general*)
FAITH-α-X   FAITH-X

S/G partitioning is a defining characteristic of positional faithfulness (Beckman 1997, 1998; Casali 1997), where a general faithfulness constraint is accompanied by separate versions reserved for prominent positions (onset, first syllable, root, prosodic head, etc.).

(19) *Positional faithfulness*

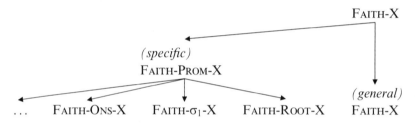

FAITH-X

(*specific*)
FAITH-PROM-X

(*general*)
...   FAITH-ONS-X   FAITH-σ_1-X   FAITH-ROOT-X   FAITH-X

Positional faithfulness theorists have shown in detail how such effects arise from rankings of the form FAITH-POS-X ≫ M ≫ FAITH-X, where positional faithfulness is ranked above general faithfulness, with some markedness constraint M intervening. If no relevant constraint intervenes, or if the ranking is reversed (i.e., general faithfulness dominates positional faithfulness), the effects are usually muted (but see Lombardi 1999 and Prince 2001 for cases where low-ranking specific constraints still have decisive power).

S/G faithfulness differentiation of a substantively different but formally similar kind was uncovered in our work on the phonological lexicon (see Ito and Mester 1995a, 1999a, 2001a, and chapter 6 above). Here faithfulness constraints targeting specific lexical strata (such as "loanwords") are ranked higher than the corresponding general faithfulness constraints. The overall result is the frequently encountered situation where marked segments and structures not found in the native vocabulary are faithfully parsed in loanwords.

(20) *Loanword faithfulness*

FAITH-X

...   FAITH-LOANWORD-X   FAITH-X

In the world of distinctive features, S/G faithfulness partitions (18), applied to marked versus unmarked feature values, yield the picture in (21).

(21) *Feature faithfulness*

Here S/G IDENT[F] produces a faithfulness analogue of the privative conception of phonological properties introduced by Trubetzkoy (1939), whereby some element literally carries a mark (such as [*aspirated*]) and its opposing member is distinguished by the absence of this mark, not by some opposing mark such as [*−aspirated*] that can be manipulated and referred to on its own (for further development in under-specificationist phonology, see, e.g., Steriade 1987; Mester and Ito 1989; Cho 1990; Lombardi 1991).

It turns out, however, that the schema (21) can in most cases not be meaningfully applied at the level of the single feature. There is no sense in which either [+voi] or [−voi] could in general be declared marked or unmarked; everything depends on the type of segment. We therefore assume, as noted earlier, that the articulation into obstruent and sonorant versions is basic to the system. The overall conception of S/G faithfulness unfolds along the lines shown in (22).

(22) *S/G voicing faithfulness*

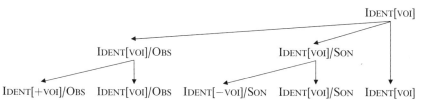

The privative effects associated with obstruent voicelessness and sonorant voicing are visible at the terminal level of IDENT constraints, namely, in the *absence* of constraints targeting unmarked properties. This is a basic difference between S/G IDENT[VOI]/OBS and the fully asymmetric IDENT[±VOI]/OBS. Whereas the former can only elevate faithfulness-to-the-marked to a higher position in the hierarchy, the latter can freely promote either the marked or the unmarked version. In this respect, then, S/G IDENT[F] is more restrictive than IDENT[±F].

The S/G faithfulness doctrine in (18) insists that such splitting of faithfulness is not just one option among many, but the only option. All partitioning must contrast an unrestricted version of a constraint with split-off versions that are in some way restricted: to items with marked values, in positions of prominence, having a special

status in the lexicon, and so on. This discourages asymmetric IDENT constraints that
divide the set of objects into mutually exclusive domains, the prominent and the
nonprominent, the marked and the unmarked, and so on, each of which would
then be ruled by its separate constraints. Rather, there is no faithfulness specific to
nonprominent positions, to unmarked values, and so on; there is only the general
version of the constraint. Thus, in positional faithfulness, constraints specific to
prominent positions (such as IDENT[F]/ONSET) contrast not with constraints specific
to nonprominent positions (such as IDENT[F]/CODA), but with position-free IDENT[F].
For distinctive features, constraints specific to marked feature values (such as
IDENT[+VOI]/OBS) contrast not with constraints specific to unmarked feature values
(such as IDENT[−VOI]/OBS), but with IDENT[VOI]/OBS.

One desirable consequence of the S/G doctrine relates to the much-discussed
FAITH-ROOT versus FAITH-AFFIX distinction (McCarthy and Prince 1995). The stipu-
lated metaranking FAITH-ROOT ≫ FAITH-AFFIX encodes the common observation
that more structures (segments, syllable types, etc.) are admitted in roots than in
affixes. Since we are concerned here only with the logic of the situation, let us simply
assume the factual correctness of the root/affix inventory asymmetry.[8] Rather than
dividing the set of morphological objects into roots and affixes, the S/G faithfulness
doctrine suggests singling out a specific subset (namely, roots) among all morphological objects, as in (23).

(23)   FAITH-X

        FAITH-ROOT-X   FAITH-X

Whereas all objects, roots and nonroots (affixes) alike, are subject to the general
FAITH-X, roots are in addition subject to the specific FAITH-ROOT-X. Hence, any
unfaithful rendition of X will always count more gravely for roots than for nonroots,
irrespective of the ranking of the constraints. This has an important advantage over
the metaranking conception of McCarthy and Prince (1995). Since FAITH-AFFIX does
not exist, the system derives, rather than stipulates, the fact that there can be no systems in which faithfulness to affixes is more important than faithfulness to roots.

7.3   Comparing Theories of IDENT

Among the areas of general phonology that provide a testing ground for different
theories of feature faithfulness, two are of special relevance. First, there is the typology of assimilation processes. When groups of adjacent segments disagreeing in some
property are under pressure to agree, which conceivable ways of resolving the conflict are attested and which are not? No less important are universals in inventory

structure, with implications of the following form: languages that have the segment or structure α always/mostly/usually also have the segment or structure β.

It turns out to be relatively easy to rule out certain conceptions of IDENT as making predictions that grossly deviate from crosslinguistic experience. Much harder is the positive task of coming up with a theory that actually does justice to all the phenomena to be accounted for.

7.3.1 The Majority Rule Test

A first issue in the theory of assimilation is the *majority rule* problem discovered by Lombardi (1999) and developed in important ways by Baković (2000). Let us follow these researchers in viewing assimilation as driven by feature agreement constraints, which we formalize as shown in (24).[9]

(24) AGREE[F]/α: "Let x and y be adjacent segments of type α, with x preceding y: then if x is [αF], so is y."

A straightforward instantiation of (24) is AGREE[VOI]/OBS, requiring adjacent obstruents to agree in voicing. We now show that the interaction of this assimilation imperative with symmetric IDENT constraints has pernicious effects. Let us consider situations where there are no positional faithfulness effects influencing the outcome (such situations clearly occur, e.g., in word-final clusters). In order for assimilation to take place at all, the ranking must be AGREE[VOI]/OBS ≫ IDENT[VOI], and in order for voicing to be otherwise contrastive, IDENT[VOI] ≫ NO-D must hold. Considering only candidates that perfectly fulfill top-ranked AGREE[VOI]/OBS (by having either uniformly voiced or uniformly voiceless obstruent clusters), we first compare obstruent clusters composed of two members, as schematically illustrated in (25).

(25)

		...	AGREE[VOI]/OBS	IDENT[VOI]	NO-D	...
a. /...ps.../	► [...ps...]					
	[...bz...]			*!	**	
b. /...pz.../	► [...ps...]			*		
	[...bz...]			*	*!*	
c. /...bs.../	► [...ps...]			*		
	[...bz...]			*	*!*	
d. /...bz.../	[...ps...]			*!		
	► [...bz...]				**	

Since no relevant constraint intervenes between agreement and faithfulness, the choice of the feature value to agree upon falls to IDENT[VOI] (i.e., in (25a,d)). In the event of a tie for IDENT[VOI] (i.e., in (25b,c)), No-D becomes active and the cluster becomes voiceless. The overall result is that all outputs are voiceless except for (25d), where the entire input sequence is voiced.

The majority rule problem arises with larger clusters, as shown in (26), where an odd-numbered cluster of obstruents agrees on a single value for [voi] by counting which of the two agreement-fulfilling outcomes involves fewer changes in voicing overall. In an even-numbered obstruent cluster, the situation is the same except that No-D serves as tiebreaker.

(26) *Wrong prediction 1: Symmetric IDENT[VOI] and "majority rule"*

		...	AGREE[VOI]/OBS	IDENT[VOI]	NO-D	...	
/...pst.../	▶ [...pst...]						
	[...bzd...]			*!**	***		
/...bst.../	▶ [...pst...]			*			*majority [−voi]: output [−voi]*
	[...bzd...]			**!	***		
/...pzt.../	▶ [...pst...]			*			
	[...bzd...]			**!	***		
/...psd.../	▶ [...pst...]			*			
	[...bzd...]			**!	***		
/...bzt.../	[...pst...]			**!			
	▶ [...bzd...]			*	***		*majority [+voi]: output [+voi]*
/...bsd.../	[...pst...]			**!			
	▶ [...bzd...]			*	***		
/...pzd.../	[...pst...]			**!			
	▶ [...bzd...]			*	***		
/...bzd.../	[...pst...]			*!**			
	▶ [...bzd...]				***		

Vote-counting scenarios like the one in (26) have never been reported in connection with actual assimilation processes. Even though the calculation is, in a general cognitive sense, entirely straightforward, it is apparently not part of the human language faculty. Critics might interpret (26) as a major malfunction of the basic framework of OT—after all, things appear to go wrong precisely because of the power of the candidate assessment system, which can rate a candidate's global well-formedness with respect to the question(s) raised by any given constraint (here, "How many voicing changes?") and then go on to compare the results across all candidates.

While there is probably a grain of truth in such criticism, the majority rule problem is hardly a suitable foundation for building a watertight case since a much more modest culprit is at hand: IDENT[VOI], the constraint that is being evaluated. We have already shown in the previous section why the lack of differentiation that goes hand in hand with symmetry can be problematic. Perhaps the root of the majority rule problem also lies here? Checking voicing faithfulness might not consist in asking undifferentiated questions about the number of voicing changes in either direction. Lombardi's (1999) and Baković's (2000) different solutions both go in this general direction (for discussion of Lombardi's proposal, see Baković 2000; Baković's own constraint-conjunctive proposal will be taken up in section 7.4). More generally, a crucial piece is missing in the world of fully symmetric feature faithfulness.

The majority rule problem thus reinforces, from a new angle, the insufficiency of symmetric IDENT[F], and one might be tempted to file it away as just another argument against a theory of feature faithfulness already compromised by the analytical insufficiencies outlined in section 7.2. But it has wider implications; as it turns out, other theories of IDENT also stumble over this issue, in their own ways. Let us first take up S/G IDENT. Continuing to assume that agreement dominates all voicing faithfulness, there are two cases to consider: (i) the S ≫ G ranking IDENT[+VOI] ≫ ... ≫ IDENT[VOI], and (ii) the G ≫ S ranking IDENT[VOI] ≫ ... ≫ IDENT[+VOI]. The second situation leads straight to the majority rule problem seen with symmetric IDENT and warrants no separate discussion. The first is more interesting. As shown in (27), except when all input obstruents are voiceless (as in the first example), the S ≫ G ranking always yields a voiced outcome. In autosegmental parlance, the result is bidirectional spreading of the marked value throughout the cluster.

(27) *Wrong prediction 2: S/G IDENT and "assimilation to the marked"*

		...	AGREE[VOI]/OBS	IDENT[+VOI]	IDENT[VOI]	No-D	...
/...pst.../	► [...pst...]						
	[...bzd...]				*!**	***	
/...bst.../	[...pst...]			*!	*		
	► [...bzd...]				**	***	

		...	AGREE[VOI]/OBS	IDENT[+VOI]	IDENT[VOI]	NO-D	...
/...pzt.../	[...pst...]			*!	*		
	▶ [...bzd...]				**	***	
/...psd.../	[...pst...]			*!	*		
	▶ [...bzd...]				**	***	
/...bzt.../	[...pst...]			*!*	**		
	▶ [...bzd...]				*	***	
/...bsd.../	[...pst...]			*!*	**		
	▶ [...bzd...]				*	***	
/...pzd.../	[...pst...]			*!*	**		
	▶ [...bzd...]				*	***	
/...bzd.../	[...pst...]			*!**	***		
	▶ [...bzd...]					***	

(27) predicts that in an obstruent cluster of any length, whenever voicing lurks in any position, the whole cluster becomes voiced (since devoicing attracts a special penalty). Voicelessness results only when all input obstruents are voiceless. This is certainly the wrong prediction to make. As Lombardi (1999) and Baković (2000) point out, the expected result is reversion to the unmarked voiceless sequence [...pst...] in all examples except the last (fully voiced and fully faithful) candidate—that is, bidirectional spreading of [−voi], not of [+voi].[10] When agreement is equally satisfied by uniform voiced and uniform voiceless outcomes, and no positional factors make any particular segment dominant, the markedness constraint NO-D, universally ranked above its counterpart against voiceless obstruents, NO-T, ought to tip the scales in favor of voicelessness. But in (27), higher-ranking IDENT[+VOI] vetoes even the slightest instance of devoicing and forestalls the desired outcome. Especially remarkable is the fact that S/G IDENT[VOI] cannot even produce a voiceless outcome by stipulation, since it has no constraint IDENT[−VOI] that could be ranked higher. The theory goes down in flames, but with honor.

Such a stipulation ensuring a voiceless outcome is certainly possible for fully asymmetric IDENT[±VOI], the most powerful variant of faithfulness under consideration here. AGREE[VOI]/OBS ≫ IDENT[−VOI] ≫ IDENT[+VOI] is one of the available rankings, and it produces uniformly voiceless outcomes, that is, assimilation to the unmarked. The problem is that it derives this correct outcome with incorrect means, as we will show.

(28) *Descriptive success, explanatory failure: IDENT[±F] forces assimilation to the unmarked*

		...	AGREE[VOI]/OBS	IDENT[−VOI]	IDENT[+VOI]	NO-D	...
/...pst.../	▶ [...pst...]						
	[...bzd...]			*!**		***	
/...bst.../	▶ [...pst...]				*		
	[...bzd...]			**!		***	
/...pzt.../	▶ [...pst...]				*		
	[...bzd...]			**!		***	
/...psd.../	▶ [...pst...]				*		
	[...bzd...]			**!		***	
/...bzt.../	▶ [...pst...]				**		
	[...bzd...]			*!		***	
/...bsd.../	▶ [...pst...]				**		
	[...bzd...]			*!		***	
/...pzd.../	▶ [...pst...]				**		
	[...bzd...]			*!		***	
/...bzd.../	[...pst...]				*!**		
	▶ [...bzd...]					***	

As (28) shows, bivalent IDENT[±F] can produce the desired agreement on [−voi], the unmarked feature value.[11] However, the derivation of this result unfortunately has nothing to do with markedness: it is rather obtained by faithfulness fiat, without NO-D making any contribution (see also the pertinent critique in Baković 2000). The stipulative nature of the solution becomes apparent when one notices that bivalent IDENT can just as easily derive the opposite result, assimilation to the marked, by reversing the ranking of the two faithfulness constraints in (28). Trying to avoid this result by freezing the ranking as IDENT[−VOI] ≫ IDENT[+VOI] would not do, for two reasons: (i) It remains unclear what relation this fixed ranking has to the independently fixed ranking of the corresponding markedness constraints. Using *u* and *m* to denote unmarked and marked values, one might contemplate IDENT[uF] ≫ IDENT[mF] as a metaranking, but the problem of redundancy seems undeniable. (ii) IDENT[−VOI] ≫ IDENT[+VOI] is descriptively the wrong ranking for Japanese, where voicing occurs without concomitant devoicing: the opposite is needed, as already shown in (10).

7.3.2 The Harmonic Completeness Test

At this point, it appears that all three theories of IDENT have failed the assimilation test, be it because their predictions are outlandish (symmetric IDENT) or at least questionable (S/G IDENT), or because of their stipulative character (IDENT[±F]). Since a stipulation that at least captures the facts is better than no analysis whatsoever, IDENT[±F] appears to have won the day, as the least of three evils. But this conclusion turns out to be premature once we consider the second broad area where any conception of feature faithfulness must prove itself, namely, inventory universals. In a significant reversal, we now find serious problems with any asymmetric conception of IDENT, and fully symmetric IDENT[F] turns out to be superior. Remarkably, its superiority lies in what was so far its major liability: its diminished power of resolution and greater restrictiveness.

The issue concerns what Prince and Smolensky (1993) have dubbed the *harmonic completeness* of segments and structure inventories in natural languages (see also chapter 6 for discussion). For example, languages are known to either contrast voiced and voiceless obstruents or have inventories with only voiceless obstruents; no human language has been reported to have voiced obstruents without having voiceless obstruents.[12] Writing *T* for *voiceless obstruent* and *D* for *voiced obstruent*, we express the inventory inclusion hierarchy as in (29a) (∅ indicates the purely hypothetical case of a language without obstruents), which excludes the inventory {D} as harmonically incomplete. In standard OT, (29a) is reflected in the universally fixed markedness ranking (29b) of the constraints against voiced and voiceless obstruents, respectively.

(29) a. {T, D} ⊃ {T} ⊃ ∅ (i.e., there is no inventory {D})

     b. No-D

         |

       No-T

With symmetric IDENT, (29a) follows directly from the markedness ranking (29b), as can be seen in (30).

(30) *Inventory hierarchy*

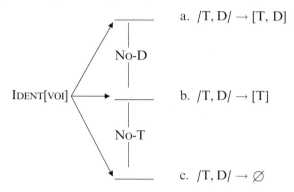

a. /T, D/ → [T, D]

b. /T, D/ → [T]

c. /T, D/ → ∅

Viewed in somewhat greater detail, these inventories arise as shown in (31a–c). To integrate the empty obstruent inventory ∅ into the typology, we assume that MAX dominates IDENT[VOI] throughout but is otherwise ranked as low as possible, following the general M ≫ F ranking default. The subscripts indicate neutralizing mappings; thus, the output element $T_{1,2}$ in (31b) corresponds to both T_1 and D_2 in the input, and so on.

(31) a.

/T_1, D_2/	F ≫ M			
	MAX	IDENT[VOI]	NO-D	NO-T
▶ [T_1, D_2]			*	*
[$T_{1,2}$]		*!		*
[$D_{1,2}$]		*!	*	
∅	*!*			

b.

/T_1, D_2/	M_1 ≫ F ≫ M_2			
	NO-D	MAX	IDENT[VOI]	NO-T
[T_1, D_2]	*!			*
▶ [$T_{1,2}$]			*	*
[$D_{1,2}$]	*!		*	
∅		*!*		

c.

/T₁,D₂/	M ≫ F			
	No-D	No-T	Max	Ident[voi]
[T₁,D₂]	*!	*		
[T₁,₂]		*!		*
[D₁,₂]	*!			*
▶ ∅			**	

The harmonically incomplete inventory {D} cannot arise because of the fixed markedness ranking No-D ≫ No-T and the compact nature of feature faithfulness. Once faithfulness overrules No-D, as in (31a), it also overrules No-T.

Asymmetric Ident theories ruin this important harmonic completeness result, essentially because their faithfulness system can easily overpower the fixed markedness ranking, canceling its prediction. As first noted in Prince 1998, the problem lies in the very existence of Ident[+voi], which makes the ranking in (32) possible, resulting in the unwanted inventory {D}.

(32) *Harmonic completeness lost: asymmetric Ident derives {D}*

/T₁,D₂/	Max	Ident[+voi]	No-D	No-T	Ident[voi]
[T₁,D₂]			*	*!	
[T₁,₂]		*!			*
▶ [D₁,₂]			*		*
∅	*!*				

Intuitively speaking, (32) is pathological in that faithfulness to marked values (Ident[+voi]) selectively overpowers No-D, whereas lower-ranked No-T remains in force (by dominating Ident[voi]). Mutatis mutandis, bivalent Ident[±F] is in the same situation as S/G Ident; that is to say, this is an argument generally favoring symmetric over asymmetric Ident. Case-specific remedies, such as denying the existence of a markedness constraint No-T against voiceless obstruents (in order to make the first candidate the winner in (32)), are unlikely to succeed. Claiming that the unmarked pole does not correspond to a markedness constraint does not recognize that the problem is entirely general and arises in all dimensions of markedness, whatever the nature of the scale and the number of points on it.

7.3.3 Not by FAITH Alone: M-Enhanced Symmetric IDENT

Considering all the evidence so far, we seem to have arrived at an impasse. Asymmetric IDENT is superior to symmetric IDENT because of its richer internal differentiation, but symmetric IDENT is superior to asymmetric IDENT because of its monolithic character, making it a single block that can be moved around in the ranking only as a unit. One way of resolving the dilemma is to build on symmetric IDENT, in order to secure the correctness of the basic typological predictions, but to add further elements from outside of faithfulness theory in order to access feature structure in greater detail.

Building on an idea first proposed by Łubowicz (2002) and further extended in Ito and Mester 1998, 2002b, Baković (2000) looks for the solution in conjunctions of faithfulness with markedness. As long as major class is preserved (here: obstruency), the effects of IDENT[−VOI] are achieved with symmetric IDENT by observing that a violation must invariably involve a segment that (i) is voiced in the output and (ii) has violated voicing faithfulness. In other words, the segment violates the conjunction IDENT[VOI]&$_{seg}$NO-D of the markedness constraint against voiced obstruents and symmetric (obstruent) voicing faithfulness. In a similar vein, the effects of IDENT[+VOI] can be reconstructed by observing that violations must involve a segment that (i) is voiceless in the output and (ii) has violated voicing faithfulness, that is, a segment violating the conjunction IDENT[VOI]&$_{seg}$NO-T.

In this constraint-conjunctive interpretation of IDENT diversification, the right predictions emerge in the assimilation case. The outcome is neither majority rule nor assimilation to the marked, but assimilation to the unmarked, as seen in (33).

(33) *IDENT[F]&NO-αF: reversal to the unmarked*

		AGREE[VOI] /OBS	IDENT[VOI]&- NO-D	IDENT[VOI]&- NO-T	IDENT[VOI]	NO-D	NO-T
/...pst.../	▶ [...pst...]						***
	[...bzd...]		*!**		***	***	
/...bst.../	▶ [...pst...]			*	*		***
	[...bzd...]		**!		**	***	
/...pzt.../	▶ [...pst...]			*	*		***
	[...bzd...]		**!		**	***	
/...psd.../	▶ [...pst...]			*	*		***
	[...bzd...]		**!		**	***	

≈ "IDENT[−VOI]"   ≈ "IDENT[+VOI]"

≈"IDENT[−VOI]"   ≈"IDENT[+VOI]"
↓   ↓

		AGREE[VOI]/OBS	IDENT[VOI]&-NO-D	IDENT[VOI]&-NO-T	IDENT[VOI]	NO-D	NO-T
/...bzt.../	► [...pst...]			**	**		***
	[...bzd...]		*!		*	***	
/...bsd.../	► [...pst...]			**	**		***
	[...bzd...]		*!		*	***	
/...pzd.../	► [...pst...]			**	**		***
	[...bzd...]		*!		*	***	
/...bzd.../	[...pst...]			*!**	***		***
	► [...bzd...]					***	

In Bakovic's theory, the ranking IDENT[VOI]&NO-D ≫ IDENT[VOI]&NO-T is invariant, since it is projected from the invariant ranking NO-D ≫ NO-T by Spaelti's (1997, 174–175) ranking principle (see section 3.3.1). In this crucial respect, the constraint-conjunctive approach is therefore more restrictive than a theory with a full-fledged IDENT[+F]/IDENT[−F] distinction, where both rankings are possible, with unwelcome results.

As shown in (34), Bakovic's theory also recaptures the harmonic completeness prediction. The markedness ranking NO-D ≫ NO-T is again effective in excluding inventories that have D but lack T as harmonically incomplete (the relevant tableaux are essentially identical to (31a–c) and are therefore omitted).

(34) *Harmonic completeness regained*

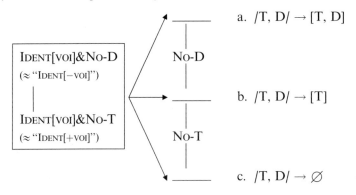

a. /T, D/ → [T, D]

IDENT[VOI]&NO-D
(≈ "IDENT[−VOI]")

NO-D

b. /T, D/ → [T]

IDENT[VOI]&NO-T
(≈ "IDENT[+VOI]")

NO-T

c. /T, D/ → ∅

The (34b) case is more properly characterized as the class of rankings (or partial rankings) {No-D, Ident[voi]&No-D} ≫ {No-T, Ident[voi]&No-T}; in other words, the twin faithfulness constraints need not be adjacent in the ranking (as an undivided Ident[voi] block) as long as their hierarchical relation is preserved.[13] Another issue of general importance concerns the ranking of the conjoined constraints in (34). Is it possible to uphold the general ranking principle that conjunctions always outrank their constituents (see section 2.2)?[14] (34) appears problematic in this respect, but Lanko Marušič (personal communication) has shown that (35), which complies with the general conjunction ranking principle, accomplishes the same as (34).

(35)

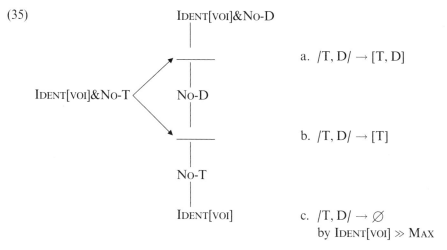

a. /T, D/ → [T, D]

b. /T, D/ → [T]

c. /T, D/ → ∅
   by Ident[voi] ≫ Max

It appears, then, that unlike the other conceptions of Ident we have considered Baković's theory passes all our tests. But as we turn back to the original issue in Japanese phonology that triggered this whole investigation of faithfulness theory, the *naga-sode*/**naga-zote* problem in section 7.1.2, once again we seem to reach an impasse.

We interpreted the voicing asymmetry noted there to mean that faithfulness to the voiced dominates faithfulness to the voiceless, making it possible to add voicing but not to remove it. We seem to have made little progress toward our goal. The invariant ranking Ident[voi]&No-D ≫ Ident[voi]&No-T, crucial as it is in excluding the unwanted assimilation to the marked, means that faithfulness to the voiceless universally outranks faithfulness to the voiced, the opposite of what was required.

The right conclusion, we suggest, is not that faithfulness theory requires further overhaul, but that faithfulness theory is being held directly responsible for too many simultaneous and irreconcilable demands. This is where the insight of Baković's constraint-conjunctive approach lies, abstracting away from its technical implementation. Diversification of faithfulness involves not successive internal subdivision, but conjunctive combination with other factors lying outside pure faithfulness. This is, of course, nothing but a reassertion of the general strategy lying behind constraint conjunction theory (see chapter 2). Instead of giving up on this theory, we should pursue this direction even more forcefully.

7.4 Sequential Markedness and Segmental Markedness

The general question we now face is why the voicing of obstruents should ever be more protected than their unmarked voicelessness. Simple markedness considerations lead us to expect the reverse, and this is what the fixed ranking IDENT[VOI]&NO-D ≫ IDENT[VOI]&NO-T correctly encodes. The crucial question is whether there are other basic markedness factors concerning voicing, besides the markedness of individual segments, that might conjoin with IDENT[VOI] and result in different effects.

7.4.1 Voicing in a Voiced Environment
While voiced obstruents have little to recommend them as individual segments, we need to figure in the sometimes opposing forces of sequential markedness. In a voiced environment, sequential markedness recommends voicing, not voicelessness, hence the crosslinguistically common processes of postvocalic or postsonorant voicing. We formalize sequential markedness as agreement constraints (see (24) in the previous section and references cited there), that is, as constraints requiring segments to agree in their values for certain features (ATR, backness, etc.) within a certain domain. What is needed here is the broadest kind of agreement constraint, as in (36).

(36) AGREE[VOI]: "Let x and y be adjacent segments, with x preceding y: then if x is [αvoi], so is y."

AGREE[VOI] bans changes in glottal state and militates against voicing contours of the forms *[+voi] [−voi] and *[−voi] [+voi]. Thus, a sequence like [ata] has two violations of AGREE[VOI]: a change in voicing from [a] to [t], and a second change in voicing from [t] to [a].[15] Except in special syllable configurations with large voiceless consonant clusters, voiceless segments normally reside in the midst of a voiced domain, just like voiced segments, surrounded by (voiced) vowels and sonorants. From this perspective, voicing an obstruent (e.g., ATA → ADA) produces a marked segment (violating NO-D), but an unmarked sequence (fulfilling AGREE[VOI]). Devoicing an obstruent, on the other hand, produces an unmarked segment (fulfilling NO-D), but a marked sequence (violating AGREE[VOI]).[16]

For our purposes here, the critical question is whether placing this sequential markedness constraint into the hierarchy of constraints responsible for *rendaku* voicing, and conjoining it with IDENT[VOI], can account for the asymmetric preference for voicing in Japanese. The underlying intuition is that in some sense, the morphophonemic *rendaku* phenomenon might be rooted in intervocalic (or intersonorant) voicing as a sequential markedness factor. As shown in (37), simply substituting AGREE[VOI] for IDENT[+VOI] in our earlier analysis is not a viable solution.

(37) *AGREE[VOI] instead of IDENT[+VOI]*

/naga + ℜ + sode/	No-D^2_m	AGREE[VOI]	REALIZE-M	IDENT[VOI]
a. naga zode	*!			*
b. actual output naga sode		**	*!	
c. wrong winner ▶ naga zote		**		**

Since AGREE[VOI] penalizes the underlying voicelessness of [s] in *naga-sode* in the same way as the derived voicelessness of [t] in *naga-zote*, the choice still comes down to REALIZE-M, which wrongly prefers the latter candidate, with its overt realization of ℜ.

7.4.2 Derived Voicing Violations: Voicing Agreement and Faithfulness

What is needed is a version of AGREE[VOI] that separates derived voicelessness from underlying voicelessness and selectively punishes the former, by focusing on candidates that violate AGREE[VOI] because of a value of voicing that is in addition a faithfulness violation. This is precisely what a composite constraint locally conjoining AGREE[VOI] with IDENT[VOI] (38) expresses.

(38) AGREE[VOI]&$_{seg}$IDENT[VOI]

We interpret AGREE[VOI] as being violated by a segment that disagrees with its predecessor in voicing. The Minimal Domain Principle (see section 5.1.1) then predicts the segment to be the domain of conjunction. When an intervocalic obstruent changes its voicing, voicing a voiceless obstruent (ATA → ADA) violates only the faithfulness constraint, but devoicing a voiced obstruent (ADA → ATA) violates both segment faithfulness and sequential markedness.

The conjoined constraint (38) penalizes voicing changes toward nonagreement. It is violated by any segment whose value for [voi] (i) disagrees with that of its predecessor and (ii) is derived, not underlying (i.e., violates faithfulness). (38) is not a pure faithfulness constraint, but a conjunction of markedness and faithfulness. Empirically, it is not exactly identical in force to IDENT[+VOI]. Output candidates such as

[ATA̩] for the input /ADA/ violate IDENT[+VOI], but not AGREE[VOI]&$_{seg}$IDENT[VOI] (as mentioned above, they are ruled out by higher-ranked constraints against voiceless sonorants).[17]

Tableau (39) shows how the new constraint makes the crucial distinction between underlyingly voiceless [s] in [...a_o...] (39b), violating low-ranked AGREE[VOI] twice, and actively devoiced [t] in context [...o_e] (39c). The latter also has two AGREE[VOI] violations, but one of them combines with an IDENT[VOI] violation involving the very same [−voi] specification and therefore registers as a violation of higher-ranked AGREE[VOI]&$_{seg}$IDENT[VOI].

(39) *Agreement-enhanced* IDENT

/naga + ℜ + sode/	No-D^2_m	AGREE[VOI]&$_{seg}$-IDENT[VOI]	REALIZE-M	IDENT[VOI]	AGREE[VOI]
a. naga zode	*!			*	
b. ▶ naga sode			*		**
c. naga zote		*!		**	**

The ranking in the tableau also reflects the basic fact that Japanese has both voiced obstruents and voiceless obstruents in its output inventory, so the faithfulness constraint IDENT[VOI] is ranked above AGREE[VOI].

As in earlier work on conjunctions of markedness and faithfulness mentioned in section 7.3.3, the approach is built on the observation that in OT, phonological derivedness is encoded as a faithfulness violation: an element of structure has changed some of its properties from its input state. For phonologically derived environments (i.e., derived by virtue of independent phonological changes), the effects of a markedness constraint M will appear to be restricted to such environments when it is conjoined with some faithfulness constraint F. The crucial point is that the output candidates violating such an M&F constraint are those unfaithful candidates that are in addition burdened with a violation of M.

For the voicing case at hand, the output candidates violating the high-ranking composite constraint are restricted to those unfaithful candidates (i.e., not faithful to the input candidate with respect to IDENT[VOI]) that also violate AGREE[VOI]. AGREE[VOI] is inactive under normal circumstances, ranking below IDENT[VOI]; but when it is conjoined with IDENT[VOI], its enhanced version takes precedence over REALIZE-M.

7.4.3 Recapitulating the Argument

In this chapter, we have discussed two approaches to the apparent asymmetry between voicing and devoicing as faithfulness violations in Japanese. The first attacks the problem directly, as a pure faithfulness issue, by making IDENT[VOI] itself in some form asymmetric. The second keeps faithfulness symmetric, but admits additional and more complex constraints that combine basic faithfulness with markedness. A specific formal expression of their interplay is the idea of conjunctions between markedness and faithfulness conjunctions. Both theories involve an extension of the general framework, whether by positing IDENT[+VOI] separate from general IDENT[VOI] or by allowing composite constraints like AGREE[VOI]&$_{seg}$IDENT[VOI], combining sequential markedness and faithfulness.

The evidence considered here, while perhaps still too limited to allow a final decision between the two theories, gives the advantage to the second one. As we have shown, asymmetric IDENT, especially in its specific/general version, while not without descriptive and theoretical merits, falters once large-scale issues are considered, such as the typology of assimilation and inventory theory. On the other hand, symmetric voicing faithfulness has conceptual merits, but seems descriptively underpowered, and it makes a serious misprediction in the area of assimilation (the "majority rule" problem).

Everything changes with the recognition that what appeared to be pure faithfulness issues might actually involve the close interweaving of faithfulness factors with markedness forces. This yields a plausible resolution to the voicing/devoicing puzzle. Viewed through the context-free lens of segmental markedness and inspecting each segment on its own, devoicing obstruents is always preferable to voicing them. But this is a myopic view of the phonological structure of connected speech, and it needs to be counterbalanced by the recognition of opposing forces in specific contexts. This leads to situations like the one in Japanese, where devoicing is excluded in voiced contexts because it leads to more marked sequences, even though it leads to less marked segments.

From this vantage point, it appears misguided to construe this whole complex of facts as a pure faithfulness issue and to then search for a theory of faithfulness able to encompass all of it directly while maintaining high standards of restrictiveness. The result is bound to be stipulatory, expressed in terms of a powerful descriptive apparatus that deprives the overall theory of its major predictions (e.g., regarding harmonic completeness). The correct answer, we submit, lies in a better understanding of the interactions between faithfulness and markedness factors, and this chapter is a small contribution toward that goal.

Chapter 8

Prosodic Anchoring

Markedness effects reflect the pressures inherent in phonetic/phonological content, but details of grammatical constituency also come into play, determining the precise way assimilations, dissimilations, and related processes unfold in larger word structures. Current understanding has taken a significant step beyond the rather unprincipled mixture of phonological and grammatical descriptions found in traditional accounts by recognizing that such effects are in an important sense phonology-internal—manifestations of a separate kind of structure organizing speech, namely, phonological constituent structure (or *prosodic structure*). While independent of grammatical structure, it is closely linked to it through the principles of grammar-prosody mapping.

In this chapter, we take a closer look at issues involved in the assignment and phonological interpretation of morphological and syntactic structure.[1] We find empirical support for the existence of prosodic structure as we turn our attention, continuing the main analytical focus of this book, to issues raised by the phonology of complex compounds in Japanese. We show that the restrictions on *rendaku* in certain types of branching structures bear on important questions regarding word structure, morphological accessibility, analogical relations between related words, and the grammar-phonology interface. We begin by illustrating the structural conditioning of *rendaku* voicing in complex compounds. Despite its initial promise, an attempt to interpret the facts along familiar output-output lines runs into surprising difficulties, and an alternative approach turns out to be superior—one that anchors the observed effects not in analogical relations to another output but in structural properties of the output form itself.

8.1 *Rendaku* Voicing in Complex Compounds

The aspect of the OCP-based analysis of *rendaku* in Ito and Mester 1986 that attracted the most attention in the subsequent phonological literature (see, e.g., McCarthy 1986; Steriade 1987; Ishihara 1989; Kenstowicz 1994) was the Lyman's

Law phenomenon—the dissimilative blocking of voicing within simple morphemes. In the original paper, however, it was a second, and at first glance more challenging, aspect that occupied center stage, namely, the failure of voicing to appear in a particular structural position in larger compound formations. To simplify terminology, we define *long compound* as any compound that properly contains another compound as a subconstituent (which we refer to as a *subcompound*). Special cases of ternary branching aside, all compounds consisting of more than two elements contain subcompounds and thus qualify as long compounds in this sense.

8.1.1 Structural Conditioning

It is easy to construct examples showing that *rendaku* voicing is productive in long compounds and can in principle apply iteratively, as in (1), marking the beginning of each noninitial element.

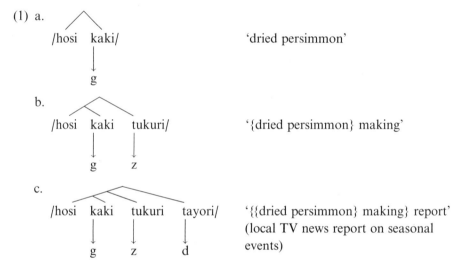

(1) a.

/hosi   kaki/   'dried persimmon'

g

b.

/hosi   kaki   tukuri/   '{dried persimmon} making'

g   z

c.

/hosi   kaki   tukuri   tayori/   '{{dried persimmon} making} report'
                                           (local TV news report on seasonal
g   z   d   events)

All such multiply voiced long compounds (see (2) for further examples) share a specific property, namely, a strictly left-branching structure. In such structures, subcompounds ({*hosigaki*} in (1b,c) and {{*hosigaki*} *zukuri*} in (1c)) are uniformly aligned with the left edge; and at all levels of structure, second members receive *rendaku* voicing.

(2) *Left-branching compounds*

hana	zono	basi	/{{hana	+ ℜ +	sono}	+ ℜ +	hasi}/
			'flower'		'garden'		'bridge'
kawa	bata	doori	/{{kawa	+ ℜ +	hata}	+ ℜ +	toori}/
			'river'		'side'		'road'
yama	zakura	dayori	/{{yama	+ ℜ +	sakura}	+ ℜ +	tayori}/
			'mountain'		'cherry'		'tidings'
umi	biraki	girai	/{{umi	+ ℜ +	hiraki}	+ ℜ +	kirai}/
			'sea'		'opening'		'dislike'
me	zamasi	dokee	/{{me	+ ℜ +	samasi}	+ ℜ +	tokee}/
			'eye'		'waking'		'clock'

Right-branching long compounds present an entirely different picture, as illustrated in (3). Here, subcompounds ({*kaoawase*}, {*kamidana*}, etc.) are aligned with the right edge of the entire compound, and *rendaku* fails to apply at the main constituent break.

(3) *Right-branching compounds*

hatu	kao	awase	/{hatu	+ ℜ +	{kao	+ ℜ +	awase}}/
	*g		'first'		'face'		'meeting'
nise	kami	dana	/{nise	+ ℜ +	{kami	+ ℜ +	tana}}/
	*g		'fake'		'divine'		'altar'
nisi	huna	basi	/{nisi	+ ℜ +	{huna	+ ℜ +	hasi}}/
	*b		'west'		'boat'		'bridge'
nuri	hasi	ire	/{nuri	+ ℜ +	{hasi	+ ℜ +	ire}}/
	*b		'lacquered'		'chopsticks'		'container'
insutanto	kitsune	udon	/{insutanto	+ ℜ +	{kitsune	+ ℜ +	udon}}/
	*g		'instant'		'fox'		'noodles'

The restriction also reveals itself in the clear intuitions of native speakers about the respective readings of minimal pairs such as *nise-zakura-dayori* and *nise-sakura-dayori* (4a,b).

(4) *A minimal pair*

a.

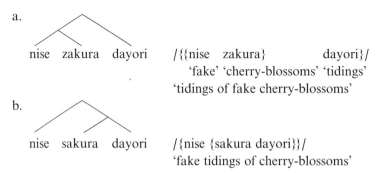

nise zakura dayori   /{{nise zakura}   dayori}/
                          'fake' 'cherry-blossoms' 'tidings'
                          'tidings of fake cherry-blossoms'

b.

nise sakura dayori   /{nise {sakura dayori}}/
                          'fake tidings of cherry-blossoms'

Inspection of (3) and (4) suggests the location of the major constituent break as the reason why *rendaku* fails in right-branching compounds. In the left-branching compound in (4a), *sakura*, which does not begin a subcompound in this case, voices to *zakura*, and *nise* 'fake' is understood as modifying only *sakura* 'cherry (blossom)'. In the contrasting right-branching case, *sakura* begins a subcompound and does not voice, and here *nise* is understood as modifying *sakura dayori*. In both cases, *tayori* 'tidings, report' voices to *dayori*.

The full generality of the branching restriction can be demonstrated with newly created compounds that are longer than three words and hence provide more room for ambiguity. A relevant test case is given in (5).[2] As a string consisting of four simplex words, it has the five possible binary grouping structures in (5a–e). The glosses are an attempt to render their (more or less plausible) interpretations, which are associated with distinct *rendaku* patterns, as indicated. As in connection with (4), native speakers have very clear intuitions regarding the possible presence and absence of *rendaku* voicing in various locations, depending on the interpretation (and associated structure) that is intended. Besides illustrating the productivity of *rendaku* itself, this shows that the restriction carries over to new cases.

(5) */nise/ /kami/ /tana/ /tukuri/ 'fake' 'god' 'shelf' 'making'*

a.

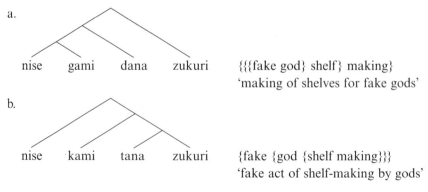

nise gami dana zukuri   {{{fake god} shelf} making}
                              'making of shelves for fake gods'

b.

nise kami tana zukuri   {fake {god {shelf making}}}
                              'fake act of shelf-making by gods'

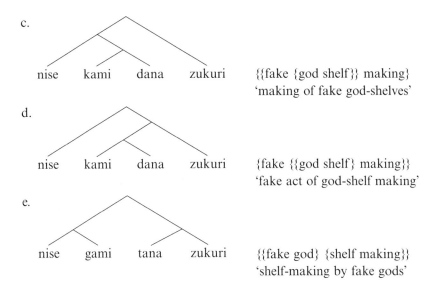

c.

nise   kami   dana   zukuri   {{fake {god shelf}} making}
                                       'making of fake god-shelves'

d.

nise   kami   dana   zukuri   {fake {{god shelf} making}}
                                       'fake act of god-shelf making'

e.

nise   gami   tana   zukuri   {{fake god} {shelf making}}
                                       'shelf-making by fake gods'

Consolidating the results in (6), where "$^+$" indicates *rendaku* voicing and "$^-$" its absence, reveals that voicing is systematically blocked at the beginning of a larger subconstituent. In typographic terms: *{$^+$.

(6) a. {{{$^-$A $^+$B} $^+$C} $^+$D}
    b. { $^-$A {$^-$B {$^-$C $^+$D}}}
    c. {{ $^-$A {$^-$B $^+$C}} $^+$D}
    d. { $^-$A {{$^-$B $^+$C} $^+$D}}
    e. { $^-$A $^+$B} {$^-$C $^+$D}}

Otsu's (1980, 219) account, the first to draw attention to this restriction on compound voicing, takes the "*{$^+$" generalization at face value and formalizes it in terms of syntactic branching (at the word level). Treating *rendaku* as a phonological rule, in the style of Chomsky and Halle 1968, Otsu adds a direct syntactic condition that limits its application to elements on right branches at the lowest level of compound structure (the Right Branch Condition).[3]

Elsewhere (Ito and Mester 1986), we argue that the Right Branch Condition, with its problematic intermingling of syntactic and phonological information, is an artifact and can be dispensed with, once the phonology of voicing in Japanese is more fully understood. We show that all effects of the condition already follow from the independently justified autosegmental interpretation of Lyman's Law, which in turn can be reduced to the autosegmental OCP operating on an underspecified voicing tier (see chapter 2). Besides a few specific assumptions laid out in the original paper, this derivation of all right branch effects from more basic principles relies on the cyclicity of *rendaku* and the OCP and, more broadly, on the general way in which phonology and morphology interact in Lexical Phonology (Kiparsky 1982, 1985).

In the present context, many of these assumptions no longer hold or can at least not be taken for granted, and it is therefore appropriate to take a fresh look at the phenomenon. We will continue to assume, in agreement with the mainstream of work on the syntax-phonology interface in the tradition of Selkirk 1980, 1984 (see also Nespor and Vogel 1986; Inkelas and Zec 1990), that phonology makes no direct reference to syntactic/morphological branching, command relations, and so on. This fundamental tenet forestalls any idea of returning to adding some kind of syntactic branching condition (or notational variants in terms of c- or m-command) to the formal statement of *rendaku* voicing.

The blocking of voicing at the beginning of subcompounds is reminiscent of the "cyclic" behavior often associated with morphologically complex constructions whose parts also occur independently. Many such cases of cyclicity have been successfully subsumed under output-output (OO) faithfulness (see, e.g., Benua 1995; McCarthy 1995; Kenstowicz 1996; Ito, Kitagawa, and Mester 1996; Ito and Mester 1997a; Steriade 1997; Burzio 1997), and it is natural to expect that a similar explanation might apply here. It comes as something of a surprise, therefore, that upon closer inspection things turn out quite differently.

8.1.2 Output-Output Correspondence and Its Shortcomings

The basic idea of OO faithfulness is straightforward and highly reminiscent of neogrammarian analogy (especially in fully developed synchronic conceptions such as Paul 1880, chap. 5): voicing is blocked in {A {B C}} (e.g., *hatu-kao-awase*) because {B C} (*kao-awase*) occurs independently, and in this occurrence B (*kao*), being initial, shows no compound voicing. This property of the initial consonant is guarded by the OO identity constraint in (7), which follows the general principle giving priority to free forms (bases) over their correspondents occurring in a morphological construction (including affixed forms and compounded forms).

(7) IDENT-OO[F]: "A form in a compounded/affixed construction is identical to its corresponding base form with respect to [F] specifications."

Formally speaking, IDENT-OO[F] is a group of constraints on the correspondence relation holding between the segments of the phonological exponent of every constituent inside a morphological construction and the segments of the phonological exponent of the corresponding free form, provided such a form exists. In order not to lose sight of the general picture over a concern with highly specific OO constraints, it is helpful to view this as part of an overall conception of OO relations as reflections of the compositional computation of phonological form: the phonological form of

a morphologically complex input is a function of the phonological form of its parts
and of their mode of combination, as expressed in (8) for the case of compounds (see
Ito and Mester 1997a, 420).

(8) φ (member₁⌢ member₂) = φ (member₁) + φ (member₂)

> The phonological output form (φ(x)) of an input that consists of the
> morphological concatenation (⌢) of two members, member₁ and member₂, is
> identical to the phonological combination (+) of the phonological output forms
> of the two members.

In current OT, this basic idea of compositionality is technically implemented as a set
of OO faithfulness constraints distributed over the constraint system.[4] The member
of this set that is relevant here is IDENT-OO[VOI], a constraint requiring the voicing
specifications of the segments of an expression occurring as part of a morphological
construction to exactly match those in its base form (i.e., its freestanding output
form, provided one exists).[5]

Since its purpose is to forestall *rendaku* in the relevant cases, IDENT-OO[VOI] ranks
above REALIZE-M, as in (9).

(9) IDENT-OO[VOI]

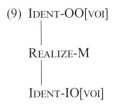

REALIZE-M

IDENT-IO[VOI]

(10) illustrates the OO account of *rendaku* blocking in right-branching compounds
with an example.

(10) nise kami dana *'fake god-shelf'*

Base: [kami dana] Input: /{nise + ℜ + {kami + ℜ + tana}}/	IDENT- OO[VOI]	REALIZE-M	IDENT- IO[VOI]
a. nise gami dana	*!		**
b. ▶ nise kami dana		*	*
c. nise kami tana	*!	**	
d. nise gami tana	*!*	*	*

Voiceless [k] in *kami-dana*, in its occurrence as a subcompound embedded in
nise kamidana, is preserved through correspondence with the voiceless [k] in the

independent base output form *kami-dana*. Thus, candidate (10b), which realizes only the second instance of the linking morpheme, wins over the other candidates, such as (10a), which realizes both instances, and (10c), which is fully faithful to the segments of the input and realizes neither. Candidate (10d) realizes the first and not the second instance of the linking morpheme, leading to a double violation of IDENT-OO.

In the left-branching counterpart to (10), both instances of the linking morpheme are realized, as shown in (11).

(11) nise gami dana *'fake-god shelf'*

Base: [nise gami] Input: /{nise + ℜ + {kami + ℜ + tana}}/	IDENT-OO[VOI]	REALIZE-M	IDENT-IO[VOI]
a. ▶ nise gami dana			**
b. nise kami dana	*!	*	*
c. nise kami tana	*!	*!*	
d. nise gami tana		*!	*

While the OO-based explanation of *rendaku* blocking at the beginning of subcompounds deals successfully with these examples, it encounters at least two serious problems. Besides the elusiveness of the notion "base" needed to secure blocking in all relevant cases, it is in other respects difficult to restrict it in the required way. Taken together, these problems indicate that, at least as far as the phonology of compounds is concerned, OO constraints do not provide the right kind of explanation.

Starting with the first point, in order to make sure that IDENT-OO exerts its blocking function in all cases, the crucial base form—itself a compound—must exist as an output. This assumption is unlikely to be fulfilled in all cases: one can easily imagine specific long compounds that are in frequent use without all of their subcompounds occurring with any frequency by themselves. For an individual speaker, their frequency might very well be zero. In other words, "independently existing" must be interpreted in some metaphorical way, but it is unclear what the metaphor is.

The problem of the missing or elusive base, which appears unsolvable at the level of individual speakers' grammars and needs to be explicitly addressed at a level like that of the speech community, is a threat for OO analyses in general (see Kiparsky 1998), whose central means of explanation is the existence of transderivationally related outputs.

Compounding raises a further issue that does not arise in the same way with affixation. The generative resources of the compounding system are akin to those of syntax. What is involved in judgments like those shown in (5) is not a finite set of forms, be they listed in some dictionary or memorized, but the tacit knowledge of a competent speaker/hearer, in the sense familiar from syntactic theory. Given the productivity and recursivity of compounding, speakers can easily create novel expressions of the form {A {B C}} and correctly withhold *rendaku* voicing from B, without {B C}'s ever having been uttered, or otherwise encountered, by itself. The problem of the missing base is therefore more serious here than in cases of affixation, which tend to be restricted and in many instances lexicalized.[6]

While the problem of the missing base means that OO faithfulness cannot guarantee blocking of voicing in all cases where it is required, the opposite situation also arises, where OO faithfulness engages in excessive blocking, barring perfectly legitimate *rendaku* forms. Consider a compound consisting of two simplex words, as in (12).

(12) kami dana *'god shelf'*

Base: [tana] Input: /{kami + ℜ + tana}/	IDENT-OO[VOI]	REALIZE-M	IDENT-IO[VOI]
kami dana	*!		*
wrong winner ▶ kami tana		*	

Since each of the compound members is an independent word, each has a base form. If so, why does the existence of the word *tana* not block *rendaku* in *kami-dana*? The corresponding problem does not arise with OO constraints in affixation cases because the affix itself is not a freely occurring element.

Excessive blocking is caused by the generality of the OO faithfulness constraint: we want blocking through analogy with the uncompounded base only for compound members that are themselves compounds, not for simplex words, but IDENT-OO[VOI] makes no such distinction.

Both of these problems are perhaps not insurmountable. In a theory where OO correspondence plays a larger role (in fact, where IO correspondence plays little or no role), all compositional computation of complex forms will depend on some type of OO correspondence. If this is the right track to pursue, then whatever solves the large-scale computability problem should be able to deal with the problems encountered here as well. To ensure a sufficient supply of base forms, one could consider using the grammar itself to compute outputs where none exist (see Kurisu 2001 for a formal proposal of this kind). Regarding the second problem, we have posited a difference in morphological category and structure, based on economy and minimality principles, between simple compounds and complex compounds, attempting a more principled explanation (see Ito and Mester 1998). But it is unclear whether having the grammar compute all base forms accords with the spirit of the OO approach, since it is in fact tantamount to reinstating the cyclic derivation in another guise. Regarding subtle but crucial differences in morphological structure, the question ultimately comes down to the existence of independent support for such structures.

We therefore do not adopt the OO approach at this point, pending its further development and solidification in theory and analysis. An alternative prosody-based approach, to be presented in the following sections, appears superior. It is directly based on the actual prosodic constituent structure of right-branching compounds, as it manifests itself in the phonetic output in other ways, besides presence or absence of compound voicing. In particular, it does not depend on questionable OO relations or special assumptions about morphological word structure.

8.2   The Internal Prosodic Structure of Compounds

The syntax-phonology interface hypothesis put forth by Selkirk (1980, 1984), and fruitfully applied and developed in many subsequent studies, severely limits the access that phonological generalizations can have to grammatical information. The basic idea is that substantive phonological restrictions, such as the blocking of voicing in some position under consideration here, must always be statable in terms of genuine phonological elements and constituents, and do not require direct reference to morphology and syntax. Corresponding to what Pullum and Zwicky (1988) have dubbed "phonology-free syntax," phonology is, in a fundamental way, "syntax-free." Just as there are no languages that move every word beginning with a nasal consonant to sentence-initial position, so there are no languages where subject noun phrases allow underlyingly nasalized vowels to appear nasalized in the output, whereas object noun phrases do not.

While phonological processes and conditions do not have such direct access to syntactic information, the influence of grammatical structure on phonological form remains massive and pervasive. For example, a word receives phrasal stress because it appears in a certain position, onset-coda syllabification differs drastically depending on the way morphemes are ordered in words, and so on. But all such influence is indirect, mediated through the basic mapping between grammatical and phonological structure, which is to a large extent regulated by the theory of anchoring in OT.

8.2.1   Left- and Right-Branching Structures and Their Prosodic Differences
For the case at hand, our basic hypothesis is that the asymmetry observed in *rendaku* voicing is a consequence of the different prosodic structures of left- and right-branching compounds. Differences in the way the two kinds of structures are parsed go back to the earliest work in prosodic phonology, when Liberman and Prince

(1977) used them to establish the superiority of the metrical conception of stress and rhythmic structure over the segmentalist tradition represented by Chomsky and Halle 1968. Well-known examples include contrasts such as {{{*la*^{1}*w degree*} *require-ment*} *changes*} versus {{*la*^{2}*w degree*} {*la*^{1}*nguage requirement*}}, where the appearance of main stress on a noninitial member is a characteristic of right-branching compound structures.

Postponing for the moment a discussion of the constraints responsible for assigning the relevant prosodic structures, we start by looking at a basic difference between Japanese compounds and those of many other languages, including English. In the latter case, in a two-word compound (e.g., *la*^{1}*nguage requi*^{2}*rement*) each member carries a separate word stress, and one of the stresses is elevated to main prominence within the compound. Each member preserves its pattern of prominence (abstracting away from Rhythm Rule effects and the like) and is therefore a separate prosodic word, whereas the whole compound forms a higher prosodic domain. Corresponding two-word compounds in Japanese behave quite differently. Special cases aside, the members do not carry separate accents; instead, there is at most one accent per compound (phonetically, a falling pitch contour), as shown in (13), repeated from section 3.2.

(13) pe^{HL}rusya + ne^{HL}ko   → perusyane^{HL}ko   'Persian cat'
      sya^{HL}kai + se^{HL}edo   → syakaise^{HL}edo   'social system'
      ya^{HL}mato + nade^{HL}siko → yamatonade^{HL}siko 'Yamato woman'
      na^{HL}ma   + tama^{HL}go   → namata^{HL}mago   'raw egg'
      a^{HL}isu   + koohi^{HL}i   → aisuko^{HL}ohii   'iced coffee'

Unlike its English counterpart, a prototypical Japanese compound does not contain members that are separate prosodic words; instead, the whole compound is a single prosodic word (see Tanaka 2001a,b for a clear exposition of the contrast). Whereas simplex grammatical words correspond to prosodic words on a more or less one-to-one basis in English, this is not the case in Japanese.

In the present study, we are not concerned with exactly how the location of the compound accent is computed, which is a very complex matter, but with the simple and uncontroversial fact that compounds constitute a single accentual domain. Compound accentuation itself has been the object of important studies including Martin 1952, McCawley 1968, Poser 1984, 1990, and Kubozono 1988, 1993. While opinions diverge as to what the default pattern is in specific areas (see Kubozono 1995 and Tanaka 2001a for discussion and analyses within OT), the main generalizations are straightforward: a compound ends up with a single accent by (i) removing any lexical accents from the first member and (ii) assigning a new accent at the compound juncture (prototypically, on the first syllable of the second member).[7]

The grammar-prosody asymmetry seen in Japanese compounds is one instance of a widely observed asymmetry (beginning with the readjustment rules of Chomsky and Halle 1968) wherein prosodic structure is flatter and shows less embedding than the grammatical structure it corresponds to. This situation is depicted in (14), where the grammatical (syntactic and morphological) structure is indicated with curly brackets, labeled *w* for *grammatical word*, and the prosodic word structure is indicated with square brackets, labeled ω.[8]

(14) Parsing into grammatical words: $\{_w\{_w X\} \{_w Y\}\}$
      Parsing into prosodic words: $[_\omega$ $]$

How then do the long compounds behave? Kubozono (1988, 1993) stresses the special prosody associated with right-branching structures in Japanese, pointing out that for certain right-branching compounds a single prosodic word is not appropriate since there are two surface accents. While a single prosodic word continues to be assigned to a left-branching compound, as in (15a), two prosodic words must be assigned to a right-branching compound, as in (15b). (From now on, we will use *γ-structure* as an abbreviation for *grammatical structure*, and *ω-structure* for *prosodic word structure*.)

(15) *One prosodic word versus two prosodic words*

                    a. Left-branching compound

      γ-structure: $\{\{\{X\} \{Y\}\} \{Z\}\}$
      ω-structure: [   ]

                    b. Right-branching compound

      γ-structure: $\{\{X\} \{\{Y\} \{Z\}\}\}$
      ω-structure: [   ] [   ]

Kubozono's (1993) example in (16) illustrates the difference with the two readings of an ambiguous compound.

(16) nihon buyoo kyookai *'Japan dance association'*

      a. ω: [o⌐   ]
          γ: $\{\{\{nihon\} \{buyoo\}\} \{kyookai\}\}$ 'association for Japanese dance'
      b. ω: [o⌐] [o⌐   ]
          γ: $\{\{nihon\} \{\{buyoo\} \{kyookai\}\}\}$ 'dance association of Japan'

Kubozono, Ito, and Mester (1997) provide the additional examples in (17) in support of the right-branching generalization.

(17) *Examples of right-branching compounds, with two accents and two ω's*

    a. ω: [o⌐] [i⌐   ]
      γ: {{nihon} {{ea} {sisutemu}}}   'Japan air system'
    b. ω: [o⌐] [a⌐   ]
      γ: {{tihoo} {{kookyoo} {dantai}}}   'local public bodies'
    c. ω: [i⌐   ] [o⌐   ]
      γ: {{nitibee} {{anpo} {zyooyaku}}}   'Japan-U.S. security treaty'
    d. ω: [a⌐   ] [i⌐   ]
      γ: {{kantoo} {{dai} {sinsai}}}   'Kanto great earthquake'
    e. ω: [o⌐   ] [a⌐   ]
      γ: {{koohaku} {{uta} {gassen}}}   'red-white song competition'

The examples in (17) do not realize the linking morpheme because of their S or F status; but the same pattern can be reproduced with Y items, as in (18), and here *rendaku* voicing manifests itself.

(18) *Exemplifying the correlation among* γ*-structure,* ω*-structure, accent, and* rendaku

    a. /niho⌐n/ /sakura/ /maturi/
      'Japan' 'cherry' 'festival'

      ω: [a⌐   ]   [o⌐] [a⌐   ]
      γ: {{{nihon} {zakura}} {matsuri}}   {{nihon} {{sakura} {matsuri}}}
      'festival for Japanese cherry   'Japanese cherry blossom
      blossoms'   festival'

    b. /ta⌐nuki/ /tani⌐/ /nobori/
      'badger' 'valley' 'climbing'

      ω: [o⌐   ]   [a⌐] [o⌐   ]
      γ: {{{tanuki} {dani}} {nobori}}   {{tanuki} {{tani} {nobori}}}
      'climbing of Badger Valley'   'valley climbing by badgers'

Both examples allow two different readings, as indicated. In the representations on the right, with right-branching γ-structures, there are two prosodic words, both carrying accents, and *rendaku* voicing is absent. In the representations on the left, with left-branching γ-structures, there is one prosodic word, with one accent, and *rendaku* voicing is present. Since Japanese allows for unaccented prosodic words (see section 3.2), one prosodic word can bear up to one accent, and two prosodic words up to two accents, and the general correlations are as in (19).

(19) *Core descriptive generalization regarding long compounds*

    Left-branching γ ≈ one ω ≈ one accent (maximally) ≈ *rendaku* voicing
    Right-branching γ ≈ two ω's ≈ two accents (maximally) ≈ no *rendaku* voicing

It is the power of these correlations, which tie together γ-structure, ω-structure, accent, and *rendaku*, that allows us to see the phonology of *rendaku* in a broader context. They constitute the strongest argument for an explanation directly built on prosody, as opposed to the OO approach contemplated in section 8.1.2.

8.2.2 Semantic Ambiguities versus Optional Rhythmic Constraints

Before turning to our analysis, we need to address one complicating factor relating to the left-branching portion of the generalization (i.e., "left-branching ≈ single prosodic word"). Kubozono (1993) points out that strictly left-branching compounds containing four or more members often show accentual variation, being either parsed into the expected single prosodic domain (20a) or split into two prosodic domains (20b).

(20) *Four-member compounds (from Kubozono 1993, 55)*

a. ω₁:	[A B C D]	[	eˈ]	[	eˈ]
b. ω₂:	[A B] [C D]	[aˈ] [	eˈ]	[oˈ] [	eˈ]
γ:	{{{A B} C} D}	{{{toonan azia} syokoku} rengoo}		{{{san kootai} kinmu} seedo}	
		'southeast-Asia-nation-union'		'three-shift-work-system'	

According to Kubozono, the unexpected (20b), with its two accent domains, results from the influence of optional rhythmic constraints disfavoring long accentual phrases and favoring binary structure. There are several factors that appear to trigger this phonological restructuring, but the crucial observation for our purposes is this: for strictly left-branching four-member compounds whose members are susceptible to *rendaku* voicing (21), there is no comparable variation, and they can only be parsed as a single prosodic domain (21a).[9]

(21) *Left-branching four-member compounds with* rendaku

a. ω₁:	[A B C D]	[	uˈ]	[	aˈ]
b. ω₂:	*[A B] [C D]	*[uˈ] [	uˈ]	*[iˈ] [	aˈ]
γ:	{{{A B} C} D}	{{{mitu bati} bako} zukuri}		{{{satuma mikan} batake} dayori}	
		/miˈtu/ /hati/ /hako/ /tukuri/		/saˈtuma/ /miˈkan/ /hatake/ /taˈyori/	
		'honey' 'bee' 'box' 'making'		'Satsuma' 'mandarin' 'field' 'report'	

What is important here is the presence of *rendaku* voicing on the third member; in other words, in the ill-formed phrasings in (21b), a new prosodic domain would start with a *rendaku*-voiced segment. Why are such prosodic restructurings excluded in long compounds with *rendaku*? Note that from a general theoretical perspective, it is quite troubling to find an optional postlexical/phrasal restructuring process (which is based on prosodic rhythm and length) crucially conditioned by compound voicing (which not only is segmental in nature but also, as we have shown, has all the properties of a deeply lexical process: grammatical conditioning, stratal restrictions, exceptions, etc.).

A closer look at the examples in (20) illustrating the accentual variation reveals that, while both avoidance of long accentual phrases and a preference for binary prosodic structures are certainly involved, another crucial factor is present that distinguishes the cases where accentual variation is possible from those where it is not. We will refer to it as *covert grammatical ambiguity*: different γ-structures with quasi-identical interpretations. In other words, what looked like a variation between two alternative prosodic parses of a single γ-structure might actually be two parses, each corresponding to a different γ-structure. Such grammatical ambiguities are frequent in long compounds because of the openness of the modifier-head relation, which is in principle unrestricted semantically and can often be further specified, in a given pragmatic context, in a number of different ways.[10] In this way, slightly different γ-structures assigned to a given compound can, coupled with suitable interpretations of the relation, lead to quasi-identical interpretations of the whole compound. Taking the putatively unambiguous {{{W X} Y} Z} compounds in (20) as examples, we find that other γ-structures—in particular, {{W X} {Y Z}}—cannot be excluded as possibilities in these cases. The differences in interpretation between the bracketing (22a) 'union of Southeast Asian nations' (ASEAN) and the alternative (22b) 'union-of-nations in Southeast Asia' are subtle and of little practical import. While the former is perhaps the semantically more natural grouping, the latter makes use of the independently existing *syokoku rengoo* 'union of nations' as a subcompound (see Spencer 1988 on the importance of such relations in bracketing paradoxes) and has superior prosody in its favor. Similar considerations apply to (22c) 'system of three-shift work' and the alternative bracketing (22d) 'system-of-work organized in three shifts'.[11]

(22) *Covert grammatical ambiguities*

a.	{{{toonan azia} syokoku} rengoo}	{{{Southeast Asia} nations} union}
b.	{{toonan azia} {syokoku rengoo}}	{{Southeast Asia} {nations union}}
c.	{{{san kootai} kinmu} seedo}	{{{three shift} work} system}
d.	{{san kootai} {kinmu seedo}}	{{three shift} {work system}}

It seems impossible to exclude the {{W X} {Y Z}} structures (22b,d) on some principled basis, in particular since their prosody is preferable, with strictly binary prosodic words that in addition constitute short accentual domains. (22) reveals that there is actually an ambiguity, with only a marginal difference in meaning, between fully left-branching γ-structures and binary-branching γ-structures. The two are depicted in (23) and (24), with their respective prosodic structures.

(23) *Left-branching γ-structure*

[A B C D]	[e⌐]	[e⌐]
{{{A B} C} D}	{{{toonan azia} syokoku} rengoo}	{{{san kootai} kinmu} seedo}
	'union of Southeast Asian nations'	'system of three-shift work'

(24) *Binary-branching γ-structure*

[A B] [C D]	[a⌐] [e⌐]	[o⌐] [e⌐]
{{A B} {C D}}	{{toonan azia} {syokoku rengoo}}	{{san kootai} {kinmu seedo}}
	'nations union of Southeast Asia'	'work system of three shifts'

If grammatical ambiguity is the source of the observed variation, then there is no need for optional prosodic restructuring. Rather, prosodic parsing proceeds exactly as expected: the reading with a left-branching γ-structure yields one prosodic domain (23), and the reading with a binary-branching structure (which necessarily includes a right-branching γ-structure) yields two prosodic domains (24).

The fact that no comparable accentual variation is ever observed in the *rendaku* cases now follows straightforwardly. They are strictly left-branching four-member compounds; hence, they have only one prosodic domain (25).

(25) *Strictly left-branching ABCD* (rendaku *on C, one prosodic domain*)

[A B C D]	[b u⌐]	[b a⌐]
{{{A B} C} D}	{{{mitu bati} bako} zukuri}	{{{satuma mikan} batake} dayori}
	'making honey bee boxes'	'report on Satsuma mandarin fields'

The crucial difference between the Sino-Japanese (and hence *rendaku*-free) compounds in (23) and (24) and the compounds consisting of Yamato words in (25) is that the segmental strings in the latter case are not covertly ambiguous between two grammatical structures: even though alternative binary-branching structures (26) are conceivable as before, the resulting split into two prosodic domains is not compatible with *rendaku* voicing, and the corresponding outputs are therefore different in their segmental makeup (26).

(26) *Binary-branching ABCD (no* rendaku *on C, two prosodic domains)*

[A B] [C D]	[u⌐] [u⌐]	[i⌐] [a⌐]
{{{A B} C} D}	{{mitu bati} {hako zukuri}}	{{satuma mikan} {hatake dayori}}
	'box making for honey bees'	'field report on Satsuma mandarins'

What appeared to be a counterexample to the left-branching generalization, then, can be attributed to a grammatical ambiguity between strictly left-branching and binary-branching structures. The upshot is that even four-member left-branching compounds, with or without *rendaku*, are always phonologically parsed into one prosodic domain, and the core generalization given in (19) (repeated here) remains valid.

(27) *Core descriptive generalization regarding long compounds*

Left-branching γ ≈ one ω ≈ one accent (maximally) ≈ *rendaku* voicing
Right-branching γ ≈ two ω's ≈ two accents (maximally) ≈ no *rendaku* voicing

As we will show in section 8.4.2, the correlation between accent and *rendaku* is somewhat more complex, requiring more distinctions on the prosodic side. Before turning to such extensions, we will develop the formal OT analysis of the basic generalization just described. The analysis addresses two main issues. First, regarding the assignment of ω-structure, we take a closer look at the anchoring constraints that give rise to the different prosody assigned to left- versus right-branching γ-structures, resulting in structures with one versus two prosodic words. Subsequently, we turn to the exact implications of the ω-structures assigned. Simply positing two prosodic words is not sufficient; we also need to formulate the constraints that prevent the *rendaku* morpheme from being realized in such cases.

8.3 Initial Anchoring and Initial Markedness

The centerpiece of our approach is a grammar-prosody interface constraint requiring that edges of grammatical constituents carry a prosodic mark. As a general idea, this goes back to Trubetzkoy's (1939) work on prosodic boundary markers (his *Grenzsignale*). In recent years, Selkirk's (1986) end-based theory of the grammar-prosody interface constitutes an important step forward: languages typically single out one edge (left or right) of a γ-constituent—w (grammatical word) or XP (maximal syntactic projection)—to the exclusion of the other edge, and require it to coincide with a prosodic boundary. Further development within OT is due to McCarthy and Prince (1993a) and Truckenbrodt (1999).

8.3.1 Anchored but Minimal

In formulating our constraint, we need to be clear about what is meant by the "edge of a constituent," since what counts as the "first/last element" depends on the level of parsing. In the present context, we can limit ourselves to the segmental level (see Spaelti 1994 for a more comprehensive conception), where we are dealing with strings of segments. Taking up the formal development in Ito, Kitagawa, and Mester 1996, for every string α we define its left (right) edge as the minimal member of the set of its nonempty initial (final) substrings, as in (28c,d).[12]

(28) *Defining* edge of a string *(α, x, y, z are nonempty strings of segments)*

  a. Begin(α) = {x | ∃y[α = xy] ∧ x ≠ ∅}   "x *begins* (is an initial substring of) α."

  b. End(α) = {x | ∃y[α = yx] ∧ x ≠ ∅}   "x *ends* (is a final substring of) α."

   c. Edge(α, L) = {x | $\forall$z[z $\in$ Begin(α) $\rightarrow$ "*Left edge:* x begins all beginnings
       x $\in$ Begin(z)]   of α."

   d. Edge(α,   R) = {x | $\forall$z[z $\in$ End(α) $\rightarrow$ "*Right edge:* x ends all endings of
       x $\in$ End(z)] α."

Next, we formulate our grammar-prosody interface constraint in (29).

(29) ANCHOR-L(w, ω): "For every left edge x of a grammatical word w, there is a
     prosodic word ω such that (an R-correspondent of) x is the left edge of ω:

$$\forall x, w[\text{Edge}(w, L) = x \rightarrow \exists\omega[\text{Edge}(\omega, L) = R(x)]]."$$

In the cases considered here, the relevant correspondence relation R is self-
correspondence, since the very same element x must be the left edge of ω, not some
image of x. This indicates that identity is a correspondence relation.[13] Anchoring
constraints like (29) are violated by left and right edges, where we can think of an
edge as a pair (α, β) with α being an edge (left or right) of β. Thus, ANCHOR-L is
violated by a pair (x, w), x = Edge(w, L), whenever there is no prosodic word ω such
that x = Edge(ω, L).

    Constraint (29) requires left-edge anchoring of a grammatical word to a prosodic
word, as schematically shown in (30), where every beginning of a grammatical word
corresponds to the beginning of a prosodic word. It restates, in the language of
anchoring, what earlier work on syntax-phonology mapping expressed as a particular setting in a principles-and-parameters-based theory. Thus, Selkirk and Tateishi
(1988, 322) propose essentially the same requirement, calling it the *Japanese Prosodic Word Parameter* ("Prosodic Word: {Left, X_{lex}}, where X_{lex} stands for lexical
item").

(30) γ-structure: {$_w$ A ... {$_w$ B ... {$_w$ C ...
     ω-structure: [$_\omega$ [$_\omega$ [$_\omega$

    While the beginnings of constituents have often turned out to be of particular
importance for the grammar-prosody interface, pointing to a dominant position of
constraints such as ANCHOR-L, corresponding right-anchoring constraints focusing
on the ends of constituents are not as active in the grammar. They are generally low-
ranking in the constraint hierarchy, or perhaps even nonexistent, as suggested by
Nelson (1998), in which case ANCHOR-L would be complemented not by ANCHOR-R,
but by a directionally neutral ANCHOR constraint.

    All else being equal, (29) leads to the assignment of a new prosodic ω whenever
the beginning of a new grammatical w has been reached. This is not yet the correct
result, indicating that further constraints must be involved. Consider the prosodic
structures assigned to a schematic two-member compound in (31).

(31) $\{_w \{_w X\} \{_w Y\}\}$

    a. $[_\omega X] [_\omega Y]$ ANCHOR-L satisfied
    b. $[_\omega X \quad Y]$ ANCHOR-L violated in constituent $\{Y\}$

Given the facts regarding accent and *rendaku* surveyed in section 8.2.1, the correct prosodic structure here is (31b), with one ω assigned to compounds made up of two simplex w's. The force of the constraint ANCHOR-L is neutralized here through domination by a member of the family of constraints NO-STRUC militating against any structure (as proposed in unpublished work by Cheryl Zoll mentioned in Prince and Smolensky 1993, 25, fn. 13, and invoked in numerous subsequent studies). We will refer to the relevant member of this family as *NO-STRUC[ω]*. As (32) shows, this constraint ranks above ANCHOR-L.

(32) *Ranking: NO-STRUC[ω] ≫ ANCHOR-L*

$\{\{X\} \{Y\}\}$	NO-STRUC[ω]	ANCHOR-L
a. [X] [Y]	**!	
b. ▶ [X Y]	*	*(Y)

The fact that the winner in (32) still violates NO-STRUC[ω] raises the question whether other candidates might do still better. Some relevant competitors are given in (33), together with a brief diagnostic.

(33) *Other relevant candidates*

c. X Y	no ω-structure: violation of LX ≈ PR (or an equivalent)
d. [X [Y]]	recursive ω's: 2 NO-STRUC[ω] violations, 1 violation of RECURSIVITY
e. [[X] [Y]]	3 NO-STRUC[ω] violations

A candidate with no ω-structure whatsoever, (33c), while steering clear of a violation of NO-STRUC[ω], violates fundamental and high-ranking constraints requiring the presence of at least some prosody making the form pronounceable, such as Prince and Smolensky's (1993) LX ≈ PR (or an equivalent thereof) requiring every lexical word to correspond to a prosodic word. Candidate (33c) also violates Truckenbrodt's (1999) constraint WRAP, requiring syntactic and morphological units to be contained in a single prosodic word; however, this violation is not decisive since, as we will show, WRAP is a dominated constraint in Japanese. Candidates (33d) and (33e) fulfill

ANCHOR-L perfectly, but the former violates RECURSIVITY and the latter has additional NO-STRUC[ω] violations. In presenting our basic analysis, we will henceforth consider only candidates that are at least parsed by ω-structure and whose parsing is nonrecursive. We will have occasion to return to the issue of recursive prosodic structure in section 8.4.2.

With NO-STRUC[ω] dominating ANCHOR-L, however, it appears a single-ω candidate will always be the winner even in longer compounds, and it seems impossible to distinguish between left-branching compounds and right-branching compounds in the required way. Focusing on the fact that the beginnings of constituents are of particular importance for the grammar-prosody interface, consider the constituent-initial elements in (34).

(34) $\{_C\{_A\ x\ldots\}\ \{_B\ y\ldots\}\}$

The element x, the leftmost element of A, is simultaneously the leftmost element of the larger constituent C; but y, the leftmost element of B, is not leftmost in any larger constituent (B and C share a right edge, but this is irrelevant). If y, the leftmost element of constituent B, is not anchored to a prosodic word, there is only one violation of ANCHOR-L, incurred by (y, B) ("y qua left edge of B"). But if x, the leftmost element of constituent A, is not anchored to a prosodic word, there are two violations of ANCHOR-L: one incurred by (x, A) ("x qua left edge of B"), and another by (x, C) ("x qua left edge of C"). In typographic terms, contiguous "{{" must be matched by "[", but a single "{" need not.

As many earlier instances in this book have indicated, locally clustered multiple violations of one and the same constraint play a special role in OT's candidate evaluation, in a way that the theory takes formal notice of. Continuing to use self-conjunction of constraints as a way of assessing special penalties to such clusters of violations, we formalize the conjunction in (35). As pointed out in connection with (29), anchoring is violated by edge elements. Given our segment-based definition of the left edge of a string in (28), the Minimal Domain Principle (see section 5.1.1) predicts the local domain of conjunction to be the segment, as indicated.

(35) ANCHOR-L$^2_{s(eg)}$: ANCHOR-L(w, ω)$\&_{seg}$ANCHOR-L(w, ω)

The conjoined constraint asserts that no element should occupy the left edge of two different w-constituents without occupying the left edge of some ω-constituent. Potential sites of ANCHOR-L^2_s violations are elements at left compound edges, which are shared between the overall compound constituent C and the individual member constituent A.[14] Whenever such w-initial x's are not ω-initial, ANCHOR-L is violated twice, amounting to an additional single violation of ANCHOR-L^2_s.

Putting the pieces of our analysis together, we have reached the familiar ranking configuration A$^2 \gg$ B $\gg$ A in (36).

(36)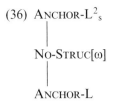

This subhierarchy explains why right-branching γ-structures ($\rightarrow$ two ω's) and left-branching γ-structures ($\rightarrow$ one ω) are assigned different prosodies, as shown in (37) and (38).

(37) *Right-branching compound (e.g.,* hatu-kao-awase*)*

{{X} {{Y} {Z}}}	ANCHOR-L^2$_s$	NO-STRUC[ω]	ANCHOR-L
a. [X Y Z]	*!	*	**(Y), *(Z)
b. ▶ [X] [Y Z]		**	*(Z)
c. [X Y] [Z]	*!	**	**(Y)
d. [X] [Y] [Z]		***!	

(38) *Left-branching compound (e.g.,* hana-zono-basi*)*

{{{X} {Y}} {Z}}	ANCHOR-L^2$_s$	NO-STRUC[ω]	ANCHOR-L
a. ▶ [X Y Z]		*	*(Y) *(Z)
b. [X] [Y Z]		**!	*(Z)
c. [X Y] [Z]		**!	*(Y)
d. [X] [Y] [Z]		**!*	

In the right-branching compound (37), the double violation of ANCHOR-L on Y triggers a violation of the self-conjoined constraint in the minimally prosodified candidate (37a) (as well as in the prosodically misaligned candidate (37c)), making (37b) the overall winner. But in the left-branching compound (38), no double violations of ANCHOR-L arise for the minimal prosodification (38a), which is therefore optimal.

The basic skeleton of the grammar-phonology interface theory proposed in (36) is very simple, with the structural markedness constraint NO-STRUC[ω] interleaved between the two anchoring constraints—above plain ANCHOR-L (hence deactivating it in the default situation), but below the enhanced ANCHOR-L^2$_s$ constraint.

This mode of explanation seems superior to any attempt, such as our previous one (Ito and Mester 1998), to set up different labels for simple and compounded grammatical words and then make other constraints sensitive to this specific difference. More importantly, (36) formalizes a simple and direct explanation for the fact that right-branching structures are prosodically special: a single γ-boundary is not sufficient to warrant starting a new ω, but two coincident γ-boundaries are. Projected into the string, each instance of γ-branching means a coincidence of γ-boundaries at a specific point. In strictly left-branching γ-structures, all γ-boundaries necessarily coincide at the left edge, so a single ω is in principle sufficient. But any kind of right branching means a coincidence of γ-boundaries somewhere in the middle of the string, and hence requires starting a new ω at that point.

The conception of the grammar-prosody interface that lies behind this approach is minimalist in the sense that it works with very few specific assumptions, and we anticipate that other parts of interface theory, besides compounds, can be simplified in a similar way. Looking beyond the technicalities of constraint self-conjunction, the general moral is that properly calculating the weight of multiple violations is more explanatory, in OT as elsewhere, than stipulating extra constraints.

8.3.2 Positional Constraints: Markedness versus Faithfulness

The interface constraints ensure that left-branching morphological structures in Japanese have one prosodic domain, and right-branching structures have two. But this is only the first half of the story: the remaining question is why this prevents the realization of the *rendaku* morpheme in the latter case. Broadly speaking, OT has developed two kinds of approaches to such questions, one in terms of positional faithfulness and one in terms of positional markedness, and their relative merits and demerits are an issue of current theoretical debate (we return to related considerations in section 8.4.1). For the case at hand, we pursue both avenues, and while the evidence in favor of one or the other is not overwhelming, we will point to some considerations favoring the markedness approach.

The cornerstone of positional faithfulness explanations is the idea that positions of prominence are singled out by being more faithful, hence richer in contrasts, where IO faithfulness is involved, than the rest.[15] Being "prominent" here means to stand out from the surroundings either phonetically (as do released consonants in onsets) or psychologically (as do beginnings of roots), and some positions, such as stressed syllables, probably fall into both categories. Positional faithfulness theory proposes that there is a well-defined set P of such prominent positions, and every faithfulness constraint F has separate, and separately rankable, versions F/p for every p ∈ P. Positional faithfulness effects arise when the ranking configuration F/p ≫ C ≫ F obtains, with F antagonistic to some constraint C.

Staying with the general theme that the beginnings of things tend to be more faithful than the rest, let us consider including the prosodic word–initial position (notated as "/[ω__") among the members of P.[16] Positional faithfulness theory then provides us with a constraint IDENT[VOI]/[ω__ specific to ω-initial elements. Ranked above REALIZE-M, it has the desired effect of preventing the linking morpheme ℜ from being realized in ω-initial position (since this always involves a breach of voicing faithfulness within the affected segment). The resulting subhierarchy in (39) has the formal structure F/p ≫ C ≫ F of positional faithfulness explanations.

(39) IDENT[VOI]/[ω__

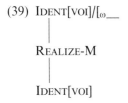

REALIZE-M

IDENT[VOI]

Since the interface constraint hierarchy of section 8.3.1 (ANCHOR-L^2_s ≫ No-STRUC[ω] ≫ ANCHOR-L) ranks above this faithfulness block, the competition is already lost for all candidates without the appropriate prosodic structuring. This is illustrated in tableaux (40) and (41), where ANCHOR-L^2_s removes candidates (e)–(h) from the competition in (40), and No-STRUC[ω] does the same for candidates (a)–(d) in (41). As a consequence, *sakura* is bound to be ω-initial in whatever candidate wins the competition in (40), but ω-internal in the one that wins in (41). The high-ranking ω-initial version of IDENT[VOI]/[ω__ does the rest, dictating that ω-initial *sakura* remains faithfully voiceless in the winning candidate (40a), violating REALIZE-M with respect to the linking morpheme ℜ. On the other hand, no special faithfulness prevents voicing of the ω-internal *zakura* in (41f).

(40) *Right-branching γ-structure*

{{yósino} + ℜ + {{sakura} + ℜ + {táyori}}}	*Interface constraints*	IDENT[VOI] /[ω__	REALIZE-M	IDENT[VOI]
a. ▶ [o⌐] [s da⌐]	...		*	*
b. [o⌐] [z da⌐]	...	*!		**
c. [o⌐] [s ta⌐]	...		**!	
d. [o⌐] [z ta⌐]	...	*!	*	*
e. [s da⌐]	*!ANCHOR-L^2_s		*	*
f. [z da⌐]	*!ANCHOR-L^2_s			**
g. [s ta⌐]	*!ANCHOR-L^2_s		**	
h. [z ta⌐]	*!ANCHOR-L^2_s		*	*

(41) *Left-branching γ-structure*

{{{yósino} + ℜ + {sakura}} + ℜ + {táyori}}	*Interface constraints*	IDENT[VOI] /[ω__	REALIZE-M	IDENT[VOI]
a. [o⌐ s] [da⌐]	*!No-Struc[ω]	*	*	*
b. [o⌐ z] [da⌐]	*!No-Struc[ω]	*		**
c. [o⌐ s] [ta⌐]	*!No-Struc[ω]		**	
d. [o⌐ z] [ta⌐]	*!No-Struc[ω]		*	*
e. [s da⌐]	. . .		*!	*
f. ▶ [z da⌐]	. . .			**
g. [s ta⌐]	. . .		*!*	
h. [z ta⌐]	. . .		*!	*

While a positional faithfulness account is easily developed along such lines, we also need to consider a fundamentally different way of construing the situation, namely, in terms of markedness. For example, coda devoicing facts can, broadly speaking, be interpreted either as "onset position faithfulness" or as "coda position markedness" (we return to this point in section 8.4.1).

Expressed in terms of OT constraints, positional markedness takes several forms. First, there are direct statements of the general form M/α creating a version of the markedness constraint M specific to position α. Since such statements say what needs to be said but cast no further light on the matter, two different ways have been explored of deriving positional markedness effects in a more principled fashion. In cases where the position has an explicit markedness constraint directed against it (such as NO-CODA), constraint conjunction offers an attractive means of understanding why the marked is banned from a marked position (see Smolensky 1995; Ito and Mester 1997b, 1998; chapter 2 above). But constraint conjunction can only give rise to a specific variety of positional markedness effects since it can only reach positions that can be pinpointed by a specific constraint, which is unlikely to exhaust all relevant positions.

Positional markedness effects of a different kind do not involve explicitly ruling out the marked in certain positions (whether by constraint conjunction or by direct stipulation). Rather, they arise because the marked is explicitly required to be aligned/anchored to certain other positions, such as prosodic heads or edges of particular constituents. This is the type of positional markedness studied in Ito and Mester 1994, 1999b, with significant further development in Zoll 1997. Generally speaking, all the positions of prominence $p \in P$ that figure in positional faithfulness accounts are available for the anchoring of marked properties. This has an important advantage over any attempt to directly outlaw marked properties in nonprominent positions. Unlike the set of prominent positions P, the elements of the complement set $\bar{P}$ have nothing in common except the very absence of prominence. In other words, there is no way of referring to the elements of $\bar{P}$ in a general form without implicitly or explicitly referring to P.[17]

A positional markedness counterpart to the faithfulness account presented earlier consists of a higher-ranked position-specific version of the basic constraint against voiced obstruents No-D, narrowed down to ω-initial position.[18] Ranked above REALIZE-M, the new constraint No-D/[ω__ prevents the linking morpheme ℜ from being realized in this position by markedness alone (underlying voicing is protected by higher-ranking IO faithfulness for voiced segments; see (46)).

(42)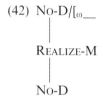

Tableaux (43) and (44) illustrate the positional markedness account. Only the candidates that successfully pass through the higher-ranking interface constraints are considered here (see the discussion in connection with (40) and (41)), so (43) shows only candidates with two prosodic words, and (44) shows only candidates with one prosodic word.

(43) *Right-branching γ-structure: two prosodic words*

{{yósino} + ℜ + {{sakura} + ℜ + {táyori}}}	No-D /[ω__	REALIZE-M	No-D
a. ▶ [oꜛ] [s daꜛ]		*	*
b. [oꜛ] [z daꜛ]	*!		**
c. [oꜛ] [s taꜛ]		**!	
d. [oꜛ] [z taꜛ]	*!	*	*

(44) *Left-branching γ-structure: one prosodic word*

{{{yósino} + ℜ + {sakura}} + ℜ + {táyori}}	No-D /[ω__	Realize-M	No-D
e. [s da⌐]		*!	*
f. ▶ [z da⌐]			**
g. [s ta⌐]		*!*	
h. [z ta⌐]		*!	*

In their overall architecture, the approaches built on faithfulness (39) and markedness (42) are similar: in both cases, a high-ranking positional constraint, which crucially relies on the ω-parsing dictated by the interface constraints, is introduced in the hierarchy above Realize-M, as shown in (45).

(45) *Positional faithfulness   Positional markedness*

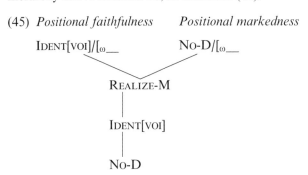

In the earlier examples illustrating the two alternatives (see (37), (38), (40), and (41)), the candidates violating the positional faithfulness constraint (for having changed underlying voicing ω-initially) also violate the positional markedness constraint (for containing voiced obstruents ω-initially), and vice versa. The two approaches do differ in how they handle candidates with underlyingly voiced ω-initial segments, but without yielding a decisive argument either way. The faithfulness approach already protects underlyingly voiced ω-initial segments such as the *g* in *geta* 'clogs' against devoicing. For the markedness approach, it must be the case that the positional constraint is dominated by the faithfulness constraint against devoicing, as shown for the simple word *geta* in (46).

(46) geta *'clogs'*

{geta}	*Faithfulness constraint against devoicing*	No-D/[_ω__
a. ▶ geta		*
b. keta	*!	

It is important to note that this does not involve any special protection of the initial segment by a positional faithfulness constraint (which would amount to a problematic redundancy for the positional markedness approach). Rather, a general and independently motivated constraint against devoicing (stated in some form—say, as IDENT[+VOI] or the conjunction AGREE[VOI]&IDENT[VOI]; see chapter 7 for detailed discussion), outranks No-D/[_ω__.

The two approaches thus seem to fare equally well in their overall empirical coverage. Comparing them from a broader perspective, not merely with respect to the narrow question of how they perform their work in the current analysis, we find that the positional markedness conception has two points in its favor. First, a markedness restriction against word-initial voiced obstruents is phonetically well motivated since obstruent voicing in this position presents significant implementational (as well as perceptual) difficulties, as is well known from elementary phonetics and cross-linguistically visible in the partial voicing of plosives in this position. The difficulty of making the onset of voicing coincide precisely with the start of the articulatory gestures for the consonant leads to significant lags in voice onset time, often resulting in scenarios where the actual phonetic cue separating the two series of stops is aspiration instead of voicing.

Second, turning to the specific case of Japanese, a positional markedness constraint against ω-initial voiced obstruents—unlike a positional faithfulness constraint specific to ω-initial position—enjoys direct empirical support from earlier stages of the language. In Old Japanese (eighth century A.D.), obstruent voicing was contrastive in internal positions, but voiced obstruents did not occur word-initially (see, e.g., Unger 1975, 8; Frellesvig 1995, 65–68). Exactly the same distributional contrast existed for the rhotic [r], which occurred only word-internally. Crosslinguistically, this is one instance of a broad pattern of "fortition" or "augmentation" characterizing prominent positions, such as the beginning of the word (cf. the ban against word-initial [ʒ] and [ŋ] in English, etc.; and see Smith 2001 and de Lacy 2001 for general discussion and exemplification).

This kind of restriction can be made sense of only as positional markedness, not as positional faithfulness—the latter would lead to more voicing contrasts initially than medially, exactly the opposite of the Old Japanese facts. Even in Modern

Japanese, ω-initial faithfulness does not sit well with the statistically still persisting underrepresentation of voiced obstruents in word-initial position (see section 2.3.1). The only descriptively adequate way of capturing the Old Japanese facts would be to protect all *medial* positions by special faithfulness, thus in effect exposing only the ω-initial position to the full force of No-D—but this is incompatible with the fundamental tenet that positional faithfulness is tropic to positions of some sort of prominence.

Given these considerations, we will adopt the positional markedness approach, summarizing the ranking of all constraints involved in (47). Further issues regarding faithfulness versus markedness will be discussed in section 8.4.1.

(47) *Summary of the positional markedness analysis*

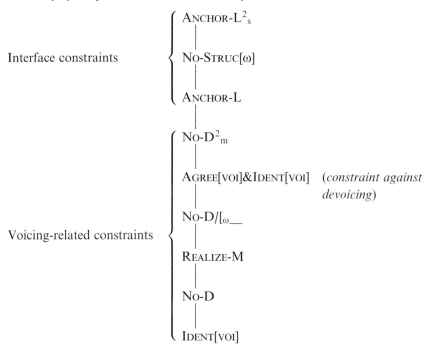

8.4 Further Issues

In this section, we first take up the general problem of overlap in analysis and empirical coverage between positional markedness and faithfulness approaches, and we discuss related issues and their theoretical implications (section 8.4.1). We then return to the prosodic structures that determine accentuation and *rendaku* realization in compounds and discuss additional factors influencing the accentual properties of long compounds that do not necessarily correlate with *rendaku* (section 8.4.2). Finally, we show that our approach anchored in tangible prosodic properties of the output form, besides its overall advantage in theory and analysis, also has an empirical point in its favor over the cyclic/derivational line of approach characteristic of past accounts (section 8.4.3).

8.4.1   Coda Devoicing Revisited

Overlap in coverage and redundancy in analysis between positional faithfulness and positional markedness are not uncommon, and there is no straightforward way of pronouncing one of them correct since they both have their virtues. For the case involving the absence of *rendaku* voicing from ω-initial position, we showed in section 8.3.2 that the markedness and faithfulness approaches also fare equally well in overall empirical coverage, and we adduced phonetic and historical arguments in favor of the latter approach.

Arguing along entirely different lines, Prince and Tesar (1999, 19–23) show that adding positional faithfulness constraints to the basic OT framework brings with it a particular kind of learning problem that positional markedness is free of. Building on earlier work (Tesar 1995; Prince 1997; Tesar and Smolensky 1998), they develop an algorithm for the acquisition of OT grammars on the basis of purely distributional evidence (i.e., without alternations and nontrivial underlying forms) that incorporates a markedness-over-faithfulness ranking bias. The problem is that for the algorithm to work correctly, when it becomes necessary to insert a faithfulness constraint into the hierarchy, the faithfulness constraint with the fewest additional consequences needs to be selected; otherwise, a nonrecoverable learning error cannot be excluded. But in a theory with the special/general relationships between faithfulness constraints characteristic of positional faithfulness, there is no general way of enabling the learner to make this selection correctly. As Prince and Tesar (1999, 22–23) show, the idea of adding a metaconstraint with the effect of always picking "the special over the general," while deceptively simple, in fact hides the real problem: namely, how to identify the existence of a special/general relation between two constraints. Far from being decidable merely by inspecting the formulation of the constraints, it depends on the details of the individual constraint hierarchy and requires a rather complex meta-analysis of the grammar itself, and of the way in which it sifts the set of candidates. No comparable problem arises for positional markedness, and while leaving the issue unresolved, Prince and Tesar (1999, 23) note that "[s]hort of complete elimination of positional faithfulness, one might nevertheless hope to minimize the problem by minimizing dependence on positional faithfulness in favor of positional markedness. . . ."

Here we turn to a relatively simple and well-studied example, namely, coda devoicing of the kind seen in Dutch and German (analyzed in section 2.2.2 in terms of constraint-conjunctive positional markedness). To focus attention on the main differences, we express the positional markedness approach here by means of the direct and unadorned statement NO-D/CODA, sidestepping any potentially distracting theoretical commitments. We are faced with the two alternative explanations for coda devoicing in (48) and (49), using the German word *grob* 'coarse' as an example. Both are position-focused, but one proceeds in terms of faithfulness, the other in terms of markedness.

In the positional faithfulness view of syllable-final devoicing, the basic generalization is that voiced obstruents are ruled out in a context-free way (NO-D ≫ IDENT[VOI]). But in positions of prominence such as onset (or "released consonant"— see Padgett 1995a; Steriade 1995a), a voicing contrast is allowed to arise. In other words, obstruent voicing is noncontrastive everywhere except in onsets.

(48) *Positional faithfulness: coda devoicing*

/gro:b/	IDENT[VOI]/ONS	NO-D	IDENT[VOI]
▶ gro:p		*	*
gro:b		**!	
kro:p	*!		**

From this perspective, there are literally no coda conditions in phonology, or other such positional markedness effects. Rather, the whole explanation is cast in terms of faithfulness and is focused on strong positions such as onsets. Codas are not singled out in any way as being weak; they are simply included among the nonstrong positions.

The positional markedness view is entirely different: here German/Dutch is characterized by a context-free voicing contrast (IDENT[VOI] ≫ NO-D), but position-specific markedness in codas (or alternatively, in unreleased consonants) neutralizes the contrast in one specific context. In other words, obstruent voicing is contrastive everywhere except in codas.

(49) *Positional markedness: coda devoicing*

/gro:b/	NO-D/CODA	IDENT[VOI]	NO-D
▶ gro:p		*	*
gro:b	*!		**
kro:p		**!	

Both theories have their limitations; and while they overlap in many cases, they are in some respects complementary. Zoll (1998) has shown that positional markedness constraints are an irreducible part of phonological theory and cannot be subsumed under faithfulness considerations. Thus, in many Australian languages the familiar limitation of vowel length to the first (and main-stressed) syllable of a prosodic word extends beyond faithfulness to cases where vowel length is not a faithfully preserved input property, but arises through an alternation triggered by another element (i.e., as a faithfulness *violation*). It is therefore an issue not of letting input vowel length through only in position p (faithfulness), but of allowing output vowel length only in position p (markedness).

For the case at hand, it is also clear that the idea of reducing all coda neutralization phenomena to the faithfulness differential between nonprominent and prominent positions cannot succeed as a general program, and for a similar reason: featurally marked codas are banned independently of faithfulness. Thus, in systems where palatalization, aspiration, voicing, and the like, are used as suprasegmental markers ("floating autosegments"; see McCarthy 1983 and Mester and Ito 1989 for examples), onsets are crosslinguistically preferred as anchors, not codas. This is not enhanced faithfulness in onset position—rather the opposite. In fact, the positional faithfulness scheme IDENT-ONS ≫ M ≫ IDENT predicts the opposite: codas should constitute ideal anchors to associate morphemic palatalization markers and the like, not onsets. Such failed predictions highlight the built-in limitations of exclusively faithfulness-based accounts. The common thread uniting the greater inventory found in prominent positions ("faithfulness") and their simultaneous greater capacity to absorb superimposed features must be sought not in faithfulness, but in a more basic phonetic/phonological factor, namely, the markedness differential between the two kinds of positions. This leads to the conclusion that positional markedness must remain a part of the theory.[19]

As an argument for a positional faithfulness account of German/Dutch syllable-final devoicing, Lombardi (2001) makes the interesting typological claim that crosslinguistically, vowel epenthesis is never used to "rescue" voiced obstruents in codas as an alternative to devoicing.[20] The idea is that the absence of epenthesis is a predictable consequence of the assumptions of positional faithfulness theory—in particular, of the absence of any positional markedness constraint against voiced obstruent codas. The core of the argument is reproduced in tableau (50).

(50) *Epenthesis candidate (c) as a perennial loser (i.e., under any ranking)*

/gro:b/	IDENT[VOI]/ONS	NO-D	IDENT[VOI]	DEP
a. gro:p		*	*	
b. gro:b		**		
harmonically bounded by (b) c. gro:bə		**		*

For an input like /gro:b/, the epenthesizing candidate (50c) [gro:bə] can never emerge as a winner, wherever DEP (here, militating against vowel insertion) is ranked, since it is harmonically bounded by (50b) [gro:b]. It does not matter that (50b) has a voiced obstruent coda—the positional faithfulness approach crucially assumes that no markedness constraint exists that is specifically directed against codas of this kind. Candidate (50b) violates only the general markedness constraint against voiced obstruents, and this violation is shared by (50c), which has an additional DEP violation.

Closer inspection reveals, however, that this argument for the superiority of the positional faithfulness approach does not quite succeed. First, from the point of view of the phonetic groundedness of constraints, the putative absence of positional markedness constraints targeting laryngeal features in syllable codas is rather surprising since such constraints would enjoy some of the best motivation that exists in this area, codas being notorious among the positions poor in cues for obstruent voicing and the like, as amply documented in the work of Steriade (1995a) and others.

Second, there are indications that the absence of a markedness constraint against voiced obstruent codas, far from being an advantage for phonological theory, is a handicap. The problem arises in connection with the supposed total absence of epenthesis as a repair strategy as in (50), which is empirically questionable. Thus, there is some evidence that at least in second language acquisition and other situations involving language contact, epenthetic vowels do indeed appear. For example, some speakers of German/Dutch, with only limited knowledge of nondevoicing languages such as French or English, have been observed to use protective epenthetic schwa-type vowels of the kind seen in (50c) to preserve word-final voiced obstruents. Barring the rather implausible claim that such euphonic adjustments are always to be analyzed as underlying vowels posited in the input, a version of OT with positional faithfulness but without coda-specific markedness constraints cannot provide a constraint ranking that generates the interlanguage produced by such speakers.

In the case of German, there is independent historical evidence along similar lines showing that the harmonic bounding relation seen in (50) is invalid. As part of a group of sweeping apocope processes characterizing the transition from Middle to New High German, adjectives, together with many other kinds of lexical items, lost their final [ə] (orthographic ⟨e⟩). This resulted in changes like *sü*[s]*e* > *sü*[s] 'sweet' and *schöne* > *schön* 'beautiful', where a final schwa is ungrammatical in the modern language. Apocope had exceptions, however, and final [ə] was preserved in a number of cases, either quasi-obligatorily, as in *müde* 'tired', *bö*[z]*e* 'evil', *lei*[z]*e* 'soft', and *träge* 'listless', or optionally, as in *ba*[ŋg]*e* 'afraid'[21] and *lo*[z]*e* 'loose'. The interesting point here is what most exceptions to apocope have in common: the consonant preceding the final vowel of the adjective was a voiced obstruent.[22]

While avoidance of apocope is not the same as across-the-board epenthesis,[23] the logic of the situation is similar. This is shown in (51), which depicts the historical stage when apocope was an active process. Here, the supposed strength of the positional faithfulness account—the harmonic bounding of (51c) by (51b) due to the absence of a NO-D/CODA constraint—becomes a liability. We can remain noncommittal regarding the identity and ranking of the constraint(s) driving apocope. The crucial point is that the nonapocopating candidate (51c), the real-world winner, has no chance of winning in this positional faithfulness scenario.

(51) *Apocope-avoiding actual output (c) wrongly declared a perennial loser:* müde 'tired'

/my:də/	IDENT[VOI]/ONS	NO-D	IDENT[VOI]	*Constraint(s) driving apocope*
a. my:t			*	
b. my:d		*		
harmonically bounded by (b) c. my:də		*		*

The problem for the positional faithfulness view is how to make sense of such facts, which are probably not restricted to this one case: since there is literally no markedness factor distinguishing voiced obstruents in onsets and in codas, what is the point of violating the apocope requirement in such cases? Positional markedness has no trouble with the situation since it is virtually built on the assumption that there is a markedness constraint specifically targeting voiced obstruent codas, which bars candidate (52b) and thus opens the way for the nonapocopating (52c).

(52) *Positional markedness ranking selecting apocope-suppressing candidate (c):*
      müde *'tired'*

/myːdə/	No-D/Coda	*Ident[voi]	No-D	*Constraint(s) driving apocope*
a. myːt		*!		
b. myːd	*!			
c. ▶ myːdə			*	*

8.4.2 *Rendaku* and Accentual Domains

Through the assignment of prosodic word structure by the interface constraints and
the positional constraint on ω-initial elements, the analysis developed in section 8.3.1
predicts that the realization of the linking morpheme ℜ in long compounds in Japanese should go hand in hand with the accentual pattern. As summarized in (53),
rendaku should correlate with one accentual domain, and absence of *rendaku* with
two accentual domains.

(53) *Accentual domains in compounds*

	a. Left-branching compound	b. Right-branching compound
γ-structure:	{{{X} {Y}} {Z}}	{{X} {{Y} {Z}}}
ω-structure:	[ ]	[ ] [ ]
	• *rendaku* on Y	• no *rendaku* on Y
	• one accentual domain	• two accentual domains

There is thus a sharp division between "lexical" prosodic structures of compounds
as in (54a) (which include ordinary two-word compounds) and the special group of
"phrasal" parses in (54b).

(54) *Lexical (single-ω) versus phrasal (double-ω) parses*

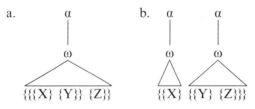

Here α denotes the prosodic constituent dominating the prosodic word ω in the prosodic hierarchy. In Japanese, α is the domain of initial lowering (labeled *accentual*

phrase by Pierrehumbert and Beckman (1988) and *minor phrase* by other authors, including McCawley (1968), Kubozono (1988, 1993), and Selkirk and Tateishi (1988)). In the general case, more than one ω can be grouped into a single α as long as only one ω is accented (see the works cited for detailed discussion).

A more thorough study of long compounds reveals, however, that this distributional parallelism between *rendaku* and accent in compounds is not complete. While it remains true that all *rendaku*-accepting forms (left-branching compounds) have at most one accent (i.e., constitute a single accentual domain), not all *rendaku*-rejecting right-branching compounds have two accentual domains, as shown by the examples in (55).

(55) Rendaku-*accent relation in long compounds*

	One accentual domain	Two accentual domains
Rendaku	a. nara zuke ga⌐kari '{Nara-pickle} business' yo zakura da⌐yori '{night-cherry} festival'	b.
No *rendaku*	c. tokusan tu⌐ke mono 'specialty {pickled-items}' zenkoku ku⌐mi ai 'nationwide {(group-) union}'	d. kyo⌐oto tukemono kyo⌐okai 'Kyoto {pickling-association}' ze⌐nkoku sakura da⌐yori 'nationwide {cherry-tidings}'

Besides (55a) and (55d), corresponding to the parses in (53a) and (53b), there is a type of parse that is in a sense intermediate, namely, (55c): a right-branching γ-structure without *rendaku* that nevertheless does not split into two accentual domains. Furthermore, Kubozono, Ito, and Mester (1997) show that the latter (single accentual domain with no *rendaku*) has two subtypes, one with a compound-specific junctural accent (see section 8.2.1 above), the other retaining the lexical accent structure of the second member. What remains impossible, however, is (55b): a long compound showing *rendaku* and splitting into two accentual domains at the same point.

The defining phonological characteristics of these four different compound types are summarized in (56).

(56) *Characteristics found in long compounds*

Compound types	(i)	(ii)	(iii)	(iv)
One accentual domain	yes	yes	yes	no
Junctural compound accent	yes	yes	no	no
Rendaku	yes	no	no	no

For the analysis to successfully accommodate both the existence of single accentual domains with no *rendaku* and the nonexistence of compounds with two accentual domains with *rendaku*, the crucial prerequisite is a fuller grasp of the range of prosodic structures found in Japanese compounds. Expanding the narrow lexical-phrasal dichotomy posited earlier in (54), we propose a more articulated overall typology of prosodic compound structures, including the option of recursive prosodic word structure. As shown in (57), at least four types are distinguished, with systematically different properties outlined in (56).

(57) *Overall prosodic typology of compound structures*

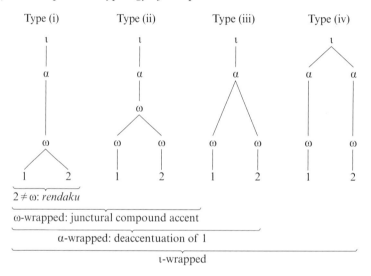

Besides the recursive ω in (ii), the basic distinction among the structures in (57) is the wrapping domain, going up the prosodic hierarchy from ω (prosodic word), to α (accentual phrase), to ι (intermediate phrase).[24] The prosodic word ω is the domain of the compound accent rule, which assigns a compound-specific accent at the juncture of the compound members. The α-phrase is the domain of deaccentuation (allowing at most one accent within it) and is furthermore characterized by an initial rising tone. The ι-phrase is the domain of the phonetic process of downstep (or catathesis), whereby each accent triggers a lowering of the following tones within the same ι-phrase.

In terms of this prosodic typology, deaccentuation of the first (nonhead) member is found in structure types (i), (ii), and (iii) of (57)—that is, in all cases except (iv), where it constitutes an α-domain by itself and therefore preserves its lexical accent. On the other hand, the assignment of a new compound-specific accent—namely, at the juncture between the two members—is an exclusive property of the ω-wrapped structures (i) and (ii).

(58) *Examples of prosodic typology of compound structures*

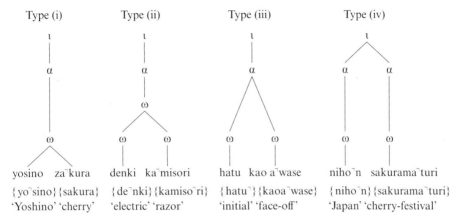

Type (i)	Type (ii)	Type (iii)	Type (iv)
yosino za⌐kura	denki ka⌐misori	hatu kao a⌐wase	niho⌐n sakurama⌐turi
{yo⌐sino}{sakura}	{de⌐nki}{kamiso⌐ri}	{hatu⌐}{kaoa⌐wase}	{niho⌐n}{sakurama⌐turi}
'Yoshino' 'cherry'	'electric' 'razor'	'initial' 'face-off'	'Japan' 'cherry-festival'

In *yosino za⌐kura* (58)(i), lexically unaccented *sakura* receives a compound accent, whereas lexically accented *yo⌐sino* is deaccented; in *denki ka⌐misori* (58)(ii), lexically accented *de⌐nki* is deaccented, whereas *kamiso⌐ri*'s accent "moves" to the junctural position. The non-ω-wrapped compound structures (58)(iii) and (iv), on the other hand, are characterized by the absence of compound-specific accentuation in their two members, except that in the α-wrapped (58)(iii) the first member *hatu⌐* is deaccented.[25] *Rendaku* is blocked whenever the second member constitutes a ω-domain, not only in (58)(iv) with its two parallel α-domains (making two accentual domains), but also in (58)(ii) and (iii), where the first (nonhead) member is deaccented, resulting in one accentual domain. This, then, is the structural reason why the empirical correlation between *rendaku* and single accent holds only in one direction: *rendaku* implies single accent (= (57)(i)), but single accent is compatible with structures allowing *rendaku* (= (57)(i)) and those disallowing *rendaku* (= (57)(ii) and (iii)).

In terms of the grammar-prosody mapping illustrated in (59), all left-branching γ-structures have a single ω-structure and fall into pattern (i), with *rendaku* realization and maximally one accent, whereas for right-branching γ-structures three prosodic parses (ii)–(iv) are in principle possible (prosodic structures are given with bracketed labels equivalent to the tree-structural format above).

(59) *Grammar-prosody mapping*

γ-structures	left-branching {{{X}{Y}}{Z}}		right-branching {{X}{{Y}{Z}}}	
	(i)	(ii)	(iii)	(iv)
p-structures	ι: [ ]	ι: [ ]	ι: [ ]	ι: [ ]
	α: [ ]	α: [ ]	α: [ ]	α: [ ][ ]
	ω: [X Y Z]	ω: [[X] [Y Z]]	ω: [X] [Y Z]	ω: [X] [Y Z]

These mapping relations raise two questions. First, why are *three* different prosodic structures allowed for right-branching compounds? And second, why are there no comparable multiple prosodic parsings of left-branching γ-structures? Answers to both questions partially emerge as we compare, for each type of γ-structure, how the four options are evaluated by the high-ranking interface constraints proposed in section 8.3.1. The tableaux in (60) and (61) show the results for left-branching and right-branching γ-structures, respectively.

(60) *Left-branching γ-structure*

{{{X} {Y}} {Z}}	ANCHOR-L^2_s	NO-STRUC[ω]	ANCHOR-L

a. ▶ ι: [   ]
   α: [   ]
   ω: [X Y   Z]
		*	*Y *Z

b.   ι: [   ]
   α: [   ]
   ω: [[X Y] [Z]]
		**!	*Y

c.   ι: [   ]
   α: [   ]
   ω: [X Y] [Z]
		**!	*Y

d.   ι: [   ]
   α: [   ] [ ]
   ω: [X Y] [Z]
		**!	*Y

(61) *Right-branching γ-structure*

{{X} {{Y} {Z}}}	Anchor-L^2_s	No-Struc[ω]	Anchor-L
a.　ι: [　　　　] α: [　　　　] ω: [X　Y　Z]	*!	*	*Z, **Y
b. ▶ ι: [　　　　] α: [　　　　] ω: [[X] [Y Z]]		**	*Z
c. ▶ ι: [　　　　] α: [　　　　] ω: [X] [Y　Z]		**	*Z
d. ▶ ι: [　　　　] α: [ ] [　　] ω: [X] [Y　Z]		**	*Z

For right-branching compounds (61), the relevant structures are tied in terms of the interface constraints seen here. Different candidates emerge as winners through the interaction of lower-ranked prosodic constraints. Thus, No-Recursivity is violated by candidate (61b); No-Struc[α] is violated by candidate (61d); and the candidates (61c,d) incur a violation of the constraint Wrap proposed by Truckenbrodt (1999), requiring syntactic/morphological units to be contained within the appropriate prosodic category. In contrast, for the left-branching compound (60) the winning prosodic structure has already been unambiguously determined by the high-ranking interface constraints, so lower-ranked constraints do not have a chance to influence the outcome.

A detailed constraint-ranking analysis determining the final winning prosodic structure for right-branching inputs lies beyond the scope of this book since it would take us too far into the analysis of accent and accentual phrases in Japanese (see Kubozono, Ito, and Mester 1997 and references cited there for relevant discussion). Among the factors triggering the parsing of second members as separate accentual domains, we find not only a branching γ-structure, but also prosodic factors. Thus, Kubozono (1995, 23) observes that a length restriction is at work: when used as the second member of a compound, items comprising more than four moras, even when monomorphemic, such as *kariforunia* 'California', form their own accentual domain and resist the imposition of an overall compound accent. Thus, *minami kariforunia* 'southern California' is unaccented, preserving the unaccentedness of the base word (compound accentuation would result in the ungrammatical *minami ka'riforunia).[26] Accentual independence of the second member does not automatically entail accentual independence of the first member; rather, the two are independent of each other. Retention of the accent of the first member is not automatic, but instead depends on a host of semantic, pragmatic, and prosodic factors.

The observation that accent pattern and *rendaku* voicing often go hand in hand has sometimes given rise to the mistaken impression that there is a direct dependency of some kind, with two accents in a compound literally causing the absence of *rendaku*, and *rendaku* literally preventing the separate accents in the two parts—sometimes even culminating in the idea that *rendaku* might itself be some kind of accent. From the current perspective, this constitutes a confusion between observations to be explained and explanatory principles. What is missing is the central piece, namely, the underlying prosodic structures that both accent and *rendaku* are responsive to. In the analysis developed here, there are no constraints linking accent and *rendaku* directly to each other, and this is necessarily so: constraints are universal and do not express language-particular correlations between observational generalizations. The overall picture that emerges is familiar from many other studies in prosodic phonology. There is no direct and exact correspondence of any kind between *rendaku* and accent. Rather, they are intrinsically connected in many ways because they are both anchored in the more abstract prosodic structures that organize speech, and a specific link is provided by the prosodic word (ω), a central element of prosodic form. As shown in section 8.3.2, voicing constraints are sensitive to edges of prosodic words, and accentual units are built on prosodic words (through independent anchoring constraints). Since the two independent processes both refer to the same prosodic structure, they often appear in the same environment. Unlike any analysis claiming direct dependence of *rendaku* and accent, ours predicts that the two will diverge in certain cases.

8.4.3 Anchoring versus Cyclicity: An Empirical Point of Difference

The proposal in section 8.3 accounts for the basic structural blocking of *rendaku* in long compounds in terms of two factors: prosodic anchoring creates internal ω-domains in long compounds, and positional markedness bans voiced obstruents initially in ω-domains. In incorporating some of the insights that set current OT apart from earlier models of phonology, the overall analysis automatically enjoys a general kind of advantage over earlier proposals. However, it is also appropriate to ask whether the new approach brings with it any direct empirical advantages (i.e., setting aside conceptual considerations and comparisons in the context of general phonological theory). In terms of analytical detail and empirical coverage, its chief rival is the cyclic OCP-based analysis we proposed in Ito and Mester 1986.

Taking Otsu's (1980) statement of structural blocking (by a prohibition clause formulated directly in terms of grammatical branching; see section 8.1.1 above) as an observation to be explained in terms of more basic principles, our 1986 cyclic analysis argues that the influence of grammatical branching is indirect, following from the fact that *rendaku* and Lyman's Law (i.e., the OCP) apply cyclically, hence retrace the structure of the compound. In this framework, the structural blocking of *rendaku* in right-branching compounds is not a separate stipulation, but one of the OCP effects triggered by the floating (and often unrealized) feature [+voi]. The basic claim is that structural blocking is already predicted by the general way in which phonology and structure interact in Lexical Phonology (Kiparsky 1982, 1985), once a proper understanding of the phonological constraint (OCP) and the morphophonemic process (*rendaku*) involved has been reached.

The current prosodic anchoring proposal concurs with the cyclic OCP-based analysis that there is no need and no place for a branching condition, and more generally, that phonology does not need the power implied by such direct reference to grammatical branching. On the other hand, the prosodic anchoring analysis differs crucially from the cyclic OCP-based analysis in that (i) there is no cyclic derivation, (ii) there is no floating feature [+voi], and (iii) the OCP is not responsible for the right-branch effects. Instead, a nonderivational structural solution is built on independently motivated prosodic form and positional markedness, where the relevant constraints interact with each other, and with the rest of the phonology, in new ways made possible by OT. Discarding all differences irrelevant for the empirical comparison, we set the two explanations side by side in (62).

(62) *Two explanations for the nonrealization of $\mathfrak{R}_1$ in right-branching compounds (example:* hatu kao awase *'first {face-meeting}, first sumo match between two* rikisi'*)*

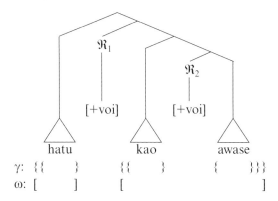

• Prosodic anchoring account: *kao* is ω-initial.
• Cyclic OCP account (Ito and Mester 1986): $\mathfrak{R}_2$'s [+voi] triggers deletion of $\mathfrak{R}_1$'s [+voi] via the OCP on the voicing tier and then disappears itself.

The two accounts agree that $\mathfrak{R}_2$ leaves no imprint on the output because the first segment [a] of *awase* cannot realize it in a distinctive way. But from this point on, the explanations diverge. For the prosodic anchoring account, $\mathfrak{R}_1$ remains unrealized because positional markedness prohibits the creation of voiced obstruents in ω-initial position. For the cyclic OCP account, even though $\mathfrak{R}_2$'s [+voi] remains unattached (and ultimately deletes by the convention of Stray Erasure), it leads to the prior disappearance of $\mathfrak{R}_1$'s [+voi] by virtue of the OCP's applying on the voicing tier.

Over large areas, the two accounts are empirically indistinguishable, but fortunately there is one class of cases in which the cyclic OCP account and the prosodic anchoring account make different predictions. As discussed in chapter 6, *rendaku* voicing is restricted to native (and nativized) items and is not found with forms from the other lexical strata of Japanese. As shown in the same context, even among native Yamato compounds, two types systematically avoid *rendaku* voicing: (i) dvandva compounds (i.e., coordinate or double-headed compounds, such as *oyako* 'parent and child'), and (ii) deverbal nominals in which the second (head) member is a transitive verb stem and the first member a noun constituting its direct object, such as *sakana-tsuri* 'fish-catching, fishing'.

Of interest here is the behavior of such *rendaku*-rejecting forms as subcompounds embedded inside larger compounds. Examples with such compounds as first and second members are given in (63) and (64), respectively.

(63) *Dvandvas and deverbal compounds as the first member of a compound*

{{oya + ko} + $\mathfrak{R}$ + kenka}   [oya ko **genka**]   {parent + child} 'family quarrel'
{{kusa + ki} + $\mathfrak{R}$ + some}   [kusa ki **zome**]   {grass + tree} 'plant dyeing'
{{kami + sori} + $\mathfrak{R}$ + kai}   [kami sori **gai**]   {hair + shave} 'razor/jackknife clam'

(64) *Dvandvas and deverbal compounds as the second member of a compound*

{kinzokusee + $\mathfrak{R}$ + {te + asi}}   [kinzokusee [te asi]]   {hands + feet} 'metal limbs'
{utyuuzin + $\mathfrak{R}$ + {oya + ko}}   [utyuuzin [oya ko]]   {parent + child} 'outer-space family'
{anzen + $\mathfrak{R}$ + {kami + sori}}   [anzen [kami sori]]   {hair + shaver} 'safety razor'

The larger compound here is a normal *rendaku*-inducing compound, and as expected we find *rendaku* voicing in (63). The difference between the cyclic OCP and prosodic anchoring approaches revolves around the nonappearance of *rendaku* in the larger compound in (64). Under the prosodic anchoring approach, the nonapplication of *rendaku* is expected, since the inner compound (e.g., *kami sori*) is mapped onto a prosodic word.[27] On the other hand, the cyclic OCP approach, in its exclusive reliance on either underlying obstruent voicing or cyclically inserted *rendaku* voicing, incorrectly predicts that *rendaku* will apply, since no *rendaku* morpheme has been inserted on the cycle of the non-*rendaku* compound. If all structural blocking of *rendaku* is to be reduced to the OCP on voicing, a principled account for this kind of case is thus lacking.[28] Here we have, then, an empirical point in favor of the current nonderivational and noncyclic proposal driven by prosodic anchoring—a reassuring result.

Epilogue

At the end of our year-long research visit to Kyoto, the old capital, we realize that we have just scratched the surface of the rich system of Japanese morphophonemics, concentrating on a few prominent aspects. We leave the last words to Sei Shōnagon (born ca. 967, from her *Makura-no sōsi* 'Pillow Book'):

春はあけぼの。やうやうしろくなりゆく、山ぎはすこしあかりて、紫だちたる雲の細くたなびきたる。

夏は夜。月のころはさらなり、闇もなほ、蛍の多く飛びちがひたる。また、ただ一つ二つなど、ほのかにうち光りて行くもをかし。雨など降るもをかし。

秋は夕ぐれ。夕日のさして、山の端いと近うなりたるに、烏の寝どころへ行くとて、三つ四つ、二つ三つなど飛び急ぐさへあはれなり。まいて、雁などの連ねたるが、いと小さく見ゆるはいとをかし。日入り果てて、風の音・虫の音など、はた言ふべきにあらず。

冬はつとめて。雪の降りたるは、言ふべきにもあらず、霜のいと白きも、またさらでも、いと寒きに、火など急ぎおこして、炭もて渡るもいとつきづきし。昼になりて、ぬるくゆるびもていけば、火桶の火も、白き灰がちになりてわろし。

清少納言「枕草子」

In the translation by Ivan Morris (1991):

In spring it is the dawn that is most beautiful. As the light creeps over the hills, their outlines are dyed a faint red and wisps of purplish cloud trail over them.

In summer the nights. Not only when the moon shines, but on dark nights too, as the fire-flies flit to and fro, and even when it rains, how beautiful it is!

In autumn the evenings, when the glittering sun sinks close to the edge of the hills and the crows fly back to their nests in threes and fours and twos; more charming still is a file of wild geese, like specks in the distant sky. When the sun has set, one's heart is moved by the sound of the wind and the hum of the insects.

In winter the early mornings. It is beautiful indeed when snow has fallen during the night, but splendid too when the ground is white with frost; or even when there is no snow or frost, but it is simply very cold and the attendants hurry from room to room stirring up the fires and bring charcoal, how well this fits the season's mood! But as noon approaches and the cold wears off, no one bothers to keep the braziers alight, and soon nothing remains but piles of white ashes.

Appendix

This appendix presents a collection of compounds exhibiting *rendaku* voicing and Lyman's Law effects. While it is not intended to be exhaustive, enough examples of various kinds have been provided to illustrate the productivity of the processes within the relevant lexical strata.

A.1 Compounds Exhibiting *Rendaku* Voicing

Undergoer	Compound	Gloss
ha$_1$	ire-ba	'insert-tooth, dentures'
ha$_1$	musi-ba	'insect-tooth, decayed tooth'
ha$_1$	tugi-ba	'connect-tooth, capped tooth, (dental) crown'
ha$_2$	oti-ba	'fallen leaves'
ha$_2$	waka-ba	'young leaves'
hae$_1$	me-bae	'bud-grow, sprout'
hae$_1$	sita-bae	'under-grow, underbrush, undergrowth'
hae$_2$	deki-bae	'result-shine, resulting appearance'
hae$_2$	mi-bae	'see-shine, appearance, vanity'
hai	hara-bai	'belly-crawl, lie on one's belly'
hai	yo-bai	'night-crawl, illicit love affair at night'
hai	yoko-bai	'side-crawl, sideways crawl'
haki	geta-baki	'clog-wear, wearing clogs'
haki	sita-baki	'under-wear, underpants'
hako	geta-bako	'clog-box, shoe rack, chest for footwear'
hako	gomi-bako	'waste-box, garbage can'
hako	ko-bako	'small-box, jewelry box, etui'
hako	kutu-bako	'shoe-box, shoe cabinet'
hako	su-bako	'nest-box, hive'
hako	suzuri-bako	'inkstone case'

Undergoer	Compound	Gloss
hako	te-bako	'hand-box, case to keep valuables'
hako	tobi-bako	'jump-box, vaulting horse'
hako	zyuu-bako	'layered box (for food)'
hana$_1$	de-bana	'out-flower, first brew of tea'
hana$_1$	hana-bana	'flower-flower, many kinds of flowers'
hana$_1$	hi-bana	'fire-flower, fire spark'
hana$_1$	ike-bana	'arrange-flower, flower arrangement'
hana$_1$	osi-bana	'push-flower, pressed flowers, dried plants'
hana$_2$	de-bana	'exit-nose, opportunity'
hana$_2$	ko-bana	'small-nose, wings of the nose'
hana$_2$	te-bana	'hand-nose, blowing one's nose with one's fingers'
hanare	hanare-banare	'separate-separate, separated, scattered'
hanare	oya-banare	'parents-separate, independence from parents'
hanare	ti-banare	'breast-separate, be weaned'
hanare	toko-banare	'bed-separate, getting out of bed'
hanare	zoku-banare	'common-separate, unworldly'
hanasi	kankyoo-banasi	'environment-story, story about the environment'
hanasi	miai-banasi	'meet-story, talk of arranged marriage'
hanasi	naga-banasi	'long-story, tedious talk'
hanasi	netto-banasi	'Internet talk'
hanasi	nise-banasi	'false-talk, fake story'
hanasi	ura-banasi	'back-story, inside story'
hanasi	wakare-banasi	'separate-story, considering divorce'
hanasi	warai-banasi	'laugh-story, funny story'
hanasi	ziman-banasi	'boast-story, boastful talk'
hanasu	te-banasu	'hand-separate, part with, separate'
hara	ko-bara	'small-stomach, belly, abdomen'
hara	sita-bara	'lower-stomach, abdomen'
hara	yoko-bara	'side-stomach, side, flank'
hara	zi-bara	'self-stomach, paying one's own way'
harai	itizi-barai	'once-pay, one-time payment'
harai	mae-barai	'before-pay, advance payment'
harami	hidari-barami	'left-side-pregnant, male birth'
harasi	ki-barasi	'feel-divert, diversion, pastime, recreation'
harasi	kokoro-barasi	'heart-divert, diversion from depressed feelings'
harasi	usa-barasi	'depression-divert, diversion from melancholy'
hari	kari-bari	'temporary-paste, provisional pasting (of walls)'
hari	sita-bari	'under-paste, undercoat, first coat'

Undergoer	Compound	Gloss
hari	te-bari	'hand-paste, pasting by oneself, gambling without money'
hasami	ita-basami	'board-put-between, in a dilemma'
hasami	ryoori-basami	'cook-shears, kitchen scissors'
hasi$_1$	hasi-basi	'edge-edge, all edges'
hasi$_2$	hi-basi	'fire-chopsticks, tongs'
hasi$_2$	wari-basi	'split-chopsticks, half-split (splittable) chopsticks'
hasi$_3$	huna-basi	'boat-bridge, pontoon bridge'
hasi$_3$	kari-basi	'provisional-bridge, temporary (makeshift) bridge'
hasika	syooni-basika	'infant-measles, children's measles'
hasira	hi-basira	'fire-pillar, pillar of flames'
hasira	kai-basira	'shell-pillar, scallops'
hasira	simo-basira	'frost-pillar, ice columns, frost columns'
hata$_1$	ido-bata	'well-side, place for housewives' gossip'
hata$_1$	kawa-bata	'riverside'
hata$_1$	miti-bata	'road-edge, roadside, wayside'
hata$_2$	te-bata	'hand-flag, small flag held by hand'
hatake	imo-batake	'potato field'
hatake	kuwa-batake	'mulberry field'
hatake	satookibi-batake	'sugarcane field'
hataraki	sita-bataraki	'under-work, hackwork, assistance'
hataraki	tada-bataraki	'free-work, working for nothing'
hataraki	tomo-bataraki	'together-work, both husband and wife working for a living'
hati$_1$	ko-bati	'small-pot, small bowl'
hati$_1$	suri-bati	'grinding-pot, earthenware mortar for grinding'
hati$_1$	ueki-bati	'planting-pot, flowerpot'
hati$_2$	hataraki-bati	'worker bee'
hati$_2$	mitu-bati	'honeybee'
hato	densyo-bato	'message-dove, carrier pigeon'
hato	yama-bato	'mountain-dove, turtledove'
hayai	te-bayai	'hand-fast, quickly, promptly'
hayasi	matu-bayasi	'pine forest'
hayasi	sugi-bayasi	'cedar forest'
he	iidasi-be	'say-start-fart, the one calling attention to a fart is the farter, the one who brings up a subject must be the first to act on it'
hee	do-bee	'earth-enclosure, mud wall, plaster wall'

Undergoer	Compound	Gloss
hee	ita-bee	'board-enclosure, wooden fence'
hera	kutu-bera	'shoe-spatula, shoehorn'
heri$_1$	huna-beri	'boat-side, side of a boat'
heri$_2$	me-beri	'notch-loss, loss in weight, depreciation'
heso	de-beso	'protruding navel'
heta	kuti-beta	'mouth-bad, poor talker'
heya	aki-beya	'empty-room, available room (in a hotel)'
heya	benkyoo-beya	'study-room, study'
hi$_1$	hi-bi	'day-day, many days'
hi$_1$	kyuuryoo-bi	'payday'
hi$_2$	kitune-bi	'fox-fire, will-o'-the-wisp, jack-o'-lantern'
hi$_2$	mukae-bi	'welcome-fire, welcoming bonfire (for departed spirits)'
hi$_2$	sita-bi	'low-fire, burn low, go out of fashion'
hi$_2$	taki-bi	'burn-fire, bonfire'
hi$_2$	tane-bi	'seed-fire, pilot light'
hie	hana-bie	'flower-cold, chilly spring weather'
hie	hie-bie	'cold-cold, chilly'
hie	ne-bie	'sleep-cold, get chilled while asleep'
hie	soko-bie	'bottom-cold, chilled to the bone, raw cold'
hikae	te-bikae	'hand-note, notebook, memorandum'
hiki	ai-biki	'meet-draw, date, assignation, rendezvous'
hiki	gomu-biki	'rubber-draw, rubberized, rubber-coated'
hiki	kaku-biki	'stroke-draw, arranged by strokes'
hiki	ki-biki	'mourning-draw, absence owing to a death in the family'
hiki	kuzi-biki	'ticket-draw, lottery drawing'
hiki	ma-biki	'interval-draw, thinning out'
hiki	ne-biki	'root-draw, uproot, redeem price reduction, discount'
hiki	on-biki	'sound-draw, looking up a kanji by its reading'
hiki	sio-biki	'salt-draw, salted fish'
hiki	te-biki	'hand-draw, guidance, guidebook, introduction'
hiki	wari-biki	'tenths-draw, ten percent discount, rebate'
hiki	zi-biki	'letter-draw, dictionary'
hira	hana-bira	'flower petal'
hiraki	mise-biraki	'store-open, opening a store, starting a business'
hiraki	ryoo-biraki	'both-open, double door'

Undergoer	Compound	Gloss
hiraki	umi-biraki	'sea-open, opening the beaches for swimmers'
hiraki	yama-biraki	'mountain-open, opening a mountain for climbers'
hirame	sita-birame	'tongue-flatfish, sole'
hire	se-bire	'back-fin, dorsal fin'
hiro	hiro-biro	'wide-wide, extensive, spacious'
hiro	se-biro	'back-wide, business suit'
hiroi	te-biroi	'hand-wide, extensive, large, spacious'
hisa	hisa-bisa	'long-long, long time, many days'
hisasi	ita-bisasi	'board-visor, wooden eaves, pent roof'
hisi	hana-bisi	'flower-rhombus, flower-shaped rhombus (family crest)'
hisi	mitu-bisi	'three-rhombus, triple diamond-shaped crest, Mitsubishi'
hitasi	mizu-bitasi	'water-soak, soaked in water, flooded'
hito	hito-bito	'man-man, people'
hito	huru-bito	'ancient-person, the deceased, old friend'
hito	miya-bito	'palace-person, noble courtier'
hito	tabi-bito	'travel-person, traveler'
hiyori	koharu-biyori	'small-spring-weather, mild autumn weather, Indian summer'
hiyori	yuki-biyori	'snow weather'
home	beta-bome	'sticky-praise, exaggerated praise, flattery'
hone	ago-bone	'chin-bone, jawbone'
hone	se-bone	'back-bone, spine'
hone	suzi-bone	'sinews-bone, structure, bone with sinews'
hooki	hane-booki	'feather-broom, feather duster'
hooki	te-booki	'hand-broom, whisk broom'
hootyoo	deba-bootyoo	'pointed-carver, kitchen knife'
hore	hitome-bore	'one-eye-love, falling in love at first sight'
hore	hore-bore	'love-love, admiringly, fondly'
hore	oka-bore	'hilltop-love, unrequited love, secret affection'
hore	unu-bore	'self-love, self-conceited'
hori	kara-bori	'empty-moat, dry moat'
hori	soto-bori	'outside-moat, outer moat'
hosi$_1$	ama-bosi	'sweet-dry, persimmon cured in the sun'
hosi$_1$	hi-bosi	'sun-dry, sun-dried'
hosi$_1$	kage-bosi	'shadow-dry, drying in the shade'
hosi$_1$	maru-bosi	'complete-dry, dried whole (fish, vegetables, etc.)'

Undergoer	Compound	Gloss
hosi₁	ni-bosi	'cook-dry, small dried sardines'
hosi₂	kin-bosi	'gold-star, dazzling victory'
hosi₂	zu-bosi	'chart-star, bull's-eye, mark'
hoso	goku-boso	'extra-thin, superfine'
hoso	hoso-boso	'thin-thin, very thinly, poorly'
hotoke	iki-botoke	'live-Buddha, living Buddha, incarnation of Buddha'
hotoke	nodo-botoke	'throat-Buddha, Adam's apple'
hue	asi-bue	'reed-flute, reed pipe'
hue	tate-bue	'vertical-flute, recorder'
hue	tuno-bue	'horn-flute, hunting horn'
hue	yoko-bue	'horizontal-flute, flute, fife'
huki₁	kara-buki	'dry-wipe, polishing with a dry cloth'
huki₂	i-buki	'breath-blow, breath'
hukin	dai-bukin	'table-dustcloth, cloth for wiping the table'
hukuro	gekkyuu-bukuro	'salary-bag, envelope containing one's monthly pay'
hukuro	kami-bukuro	'paper bag'
hukuro	te-bukuro	'hand-bag, gloves, mittens'
hukuro	uki-bukuro	'float-bag, swimming float'
humi₁	kana-bumi	'kana-letter, publication in kana alone'
humi₁	koi-bumi	'love letter'
humi₂	ne-bumi	'price-tread, evaluation, setting prices'
humi₂	se-bumi	'depth-tread, first trial, measuring the river depths'
huna	kan-buna	'cold-crucian, crucian carp caught in midwinter'
hune	hiki-bune	'draw-boat, tugboat'
hune	ko-bune	'small boat'
hune	ni-bune	'load-boat, freighter, lighter'
hune	yu-bune	'hot-water-vessel, bathtub'
huri₁	ke-buri	'feel-movement, sign, indication'
huri₁	mi-buri	'body-movement, gesture'
huri₁	te-buri	'hand-movement, gestures of hands or arms'
huri₂	ko-buri	'small-fall, light rain'
huri₂	yoko-buri	'horizontal-fall, driving rain'
huro	asa-buro	'morning-bath, taking a bath in the morning'
huro	kama-buro	'pot-bath, bath made of iron'
huro	sio-buro	'salt-bath, saltwater bath'
husoku	mizu-busoku	'water-lack, shortage of water'

Undergoer	Compound	Gloss
husoku	ne-busoku	'sleep-lack, lack of sleep'
husoku	suimin-busoku	'sleep-lack, lack of sleep'
husoku	te-busoku	'hand-lack, be short of help'
husoku	undoo-busoku	'exercise-lack, lack of exercise'
huta	age-buta	'raise-lid, trapdoor'
huta	nabe-buta	'pot-lid, lid'
hute	hute-bute	'saucy-saucy, impudent, shameless'
huti	gaku-buti	'frame-edge, picture frame'
huti	kin-buti	'gold-edge, gilded rims'
huto	hone-buto	'bone-thick, thick boned'
hutoi	zu-butoi	'mark-thick, audacious, impudent'
$hyoosi_1$	san-byoosi	'three-beat, three-timed, all-around'
$hyoosi_1$	te-byoosi	'hand-beat, beat time with the hands'
$hyoosi_2$	kawa-byoosi	'leather-cover, leather binding'
$hyoosi_2$	ura-byoosi	'reverse-cover, back cover'
kae	ido-gae	'well-change, changing wells, changing allegiance'
kae	kura-gae	'saddle-change, changing jobs, changing quarters (geisha)'
kaeri	hi-gaeri	'day-return, day trip'
kaeru	ama-gaeru	'rain-frog, tree frog'
kaeru	ao-gaeru	'green-frog, green tree frog'
kaeru	gama-gaeru	'toad-frog, toad'
kai	baka-gai	'stupid-clam, surf clam'
kai	hora-gai	'boast-clam, trumpet shell'
kaisya	zidoosya-gaisya	'car company'
kakari	oo-gakari	'big-involve, large-scaled'
kakari	te-gakari	'hand-involve, clue, track'
kakasi	nise-gakasi	'false scarecrow'
kakato	kinzoku-gakato	'metal heels'
kake	too-gake	'far-run, long gallop, horseback ride'
kake	zookin-gake	'dustcloth-wiping, wiping with a dustcloth'
kakeru	kokoro-gakeru	'heart-hang, intend, bear in mind'
kakeru	te-gakeru	'hand-hang, handle, deal with'
$kaki_1$	migi-gaki	'right-write, writing from right to left'
$kaki_1$	te-gaki	'hand-write, handwritten'
$kaki_1$	yoko-gaki	'horizontal-write, writing horizontally'
$kaki_2$	hito-gaki	'person-fence, crowd'
$kaki_2$	ike-gaki	'live-fence, hedge'

Undergoer	Compound	Gloss
kaki$_2$	isi-gaki	'stone-fence, stone wall'
kaki$_3$	hosi-gaki	'dried persimmon'
kaki$_3$	huyu-gaki	'winter persimmon'
kaki$_3$	sibu-gaki	'astringent persimmon'
kama	ato-gama	'after-pot, successor'
kama	aturyoku-gama	'pressure-pot, pressure cooker'
kama	maru-gama	'round pot'
kama	tya-gama	'tea-pot, teakettle'
kamae	mon-gamae	'gate-appearance, gate front'
kame	umi-game	'sea turtle'
kame	zeni-game	'coin-turtle, baby turtle'
kami$_1$	kami-gami	'god-god, gods'
kami$_1$	uzi-gami	'family-god, guardian god'
kami$_2$	te-gami	'hand-paper, letter'
kami$_2$	tiri-gami	'dust-paper, tissue paper'
kami$_3$	arai-gami	'wash-hair, (newly) washed hair'
kami$_3$	sage-gami	'down-hair, hair hanging down (the back)'
kanasii	ura-ganasii	'back-sad, sad, sorrowful'
kane$_1$	hiki-gane	'draw-metal, trigger, gunlock'
kane$_1$	ko-gane	'yellow-metal, gold'
kane$_1$	me-gane	'eye-metal, spectacles, glasses'
kane$_1$	nise-gane	'false-money, counterfeit money'
kane$_1$	nobe-gane	'sheet-metal, dagger, sword'
kane$_2$	ki-gane	'feel-combine, hesitance, having scruples'
kane$_3$	kane-gane	'before-before, since long ago'
kani	kabuto-gani	'helmet-crab, horseshoe crab'
kanna	maru-ganna	'round plane (tool)'
kao	anzi-gao	'worry-face, worried look'
kao	maru-gao	'round-face, moon face'
kao	yoko-gao	'side-face, face in profile'
kao	yuu-gao	'evening-face, moon flower'
kappa	ama gappa	'rain cape'
karasu	tabi-garasu	'travel-crow, transient, wanderer, traveled man'
kari$_1$	ma-gari	'space-borrow, renting a room'
kari$_1$	osi-gari	'press-borrow, forced to borrow'
kari$_2$	taka-gari	'eagle hunting'
karu	karu-garu	'light-light, lightly, thoughtlessly'
karu	ki-garu	'feel-light, cheerful, buoyant, lighthearted'

Undergoer	Compound	Gloss
karuta	iroha-garuta	'iroha-cards, syllabary playing cards'
kasa	ama-gasa	'rain umbrella'
kasa	hi-gasa	'sun umbrella'
kasane	kasane-gasane	'repeat-repeat, repeatedly, doubly'
kasane	nimai-gasane	'two-layer-repeat, wearing two layers of clothing'
$kasi_1$	nama-gasi	'fresh-cake, sweets, pastry'
$kasi_1$	tya-gasi	'tea-cake, refreshments'
$kasi_2$	ma-gasi	'space-rent, renting out a room'
kasira	hata-gasira	'flag-head, boss, leader'
kasira	kasegi-gasira	'earn-head, biggest earner'
$kata_1$	kumo-gata	'cloud-shape, cloud formations'
$kata_1$	maru-gata	'round-shape, circle, circular form'
$kata_1$	te-gata	'hand-shape, note, bill, draft'
$kata_2$	aku-gata	'evil-person, villain's part'
$kata_2$	kata-gata	'person-person, persons (honorific)'
$kata_2$	oku-gata	'interior-person, lady, nobleman's wife'
$kata_3$	nade-gata	'stroke-shoulder, sloping shoulders'
katai	te-gatai	'hand-hard, safe, reliable, of good reputation'
kataki	koi-gataki	'love-rival, rival in love'
$kawa_1$	tani-gawa	'valley-river, mountain stream'
$kawa_2$	ke-gawa	'hair-skin, fur'
kawaki	nama-gawaki	'fresh-dry, half wet'
kawase	densin-gawase	'telegraph-pay, telegraphic transfer/remittance'
kayoi	zyuku-gayoi	'school-commute, going to a prep school'
ke	aka-ge	'red hair'
ke	eda-ge	'branch-hair, split end of hair'
ke	mayu-ge	'eyebrow-hair, eyebrow'
ke	ubu-ge	'baby-hair, soft, downy hair (such as on one's cheek)'
keeko	butukari-geeko	'hit-practice, practice running against the sumo opponent'
keeko	de-geeko	'go-out-practice, practice at another sumo stable'
kenka	oyako-genka	'parent-child-quarrel, quarrel between parent and child'
kesiki	yuu-gesiki	'evening-scene, landscape scenery in the evening'
kesyoo	usu-gesyoo	'light makeup'
ki_1	ki-gi	'tree-tree, trees'
ki_1	makura-gi	'pillow-wood, (railroad) crosstie'

Undergoer	Compound	Gloss
ki_1	taki-gi	'burn-wood, firewood'
ki_2	mizu-gi	'water-wear, bathing suit'
ki_2	ubu-gi	'baby-wear, baby clothes'
kie	kie-gie	'vanish-vanish, on the point of vanishing'
kiki	hito-giki	'person-hear, reputation, respectability'
kiki	nama-giki	'raw-hear, being inattentive'
kiki	sita-giki	'under-hear, inquiring beforehand'
kiku	hina-giku	'doll-chrysanthemum, daisy'
kiku	natu-giku	'summer-chrysanthemum, early chrysanthemum'
kiku	no-giku	'field-chrysanthemum, wild chrysanthemum, aster'
kiku	zan-giku	'remain-chrysanthemum, late chrysanthemum'
kime	tuki-gime	'month-determine, monthly'
kimi	waka-gimi	'young-lord, prince'
kimo	ara-gimo	'rough-liver, guts'
kimo	iki-gimo	'live-liver, liver taken from a living animal'
kinu	aya-ginu	'twill-silk, twilled silk fabric'
kinu	e-ginu	'picture-silk, silk canvas'
kirai	onna-girai	'woman-hater, misogynist'
$kire_1$	ha-gire	'tooth-cut, the feel when biting, manner of enunciation'
$kire_1$	ki-gire	'wood-cut, piece of wood'
$kire_1$	kire-gire	'cut-cut, pieces, scraps'
$kire_1$	koma-gire	'fine-cut, small pieces'
$kire_1$	tane-gire	'seed-cut, running out of seeds'
$kire_1$	te-gire	'hand-cut, severing connections or relations'
$kire_2$	huru-gire	'old-cloth, rags'
$kire_2$	huti-gire	'border-cloth, border strip'
$kiri_1$	atu-giri	'thick-cut, thick slice'
$kiri_1$	hi-giri	'day-cut, fixed or appointed date'
$kiri_1$	ku-giri	'phrase-cut, end, stop, punctuation'
$kiri_1$	maru-giri	'round-cut, round gimlet'
$kiri_1$	sen-giri	'thousand-cut, small pieces or strips of vegetables'
$kiri_1$	wa-giri	'circle-cut, round slices'
$kiri_1$	wan-giri	'one-cut, hanging up after letting the phone ring once'
$kiri_1$	yotu-giri	'four-cut, cutting into four, photograph size'
$kiri_2$	kawa-giri	'river-fog, mist over the river'
$kiri_2$	yama-giri	'mountain-fog, mountain mist'

Undergoer	Compound	Gloss
kiri$_2$	yo-giri	'night-fog, night mist'
kiru	ne-giru	'price-cut, driving a bargain, haggling'
kiru	yoko-giru	'horizontal-cut, crossing (e.g., a field), traversing'
kisi	kawa-gisi	'river-shore, riverside, riverbank'
kisya	yo-gisya	'night train'
kitanai	kuti-gitanai	'mouth-dirty, foulmouthed, abusive'
kitanai	usu-gitanai	'light-dirty, dirty-looking, untidy'
kiwa	de-giwa	'out-edge, the time of setting out'
kiwa	hae-giwa	'grow-edge, hairline'
kiwa	hike-giwa	'retreat-edge, closing time'
kiwa	ma-giwa	'place-edge, at the point of, on the verge of'
kiwa	mizu-giwa	'water-edge, beach, water's edge'
kiwa	ne-giwa	'sleep-edge, on the verge of sleep, just falling asleep'
kiwa	same-giwa	'wake-edge, on the verge of waking'
kiwa	seto-giwa	'strait-edge, brink, critical moment'
kiwa	sini-giwa	'die-edge, on the verge of death'
kiwa	te-giwa	'hand-edge, performance, skill, tact'
kiwa	yama-giwa	'mountain-edge, ridge of a mountain, near a mountain'
ko	huta-go	'two-child, twin'
ko	mai-go	'stray-child, missing child'
ko	mizu-go	'water-child, aborted child, stillborn child'
ko	osie-go	'teach-child, (one's) student'
koe$_1$	kake-goe	'throw-voice, yell, shout'
koe$_1$	koe-goe	'voice-voice, many voices'
koe$_1$	ko-goe	'small-voice, low voice, whisper'
koe$_1$	naki-goe	'cry-voice, crying voice'
koe$_1$	sakebi-goe	'shout-voice, yell, scream'
koe$_1$	sinobi-goe	'secret-voice, whispering'
koe$_1$	uta-goe	'song-voice, singing voice'
koe$_1$	yobi-goe	'call-voice, call, hail, yell'
koe$_1$	zi-goe	'self-voice, one's natural voice'
koe$_2$	kan-goe	'winter-manure, night soil stored in midwinter'
koe$_2$	simo-goe	'under-manure, night soil, dung, muck'
koi$_1$	hi-goi	'red-carp, golden carp'
koi$_1$	ma-goi	'true-carp, black carp, black koi'
koi$_2$	ama-goi	'rain-seek, praying for rain'
koi$_2$	inoti-goi	'life-seek, pleading for (one's) life'

Undergoer	Compound	Gloss
kokoro	otome-gokoro	'maiden-heart, feelings of a girl'
kokoro	sita-gokoro	'under-heart, secret desire beneath the surface'
koma	koma-goma	'fine-fine, minutely, in detail'
koma	te-goma	'hand-piece, game pieces under one's control'
kome	ko-gome	'small-rice, crushed rice'
kome	moti-gome	'glutinous-rice, sticky rice to make rice cake'
komi	iki-gomi	'spirit-include, ardor, enthusiasm'
konasi	atama-gonasi	'head-manage, (scold) unsparingly'
konasi	hara-gonasi	'stomach-manage, aid to digestion'
konomi	onna-gonomi	'woman-liking, woman's favorites'
koori	hana-goori	'flower-ice, flowers surrounded by ice'
koosi	de-goosi	'out-lattice, projecting lattice, latticed bay window'
kori	kori-gori	'repent-repent, have enough of, learn by experience'
koro	hi-goro	'day-period, normally, habitually'
koro	ima-goro	'now-period, about this time'
koro	itu-goro	'when-period, about when, how soon'
koro	mi-goro	'see-period, best time to see'
koro	ne-goro	'price-period, reasonable price'
koro	tabe-goro	'eat-period, good for eating, in season'
koro	te-goro	'hand-period, moderate, handy'
koro	tika-goro	'near-period, lately, recently, nowadays'
koromo	ha-goromo	'feather-robe, robe of feathers (worn by fairies)'
korosi	hito-gorosi	'person-kill, homicide'
korosi	mi-gorosi	'look-kill, leave a person in the lurch'
korosi	mina-gorosi	'all-kill, massacre'
korosi	onna-gorosi	'woman-kill, lady-killer'
kosi$_1$	ebi-gosi	'shrimp-waist, stooped'
kosi$_1$	maru-gosi	'round-waist, unarmed'
kosi$_1$	oyobi-gosi	'bent-waist, indecisive attitude'
kosi$_1$	tuyo-gosi	'strong-waist, firm or tough stance'
kosi$_2$	atama-gosi	'head-go-over, going over a person's head'
kosi$_2$	natu-gosi	'summer-go-over, surviving the summer'
kotatu	denki-gotatu	'electric-heater, electric footwarmer, electric kotatsu'
kotatu	hori-gotatu	'dig-heater, kotatsu on dug-out flooring'
koto$_1$	gee-goto	'art-thing, accomplishments'
koto$_1$	koto-goto	'thing-thing, in everything, in every way'
koto$_1$	kuse-goto	'habit-thing, crookedness, unlawfulness, calamity'

Undergoer	Compound	Gloss
koto$_1$	mi-goto	'see-thing, splendid, magnificent, admirable'
koto$_1$	nani-goto	'what-thing, what, something'
koto$_1$	narai-goto	'learn-thing, private lessons'
koto$_1$	si-goto	'do-thing, work, occupation, employment'
koto$_2$	ko-goto	'small-say, scolding, finding fault'
koto$_2$	kuri-goto	'repeat-say, tedious talk, repetition, complaint'
koto$_2$	naki-goto	'cry-say, complaint'
koto$_2$	ne-goto	'sleep-say, talking in sleep, nonsense'
koto$_2$	sora-goto	'sky-say, falsehood, lie'
koto$_2$	tawa-goto	'funny-say, nonsense, silly things, joke'
koto$_2$	zare-goto	'play-say, nonsense, silly things, wanton sporting'
koto$_3$	o-goto	'small-koto, small-sized koto'
koto$_3$	tate-goto	'vertical-koto, harp'
kowa	kowa-gowa	'fear-fear, fearfully, timidly, cautiously'
koya	kari-goya	'temporary-shed, booth, shack, hut, shed'
koya	usagi-goya	'rabbit-shed, rabbit hutch'
koya	usi-goya	'cow-shed, cattle barn'
koyomi	hana-goyomi	'flower calendar'
kui$_1$	inu-gui	'dog-eat, sloppy eater'
kui$_1$	tomo-gui	'together-eat, cannibalism (in animals), mutual destruction'
kui$_2$	boo-gui	'stick-pole, post, stake'
kui$_2$	hasi-gui	'bridge-pole, bridge pillar'
kuki	ha-guki	'tooth-stem, gum, tooth ridge'
kuma	ana-guma	'hole-bear, badger'
kuma	kuma-guma	'corner-corner, nooks and corners'
kumi	aka-gumi	'red-group, team with red banner, women's team'
kumi	en-gumi	'relation-group, betrothal, alliance'
kumi	ki-gumi	'wood-group, wooden framework'
kumi	yoko-gumi	'horizontal-group, horizontal typesetting'
kumo	ama-gumo	'rain-cloud, precipitation cloud, rain-laden cloud'
kumo	maki-gumo	'whirl-cloud, cirrus (cloud)'
kumo	yoko-gumo	'horizontal-cloud, wall or bank of clouds'
kuni	kuni-guni	'country-country, countries'
kuni	yuki-guni	'snow country'
kura$_1$	ana-gura	'hole-storage, cellar'
kura$_1$	kane-gura	'money-storage, vault, provider of funds'
kura$_2$	ni-gura	'load-saddle, packsaddle'

Undergoer	Compound	Gloss
kurasi	hitori-gurasi	'single-live, living by oneself'
kure	hi-gure	'sun-dark, twilight, sunset, dusk, evening'
kure	kure-gure	'repeat-repeat, repeatedly'
kuri$_1$	ama-guri	'sweet-chestnut, broiled sweet chestnuts'
kuri$_1$	wari-guri	'break-chestnut, rubble, broken stone'
kuri$_2$	kane-guri	'money-get, financing, raising funds'
kuri$_2$	te-guri	'hand-get, reeling in, passing from hand to hand'
kuro	iro-guro	'color-black, dark complexion'
kuro	kuro-guro	'black-black, pitch black'
kuro	oha-guro	'tooth-black, blackened teeth'
kuruma	kaza-guruma	'wind-wheel, windmill'
kuruma	ni-guruma	'load-wheel, cart'
kurumi	no-gurumi	'field-walnut, wild walnut'
kusa	hosi-gusa	'dry-grass, hay, dry grass'
kusa	ii-gusa	'say-grass, one's words or remarks, an excuse'
kusa	natu-gusa	'summer grass'
kusa	no-gusa	'field-grass, wild grasses'
kusa	ti-gusa	'thousand-grass, great variety of flowering plants'
kuse	kuti-guse	'mouth-habit, way of saying, favorite phrase'
kuse	ne-guse	'sleep-habit, sleeping habit'
kuse	waru-guse	'bad-habit, vice'
kusi	kana-gusi	'metal-skewer, iron skewer'
kusi	tama-gusi	'jewel-skewer, branch of a sacred tree'
kuso	ma-guso	'horse dung'
kusuri	ke-zome-gusuri	'hair-dye-medicine, hair-dyeing lotion'
kusuri	nomi-gusuri	'swallow-medicine, internal medicine'
kusuri	ti-dome-gusuri	'blood-stop-medicine, styptic medicine'
kuti	de-guti	'go-out-mouth, exit, gateway, outlet'
kuti	gama-guti	'toad-mouth, pouch, purse'
kuti	hi-guti	'fire-mouth, burner, origin of a fire'
kuti	kage-guti	'shadow-mouth, malicious gossip, backbiting'
kuti	kawa-guti	'river-mouth, mouth of river, estuary'
kuti	kin-guti	'gold-mouth, gold paper wrapped around cigarette tip'
kuti	kuti-guti	'mouth-mouth, each entrance, every mouth, unanimously'
kuti	nikumare-guti	'hated-mouth, words that make oneself hated, bad-mouthing'

Undergoer	Compound	Gloss
kuti	nomi-guti	'drink-mouth, tap, faucet, spigot'
kuti	seme-guti	'attack-mouth, method of attack, place of attack'
kuti	te-guti	'hand-mouth, modus operandi, criminal technique, trick'
kuti	to-guti	'door-mouth, door'
kuti	tuge-guti	'tell-mouth, telltale'
kuti	waru-guti	'bad-mouth, bad-mouthing, insult, slander'
kutu	ama-gutu	'rain-shoe, overshoes'
kutu	kawa-gutu	'leather shoe'
kutu	ki-gutu	'wood-shoe, clogs'
kutu	naga-gutu	'long-shoe, boots'
saiku	kawa-zaiku	'leather-ware, leather workmanship'
sakana	yaki-zakana	'burn-fish, broiled fish'
sakari	hana-zakari	'flower-peak, in full bloom'
sakari	hataraki-zakari	'work-peak, in prime of life'
$sake_1$	ama-zake	'sweet-sake, sweet drink made from fermented rice'
$sake_1$	huru-zake	'old-sake, well-cured sake, last year's sake'
$sake_1$	inaka-zake	'country-sake, locally brewed sake'
$sake_1$	ki-zake	'pure-sake, sake served chilled'
$sake_1$	ne-zake	'night-sake, nightcap, drink before sleeping'
$sake_2$	sio-zake	'salt-salmon, salted salmon'
saki	saki-zaki	'far-far, in the distant future'
sakura	nihon-zakura	'Japanese cherry blossoms'
sakura	nise-zakura	'fake cherry blossoms'
sakura	yamato-zakura	'Yamato cherry blossoms, *Prunus yedoensis*'
sakura	yama-zakura	'mountain-cherry, wild cherry'
sakura	yosino-zakura	'Yoshino cherry blossoms'
sama	bu-zama	'bad-state, unsightly, clumsy, uncouth'
sama	ne-zama	'sleep-state, sleeping posture'
sama	sama-zama	'various-various, diverse, of all kinds'
sama	simo-zama	'low-state, lower classes, common people'
samasi	me-zamasi	'eye-open, eye-opener, alarm clock'
$same_1$	hitokui-zame	'man-eating shark'
$same_2$	same-zame	'sorrow-sorrow, sorrowfully, anguishedly'
$same_3$	yu-zame	'bath-chill, feeling chilly after taking a bath'
samu	samu-zamu	'cold-cold, desolate, wintry'
samu	yo-zamu	'night-cold, cold night'
samui	hada-zamui	'skin-cold, chilly'

Undergoer	Compound	Gloss
sao	hata-zao	'flag-pole, flagstaff, flagpole'
sao	tugi-zao	'connect-pole, jointed fishing rod'
sara	hai-zara	'ash-dish, ashtray'
sara	hi-zara	'fire-dish, fire grate, chafing dish, pipe bowl'
sara	ki-zara	'wood-dish, wooden plate'
sara	ko-zara	'small-dish, small serving dish'
sarasi	ama-zarasi	'rain-expose, weather (rain) beaten'
sarasi	arai-zarasi	'wash-expose, threadbare, worn'
saru	nihon-zaru	'Japan-ape, Japanese monkey, macaque'
saru	te-naga-zaru	'hand-long-ape, long-armed ape, gibbon'
saru	yama-zaru	'mountain-ape, monkey, rustic, boor'
sasa	kuma-zasa	'bear-bamboo, low and striped bamboo'
sasi	hi-zasi	'sun-point, sunlight, rays of the sun'
sasi	kusi-zasi	'skewer-point, skewered'
sasi	mana-zasi	'eye-point, look'
sasi	na-zasi	'name-point, nomination, calling names'
sasu	me-zasu	'eye-aim, aiming at, having an eye on'
sata	kitigai-zata	'mad-affair, sheer madness'
sata	omote-zata	'public-affair, making public'
sata	tori-zata	'take-affair, rumor'
sato	ura-zato	'back-village, village by the sea'
satoo	aka-zatoo	'red-sugar, brown sugar'
sawari	hada-zawari	'skin-touch, feel'
sawari	me-zawari	'eye-touch, eyesore'
sawari	mimi-zawari	'ear-touch, jarring'
sawari	te-zawari	'hand-touch, feeling rough or soft to the touch'
saya	ne-zaya	'price-sheath, margin, spread (in prices)'
se	neko-ze	'cat-back, stoop, hunchback'
se	uwa-ze	'above-back, height'
seki	kara-zeki	'dry-cough, hacking cough'
sema	te-zema	'hand-narrow, small, narrow'
seme	hi-zeme	'fire-attack, attacking with fire, torture by fire'
seme	mizu-zeme	'water-attack, inundating a castle, water torture'
seme	yo-zeme	'night-attack, attacking at night'
semi	natu-zemi	'summer cicada'
sikake	iro-zikake	'love-device, pretense of love'
siki	sita-ziki	'under-place, pad, pinned under, crushed beneath'
sima$_1$	sima-zima	'island-island, islands'

Undergoer	Compound	Gloss
sima$_2$	yoko-zima	'horizontal-stripe, lateral stripes'
simari	to-zimari	'door-close, lockup'
sime	ne-zime	'sound-squeeze, tuning'
simo	simo-zimo	'low-low, lower classes, common people'
sina	te-zina	'hand-thing, jugglery, magic, tricks'
sini	inu-zini	'dog-death, useless death'
sirami	toko-zirami	'bed-louse, floor louse'
sirase	yume-zirase	'dream-notice, revelation in a dream'
siri	don-ziri	'complete-bottom, tail end'
siro$_1$	ao-ziro	'blue-white, pale white'
siro$_2$	ne-ziro	'root-castle, stronghold, citadel'
sirusi	hata-zirusi	'flag-mark, design on a flag, ensign'
sita$_1$	neko-zita	'cat-tongue, aversion to hot food'
sita$_2$	sita-zita	'low-low, lower classes, common people'
sitaku	tabi-zitaku	'trip-prepare, preparation for a trip'
siwa	ko-ziwa	'small-wrinkle, fine wrinkles'
soe	kai-zoe	'help-accompany, helper, assistant'
soe	kuti-zoe	'mouth-accompany, recommendation'
soe	maki-zoe	'roll-accompany, getting entangled in'
soi	noti-zoi	'after-accompany, one's second wife'
soi	umi-zoi	'sea-accompany, coastlands'
soko	age-zoko	'raise-bottom, false bottom'
soko	atu-zoko	'thick-bottom, thick-soled footwear'
soko	don-zoko	'complete-bottom, very bottom, pits'
soko	kawa-zoko	'river-bottom, riverbed'
soko	kutu-zoko	'shoe-bottom, shoe sole'
soko	oku-zoko	'deep-bottom, depth, bottom (of one's heart)'
soko	tani-zoko	'valley-bottom, bottom of a ravine'
some	ti-zome	'blood-dye, bloodstained'
some$_1$	kata-zome	'shape-dye, stencil dyeing'
some$_1$	ke-zome	'hair-dye, hair coloring'
some$_2$	de-zome	'come-out-first, debut'
some$_2$	ki-zome	'wear-first, wearing new clothes for the first time'
son	maru-zon	'round-loss, total loss'
sono	hana-zono	'flower garden'
soosi	e-zoosi	'picture book'
soosi	kana-zoosi	'kana-book, story book in kana'
sora	aki-zora	'autumn sky'

Undergoer	Compound	Gloss
sora	ama-zora	'rain-sky, sky threatening of rain'
sora	natu-zora	'summer sky'
sora	samu-zora	'cold-sky, cold weather'
sora	taka-zora	'high-sky, high altitude'
sora	yo-zora	'night sky'
sore	sore-zore	'that-that, each, respectively'
sori$_1$	inu-zori	'dogsled'
sori$_2$	saka-zori	'reverse-shave, shaving against the grain'
sori$_2$	sita-zori	'under-shave, barber's apprentice'
su	awase-zu	'combine-vinegar, flavored vinegar'
su	syokuyoo-zu	'food-vinegar, cooking vinegar'
su	ume-zu	'plum vinegar'
sue	sue-zue	'end-end, in the future'
suiryoo	ate-zuiryoo	'hit-estimate, guesstimate'
suki	de-zuki	'go-out-fond, fond of going out'
suki	suki-zuki	'like-like, likes and dislikes, matter of taste'
suki	yoko-zuki	'horizontal-like, crazy about but not good at'
sumai	kari-zumai	'temporary-live, temporary residence'
sumai	wabi-zumai	'simple-live, humble dwelling'
sumi	sumi-zumi	'corner-corner, every nook and corner'
sure	kinu-zure	'silk-rub, rustling of clothes'
sure	kura-zure	'saddle-rub, saddle sores'
sure	waru-zure	'bad-rub, oversophistication'
suri	kari-zuri	'temporary-print, proof printing'
suri	sita-zuri	'under-print, proof printing'
suri	te-zuri	'hand-print, printing by hand'
susi	maki-zusi	'roll-sushi, rolled sushi'
susi	osi-zusi	'press-sushi, pressed sushi'
susuki	yama-zusuki	'mountain-eulalia, mountain pampas grass'
sute	kake-zute	'hang-abandon, stop paying installments'
syaku	te-zyaku	'hand-serve, help oneself to sake'
syasin	kao-zyasin	'face-photo, portrait'
ta	ina-da	'rice-field, rice paddy'
ta	kakusi-da	'hide-field, hidden rice paddy (to avoid taxation)'
taka	en-daka	'yen-high, high-valued yen'
taka	kasegi-daka	'earn-high, earnings'
taka	taka-daka	'high-high, at most'
takara	ko-dakara	'child-treasure, blessed with children'

Undergoer	Compound	Gloss
take	ao-dake	'green bamboo'
take	sao-dake	'pole-bamboo, bamboo pole'
taki	me-daki	'woman-waterfall, lesser of a pair of waterfalls'
tako	su-dako	'vinegar-octopus, cooked octopus in vinegar'
tako	yude-dako	'boiled octopus'
tama	aku-dama	'bad-ball, bad character, villain'
tama	ame-dama	'candy-ball, toffees'
tama	bii-dama	'beads-ball, marble'
tama	hi-dama	'fireball'
tama	me-dama	'eyeball'
tama	ote-dama	'hand-ball, game using juggling bags'
tama	sore-dama	'go-astray-ball, stray bullet'
tama	te-dama	'hand-ball, trifle with (a person)'
tama	yari-dama	'pike-ball, make a victim of'
tama	zyuzu-dama	'rosary-ball, rosary beads'
tamari	hi-damari	'sun-gather, sunny spot'
tamasii	makezi-damasii	'lose-not-spirit, unyielding spirit'
tamasii	yamato-damasii	'Yamato spirit'
tamesi	ude-damesi	'arm-try, trial of strength'
tana	garasu-dana	'glass shelf'
tana	kami-dana	'god-shelf, house altar'
tana	to-dana	'door-shelf, closet, locker'
tane	hi-dane	'fire-seed, live coals, remains of fire'
tane	ko-dane	'child-seed, children, descendants'
tane	tuya-dane	'romance-seed, love affair'
tani	tanuki-dani	'badger valley'
tanomi	hito-danomi	'person-ask, reliance on others'
tanomi	kami-danomi	'god-ask, pray for divine aid'
tansu	tya-dansu	'tea-chest, cabinet for tea utensils'
tansu	yoohuku-dansu	'wardrobe-chest, drawers for clothes'
tanuki	yama-danuki	'mountain badger'
taore	kui-daore	'eat-collapse, financially ruinous extravagance in food'
taosi	yoko-daosi	'side-fall, fall down sideways'
tara	hi-dara	'dried cod'
tare	ama-dare	'rain-drip, raindrops'
tasuke	hito-dasuke	'people-help, act of charity'
tasuke	te-dasuke	'hand-help, helping hand'

Undergoer	Compound	Gloss
tasuki	siro-dasuki	'white sash'
tataki	hukuro-dataki	'bag-hit, ganging up and giving a person sound beating'
tatami	age-datami	'raise-tatami, tatami finished on both sides'
tatami	ao-datami	'blue-tatami, new tatami'
tatami	isi-datami	'stone-tatami, stone pavement'
tate	doru-date	'dollar-build, dollar base'
tate	en-date	'yen-build, yen base'
tate	ki-date	'spirit-stand, disposition, nature'
tate	te-date	'hand-stand, means, method'
tate	usiro-date	'back-stand, backer, patron'
tati$_1$	hara-dati	'stomach-stand, infuriate'
tati$_2$	sio-dati	'salt-abstain, abstaining from salty food'
tatu	awa-datu	'bubble-stand, bubble, foam'
tatu	tabi-datu	'trip-stand, go on a journey'
tawara	kome-dawara	'rice-bag, straw rice bag'
tayori	eeyoo-dayori	'nutrition-tidings, communication about nutrition'
tayori	kisetu-dayori	'season-tidings, season's greetings'
tayori	sakura-dayori	'cherry-tidings, tidings of cherry blossoms'
tayori	supootu-dayori	'sports-tidings, talk about sports'
tayori	ume-dayori	'plum-tidings, tidings of plum blossoms'
te	hito-de	'person-hand, (pass into) another hand'
te	kuma-de	'bear-hand, rake'
te	su-de	'bare-hand, empty-handed'
tera	huru-dera	'old temple'
tera	uzi-dera	'family-temple, shrine built to a guardian deity'
tera	yama-dera	'mountain temple'
tera	zen-dera	'Zen temple'
ti	hana-zi	'nosebleed'
tie	saru-zie	'monkey-wits, shallow cunning, shallow cleverness'
tie	waru-zie	'bad-wits, guile, serpentine wisdom'
tika	ma-zika	'space-near, proximity, soon'
tika	te-zika	'hand-near, nearby, familiar'
tika	tika-zika	'near-near, soon'
tikara	baka-zikara	'fool-strength, brute force'
to	ama-do	'rain door'
to	ami-do	'screen door'
to	kuguri-do	'ducking-door, side door'

Undergoer	Compound	Gloss
to	sugi-do	'cedar-door, door made of cedar'
toi	ama-doi	'rain gutter'
tokee	me-zamasi-dokee	'eye-opening-clock, alarm clock'
toki	de-doki	'leave-time, time of departure'
toki	hike-doki	'close-time, closing time'
toki	ima-doki	'now-time, present, nowadays'
toki	toki-doki	'time-time, sometimes'
toko	hi-doko	'fire-bed, fire grate'
tokoro	de-dokoro	'leave-place, source, outlet'
tokoro	tokoro-dokoro	'place-place, in various places'
tomari	su-domari	'bare-lodge, overnight stay without meals'
tome	eki-dome	'station-stop, delivery of freight to a station'
tome	ha-dome	'tooth-stop, brake'
tome	ti-dome	'blood-stop, styptic'
toohu	yu-doohu	'hot tofu'
tooi	en-dooi	'relation-far, late marriage, little prospect of marriage'
toori	zikan-doori	'time-exact, punctually'
tora	ko-dora	'small-tiger, drinker'
tora	mesu-dora	'female tiger'
tori$_1$	huti-dori	'border-take, hemming, bordering'
tori$_1$	ma-dori	'space-take, plan of a house, arrangement of rooms'
tori$_1$	te-dori	'hand-take, real income, after-tax take-home pay'
tori$_1$	yoko-dori	'side-take, usurpation, snatching, seizure'
tori$_2$	kaza-mi-dori	'wind-see-bird, weather vane bird'
tori$_2$	umi-dori	'sea bird'
toru	hima-doru	'time-take, take time'
tosi	hebi-dosi	'snake-year, year of the snake'
tuka$_1$	ari-zuka	'ant-mound, anthill'
tuka$_1$	kai-zuka	'shell-mound, shell heap'
tuka$_2$	ko-zuka	'small-handle, knife attached to the sheath of a sword'
tukai	hude-zukai	'brush-use, penmanship'
tukami	te-zukami	'hand-grasp, seize by hand'
tuke$_1$	gimu-zuke	'duty-attach, obligation'
tuke$_1$	iti-zuke	'place-attach, placement, fixed position'
tuke$_1$	kaku-zuke	'grade-attach, grading, rating, classification'

Undergoer	Compound	Gloss
tuke₁	ki-zuke	'care-attach, care of (c/o)'
tuke₁	yoko-zuke	'side-attach, coming alongside'
tuke₂	nara-zuke	'Nara pickles'
tuke₂	na-zuke	'greens-pickle, pickled vegetables'
tuke₂	sio-zuke	'salt-pickle, pickling in salt'
tuke₂	su-zuke	'vinegar-pickle, pickling in vinegar'
tuki	kiku-zuki	'chrysanthemum-moon, ninth month in the lunar calendar'
tuki	mika-zuki	'third-day-moon, new moon, crescent'
tuki	oboro-zuki	'hazy-moon, misty moonlit night'
tuki	tuki-zuki	'month-month, monthly'
tuku	kan-zuku	'feel-attach, suspect, sense, scent'
tuku	ki-zuku	'attention-attach, notice, realize'
tuku	ko-zuku	'little-attach, poke, push'
tuku	ne-zuku	'root-attach, take root'
tuku	tika-zuku	'near-attach, acquaint'
tuku	tuku-zuku	'thorough-thorough, thoroughly, utterly'
tukuri	te-zukuri	'hand-made, homemade'
tukusi	kokoro-zukusi	'heart-render, heart effort, kindness'
tuma	hito-zuma	'man-wife, another man's wife'
tumari	te-zumari	'hand-choke, be pinched for money'
tume₁	go-zume	'back-fill, rear guard'
tume₁	kan-zume	'can-fill, canning, canned goods'
tume₁	migi-zume	'right-fill, right justified'
tume₁	zi-zume	'letter-fill, number of characters, manuscript paper'
tume₂	ke-zume	'kick-nail, spur, cockspur'
tume₂	ko-zume	'small-nail, half-moon of a fingernail'
tumi	ni-zumi	'load-pile, loading'
tumi	sita-zumi	'low-pile, goods in the lower layer, lower-class people'
tuna	hiki-zuna	'pull-rope, tow rope, bell rope'
tuna	ido-zuna	'well rope'
tuna	ta-zuna	'hand-rope, bridle, reins'
tuna	yoko-zuna	'side-rope, sumo grand champion'
tune	tune-zune	'usual-usual, always, usually'
tura	soto-zura	'outside-face, exterior, surface, outward appearance'
tura	zi-zura	'letter-face, appearance of kanji/writing'

Undergoer	Compound	Gloss
ture	miti-zure	'road-take-along, traveling companion'
turi	iso-zuri	'beach-fishing, fishing from rocks by the shore'
turi	oki-zuri	'open sea-fishing, offshore fishing'
turi	te-zuri	'hand-fishing, handline fishing'
turu₁	imo-zuru	'potato-vine, sweet potato vines'
turu₁	te-zuru	'hand-vine, connections, contacts, influence'
turu₁	yumi-zuru	'bowstring'
turu₂	ori-zuru	'fold-crane, origami folding crane'
turu₂	tantyoo-zuru	'Manchurian crane, *Grus japonensis*'
tuti	kana-zuti	'metal-hammer, iron hammer'
tuti	ko-zuti	'small-hammer, gavel'
tutu	i-zutu	'well-pipe, well curb'
tuyoi	kokoro-zuyoi	'heart-strong, feeling secure'
tyawan	yunomi-zyawan	'tea-drinking cup'

A.2   Compounds Exhibiting Lyman's Law Effects

Nonundergoer	Compound	Gloss
haba	hiro-haba	'broad-width, double-width cloth or fabric'
haba	kata-haba	'shoulder width (breadth)'
haba	kawa-haba	'river-width, width of a river'
haba	mi-haba	'body-width, width of a garment'
haba	mune-haba	'chest-width, breadth of the chest'
haba	oo-haba	'big-width, full width, large scale, drastic'
haba	yoko-haba	'side-width, breadth, width'
hada	aka-hada	'red-skin, grazed skin, bare of trees'
hada	are-hada	'rough skin'
hada	hito-hada	'person-skin, skin, body warmth'
hada	iwa-hada	'rock-skin, bare rock'
hada	kata-hada	'shoulder-skin, bare shoulder'
hada	ki-hada	'tree-skin, bark of a tree'
hada	moro-hada	'straight-skin, strip oneself to one's waist'
hada	moti-hada	'rice-cake-skin, soft, smooth skin'
hada	same-hada	'shark-skin, fish skin'
hada	su-hada	'bare-skin, naked body, natural complexion'
hada	tori-hada	'bird-skin, gooseflesh, pimples'
hada	yama-hada	'mountain-skin, bare surface of a mountain'
hada	yawa-hada	'soft-skin, fair skin'

Nonundergoer	Compound	Gloss
hada	yuki-hada	'snow-skin, snow's surface, lily-white skin'
hada	zi-hada	'earth-skin, texture, grain'
hage	maru-hage	'round-bald, complete baldness'
hage	waka-hage	'young-bald, premature baldness'
hagi₁	kake-hagi	'hook-attach, invisible mending of clothes'
hagi₁	tugi-hagi	'join-attach, patching'
hagi₂	oi-hagi	'chase-pull-off, highway robber'
hagure	kui-hagure	'eat-go-astray, missing one's meal'
hakobi	hude-hakobi	'brush-carry, penmanship'
hazi	aka-hazi	'red-shame, disgrace'
hazi	sini-hazi	'die-shame, shameful death'
hazime	goyoo-hazime	'business-begin, opening of offices for the year'
hazime	te-hazime	'hand-begin, in the beginning'
hazu	te-hazu	'hand-expected, a plan, arrangements'
hazure	mato-hazure	'mark-miss, missing the mark'
hazure	miti-hazure	'road-miss, outskirts of town'
hebi	garagara-hebi	'rattlesnake'
hebi	kuro-hebi	'black snake'
hebi	sima-hebi	'striped-snake, garter snake'
hebi	umi-hebi	'sea-snake, sea serpent'
hibari	kusa-hibari	'grass-lark, grass cricket, *Paratrigonidium bifasciatum*'
hida	yama-hida	'mountain-crease, folds of a mountain'
hida	yoko-hida	'vertical-crease, vertical fold'
hidoi	te-hidoi	'hand-harsh, harshly, mercilessly'
hige	ago-hige	'chin-beard, goatee'
hige	kuti-hige	'mouth-beard, mustache'
hige	tora-hige	'tiger-beard, bristly beard or mustache'
hige	yagi-hige	'goat-beard, goatee'
hituzi	ko-hituzi	'child-sheep, lamb'
hiza	kata-hiza	'side-knee, (kneel on) one knee'
hiza	tate-hiza	'stand-knee, sitting with one knee drawn up'
hizi	kata-hizi	'side-elbow, (rest on) one elbow'
hodoki	te-hodoki	'hand-untie, initiating, teaching
huda	ai-huda	'match-sign, check'
huda	aka-huda	'red-sign, goods sold, clearance sale'
huda	e-huda	'picture-sign, face or picture card'
huda	hana-huda	'flower-sign, floral playing cards'

Nonundergoer	Compound	Gloss
huda	hari-huda	'paste-sign, poster, notice'
huda	hiki-huda	'pull-sign, circular, announcement flier'
huda	ire-huda	'enter-sign, bid, tender'
huda	kake-huda	'hang-sign, placard'
huda	kiri-huda	'cut-sign, trump card'
huda	na-huda	'name-sign, nameplate, nametag'
huda	ne-huda	'price-sign, price tag (mark, label)'
huda	ni-huda	'load-sign, label, tag'
huda	nise-huda	'fake-sign, counterfeit money, forged document'
huda	nuri-huda	'lacquered sign'
huda	sage-huda	'hang-sign, tag, label'
huda	siti-huda	'pawn-sign, pawn ticket'
huda	tate-huda	'stand-sign, notice, bulletin board'
huda	te-huda	'hand-sign, hand (in cards), visiting card'
huda	tomi-huda	'fortune-sign, lottery ticket'
huda	tori-huda	'take-sign, card(s) to be picked up'
huda	tuke-huda	'attach-sign, tag, label'
huda	tuzi-huda	'crossroads-sign, street corner bulletin board'
hude	e-hude	'picture-brush, paintbrush'
hude	hito-hude	'one-brush, a few lines, stroke of pen'
hugu	tora-hugu	'tiger globefish'
husagi	ana-husagi	'hole-clogging, stopgap'
husagi	basyo-husagi	'place-clogging, obstruction'
kaba	sira-kaba	'white birch'
kabe	ita-kabe	'board-wall, wooden wall'
kabe	nama-kabe	'fresh-wall, undried wall'
kabe	sira-kabe	'white-wall, white plaster wall'
kabe	tuti-kabe	'earth-wall, mud wall'
kabi	ao-kabi	'blue-mold, penicillium'
kabi	kuro-kabi	'black-mold, bread mold, *Aspergillus niger*'
kabu	huru-kabu	'old-stock, old-timer, veteran, senior'
kabu	kara-kabu	'empty-stock, fictitious stock'
kabu	kiri-kabu	'cut-stock, stump, stubble'
kabu	ko-kabu	'child-stock, new bulb, new stocks'
kabu	moti-kabu	'hold-stock, stock holdings, one's shares'
kabu	ninki-kabu	'favorite-stock, popular stocks'
kabu	oya-kabu	'parent-stock, parent root or stock'
kabu	sin-kabu	'new-stock, new stocks or shares'

Nonundergoer	Compound	Gloss
kabu	zatu-kabu	'miscellaneous-stock, assorted stocks'
kabu	zitu-kabu	'actual-stock, shares actually traded'
kabuto	tetu-kabuto	'iron helmet'
kado$_1$	hito-kado	'one-point, full-fledged, considerable'
kado$_2$	magari-kado	'turn-corner, turning point'
kado$_2$	mati-kado	'street corner'
kagami	mizu-kagami	'water-mirror, one's image in the water'
kagami	te-kagami	'hand mirror'
kage	hi-kage	'sun shadow'
kage	hito-kage	'man-shadow, silhouette'
kage	hosi-kage	'star-shadow, starlight'
kage	tuki-kage	'moon-shadow, moonlight'
kage	yama-kage	'mountain-shadow, mountain recess/shelter'
kage	yuu-kage	'evening-shadow, light of the setting sun'
kagi$_1$	ai-kagi	'match-key, passkey, duplicate key'
kagi$_2$	te-kagi	'hand-hook, cargo hook'
kago	kuzu-kago	'trash-basket, wastebasket'
kago	musi-kago	'insect cage'
kago	te-kago	'handbasket'
kago	tori-kago	'birdcage'
kago	turi-kago	'fish-basket, angler's basket, gondola'
kamado	seeyoo-kamado	'western-oven, Western kitchen range'
kasegi	de-kasegi	'leave-earn, working away from home'
kasegi	genkoo-kasegi	'manuscript-earn, living on one's writing'
kasegi	zikan-kasegi	'time-earn, holding out, stalling, putting off'
kawazu	ao-kawazu	'green frog'
kaze$_1$	aki-kaze	'autumn breeze'
kaze$_1$	asa-kaze	'morning breeze'
kaze$_1$	ha-kaze	'leaf-wind, breeze rustling through leaves'
kaze$_1$	hama-kaze	'beach-wind, sea breeze'
kaze$_1$	haru-kaze	'spring breeze'
kaze$_1$	kami-kaze	'god-wind, divine wind, kamikaze'
kaze$_1$	kara-kaze	'dry wind'
kaze$_1$	kawa-kaze	'river-wind, breeze off a river'
kaze$_1$	kita-kaze	'north wind'
kaze$_1$	koi-kaze	'love-wind, love's zephyr'
kaze$_1$	ma-kaze	'devil-wind, storm caused by devil, evil wind'
kaze$_1$	matu-kaze	'pine-wind, (sound of) wind through pine trees'

Nonundergoer	Compound	Gloss
kaze$_1$	nisi-kaze	'west wind'
kaze$_1$	oi-kaze	'chase-wind, tailwind, fair or favorable wind'
kaze$_1$	oo-kaze	'strong-wind, gale'
kaze$_1$	sima-kaze	'island wind'
kaze$_1$	sio-kaze	'salt-wind, sea breeze'
kaze$_1$	soyo-kaze	'gentle breeze'
kaze$_1$	suzu-kaze	'cool breeze'
kaze$_1$	tani-kaze	'valley wind'
kaze$_1$	umi-kaze	'sea breeze'
kaze$_1$	ura-kaze	'back-wind, back sea breeze'
kaze$_1$	yama-kaze	'mountain wind'
kaze$_1$	yo-kaze	'night wind'
kaze$_1$	yoko-kaze	'side-wind, crosswind'
kaze$_2$	hana-kaze	'nose-cold, head cold'
kaze$_2$	natu-kaze	'summer cold'
kaze$_2$	otahuku-kaze	'fat-faced-woman-cold, mumps'
kaziri	nama-kaziri	'raw-bite, superficial knowledge'
kazu	hito-kazu	'person-number, number of people'
kazu	kazu-kazu	'number-number, many'
kazu	kuti-kazu	'mouth-number, number of dependents'
kibi	satoo-kibi	'sugarcane'
kizu	huru-kizu	'old wound'
kizu	kami-kizu	'bite wound'
kizu	sasi-kizu	'stab-wound, puncture wound'
kizu	suri-kizu	'scratch-wound, graze, abrasion'
kizu	tama-kizu	'bullet wound'
kobu	tikara-kobu	'strength-bump, well-developed biceps'
koge	kuro-koge	'black-burn, scorched black'
kosogi	ne-kosogi	'root-scrape off, root and all, completely'
kotoba	kaki-kotoba	'write-word, written language'
kubi	asi-kubi	'foot-neck, ankle'
kubi	eri-kubi	'collar-neck, nape of neck'
kubi	gan-kubi	'pipe-head, bowl of a pipe'
kubi	kama-kubi	'gooseneck (snake)'
kubi	maru-kubi	'round-neck, round-necked T-shirt'
kubi	nama-kubi	'raw-head, freshly severed head'
kubi	ne-kubi	'sleep-head, (cut off) head of a sleeping person'
kubi	nise-kubi	'fake-head, substitute (severed) head'

Nonundergoer	Compound	Gloss
kubi	te-kubi	'hand-neck, wrist'
kubi	uti-kubi	'hit-head, decapitation'
kuda	te-kuda	'hand-pipe, trick'
kudasi	hara-kudasi	'stomach-lowering, diarrhea'
kugi	ai-kugi	'match-nail, double-pointed nail'
kugi	inu-kugi	'dog-nail, spike'
kuguri	inu-kuguri	'dog-pass, dog door'
kuguri	tainai-kuguri	'womb-pass, pass through womb of Buddha statue'
kurabe	see-kurabe	'height-compare, measure one's height with another'
kurabe	tikara-kurabe	'strength-compare, strength contest'
kurage	denki-kurage	'electric jellyfish'
kuzi	atari-kuzi	'hit-raffle-ticket, (winning) prize ticket'
kuzi	kara-kuzi	'empty-raffle-ticket, (draw) a blank'
kuzu	ito-kuzu	'thread-waste, fluff, piece of thread'
kuzu	kami-kuzu	'paper-waste, wastepaper'
kuzu	kana-kuzu	'metal-waste, scrap metal'
kuzu	noko-kuzu	'saw-waste, sawdust'
kuzu	pan-kuzu	'bread-waste, bread crumb'
kuzu	tati-kuzu	'cut-waste, waste pieces (of cut cloth)'
kuzure	ne-kuzure	'prize-collapse, drop in prices'
kuzure	soo-kuzure	'all-collapse, sweeping crash in stock'
kuzure	yama-kuzure	'mountain-collapse, mountain slide, landslide'
sabaki	asi-sabaki	'leg-handle, legwork'
sabaki	mae-sabaki	'front-handle, maneuver at onset of sumo match'
sabaki	te-sabaki	'hand-handle, handle skillfully'
sabi	aka-sabi	'red rust'
sabi	kana-sabi	'metal rust'
sabisii	ura-sabisii	'back-lonely, lonesome'
sage	kaku-sage	'grade-lower, demotion, downgrading'
sage	te-sage	'hand-lower, handbasket'
sage	tin-sage	'pay-lower, pay cut'
sagi	sira-sagi	'white-heron, snowy egret'
sawagi	kara-sawagi	'empty-uproar, commotion about nothing'
sawagi	muna-sawagi	'breast-uproar, uneasiness, have a presentiment'
sawagi	oo-sawagi	'big-uproar, hubbub, racket'
sazi	oo-sazi	'big-spoon, tablespoon'
sazi	tya-sazi	'teaspoon'

Nonundergoer	Compound	Gloss
sezi	kara-sezi	'empty-compliment, flattery, lip service'
siba₁	hira-siba	'flat-grass, sod'
siba₂	siba-siba	'often-often, frequently, again and again'
sibu	kaki-sibu	'persimmon-sour, astringent persimmon juice'
sibu	sibu-sibu	'sour-sour, reluctantly'
simezi	murasaki-simezi	'purple-champignon, *Lyophyllum aggregatum*'
sinogi	itizi-sinogi	'once-enduring, makeshift, temporary expedient'
sinogi	kuti-sinogi	'mouth-enduring, barely making a living'
sinogi	taikutu-sinogi	'tedium-enduring, timekiller'
sirabe	kote-sirabe	'small-hand-investigation, test, tryout'
sirabe	sita-sirabe	'under-investigation, preliminary inquiry'
sirabe	syooko-sirabe	'evidence-investigation, taking of evidence'
sirube	miti-sirube	'road-guide, road signpost'
sizuka	mono-sizuka	'thing-quiet, serene, composed'
soba	kake-soba	'pour-on-soba, soba in hot broth'
soba	yaki-soba	'fry-soba, fried soba'
soba	zaru-soba	'bamboo-basket-soba, soba on a bamboo plate'
sode	han-sode	'half-sleeve, short-sleeved'
sode	hiro-sode	'wide-sleeve, wide-sleeved'
sode	huri-sode	'hang-sleeve, long-sleeved kimono'
sode	kaku-sode	'square-sleeve, square-sleeved'
sode	ko-sode	'small-sleeve, wadded silk garment'
sode	naga-sode	'long-sleeve, long-sleeved'
sode	tome-sode	'fasten-sleeve, married woman's ceremonial kimono'
sode	tutu-sode	'tube-sleeve, tight-sleeved'
suberi	hatu-suberi	'first-slide, skiing on New Year's Day'
suberi	yoko-suberi	'side-slide, slip sideways'
suberi	zi-suberi	'earth-slide, landslide'
sudare	take-sudare	'bamboo screen'
sudare	tama-sudare	'bead screen'
sugata	hatu-sugata	'first-figure, person in New Year's outfit'
sugata	tabi-sugata	'journey-figure, traveling attire'
sugata	usiro-sugata	'back-figure, figure from behind, person's back'
sugi₁	hiru-sugi	'noon-pass, after noon'
sugi₁	kuti-sugi	'mouth-pass, eking out a living, livelihood'
sugi₂	ito-sugi	'thread-cedar, cypress'
susugi	kuti-susugi	'mouth rinse'
suzi	hito-suzi	'one-line, earnestly, straightforwardly'

Nonundergoer	Compound	Gloss
suzi	ie-suzi	'family-line, lineage, pedigree'
suzi	kin-suzi	'gold-line, golden stripes'
suzi	tame-suzi	'benefit-line, patron'
suzi	te-suzi	'hand-line, having a natural aptitude'
suzi	yoko-suzi	'side-line, transversal, lateral stripes'
suzumi	yuu-suzumi	'evening cool'
taba	hana-taba	'flower-bundle, bunch of flowers, bouquet'
taba	kagi-taba	'key-bundle, bunch of keys'
taba	mugi-taba	'wheat-bundle, wheat sheaf, stacked wheat'
taba	satu-taba	'money-bundle, roll of banknotes'
$tabi_1$	hito-tabi	'one-time, once, on one occasion'
$tabi_1$	huta-tabi	'two-time, again, once more'
$tabi_1$	iku-tabi	'how-many-times, how often'
$tabi_1$	tabi-tabi	'time-time, often, repeatedly'
$tabi_2$	hitori-tabi	'single-travel, solitary journey'
$tabi_2$	huna-tabi	'boat-travel, trip by boat'
$tabi_2$	mata-tabi	'crotch-travel, wandering life of a gambler'
$tabi_2$	naga-tabi	'long-travel, long trip'
$tabi_3$	zika-tabi	'earth-down-socks, workman's socks worn without shoes'
tabu	mimi-tabu	'earlobe'
tada	tada-tada	'just-just, simply'
tade	yanagi-tade	'willow smartweed'
taguri	turu-taguri	'vine pulling'
tamago	yude-tamago	'boiled egg'
tamago	zi-tamago	'earth-egg, locally produced egg'
tigai	te-tigai	'hand-wrong, something amiss, hitch'
tigire	tigire-tigire	'break-break, torn to pieces'
tobi	issoku-tobi	'one-foot-jump, (with) one bound'
tobi	kyoku-tobi	'acrobatic-jump, fancy dive'
tobi	sandan-tobi	'three-step-jump, triple jump'
tobi	taka-tobi	'high-jump, high leap, capriole'
tobi	tobi-tobi	'jump-jump, skipping, alternately'
todoki	hu-todoki	'non-careful, rude, insolent'
toge	saka-toge	'up-thorn, reverse thorn'
tokage	ao-tokage	'green lizard'
tokage	hi-tokage	'fire-lizard, salamander'
tonbo	aka-tonbo	'red dragonfly'
tonbo	take-tonbo	'bamboo-dragonfly, small wooden toy'

Nonundergoer	Compound	Gloss
tozi	kari-tozi	'temporary-bind, temporary paper binding'
tozi	kawa-tozi	'leather-bind, leather binding'
tozi	yoko-tozi	'side-bind, binding a book in an oblong shape'
tuba	nama-tuba	'raw-sputum, saliva in one's mouth'
tuba	tan-tuba	'phlegm-sputum, spittle, expectoration'
tubaki	kan-tubaki	'cold-camellia, winter camellia'
tubaki	yama-tubaki	'mountain camellia'
$tubo_1$	huzi-tubo	'wisteria-jar, acorn shell'
$tubo_1$	kesi-tubo	'erase-jar, charcoal extinguisher'
$tubo_1$	kotu-tubo	'bone-jar, funerary urn'
$tubo_1$	sumi-tubo	'ink-jar, ink bottle'
$tubo_1$	taki-tubo	'waterfall-jar, basin under waterfall'
$tubo_1$	tako-tubo	'octopus-jar, octopus trap'
$tubo_1$	tan-tubo	'phlegm-jar, spittoon, cuspidor'
$tubo_1$	tya-tubo	'tea jar'
$tubo_2$	nobe-tubo	'total-*tsubo* (square units), total floor space'
$tubo_2$	tate-tubo	'build-*tsubo*, floor space'
tubu	ama-tubu	'raindrop'
tubu	awa-tubu	'millet grain'
tubu	hito-tubu	'one grain'
tubu	ko-tubu	'small grain'
tubu	suna-tubu	'sand grain'
tubu	tubu-tubu	'grain-grain, beaded, pimpled'
tubusi	goku-tubusi	'grain-waste, good-for-nothing fellow, idler'
tubusi	zikan-tubusi	'time-waste, wasting time'
tuge	inu-tuge	'dog-boxwood, Japanese holly'
$tugi_1$	eda-tugi	'branch-join, cleft grafting'
$tugi_1$	hone-tugi	'bone-join, bonesetting'
$tugi_1$	yaki-tugi	'burn-join, piecing broken china together by baking'
$tugi_2$	tugi-tugi	'next-next, in succession, one after another'
tumugi	siro-tumugi	'white pongee'
tunagi	tamago-tunagi	'egg-fasten, binding with egg'
tunagi	zyuzu-tunagi	'rosary-link, tied in a row'
tutuzi	yama-tutuzi	'mountain azalea'
tuzi	yotu-tuzi	'four-crossing, crossroads, intersection'
tuzuki	te-tuzuki	'hand-continue, formalities, procedure, steps'
tuzumi	sita-tuzumi	'tongue-drum, smacking one's lips'

Notes

Chapter 1

1. The system is largely a faithful rendition of the native kana syllabary in Roman letters. Linguistically sophisticated Japanese-language textbooks, such as those authored by Eleanor Harz Jorden (e.g., Jorden 1963), also rely on a modified version of the Kunrei system.

2. Here we are in general agreement with other students of Japanese. For example, Unger (1986) argues that "Kunrei romanization is more appropriate for the representation of Japanese in Latin letters than Hepburn romanization because it more accurately reflects the morphophonemic structure of *Yamato-kotoba* and *kango*, which comprise the two most important strata of the Japanese lexicon."

Chapter 2

1. The representations are simplified in abstracting away from the possibility of intervening resonants and long vowels. The central restriction was known to the ancient grammarians and appears in all standard handbooks (e.g., Whitney 1889). Since the case serves mainly illustrative purposes, we are not concerned with details of the phonetics and phonology of aspiration in Sanskrit (in particular, the distinction between voiced and voiceless aspirates), but simply take the dissimilation to affect all segments with the feature specification [+aspirated].

2. Allen (1951) provides the first formal treatment of these alternations within modern linguistics, using it to motivate a nonlinear model of phonological structure. Autosegmental OCP-based analyses appear in Borowsky and Mester 1983 and Kaye and Lowenstamm 1985, among others.

3. Multiple linking involving nonadjacent positions, as in (3c), raises issues of its own and is for many features (such as voicing) arguably out of the question (see Archangeli and Pulleyblank 1994; Ito, Mester, and Padgett 1995). More recently, a strictly localist position has been proposed, disallowing gapped configurations as a matter of principle (see Gafos 1996; Walker 1998; Ní Chiosáin and Padgett 2001).

4. As in cases classified as "dissimilative deletions" in neogrammarian handbooks (e.g., Latin *lanterna* > *laterna* 'lantern'), where consonants in weak positions disappear under the pressure of identical consonants in the local environment. See Paul 1880, 65–66, for example, for characterization and examples.

5. See Steriade 1987, Mester and Ito 1989, Cho 1990, and Lombardi 1991, among others, for versions of the privative approach within underspecification theory.

6. As first proposed in Clements 1985 and followed in many other works (see Clements and Hume 1995 for an overview).

7. See Kiparsky 1982, Archangeli 1984, Steriade 1987, and Mester and Ito 1989, among others, for specific proposals and arguments.

8. As proposed in McCarthy 1981, 1986.

9. See McCarthy and Prince 1993b, Kiparsky 1998, and Ito and Mester 2001b, 2002a, 2003 on the issue of a derivational relation between lexical and postlexical phonology, and perhaps even further level distinctions.

10. The occurrence of redundant phonetic aspiration in environments of fortition is a separate matter and not at issue here.

11. We will continue to use an "autosegmental" mode of representation, with features such as [aspirated] occupying a separate horizontal area in diagrams, for visual clarity. Linking lines here simply express that a segment has a certain property, without further geometric or other implications about tiers, planes, class nodes, and so on. While the current status of autosegmentalism as a theory within OT phonology is an important topic in itself, our investigation and its results have little bearing on the issue.

12. In particular, the markedness threshold idea is not intended to cover all phenomena involving multiple occurrences of linguistic elements, such as haplology and other repetition-avoiding patterns (see Yip 1998 for an important study), as exemplified by the following case (from German, based on the homonymy of *morgen*, which means both 'tomorrow' and 'morning'):

(i)   gestern morgen   'yesterday morning'
      heute morgen   'this morning'
   *morgen morgen   'tomorrow morning' ($\rightarrow$ morgen früh)

13. This should not be taken to exclude *adjacency* as a predicate expressing a locality condition on dissimilation; see section 3.3.3 for an example.

14. Besides the method based on harmonic alignment of prominence scales developed by Prince and Smolensky (1993) to express optimal slot-filler relations in syllabification and elsewhere, which is more limited in scope (see Aissen 1999 for an application in a syntactic context).

15. Presentations of Smolensky's constraint conjunction theory in the published literature include Kirchner 1996 and Suzuki 1997. Hewitt and Crowhurst (1996) propose a similarly named operation with different effects: the derived constraint is violated whenever *either* (not *both*) of the individual constraints is violated (this proposal is also made use of in Downing 1998). The potential for terminological confusion stems from the fact that the operation of *local conjunction*, when applying to C_1 and C_2, as in (12), derives a constraint ($C_1 \&_\delta C_2$) that, in terms of standard propositional logic, is equivalent to $C_1 \lor C_2$, the *logical disjunction* of C_1 and C_2: false if and only if both disjuncts (i.e., both C_1 and C_2) are false. Conversely, a conceivable operation of (inclusive) *local disjunction*, deriving a constraint $C_1 \lor_\delta C_2$ violated if either C_1 or C_2 is violated in some domain δ, is equivalent to $C_1 \land C_2$, the *logical conjunction* of C_1 and C_2: false if and only if either $*C_1$ or $*C_2$ (or both) are false. See also note 25 for related discussion.

16. See chapter 5 for further discussion of the relevant domains and of the important question to what extent the δ-domain of a conjunction is predictable on the basis of its constituents.

17. These issues clearly deserve further study; see Baković 2000 for important discussion.

18. See Ito and Mester 1997b for further details of the constraint-conjunctive positional markedness analysis presented below, and see section 8.4.1 for discussion of alternative positional faithfulness approaches to such distributional asymmetries.

19. The highly regulated modern spelling conventions strive to keep the spellings of morphemes constant across contexts and abstract away from all devoicing: ⟨Rad⟩ for [raːt] 'wheel', and so on. Earlier spelling conventions (e.g., the various Middle High German spelling traditions and the preregulation practice in the modern period, not to mention the spelling mistakes frequently made by contemporary school children) indicate devoicing in an explicit way. In Modern German, the neutralization of the voiced/voiceless contrast in words with syllable-final obstruents is usually regarded as complete (spelling pronunciations, hypercorrection, and language interference effects aside), eliminating any consistent and reliable cue to point to the underlying value. Occasional claims that neutralization is incomplete (see, e.g., Port and O'Dell 1985; Port and Crawford 1989) are likely to involve the interference of extraneous factors (for discussion, see Fourakis and Iverson 1984; Manaster Ramer 1996).

20. Here and throughout this book, *No-D* is used as a mnemonic label for the markedness constraint against all voiced obstruents (*D* can be thought of as abbreviating *dakuon* (濁音), the Japanese term for voiced obstruents (lit. 'turbid sound')). In earlier work (Ito and Mester 1998), we referred to this constraint as "VOP" ("Voiced Obstruent Prohibition").

21. The larger issue here is the crosslinguistic failure of "overkill" candidates like [liː] to win in such competitions. See section 8.4.1 for discussion, in connection with the positional faithfulness approach to coda devoicing (Lombardi 2001).

22. There is also a conjunction $\text{ONSET}\&_\delta\text{No-D}$ with $\delta = \sigma$, but this is no more than a purely formal possibility (see our earlier discussion of this issue)—that is, one of the many syntactically possible conjunctions that are never active in grammars, for reasons of locality. The syllable as a whole is not an appropriate domain where onsetlessness and voiced obstruenthood could add up, resulting in unattested coda devoicing exclusively in onsetless syllables (i.e., /ed/ → [et] alongside /ted/ → [ted]). This is similar to the often-cited fact that there are few, if any, solid cases of onsetlessness interacting with codafulness in the syllable domain (i.e., /ted/ → [ted] but /ed/ → [e]). These examples do not argue against constraint conjunction as a formal tool for building derived constraints; they only show that it does not come with a substantive theory of locality written on its sleeve (see chapter 5 for further discussion).

23. With local conjunction as a recursive operation, ternary (and higher) conjunction such as $(\text{No-}\varphi\&_\delta\text{No-}\varphi)\&_\delta\text{No-}\varphi = \text{No-}\varphi^2\&_\delta\text{No-}\varphi = \text{No-}\varphi^3{}_\delta$ are formally derivable. In the example given, the third violation of No-φ would be the fatal one. No convincing evidence has been found so far that $\text{No-}\varphi^3$ is ever linguistically operative separate from $\text{No-}\varphi^2$, which tends to support the old idea in generative linguistics (cf. syntactic movement theory) that the genuine contrast in grammars is not "1 vs. 2 vs. 3 vs. 4 vs. . . .", but "1 vs. greater than 1."

24. We will henceforth sometimes omit the domain index δ when the identity of the local domain is not at issue.

25. Departing from strict Smolenskian theory with its local conjunction operator "&", another approach to building composite constraints out of simple ones employs Boolean operations on constraint statements (Downing 1998; Hewitt and Crowhurst 1996). This approach is not suitable here because it does not have the means to express the crucial self-conjunctive nature of OCP-type dissimilation. Recall that in propositional logic, both the

conjunction C∧C and the disjunction C∨C are equivalent to C (e.g., *It is raining and it is raining* is true if and only if *It is raining* is true, and the same holds for *It is raining or it is raining*). Therefore, neither C∧C nor C∨C can do the work of C&ₛC.

26. The question is moot in this case since lexicon optimization will weed out input forms like the hypothetical /bʰidʰ/, whose output would *always* neutralize with that of some other input (see Prince and Smolensky 1993, 191–196; Ito, Mester, and Padgett 1995, 588–594).

27. We return to reduplicated forms involving Grassmann-style deaspiration in section 3.3.4.

28. It is interesting to note that the kana syllabary of Japanese has a direct and systematic representation of voicing in the form of the diacritic *dakuten* (lit. 'turbid points') on a kana, which is used to indicate voicing of consonants: た/だ [ta/da], く/ぐ [ku/gu], and so on. The *dakuten* is used in a strictly contrastive way (i.e., when the consonant is a voiced obstruent contrasting with a voiceless one, as in the examples just given), and not with redundantly voiced sonorants.

29. The general duplication problem was first systematically discussed by Kenstowicz and Kisseberth (1977) for cases like Yawelmani Yokuts, where morpheme structure constraints duplicate the effects of phonological rules.

30. For a recent proposal along similar lines making use of an abstract autosegmental *rendaku* marker with crucial underspecification, see Kuroda 2002.

31. /h/ does not occur intervocalically inside morphemes, hence its absence from C₂ position.

32. The fact that CDD forms are excluded as thoroughly as DDC forms is also of interest, in connection with Frisch, Broe, and Pierrehumbert's (1995) hypothesis that later position in the word can weaken the stringency of co-occurrence restrictions. For the distribution of obstruent voicing in Japanese, no such "weakening downstream" of the restriction is in evidence.

33. The common word *budoo* 'grapes' (葡萄) comes closest to being a genuine exception, yet the way it is written already casts serious doubt on its status as a monomorphemic and native form. As a reviewer notes, it is "famous as an example of a word written with two characters ... that are both used only to write that word. The usual explanation is that the Chinese word was a borrowing and that the two characters were created to write it in order to maintain the one-to-one match between syllables and characters in Chinese orthography. As was often the case, the word and the characters were borrowed into Japanese together."

34. As pointed out earlier, here and throughout this book we differentiate IDENT and similar faithfulness constraints into their feature-specific instantiations only when the point being discussed warrants this degree of detail. For further discussion of the IDENT family of constraints, see chapter 6.

35. These mostly reflect the situation in their language of origin. See Ito and Mester 1996b and Kurisu 2000 for examples and analysis.

36. Also known as *mimetics*. In McCawley's (1968, 64) characterization, they "function syntactically as manner adverbs and may refer to just any aspect (visual, emotional, etc.) of the activity involved, rather than just its sound."

37. Even this might be granting too much to the first view, however, since there is no evidence, for example, showing that all multiply voiced ideophones are of recent origin.

38. The argument in Rice 1997 for a position close to the first view involves incorrect assumptions about the Japanese facts. See Ito, Mester, and Padgett 2001 for clarification.

Chapter 3

1. The issue of local self-conjunction of constraints affecting prosodic properties like stress and length is raised by Kirchner (1996, 346) (see also Kager's (1994) Parse-2 constraint). It is further explored by Alderete (1997), who takes up proposals made by Odden (1994) and develops an articulated theory of adjacency relations.

2. As the handbooks are careful to point out (see Leumann 1977, 184; Sihler 1995, 322), degemination in Latin sometimes occurs before other kinds of heavy syllables, that is, without a following second geminate.

(i) kanna 'reed' kanaalis 'channel' *kannaalis
    farr- 'spelt' fariina 'meal, flour' *farriina
    kurrus 'chariot' kuruulis 'relating to a chariot' *kurruulis
    pollen 'fine flour' polenta 'barley-groats' *pollenta

If these facts are part and parcel of the same phenomenon as geminate dissimilation, they might be taken to point to a direct prosodic/rhythmic factor (e.g., some version of No-Clash), potentially undermining the OCP-based analysis in the text. On the other hand, it is equally conceivable that the OCP explanation extends to the cases above. The sporadically dissimilating marked property might be "heavy syllable," with dissimilation preferentially affecting the most marked structure, namely, the consonantal geminate.

3. In the Latin case just considered, it is also likely that, in order for degemination to take place, the consonants have to occupy adjacent syllables. Thus, the special superlative formation found with adjectives in -ilis, as in *fakilis* 'easy', *fakillimus* 'easiest', does not trigger degemination in *diffikilis* 'difficult', *diffikillimus* 'most difficult', **difikillimus*. Setting aside paradigm uniformity considerations, this might point to an additional locality factor for the double geminate constraint (7).

4. There are further facts and subgeneralizations that a full analysis needs to factor in. Unlike voiceless obstruents, voiced obstruents usually only geminate when they are absolutely word-final in English (e.g., [paddo] 'pad' vs. [pudingu] 'pudding', and [daburu] 'double' vs. [kappuru] 'couple'), and word-internal [t] (often flapped in American English intervocalically before an unstressed syllable) frequently resists gemination (e.g., [bataa] 'butter', but also [batterii] 'battery'). This is why (10) does not include gemination contrasts for [t] and for voiced geminates, which would have little probative value. See Katayama 1998 for a treatment of the phonology of gemination in Japanese loanwords where these factors are analyzed in detail, and Kawagoe and Arai 2002 for recent experimental results.

5. Except for obvious compounds like [uddopekkaa] 'woodpecker' and [eggunoggu] 'eggnog'.

6. But compare the clipped form [pokke], where degemination of [kk] is no longer triggered by a following geminate in the word. A reviewer points out that gemination of voiceless obstruents is sometimes avoided toward the beginning of long loanwords (cf. [fakusimiri] 'facsimile' with single [k] and the short form [fakkusu] 'fax' with [kk]), and it is indeed conceivable that this positional factor contributes to the nonco-occurrence of geminates. However, since geminates can clearly appear both in antepenultimate/penultimate ([batterii] 'battery', etc.) and in penultimate/final position ([samitto] 'summit', etc.), it is difficult to see how this factor could alone be responsible for the fact that geminates never seem to co-occur in these two positions (*[pokketto], etc.).

7. All researchers who have dealt with this area of loanword phonology have observed this directionality effect: gemination after a lax vowel preferentially targets the rightmost voiceless plosive in a word. Alternatives to the alignment treatment chosen here for expository purposes are worth investigating and might reveal more fundamental factors, such as a preference for heavy penults, which, as Haruo Kubozono has pointed out to us, will attract the pitch accent. In her model of loanword phonology based on Sympathy Theory (see, e.g., Davis 1997; Ito and Mester 1997b; Karvonen and Sherman 1998; Walker 1998; McCarthy 1999), Katayama (1998, 136–140) attributes the directional bias to a constellation of factors that include, besides input specification of moras, the results of the sympathy candidate selection process, which turn out to depend on whether the consonant is word-final or preconsonantal in the source word.

8. We assume that all other relevant IDENT constraints (as well as MAX, etc.) dominate IDENT[μ], such that degemination is the only viable repair strategy. It is also conceivable that Amharic degemination is not a general phonological process, but an allomorphic one (similar to Latin *l*-dissimilation in section 3.3.3). In this case, the antagonistic constraint would not be a faithfulness constraint (here IDENT[μ]), but an allomorph preference constraint.

9. As John Alderete, Joe Pater, Philip Spaelti, and Keiichiro Suzuki have independently pointed out to us, the new conception of the OCP as enhanced markedness makes sense of another case that remained recalcitrant under the classical conception: the dissimilation of NC combinations found in several languages of Austronesia (including Manga Mbula and Timugon Murut) and Australia (Gurindji and other languages of the northern desert fringe, as well as Gooniyandi; see Evans 1995 and work cited there). Alderete (1997) also discusses cases of nonautosegmental dissimilation, whose effects cannot be derived by the traditional OCP.

10. The relevance of this kind of case was first pointed out to us by Koichi Tateishi.

11. The output of the phonology, as given here, is simplified in abstracting away from tonal information (especially boundary tones) that is predictable on the basis of the prosodic representation. We assume the essential correctness of the basic division of labor between phonology and phonetics argued for in most of the recent work on accent and intonation, which involves phonological output structures with very few strategically placed tonal markings, leaving the task of filling in the tonal contour of the whole string to an algorithm for phonetic realization that operates with continuous values, assigning F0 values to phonological tone markings and interpolating between them. Poser (1984) and Pierrehumbert and Beckman (1988) develop detailed arguments for the superiority of this view in the case of Japanese, showing in particular that there is significant evidence against phonological tone spreading and default tone assignment mechanisms invoked in earlier studies to achieve some kind of full tonal specification in the output of the phonology.

12. Building the analysis on the basic markedness constraint No-HL does not necessarily imply that it is otherwise active in the accentual phonology of Japanese (even though it is a remarkable fact that a significant portion of Japanese words are unaccented). While an accentual fall constitutes a marked structure, its presence might be demanded by higher-ranking constraints favoring the presence of an accentual head.

13. A certain class of accentually independent prefixes preserves its accent. When these prefixes are combined with accented stems, this leads to the occurrence of two accents, as in *mo*[HL]*to-dai*[HL]*zin* 'former minister'. As Poser (1990) has shown, the correct prosodic analysis here involves more than one prosodic word.

14. See Smith 1998 for a treatment of this and other noun/verb faithfulness contrasts.

15. Under the metaranking scheme FAITH-ROOT $\gg$ FAITH-AFFIX proposed by McCarthy and Prince (1995, 364), the constraints would be ranked as NO-HL$^2{}_\omega$ $\gg$ IDENT-ROOT $\gg$ IDENT-AFFIX $\gg$ NO-HL. We have opted here for the positional faithfulness approach with the prominent version of the constraint IDENT-ROOT and the general version IDENT, which does not require a specific ranking and hence avoids the need to impose a metaranking scheme from the outside. If extensions of faithfulness constraints are limited to prominent positions, there is no category FAITH-AFFIX, and hence no need to stipulate its relative ranking with respect to FAITH-ROOT. We return to this issue in chapter 7.

16. See Padgett 2002 for related discussion and proposals to eliminate constraint conjunction in favor of universal constraint subhierarchies that are grounded in phonetic or psycho-linguistic scales.

17. This point goes back to observations by Curt Rice and Andrew Dolbey (personal communications).

18. The replacement of gutturals by palatals, as in (42c), is a general feature of Sanskrit reduplication.

19. Adoption of the theory of existential faithfulness developed by Struijke (2000; see also Spaelti 1997) might be crucial in this context since it gives a more principled answer than McCarthy and Prince's model to the question of why a dissimilative reversal to the unmarked state is so frequent in reduplication. If both the base segment and its reduplicative copy are correspondents of a given input segment, IDENT-IO[F] is fulfilled even when the copy dissimilates to the unmarked value for F.

Chapter 4

1. Except in unassimilated loans, [h] is almost exclusively found in morpheme-initial position and therefore does not appear in the following tables as C_2 and C_3.

2. As a reviewer reminds us, *sitaku* (written with two characters: 支度) is etymologically Sino-Japanese and belongs more properly in the Common Sino-Japanese stratum discussed in chapter 6.

3. Mimetic reduplication in Japanese has been taken up in the reduplication literature by McCarthy and Prince (1995), who present an ingenious analysis attributing the inapplicability of prosodic-word-internal *g*-nasalization in mimetic reduplications (*goro-goro*, **goro-ŋoro*, etc.) to the underapplication of an allophonic process (simply put, the internal [g] resists nasalization in order to stay similar to its mate in word-initial position, which cannot nasalize by virtue of its position). Elsewhere (Ito and Mester 2002a), we argue instead that the non-nasalized second [g] of *goro-goro*, and the like, is not a case of underapplication, but one of expected nonapplication, on the basis of prosodic constituency: the second part has independent prosodic word status, and its initial segment is therefore not "internal" in the required sense (as we will show in chapter 7, this also immediately explains why *rendaku* cannot apply in this position). Removing allophonic *g*-nasalization in Japanese from the list of under-applying processes is a welcome result for the overall typology of underapplication because it removes a putative counterexample to the otherwise valid restriction that only genuinely lexical processes, not allophonic processes, can underapply (as predicted in various versions of Lexical Phonology—see, e.g., Kiparsky 1986; Mester 1986).

4. This also held for earlier periods of Japanese, according to Unger (2000, 17). No historical stage of the language is empirically accessible where *rendaku* voicing is automatic.

5. There are some Sino-Japanese forms that at first glance seem to show *rendaku*-like behavior in that the second member is voiced. Pairs like 神学 *sin-gaku*/雷神 *rai-zin* 'divinity study'/ 'thunder god' or 大会 *tai-kai*/莫大 *baku-dai* 'large meeting, conference'/'extremely large' may give the impression that *rendaku* is also operative in root compounding. However, the voiced versions are (unpredictable) allomorphic variants that also appear initially, as in 神宮 *zin-guu* 'divine-palace, shrine' or 大学 *dai-gaku* 'grand-school, university'. Other cases of unpredictable voiced/voiceless allomorphs include 土地 *to-ti*/土曜日 *do-yoo-bi* 'land'/'Saturday', 分離 *bun-ri*/ 分別 *hun-betu* 'separation'/'discretion', 示唆 *si-sa*/示談 *zi-dan* 'suggestion'/'private settlement', 台風 *tai-huu*/台形 *dai-kei* 'typhoon'/'trapezoid', 次第 *si-dai*/次官 *zi-kan* 'circumstance'/'vice-minister', 上人 *syoo-nin*/上達 *zyoo-tatu* 'holy priest'/'progress', which are the results of separate waves of borrowings from Chinese, in different time periods and often from different prestige dialects of the language, following the dynastic history of the country. The overall pattern is reminiscent of the borrowings from Romance that entered the English language at different periods, resulting in doublets such as *royal*/*regal*, *hostel*/*hotel*. Similar doublets occur in Sino-Japanese, such as 強力 *kyoo-ryoku*/*goo-riki* 'strong power'; see Vance 1987, 167–169, for further examples and discussion.

6. Although most of these compounds come from the source language (Chinese, Greek/Latin), new root compounds are also formed in the borrowing language. The examples in (13) are compounds formed in Japanese in the last century, as are *tele-vision* and *micro-phone* in modern Western languages.

7. On strictly logical grounds, there could exist a constraint, hidden away at the bottom of the ranking in all other grammars, that leaps into a dominant position in the grammar of Japanese alone, commanding junctural voicing in compounds. However, this line of reasoning is an abuse rather than a use of the OT concept of violable universal constraints since it undermines the very idea of UG, turning it into a disjunctive list of language-particular stipulations dressed up as pseudo-universal constraints.

8. Elsewhere (Ito and Mester 1986, 57), we have also advocated this interpretation of *rendaku*, stating that "*rendaku* is essentially a morphological process introducing a linking morpheme in a certain morphological context" (an important element of our analysis overlooked in some subsequent work, such as Ohno 2000). Even for Old Japanese, the inherently morphological nature of *rendaku* and the nonviability of a strictly phonological account have been well established since the appearance of Unger 1975.

9. Unlike *rendaku* voicing (see chapter 7), linking -*s*- in German is not restricted to compounds with simplex second members, as shown by examples like [*Bildung-s*-[*gesamt-plan*]] 'educational overall plan' and [[*Recht-schreibung-s*]-[*blitz*-[*wörter-buch*]]] 'orthographic quick-look-up dictionary', perhaps suggesting a contrast in structure: suffixal in German ([[A-*s*] B]), but prefixal in Japanese ([A [ℜ-B]]). Note that linking -*s*- can also appear with complex first members: [[*Arbeits-beschaffung-s*]-[*mass-nahmen*]] 'work provision measures' (i.e., 'measures taken to provide work').

10. While the presence or absence of linking -*s*- is lexically fixed for each compound, sometimes the same noun exhibits different behavior as a member of different compounds, usually coupled with a difference in meaning. Thus, for *Land* 'country', we find [*Land*][*haus*] 'country home' without linking -*s*- (*Land* = 'countryside') alongside [*Land-es*][*vorwahl*] 'country code'

with linking -s- (*Land* = 'country'). A large electronic dictionary lists 61 compounds of the first kind and 59 of the second (besides 4 examples with the archaic variant *Lands-*, as in *Land-s-leute* 'compatriots').

11. The material in this paragraph is largely based on an e-mail survey conducted by Andrea Krott (see LINGUIST List 10.1477 "Linking Elements in Compounds," 7 October 1999).

12. Drawing attention to a psycholinguistic study (Kozman 1998), a reviewer reminds us of the numerous counterexamples to this restriction (some included in later chapters, such as *hosigaki-zukuri* 'dried persimmon making' in section 8.1.1). It is conceivable that a deeper morphosyntactic and semantic study of the factors at work, taking into account the classical work of Kageyama (1982) on dvandvas and Sugioka (1984) on OV compounds and building on recent models of argument structure distinguishing "process" from "result" readings, may lead to a reduction in the number of genuine exceptions.

13. It is an interesting open question whether this formally necessitates the full expressive power of featural correspondence, or whether strictly IDENT-based correspondence theory (especially in Struijke's (2000) existential quantified interpretation) is sufficient (see also Baković 2000 for relevant discussion). We return to some aspects of this issue in chapter 7.

14. Named after Benjamin Lyman, whose 1894 paper contained the first explicit statement of the generalization in the work of a non-Japanese scholar. While it is true that the restriction was first noted, with respect to an Old Japanese text (see Vance 1987, 136), in the work of the eighteenth-century Japanese philologist Moto'ori Norinaga (本居宣長), in connection with his edition and interpretation of the *Kojiki* (古事記 'Record of Ancient Matters', eighth century), Martin (1952, 49) emphasizes the importance of Lyman's paper, the starting point of all modern work on the topic ("[d]espite serious shortcomings in his principal argument, Lyman presents an attempt at systemization of the synchronic alternation which has certain merits").

15. The examples in (33b) undermine the idea of explaining the most well-known exception to Lyman's Law in compounds—namely, *hasigo* 'ladder' in compounds such as *nawa-basigo* 'rope ladder'—by claiming that the intervening voiceless [s] in position C_2 makes the voicing of C_3 invisible for C_1 (see Haraguchi 2001). While such a classical opacity account works well for this one form, it overshoots the mark by turning the exception into the rule, and vice versa: no other trisyllables of this shape show *rendaku*—that is, the voiceless obstruent in C_2 position behaves transparently (see section 6.2.2 for further discussion of *nawa-basigo* and other exceptions to Lyman's Law). Looking beyond compound voicing, if voiceless obstruents in C_2 position were indeed opaque, we should expect free co-occurrence of voiced obstruents in morpheme structure in positions C_1 ands C_3 of trisyllables whose medial C_2 is a voiceless obstruent, contrary to the facts (see section 2.3.1). Regarding the form *waka ziraga* 'prematurely gray hair' (from *siraga* 'gray hair'), another putative exception to Lyman's Law sometimes mentioned in the literature, Vance (1987) is certainly correct in noting that the only variant found in contemporary speech is *waka siraga*, without *rendaku* voicing.

16. Note, for example, the locality issue in forms like *gake-buti* 'cliff edge', where [g] and [b] must be linked to a single [+voi] across a voiceless [k] (as well as across the voiced vowels).

17. Not all compounds with *ame* as second member show the linking -s-: for example, *oo-ame* 'heavy rainfall' (cf. *ko-same* 'light rain').

18. Another example is *ao* 'blue', *massao* 'deep blue', which additionally involves gemination of *s* owing to an independent prosodic requirement on the *ma* prefix (e.g., *kuro* 'black', *makkuro* 'pitch black').

Chapter 5

1. While it is convenient to view the segment as the tail end of both hierarchies, with segments being elements of both morphemes and syllables, it is not the case that morphemes must consist of segments (cf. the feature-sized *rendaku* linking morpheme).

2. We treat the position of a segment as one of its properties (a "role") that can be locally inspected, alongside its other features. Thus, "/__]$_\sigma$" denotes one of the properties of a syllable-final consonant. We return to this issue below; see (7) and (8).

3. Since American English [ɹ] behaves in other respects like a vocalic segment (see Kahn 1976 on flapping), its word-initial appearance in words like *err*, *irk*, *earn*, or *earl* is not too surprising.

4. This might reflect a more fundamental difference between self-conjunctions and other conjunctions (see Nathan 2001 for relevant discussion). Here we will focus on our analytical goals in connection with Japanese, which lead to some a priori unanticipated empirical findings about potential dissimilation domains.

5. A rather different option would be "pair of segments," but such a construct does not constitute an independently recognized domain.

6. McCarthy's (1986) version of the autosegmental OCP goes so far as to encode the primacy of the morpheme as a domain in the very form of phonological representations, by means of the Morpheme Tier Hypothesis, which postulates a separate tier for the melodic content of each morpheme. The resulting "morphemic" geometry is independent of the geometry of features (see Schlindwein 1986; Prince 1987; McCarthy 1989).

7. Unger refers to earlier work by Ramsey and Unger (1972) and Miyake (1932), and the latter in turn credits Ishizura Tatsumaro (古言清濁 [*Kogen seidaku*], 1801) with the original observation.

8. Setting aside three special cases, all involving names of deities.

9. That is, provided m$_2$ begins with a voiceless obstruent in isolation. We will henceforth presuppose this obvious qualification.

10. Nonrecursivity of conjunction has been suggested by Baković (2000, 28), for reasons different from the ones contemplated here.

Chapter 6

1. *Latinate* as a term expressing the synchronic relevance of a stratal division in English was introduced and motivated in Aronoff 1976; see Aronoff and Fuhrhop 2002 for new evidence along similar lines in English and German.

2. Comparable cases of morphophonemic processes focused on the native vocabulary are quite frequent. As an example, consider umlaut in German. It is triggered by certain suffixes, such as plural-forming -*e* (*Bach*, *Bäche* 'creeks'), diminutive-forming -*chen* (*Sohn*, *Söhnchen* 'son'), and adjective-forming -*lich* (*Mund*, *mündlich* 'by mouth/orally'). Like *rendaku*, umlaut has exceptions, both sporadic and systematic (thus, it usually does not apply to personal names: *Karl*, *Karlchen*, *Kärlchen); and while it sometimes applies to nonnative words (such as *Person*, *Persönchen*, *Personchen 'person (diminutive)'), it is generally not found with ostensibly foreign items (*Hairshop*, *Hairshopchen*, *Hairshöpchen 'hair shop'; *Hotdog*, *Hotdogchen*, *Hotdögchen 'hot dog'; *Boom*, *Boomchen*, *B[y:]*mchen* 'boom').

3. Some of the material presented in this chapter appears, in a different form, in Ito and Mester 2001a.

4. It was in a case study of this system that Fries and Pike (1949), swimming against the tide of discovery procedure–based American structuralism, developed a model of "coexistent systems in phonology," an important precursor of current theories of lexical stratification.

5. Halle and Mohanan 1985 is one of the few studies to even attempt a rule-based analysis (in a version of Lexical Phonology). For a critical assessment, see Pinker 1999.

6. The cover term *FAITH* here subsumes different types of processes: feature manipulation and whole segment deletion. Meade (1998) shows that the internal hierarchy of the relevant faithfulness constraints is DEP $\gg$ MAX $\gg$ IDENT. This relative ranking is preserved in all FAITH$_n$ constraint families owing to the principle of Ranking Consistency (Ito and Mester 1999a), which maintains that it must always be possible to "fold up" the many specific faithfulness constraint *tokens* (F1$_a$, F2$_a$, F1$_b$, F2$_b$, etc.) into a single consistently ranked hierarchy of faithfulness constraint *types* (F1 $\gg$ F2); see Ito and Mester 1999a for further explication and discussion. Given Ranking Consistency, the schema in (8) accurately characterizes the Jamaican Creole situation.

7. We continue to refer to the faithfulness constraint involved simply as *IDENT*, in the interest of succinctness and in order to avoid cluttering the tableaux with unnecessary details. Since the examples to be discussed all involve voicing, readers who prefer featurally specific IDENT constraints can substitute IDENT[VOI]. The question of further articulations of IDENT in terms of specific feature values will be taken up in detail in chapter 7.

8. The two columns under S are etymologically both Sino-Japanese (i.e., historical loans from Chinese), but their phonological behavior differs slightly, as we will show. The distinction will be an important factor in our analysis of stratal faithfulness. Elsewhere (Ito and Mester 1995, 198–205), we show that the class of F items does not constitute a uniform stratum, but is best thought of as the cumulative totality of the items occupying less and less central areas of the lexicon. This nonuniformity is acknowledged by the split into unassimilated and assimilated F items, but many finer distinctions are hidden beneath this coarse classification: the less nativized an item is, the more it disobeys lexical constraints and the farther it lies toward the periphery of lexical space. Viewed in this light, the "splitting" of the Sino-Japanese stratum falls into the same pattern. We return to this important point below.

9. Thus, some words that to modern speakers feel like typical Y items, such as *uma* 'horse' or *hude* 'brush', are most likely very early borrowings from Chinese, mediated through Korean (Sansom 1928, 29–30). They are no longer recognizable as such because they do not follow the tight structural limitations of S forms. The latter, if disyllabic, invariably end in [u] or [i] (even this choice is largely predictable, given the epenthetic origin of these vowels—see Martin 1952; Tateishi 1990; Ito and Mester 1996b; Kurisu 2000).

10. The fact that S morphemes never contain two voiced obstruents can, in a broader perspective, be seen as a small part of the radical restriction rooted in a combination of historical and phonotactic factors, namely, the monosyllabism of the Chinese originals and the very limited coda possibilities of Japanese. If monosyllabic, an S morpheme is either an open syllable or closed by a nasal; if it is expanded to a disyllable by a (historically epenthetic) final vowel, the onset of the second syllable is restricted to /t/ and /k/ in Modern Japanese (see Ito and Mester 1996b and references cited there, and see especially Kurisu 2000 for recent discussion and analysis). Since there is no way for an S morpheme to contain more than two

consonants or for the second consonant to be a voiced obstruent, there is also no way of violating the multiple voicing restriction. This, however, does not alter the fact that S morphemes always obey the constraint No-D^2_m, which is all that matters here.

11. See section 7.2 for discussion of such special/general relations between faithfulness constraints.

12. See note 33, chapter 2.

13. This is one of the most common ways for syllable structure canons to expand over time. For example, in Hindi-Urdu, nasals are generally homorganic with following stops (see Ohala 1983; Kaye 1997): *tamba* 'copper', *gend* 'ball', *p^{h}əŋki* 'handful', *dʒəṇḍa* 'flag', and so on. Heterorganic clusters have arisen through a general process of ə-syncope in two-sided open syllables, as in /nəmək-in/ → *nemkin* 'salty' (cf. *nəmək* 'salt').

14. (28) does not indicate the results of place assimilation in the nasal. The alternation of /h/ with a labial stop (postnasally and in gemination) is a regular feature of Japanese phonology.

15. The lack of voicing here is surprising on grounds of frequency. It might be functionally motivated by the need to keep the form distinct from *san-gai* 'third floor' (from /kai/).

16. A somewhat fanciful OO-based account might capitalize on the fact that there is another S word denoting the number 4 that cannot trigger voicing—namely, *si*. By a taboo of relatively recent origin, *si* is avoided in many collocations because of its homonymy with *si* 'death'. Whatever the merits of this kind of analogy, which falls somewhere in the gray zone between anecdote and analysis, it reinforces the point that postnasal voicing in the S vocabulary does not represent regular phonology.

17. The stem node does not play a role here and is therefore suppressed from the representation (see chapter 3 for a full representation).

18. These were for the first time systematically noted in McCawley 1968; see Ito and Mester 1996b for an analysis.

19. While stratum-specific faithfulness provides a description of the fact, for example, that *rendaku* applies to Y items but not to S and F items, a reviewer points out that it does not by itself explain why this should be so. This point is well taken, and indeed the analysis is not intended to provide such an explanation (which we believe to be synchronically nonexistent). From a historical perspective, we agree with the usual view (see, e.g., Unger 1975) that links the occurrence of *rendaku* in native compounds to the fact that obstruent voicing was not contrastive in initial position in native words in Old Japanese (see also sections 2.3.1 and 7.3), whereas it was always fully contrastive in loans from Chinese.

20. Hybrid forms with *rendaku* exist both as well-established items and as recent productive formations. For example, the form /zyuu+hako/ → *zyuubako* (S+Y) 'layered (food) boxes' is a prime example of *zyuubako yomi* 'mixed reading, impure pronunciation'. A new hybrid form is /wan + kiri/ → *wangiri* (F+Y) 'one + hang up', referring to a money-saving technique whereby young cell phone users hang up after one ring so the recipient will call the number back.

21. As a reviewer reminds us, it is true that there are morphemes such as *ki* 'tree' that appear without *rendaku* in approximately 50% of the attested cases. Rosen (2001, 72) contrasts *aoki* 'green tree, laurel' with *yanagi* 'weir tree, willow', and so on. But another central finding of Rosen's study is important. The irregular applications of *rendaku* in this case, and similar ones, are not randomly distributed across all compounds with *ki* as second member. Rather, they

follow a prosodic criterion: they cluster in "short" compounds (where neither member is longer than a single foot, i.e., two moras; see the examples above) and are absent from "long" compounds (where at least one member is longer than a single foot, i.e., comprises three moras or more: *tokiwagi* 'evergreen', *tomarigi* 'resting tree, perch', etc.). Rosen's explanation is that the compounds in the first group, but not the second, are amenable to listing as lexical exceptions. In addition, according to native-speaker intuition, nonce formations are unlikely to contain unvoiced *ki*. For example, imagine a "daddy tree," a "mommy tree," and a "baby tree" presented in a children's story. Our consultants came up with *papagi*, *mamagi*, and *aka-tyangi* and were not happy with *papaki*, *mamaki*, and *akatyanki*. Even in unfavorable cases of 50% nonapplication (in terms of forms listed in the dictionary) such as *ki*, where it is at first glance hopeless to try to distinguish between "rule" and "exception," there are still empirical indications that *rendaku* represents the rule and not the exception.

22. Another familiar Yamato look-alike is *tabako* 'tobacco', whose resistance to compound voicing (*maki tabako* 'rolled tobacco', **maki dabako*) is plausibly a result of the multiple voicing constraint No-D^2_m, which becomes active once the item loses its F indexation. But since F indexation itself forestalls *rendaku* through higher-ranked faithfulness, no conclusive argument can be made.

23. Similar cases are familiar from other languages, as demonstrated, for example, by Aronoff and Fuhrhop (2002, 486) for the German suffix *-ität*: even though historically a loan from Latin, it behaves like a native suffix.

24. The tendency of two-root combinations such as *tyawan* 茶碗 in (48) to undergo *rendaku* generally does not transfer to single roots such as *tya* 茶, as shown by contrasts such as *yunomi-zyawan* versus *nihon-tya* (**nihon-zya*) 'Japanese tea'.

25. *Minimal free form* may be more appropriate than *morpheme* to indicate the domain of the double voicing constraint. A perceptive reviewer points out that the identification of collocations of two bound roots with morphemes that is part of Takayama's hypothesis is not complete, since there is no prohibition against combinations of two voiced obstruent-initial S roots, deriving forms that are impossible as native morphemes, as shown by examples like *goodoo* 合同 'association', *zyooge* 上下 'up and down', *byoobu* 屏風 'screen', and *gyoogi* 行儀 'behavior' (the latter a CS item taking the native honorific prefix *o-*). Besides pointing to the need for an even more fine-grained domain structure, this turns out to constitute further evidence, in light of the next chapter, that faithfulness to voicing values must in some way distinguish between devoicing and the addition of voicing that is part of the *rendaku* process. This is clearly an area where further exploration may yield interesting results (see also chapter 4 for discussion of the domain question for self-conjoined markedness that leads to dissimilation).

Chapter 7

1. There are, however, occasional proposals addressing specific problems in serialist theory that prefigure modern faithfulness, such as the *Aspects* theory requirement (Chomsky 1965) that deletions must be recoverable, or the Projection Principle of Government-Binding theory (Chomsky 1981). In phonology, Hale 1973 is a seminal study of input-output disparities and their importance for synchronic and diachronic analysis; it is also the source of most of the factual information about the phonological system of the Australian language Lardil, which figures prominently in Prince and Smolensky's (1993) development and justification of faithfulness constraints.

2. An *if-then* formulation has been chosen instead of McCarthy and Prince's (1995) *if and only if* version in the interest of consistency, given that the [+voi]-specific instantiation of IDENT given below in (11) requires a conditional, not a biconditional. For the general (value-neutral) instantiation, differences arise only in cases of input underspecification, which are not of central importance in the present context.

3. For example, whether it deals correctly with voicing faithfulness when obstruents alternate with sonorants, and in similar less straightforward scenarios.

4. Or rather, *high-ranking position*: a phonetic process devoicing high vowels in voiceless environments is a common feature of many dialects of Japanese, including the standard ("Tokyo") variety. For a comprehensive study of vowel devoicing and what it reveals about the interface between phonology and phonetics in OT, see Tsuchida 1997.

5. The last restriction expresses the strong form of Lyman's Law (see chapter 5). Given the law of initials in Old Japanese that excluded free morphemes beginning with voiced obstruents, all such voicing is *rendaku*-derived. The vowel symbols express distinctions in Old Japanese that are lost in the modern language.

6. This is a basic difference between faithfulness and markedness (cf. the OCP effects studied in this book, which manifest domain-conjoined markedness), plausibly related to their very different grounding. Whereas markedness constraints target overt properties of outputs involving articulatory and perceptual complexities, faithfulness constraints focus on the much more abstract grammatical relations between two levels of representation, such as input and output.

7. That is, apart from the devoicing affecting mainly (but not exclusively) high vowels in voiceless environments, which shows properties characteristic of phonetic processes, such as gradualness and optionality.

8. This would mean, among other things, that all apparent counterexamples, like those found in Turkana ATR harmony (Noske 2000) or in the templatic morphology of Modern Hebrew (Ussishkin 2000), must involve other factors. See also Revithiadou 1999 for an approach in terms of headedness to morphological faithfulness asymmetries, based on a detailed study of accent systems; and see Ussishkin and Wedel 2002 for an attempt to advance the understanding of root-affix inventory asymmetries by making contact with more fundamental psychological factors.

9. Baković (2000) makes the interesting observation that agreement constraints are formally similar to correspondence constraints, a similarity that is especially striking in the formulation in (24). This affinity, which deserves further exploration, casts an interesting light on the conjunction between agreement and faithfulness proposed in section 7.3.3.

10. The empirical argument is somewhat complicated by the fact that voicing assimilation is overwhelmingly controlled by positional factors (onsets are decisive, not markedness), giving it a directional bias. Swedish is an example showing bi-directional devoicing, that is, agreement on the unmarked value (see Lombardi 1999, 285; Baković 2000, 58). Note that our point is not that assimilation to the marked never happens, but rather that it is wrong as a general recipe. This is not to say that spreading of the marked value is never found in assimilation outside of local assimilation of laryngeal features, as considered here. There are well-known prima facie cases including consonantal place (coronals assimilating to labials and velars but not vice versa, as in Catalan—see Kiparsky 1985; Herrick 2001) or vowel features (as in dominant/

recessive [ATR] vowel harmony systems—but see Baković 2000 for an attempt to analyze the latter as agreement on the unmarked value). The failure of most current theories to draw the right distinctions in this area is perhaps due to the fact that the role of contrast is not sufficiently appreciated (for recent proposals, see, e.g., Flemming 1995; Ní Chiosáin and Padgett 2001; Padgett 2003).

11. Correctly excluding the last case, where all input segments already happen to agree on [+voi], the marked value.

12. We use voicing here as a simple example. However, the issue goes beyond the two values of such bivalent features and extends to groups of features such as [Place] and [Laryngeal], whose role in phonological processes is in many ways akin to that of multivalent features (for discussion, see McCarthy 1988; Padgett 1995b).

13. This is an important point. Baković's theory avoids majority rule and derives harmonic completeness without needing to require "indivisibility" (i.e., the literal adjacency of the various parts of voicing faithfulness in the ranking), which is unlikely to survive in the empirical world. This is an advantage over the theory developed by Prince (2001), which constructs "IDENT[F]" as an indivisible internally ranked block IDENT[αF] $\gg$ IDENT[$-\alpha$F].

14. We are indebted to the participants in our course at the Düsseldorf Summer School in Linguistics 2002 for discussion of this point and related ones, especially to Lev Blumenfeld, Andrew Koontz-Garboden, and Lanko Marušič.

15. In functional parlance, (36) is a member of the AVOID-EFFORT family of constraints studied in Steriade 1995a (see also other work cited there).

16. Devoicing the vowels instead, as in [ḀTḀ], also fulfills AGREE[VOI], but the candidate violates a universally high-ranking markedness constraint against voiceless sonorants and is a serious contender only under very special circumstances.

17. In terms of the theory of comparative markedness developed by McCarthy (2002a), the conjunction captures the effects of the "new" $_N$AGREE[VOI], which penalizes derived nonagreement but has nothing to say about input-given nonagreement.

Chapter 8

1. To avoid constantly using disjunctions like *syntactic or morphological*, we will often make informal use of the term *grammatical* in its traditional meaning, where it is restricted to the nonphonological parts of the overall linguistic system. The latter is also referred to as a *grammar* in the technical sense (as in *generative grammar*, *Universal Grammar*, etc.), where the term stands for a formal structure comprising syntax, morphology, semantics, and phonology. Since it will in general be clear from the context what is intended, we hope our usage will not give rise to ambiguity.

2. While the whole compound is a nonce formation, *kamidana* is an established compound meaning 'shelf for the family gods, house altar'.

Further examples of four-member compounds showing the same kind of ambiguity, kindly provided to us by Isao Ueda (personal communication), include *ihoo-kome-tonya-kakushi* 'illegal-rice-wholesaler-hiding', *kamo-kawa-sakana-tori* 'Kamo-River-fish-catch', *nise-kane-kakushi-fuutoo* 'fake-money-hiding-envelope', *inaka-tsukuri-sake-tokkuri* 'country-side-made-sake-decanter', *oo-karasu-saiku-kirai* 'big-crow-craft-hating', and *natsu-kusa-fue-keeko* 'summer-grass-flute-practice'.

3. See Tsujimura 1996, 59–63, for a recent version of this type of analysis, and Kozman 1998 for some experimental results.

4. These are in principle subject to free reranking in individual grammars, yielding a vast set of possible grammars. It is to be hoped that restrictions can be imposed, or a different conception emerges, reducing this set to more realistic proportions.

5. For reasons perhaps related to the first of the problems discussed below, compounds have rarely figured in the literature on OO faithfulness. Some influential models, such as those of Benua (1997) and Baković (2000), even formalize OO constraints in such a way that they are directly triggered by particular affixes and affix classes (level I vs. level II), a conception too narrow to extend to compounds in a natural way. What is actually involved in the case at hand is not OO identity in the general sense defined in (7), but a version specifically governing compounds and their parts, to the exclusion of affixal constructions.

6. Actual OO relations in compounded forms, where they exist, are predicted to vary considerably, since the base forms different speakers have access to on different occasions are bound to be different. This is precisely the finding in Ito and Mester 1997a concerning the OO-faithfulness-governed [g]~[ŋ] alternation in compounds. There is no similar variation in the *rendaku* restriction here under discussion, reinforcing the suspicion that different mechanisms are at work.

7. Further complications are caused by two independent patterns conflicting with accent at the compound boundary: (i) preservation in situ of the second member's lexical accent (if non-final), and (ii) the strong tendency of compounds to become unaccented under specific conditions (in particular, when the second member bears final accent in the input (Kubozono, Ito, and Mester 1997, 149–150) and when the whole compound is exactly four moras long (Tanaka 2001b, 178–179).

8. Our notation differs in nonessential ways from the notation frequently encountered in literature on the syntax-phonology interface, where (following the notational conventions of syntactic work) square brackets indicate grammatical structure. We have adopted the notation in the text for the sake of consistency with the rest of the book; no specific difference with respect to the previous literature, theoretical or descriptive, is intended.

9. Thanks to Haruo Kubozono for a thorough discussion of these issues.

10. That is, apart from cases where the relation is filled by a standard thematic role assigned to an argument, as in *carpet weaver* (at least in its most direct interpretation—even here it is certainly possible, depending on background and context, to interpret *carpet* as a nonargument). In order to appreciate the semantic openness of the relation between compound members in the general case, it is useful to consider, for example, the enormous range of meanings that are possible for a nonce formation like *Sunday car*.

11. The remarks on covert structural ambiguities in compounds in this section owe much to a discussion with Mats Rooth regarding German (and corresponding English) compounds. Consider the example Ato^2m-$waffen$-spe^1rr-$vertrag$ 'nuclear weapons nonproliferation treaty', which is sometimes used to illustrate the compound stress rule in German. Its stress pattern seems to require the bracketing $\{\{W^2\ X\}\ \{Y^1\ Z\}\}$, but its most natural semantic grouping is clearly $\{\{\{W\ X\}\ Y\}\ Z\}$—that is, 'treaty regarding the nonproliferation of nuclear weapons', not 'nonproliferation treaty concerning nuclear weapons'. But the second bracketing facilitates smooth binary prosodic parsing, does not lead to a significantly different interpretation, and points to *Sperr-vertrag* as an independently existing compound.

12. We restrict ourselves to nonempty substrings since we are not making use of McCarthy and Prince's (1993a) opposite-edge alignment option and remain agnostic regarding its existence.

13. This is probably what is intended by McCarthy and Prince's (1995) statement that "correspondence is reflexive."

14. Or, to use the more pedantic but more precise terminology introduced earlier in connection with (29), the two left-edge pairs (x, w_1) and (x, w_2) share their first element x.

15. See Padgett 1995a, Beckman 1997, 1998, Casali 1997, Lombardi 1999, and other contributions to the positional faithfulness literature for many cases of this kind, and see also chapter 7.

16. Since there are other reasons to prefer the markedness explanation to be presented below, we will not dwell on the questionable aspects of this assumption (e.g., for the case of prefixed words). In a language like Japanese, which has few prefixes, it is empirically difficult to separate putative cases of ω-initial faithfulness from cases of root-initial faithfulness.

17. Reference to the set of prominent positions P is sometimes seen as an exclusive privilege of positional faithfulness, leaving positional markedness in the unenviable position of having to somehow enumerate the complement set $\overline{P}$. This is a misunderstanding of positional markedness since it fails to appreciate the important role of alignment/anchoring constraints assigning particular marked properties to the very same set of prominent positions P (including beginnings and heads of constituents). Both types of positional constraints can therefore refer to the same set P, and the issue is tangential to the point under discussion.

18. It is difficult to reduce this constraint to a constraint conjunction since this would require an independently existing constraint against beginnings of prosodic words. While it is not inconceivable to refashion No-Struc[ω] in this direction (cf. also the No-Head constraint recruited as a conjunct in Smolensky 1997), this is not altogether likely, and a more promising approach might involve the enhancement constraints investigated by Smith (2001).

19. Kager (1999) lays out further reasons why any attempt to interpret all positional markedness effects as positional faithfulness is impossible.

20. Lombardi (2001) also draws attention to the crosslinguistic absence of "overkill" effects in such cases, such as wholesale consonant deletion (which would result in [gro:] for the input /gro:b/, instead of [gro:p]). For a feature like [voi], languages do not seem to delete a segment where a simple change in one feature value of the segment in question is sufficient. This might be explained as a case of harmonic bounding in a richer version of feature faithfulness, where deleting a segment incurs a Max[F] violation for every feature F. If so, it seems to pinpoint a deficiency in the strongly segment-focused Ident-based system of faithfulness constraints introduced by McCarthy and Prince (1995), who regard features strictly as attributes of segments, following Chomsky and Halle (1968) in this respect. Alternative theories have been developed preserving a more autosegmentalist perspective in which segment deletion/insertion always triggers Max/Dep-Feature violations, in addition to Max/Dep-Segment violations (see, e.g., Walker 1997; Lombardi 1998). In such theories, candidates deleting segments are in general harmonically bounded by feature-changing candidates.

21. In contemporary German: ba[ŋ]e, without [g].

22. The preservation of voicing in these cases is not motivated by any kind of *Homonymenflucht* ('flight from homonymy') since there are no actual lexical contrasts in danger of being

neutralized. We should also note that the presence of [ə] after root-final voiced obstruents in adjectives is not a synchronic requirement of Modern German, as shown by examples like *grob* 'rough' or *wild* 'wild'.

23. MAX/DEP-FEATURE theories in fact predict that full-scale segment epenthesis should be relatively rare in situations where a simple change from voiced to voiceless would also be sufficient to resolve the problem. The reason becomes clear from a numerical comparison between the many DEP[F] violations incurred by epenthesis and the single MAX[VOI] violation incurred by devoicing. All that it takes for a grammar to end up rewarding feature deletion over segment epenthesis is to rank *one* of the numerous DEP[F] constraints above MAX[VOI], and there are many ways for this to happen. But there is essentially only one way of rewarding segment epenthesis over feature deletion: MAX[VOI] must outrank *every* DEP[F] constraint.

24. The terminology here follows Pierrehumbert and Beckman 1988. The accentual and intermediate phrases are referred to as *minor* and *major* phrases, respectively, in Selkirk and Tateishi 1988.

25. According to Kubozono, Ito, and Mester (1997), other compounds in this category include *isoppu monoga⌐tari* (from *iso⌐ppu* 'Aesop' and *monoga⌐tari* 'storytelling') and *tihoo saibansyo⌐* (from *tiho⌐o* 'regional' and *saibansyo⌐* 'courthouse'). As these authors show with examples like *densi kenbikyoo*, deaccentuation of the first member (the lexically accented *densi⌐* 'electron') can occur even when the second member (here *kenbikyoo* 'microscope') is unaccented and still resists the assignment of junctural compound accent.

26. This length restriction can perhaps be rationalized in terms of the prosodic word binarity principle proposed in Ito and Mester 1992 (further developed as hierarchical alignment in Ito, Kitagawa, and Mester 1996 and Ussishkin 2000), which characterizes items longer than two feet (= four moras) as noncanonical prosodic words. Phonetic evidence for the importance of a four-mora limit for canonical prosodic words appears in experiments reported in Mori 2001.

27. Whether or not the initial member (such as *anzen*) is itself an independent prosodic word is not relevant for *rendaku* (see section 8.4.2 for a more detailed prosodic typology of compound structures in Japanese).

28. That is, apart from an ad hoc stipulation requiring (not just permitting, qua richness of the base) an inaudible *rendaku* morpheme to be present even where it can never be realized, as in dvandva compounds (for further discussion, see also Ito and Mester 1986, 66, fn. 17; Han 1994).

References

Aissen, Judith. 1999. Markedness and subject choice in Optimality Theory. *Natural Language and Linguistic Theory* 17, 673–711.

Akinaga, Kazue. 1960. Tokyo akusento hôsoku ni tsuite [On the laws of Tokyo accent]. In *Meikai nihongo akusento jiten* [Japanese accent dictionary], edited by Haruhiko Kindaichi, 1–68. Tokyo: Sanseido.

Alderete, John. 1997. Dissimilation as local conjunction. In *NELS 27*, edited by Pius N. Tamanji and Kiyomi Kusumoto, 17–32. Amherst: University of Massachusetts, GLSA.

Allen, W. Sidney. 1951. Some prosodic aspects of retroflexion and aspiration in Sanskrit. *Bulletin of the School of Oriental and African Studies* 13, 939–946.

Archangeli, Diana. 1984. Underspecification in Yawelmani phonology and morphology. Doctoral dissertation, MIT.

Archangeli, Diana. 1986. The OCP and Nyangumarda buffer vowels. In *Proceedings of NELS 16*, edited by Charles Jones and Peter Sells, 34–46. Amherst: University of Massachusetts, GLSA.

Archangeli, Diana, and Douglas Pulleyblank. 1987. Minimal and maximal rules: Effects of tier scansion. In *Proceedings of NELS 17*, edited by Joyce McDonough and Bernadette Plunkett, 16–35. Amherst: University of Massachusetts, GLSA.

Archangeli, Diana, and Douglas Pulleyblank. 1994. *Grounded Phonology*. Cambridge, Mass.: MIT Press.

Aronoff, Mark. 1976. *Word formation in generative grammar*. Cambridge, Mass.: MIT Press.

Aronoff, Mark. 1998. Isomorphism and monotonicity: Or the disease model of morphology. In *Morphology and its relation to phonology and syntax*, edited by Steven G. Lapointe, Diane K. Brentari, and Patrick M. Farrell, 411–418. Stanford, Calif.: CSLI Publications.

Aronoff, Mark, and Nanna Fuhrhop. 2002. Restricting suffix combinations in German and English: Closing suffixes and the monosuffix constraint. *Natural Language and Linguistic Theory* 20, 451–490.

Baković, Eric. 2000. Harmony, dominance, and control. Doctoral dissertation, Rutgers University.

Beckman, Jill N. 1997. Positional faithfulness, positional neutralization, and Shona vowel harmony. *Phonology* 14, 1–46.

Beckman, Jill N. 1998. Positional faithfulness. Doctoral dissertation, University of Massachusetts, Amherst.

Benua, Laura. 1995. Identity effects in morphological truncation. In *Papers in Optimality Theory*, edited by Jill N. Beckman, Laura Walsh, and Suzanne Urbanczyk, 77–136. Amherst: University of Massachusetts, GLSA.

Benua, Laura. 1997. Transderivational identity: Phonological relations between words. Doctoral dissertation, University of Massachusetts, Amherst.

Bloch, Bernard. 1950. Studies in colloquial Japanese, IV: Phonemics. *Language* 26, 86–125.

Borowsky, Toni, and Armin Mester. 1983. Aspiration to roots: Remarks on the Sanskrit diaspirates. In *CLS 19*, edited by Amy Chukerman, Mitchell Marks, and John F. Richardson, 52–63. Chicago: University of Chicago, Chicago Linguistic Society.

Burzio, Luigi. 1997. Cycles, non-derived-environment blocking, and correspondence. Ms., Johns Hopkins University.

Casali, Roderic F. 1997. Vowel elision in hiatus contexts: Which vowel goes? *Language* 73, 493–533.

Cho, Young-mee Yu. 1990. Parameters of consonantal assimilation. Doctoral dissertation, Stanford University.

Chomsky, Noam. 1965. *Aspects of the theory of syntax.* Cambridge, Mass.: MIT Press.

Chomsky, Noam. 1981. *Lectures on government and binding.* Dordrecht: Foris.

Chomsky, Noam. 1995. *The Minimalist Program.* Cambridge, Mass.: MIT Press.

Chomsky, Noam, and Morris Halle. 1968. *The sound pattern of English.* New York: Harper and Row.

Chung, Sandra. 1983. Transderivational constraints in Chamorro phonology. *Language* 59, 35–66.

Clements, G. N. 1985. The geometry of phonological features. *Phonology Yearbook* 2, 225–252.

Clements, G. N., and Elizabeth V. Hume. 1995. The internal organization of speech sounds. In *The handbook of phonological theory*, edited by John A. Goldsmith, 245–306. Oxford: Blackwell.

Clements, G. N., and Samuel Jay Keyser. 1982. *CV phonology.* Cambridge, Mass.: MIT Press.

Davidson, Lisa, and Rolf Noyer. 1997. Loan phonology in Huave: Nativization and the ranking of faithfulness constraints. In *Proceedings of the Fifteenth West Coast Conference on Formal Linguistics*, edited by Brian Agbayani and Sze-Wing Tang, 65–79. Stanford, Calif.: CSLI Publications.

Davis, Stuart. 1991. Coronals and the phonotactics of nonadjacent consonants in English. In *The special status of coronals: Internal and external evidence*, edited by Carole Paradis and Jean-François Prunet, 49–60. San Diego, Calif.: Academic Press.

Davis, Stuart. 1997. The flowering of Optimality Theory: Ponapean nasal substitution and the problem of intermediate forms. Ms., Indiana University.

DeCamp, David. 1971. Toward a generative analysis of a post-creole continuum. In *Pidginization and creolization of languages*, edited by Dell Hymes, 349–370. Cambridge: Cambridge University Press.

de Lacy, Paul. 2001. Prosodic markedness in prominent positions. Ms., University of Massachusetts, Amherst.

Downing, Laura. 1998. On the prosodic misalignment of onsetless syllables. *Natural Language and Linguistic Theory* 16, 1–52.

Evans, Nick. 1995. Current issues in the phonology of Australian languages. In *The handbook of phonological theory*, edited by John A. Goldsmith, 723–761. Oxford: Blackwell.

Flemming, Edward S. 1995. Auditory representations in phonology. Doctoral dissertation, University of California, Los Angeles.

Fourakis, Marios, and Greg Iverson. 1984. On the "incomplete neutralization" of German final obstruents. *Phonetics* 41, 140–149.

Frellesvig, Bjarke. 1995. *A case study in diachronic phonology: The Japanese onbin sound changes*. Aarhus, Denmark: Aarhus University Press.

Fries, Charles C., and Kenneth Pike. 1949. Coexistent phonemic systems. *Language* 25, 29–50.

Frisch, Stefan, Michael, Broe, and Janet Pierrehumbert. 1995. The role of similarity in phonology: Explaining OCP-Place. In *Proceedings of the 13th International Conference of the Phonetic Sciences*, vol. 3, edited by Kjell Elenius and Peter Branderud, Stockholm: KTH and Stockholm University. 544–547.

Fukazawa, Haruka. 1998. Multiple input-output faithfulness relations in Japanese. Ms., University of Maryland, College Park. [Available on Rutgers Optimality Archive, http:// roa.rutgers.edu, ROA-260-0598.]

Fukazawa, Haruka, and Mafuyu Kitahara. 2001. Domain-free OCP and *rendaku*. In *Proceedings of the 2001 International Conference on Phonology and Morphology*, edited by the Phonology-Morphology Circle of Korea, 58–66. Seoul: Korea Research Foundation.

Fukazawa, Haruka, Mafuyu Kitahara, and Mitsuhiko Ota. 1998. Lexical stratification and ranking invariance in constraint-based grammars. Ms., University of Maryland, College Park, Indiana University, and Georgetown University. [Available on Rutgers Optimality Archive, http://roa.rutgers.edu, ROA-267-0698.]

Fukuda, Suzy, and Shinji Fukuda. 1994. To voice or not to voice: The operation of *rendaku* in the Japanese developmentally language-impaired. In *Linguistic aspects of familial language impairment*, edited by John Matthews, 178–193. Special issue of *McGill working papers in linguistics/Cahiers linguistiques de McGill*. Montreal, Quebec: McGill University, Department of Linguistics.

Gafos, Adamantios. 1996. The articulatory basis of locality in phonology. Doctoral dissertation, Johns Hopkins University. [Published, New York: Garland, 2000.]

Grimm, Jakob. 1822. *Deutsche Grammatik*, vol. 1. 2nd ed. Göttingen: Dieterichsche Buchhandlung.

Hale, Kenneth. 1973. Deep-surface canonical disparities in relation to analysis and change: An Australian example. In *Current trends in linguistics*, edited by Thomas Sebeok, 401–458. The Hague: Mouton.

Halle, Morris, and K. P. Mohanan. 1985. Segmental phonology of Modern English. *Linguistic Inquiry* 16, 57–116.

Hamano, Shoko. 1986. The sound-symbolic system of Japanese. Doctoral dissertation, University of Florida, Gainesville.

Hamano, Shoko. 1998. The sound-symbolic system of Japanese. Stanford, Calif.: CSLI Publications.

Hamano, Shoko. 2000. Voicing of obstruents in Old Japanese: Evidence from the sound-symbolic stratum. *Journal of East Asian Linguistics* 9, 207–225.

Han, Eunjoo. 1994. Prosodic structure in compounds. Doctoral dissertation, Stanford University.

Hansson, Gunnar. 2001. Theoretical and typological issues in consonant harmony. Doctoral dissertation, University of California, Berkeley.

Haraguchi, Shosuke. 1977. *The tone pattern of Japanese: An autosegmental theory of tonology.* Tokyo: Kaitakusha.

Haraguchi, Shosuke. 2001. On *rendaku.* In *Phonological studies,* edited by the Phonological Society of Japan, 9–32. Tokyo: Kaitakusha.

Harris, John. 1994. *English sound structure.* Oxford: Blackwell.

Herrick, Dylan. 2001. Catalan phonology: Cluster simplification and nasal place assimilation. In *Selected papers from the 30th Linguistic Symposium on Romance Languages,* edited by Joaquim Camps and Caroline Wiltshire, 69–84. Amsterdam: John Benjamins.

Hewitt, Mark, and Megan Crowhurst. 1996. Conjunctive constraints and templates in Optimality Theory. In *NELS 26,* edited by Jill N. Beckman, 101–116. Amherst: University of Massachusetts, GLSA.

Inkelas, Sharon, and Draga Zec, eds. 1990. *The phonology-syntax connection.* Stanford, Calif.: CSLI Publications.

Ishihara, Masahide. 1989. The Morpheme Plane Hypothesis and plane internal phonological domains. In *Coyote papers: Arizona Phonology Conference Proceedings,* vol. 2, edited by S. Lee Fulmer, Masahide Ishihara, and Wendy Wiswall, 64–83. Tucson: University of Arizona, Department of Linguistics.

Ito, Junko. 1986. Syllable theory in prosodic phonology. Doctoral dissertation, University of Massachusetts, Amherst. [Published, New York: Garland, 1988.]

Ito, Junko. 1989. A prosodidic theory of epenthesis. *Natural Language and Linguistic Theory* 7, 217–259.

Ito, Junko, Yoshihisa Kitagawa, and Armin Mester. 1996. Prosodic faithfulness and correspondence: Evidence from a Japanese argot. *Journal of East Asian Linguistics* 5, 217–294.

Ito, Junko, and Armin Mester. 1986. The phonology of voicing in Japanese: Theoretical consequences for morphological accessibility. *Linguistic Inquiry* 17, 49–73.

Ito, Junko, and Armin Mester. 1992. Weak layering and word binarity. Report 92-09, Linguistics Research Center, University of California, Santa Cruz.

Ito, Junko, and Armin Mester. 1994. Reflections on CodaCond and alignment. In *Phonology at Santa Cruz 3,* edited by Jason Merchant, Jaye Padgett, and Rachel Walker, 27–46. Santa Cruz: University of California, Santa Cruz, Linguistics Research Center.

Ito, Junko, and Armin Mester. 1995a. The core-periphery structure of the lexicon and constraints on reranking. In *Papers in Optimality Theory,* edited by Jill N. Beckman, Laura Walsh, and Suzanne Urbanczyk, 181–210. Amherst: University of Massachusetts, GLSA.

Ito, Junko, and Armin Mester. 1995b. Japanese phonology. In *The handbook of phonological theory,* edited by John Goldsmith, 817–838. Oxford: Blackwell.

Ito, Junko, and Armin Mester. 1996a. Rendaku I: Constraint conjunction and the OCP. Handout of talk at the Kobe Phonology Forum. [Available on Rutgers Optimality Archive, http://roa.rutgers.edu, ROA-144-0996.]

Ito, Junko, and Armin Mester. 1996b. Stem and word in Sino-Japanese. In *Phonological structure and language processing: Cross-linguistic studies*, edited by Takahi Otake and Anne Cutler, 13–44. Berlin: Mouton de Gruyter.

Ito, Junko, and Armin Mester. 1997a. Correspondence and compositionality: The ga-gyo variation in Japanese phonology. In *Derivations and constraints in phonology*, edited by Iggy Roca, 419–462. Oxford: Oxford University Press.

Ito, Junko, and Armin Mester. 1997b. Sympathy theory and German truncations. In *Selected phonology papers from Hopkins Optimality Theory Workshop 1997/University of Maryland Mayfest 1997*, edited by Viola Miglio and Bruce Morèn, 117–139. University of Maryland working papers in linguistics 5. College Park: University of Maryland, Department of Linguistics.

Ito, Junko, and Armin Mester. 1998. Markedness and word structure: OCP effects in Japanese. Ms., University of California, Santa Cruz. [Available on Rutgers Optimality Archive, http://roa.rutgers.edu, ROA-255-0498.]

Ito, Junko, and Armin Mester. 1999a. The phonological lexicon. In *The handbook of Japanese linguistics*, edited by Natsuko Tsujimura, 62–100. Oxford: Blackwell.

Ito, Junko, and Armin Mester. 1999b. Realignment. In *The prosody-morphology interface*, edited by René Kager, Harry van der Hulst, and Wim Zonneveld, 188–217. Cambridge: Cambridge University Press.

Ito, Junko, and Armin Mester. 2001a. Covert generalizations in Optimality Theory: The role of stratal faithfulness constraints. In *Proceedings of the 2001 International Conference on Phonology and Morphology*, edited by the Phonology-Morphology Circle of Korea, 3–33. Seoul: Korea Research Foundation.

Ito, Junko, and Armin Mester. 2001b. Structure preservation and stratal opacity in German. In *Segmental phonology in Optimality Theory: Constraints and representations*, edited by Linda Lombardi, 261–295. Cambridge: Cambridge University Press.

Ito, Junko, and Armin Mester. 2002a. Lexical and postlexical phonology in Optimality Theory: Evidence from Japanese. In *Resolving conflicts in grammars*, edited by Gisbert Fanselow and Caroline Féry, 183–207. *Linguistische Berichte* Sonderheft II.

Ito, Junko, and Armin Mester. 2002b. One phonology or many? Issues in stratal faithfulness theory. In *Phonological Studies 5*, edited by The Phonological Society of Japan, 121–126. Tokyo: Kaitakusha.

Ito, Junko, and Armin Mester. 2003. On the sources of opacity in OT: Coda processes in German. In *The syllable in Optimality Theory*, edited by Caroline Féry and Ruben van de Vijver, 271–303. Cambridge: Cambridge University Press.

Ito, Junko, Armin Mester, and Jaye Padgett. 1995. Licensing and underspecification in Optimality Theory. *Linguistic Inquiry* 26, 571–614.

Ito, Junko, Armin Mester, and Jaye Padgett. 2001. Alternations and distributional patterns in Japanese phonology. *Journal of the Phonetic Society of Japan* 5, 54–60.

Iwai, Melissa. 1989. A prosodic analysis of Japanese loanwords. B.A. thesis, University of California, Santa Cruz.

Iwanami. 1992. *Gyakubiki koozien* [Reverse lookup comprehensive dictionary]. Tokyo: Iwanami.

Jakobson, Roman. 1939. Observations sur le classement phonologique des consonnes. In *Proceedings of the 3rd International Congress of Phonetic Sciences*, 34–41.

Jorden, Eleanor Harz. 1963. *Beginning Japanese*. 2 vols. With the assistance of Hamako Ito Chaplin. New Haven, Conn.: Yale University Press.

Kager, René. 1994. Generalized alignment and morphological parsing. Ms., Research Institute of Language and Speech, Utrecht University. [Available on Rutgers Optimality Archive, http://roa.rutgers.edu, ROA-36-1094.]

Kager, René. 1999. *Optimality Theory*. Cambridge: Cambridge University Press.

Kager, René. 2000. Surface opacity of metrical structure in Optimality Theory. In *The derivational residue in phonology*, edited by Ben Hermans and Marc van Oostendorp, 207–245. Amsterdam: John Benjamins.

Kageyama, Taro. 1982. Word formation in Japanese. *Lingua* 57, 215–258.

Kahn, Daniel. 1976. Syllable-based generalizations in English phonology. Doctoral dissertation, MIT.

Karvonen, Dan, and Adam Sherman [Ussishkin]. 1998. Opacity in Icelandic revisited: A sympathy account. In *NELS 28*, edited by Pius N. Tamanji and Kiyomi Kusumoto, 189–201. Amherst: University of Massachusetts, GLSA.

Katayama, Motoko. 1995. Loanword accent and minimal reranking in Japanese. In *Phonology at Santa Cruz: Papers on stress, accent, and alignment*, edited by Rachel Walker, Ove Lorentz, and Haruo Kubozono, 1–12. Santa Cruz: University of California, Santa Cruz, Linguistics Research Center.

Katayama, Motoko. 1998. Optimality Theory and Japanese loanword phonology. Doctoral dissertation, University of California, Santa Cruz.

Kawagoe, Itsue, and Masako Arai. 2002. Consonant gemination in loanwords. *Journal of the Phonetic Society of Japan* 6, 53–66.

Kaye, Alan S. 1997. Hindi-Urdu phonology. In *Phonologies of Asia and Africa*, vol. 2, edited by Alan S. Kaye, 637–652. Winona Lake, Ind.: Eisenbrauns.

Kaye, Jonathan, and Jean Lowenstamm. 1985. A non-linear treatment of Grassmann's Law. In *Proceedings of NELS 15*, edited by Steve Berman, Jae-Woong Choe, and Joyce McDonough, 220–233. Amherst: University of Massachusetts, GLSA.

Kenko. 1332. *Tsurezuregusa* [Essays in idleness]. Translated by Donald Keene. New York: Columbia University Press, 1967.

Kenstowicz, Michael. 1994. *Phonology in generative grammar*. Oxford: Blackwell.

Kenstowicz, Michael. 1996. Base-identity and uniform exponence: Alternatives to cyclicity. In *Current trends in phonology*, edited by Jacques Durand and Bernard Laks, 363–394. Paris-X and Salford: University of Salford Publications.

Kenstowicz, Michael. 1997. Uniform exponence: Exemplification and extension. In *Selected phonology papers from Hopkins Optimality Theory Workshop 1997/University of Maryland Mayfest 1997*, edited by Viola Miglio and Bruce Morèn, 139–155. University of Maryland Working Papers in Linguistics 5. College Park: University of Maryland, Department of Linguistics.

Kenstowicz, Michael, and Charles Kisseberth. 1977. *Topics in phonological theory*. New York: Academic Press.

Kiparsky, Paul. 1965. Phonological change. Doctoral dissertation, MIT.

Kiparsky, Paul. 1982. Lexical phonology and morphology. In *Linguistics in the morning calm*, edited by In-Seok Yang, 3–91. Seoul: Hanshin.

Kiparsky, Paul. 1985. Some consequences of Lexical Phonology. *Phonology* 2, 85–138.

Kiparsky, Paul. 1986. The phonology of reduplication. Ms., Stanford University.

Kiparsky, Paul. 1998. Paradigm effects and opacity. Ms., Stanford University.

Kirchner, Robert. 1996. Synchronic chain shifts in Optimality Theory. *Linguistic Inquiry* 27, 341–350.

Kitahara, Mafuyu. 2001. Category structure and function of pitch accent in Tokyo Japanese. Doctoral dissertation, Indiana University.

Komatsu, Hideo. 1981. *Nihongo no on'in* [Japanese phonology]. Tokyo: Chuokoronsha.

Kozman, Tam. 1998. The psychological status of syntactic constraints on *rendaku*. In *Japanese/Korean linguistics*, vol. 8, edited by David J. Silva, 107–120. Stanford, Calif.: CSLI Publications.

Kubozono, Haruo. 1988. The organization of Japanese prosody. Doctoral dissertation, University of Edinburgh.

Kubozono, Haruo. 1993. *The organization of Japanese prosody*. Tokyo: Kurosio.

Kubozono, Haruo. 1995. Constraint interaction in Japanese phonology: Evidence from compound accent. In *Phonology at Santa Cruz: Papers on stress, accent, and alignment*, edited by Rachel Walker, Ove Lorentz, and Haruo Kubozono, 21–38. Santa Cruz: University of California, Santa Cruz, Linguistics Research Center.

Kubozono, Haruo, Junko Ito, and Armin Mester. 1997. On'inkôzô-kara mita go-to ku-no kyôkai: Fukugô-meishi akusento-no bunseki [The word/phrase boundary from the perspective of phonological structure: The analysis of nominal compound accent]. In *Bunpô-to onsei. Speech and Grammar*, edited by S. L. R. Group, 147–166. Tokyo: Kurosio.

Kurisu, Kazutaka. 2000. Richness of the base and root fusion in Sino-Japanese. *Journal of East Asian Linguistics* 9, 147–185.

Kurisu, Kazutaka. 2001. The phonology of morpheme realization. Doctoral dissertation, University of California, Santa Cruz. [Available on Rutgers Optimality Archive, http://roa.rutgers.edu, ROA-490-0102.]

Kuroda, S.-Y. 2002. Rendaku. In *Japanese/Korean linguistics*, vol. 10, edited by Noriko Akatsuka and Susan Strauss, 337–350. Stanford, Calif.: CSLI Publications.

Leben, William. 1973. Suprasegmental phonology. Doctoral dissertation, MIT.

Leslau, Wolf. 1997. Amharic phonology. In *Phonologies of Asia and Africa*, vol. 1, edited by Alan S. Kaye, 399–430. Winona Lake, Ind.: Eisenbrauns.

Leumann, Manu. 1977. *Lateinische Laut- und Formenlehre*. Munich: C. H. Beck'sche Verlagsbuchhandlung.

Levin, Juliette. 1985. A metrical theory of syllabicity. Doctoral dissertation, MIT.

Liberman, Mark, and Alan Prince. 1977. On stress and linguistic rhythm. *Linguistic Inquiry* 8, 249–336.

Lombardi, Linda. 1991. Laryngeal features and laryngeal neutralization. Doctoral dissertation, University of Massachusetts, Amherst.

Lombardi, Linda. 1998. Evidence for MaxFeature constraints from Japanese. Ms., University of Maryland, College Park.

Lombardi, Linda. 1999. Positional faithfulness and voicing assimilation in Optimality Theory. *Natural Language and Linguistic Theory* 17, 267–302.

Lombardi, Linda. 2001. Why place and voice are different: Constraint-specific alternations in Optimality Theory. In *Segmental phonology in Optimality Theory: Constraints and representations*, edited by Linda Lombardi, 13–45. Cambridge: Cambridge University Press.

Łubowicz, Anna. 2002. Derived environment effects in Optimality Theory. *Lingua* 112, 243–280.

Lyman, Benjamin S. 1894. Change from surd to sonant in Japanese compounds. *Oriental Studies of the Oriental Club of Philadelphia*, 1–17.

Maddieson, Ian. 1984. *Patterns of sounds.* Cambridge: Cambridge University Press.

Manaster Ramer, Alexis. 1996. A letter from an incompletely neutral phonologist. *Journal of Phonetics* 24, 477–489.

Martin, Samuel E. 1952. *Morphophonemics of standard colloquial Japanese.* Language Dissertation 47. Baltimore, Md.: Linguistic Society of America.

McCarthy, John. 1981. A prosodic theory of nonconcatenative morphology. *Linguistic Inquiry* 12, 373–418.

McCarthy, John. 1983. Consonantal morphology in the Chaha verb. In *Proceedings of the Second West Coast Conference on Linguistics*, edited by Michael Barlow, Daniel Flickinger, and Michael Wescoat, 176–188. Stanford, Calif.: Stanford University, Stanford Linguistics Association.

McCarthy, John J. 1986. OCP effects: Gemination and antigemination. *Linguistic Inquiry* 17, 207–263.

McCarthy, John J. 1988. Feature geometry and dependency: A review. *Phonetica* 43, 84–108.

McCarthy, John J. 1989. Linear order in phonological representation. *Linguistic Inquiry* 20, 71–99.

McCarthy, John J. 1995. Extensions of faithfulness: Rotuman revisited. Ms., University of Massachusetts, Amherst. [Available on Rutgers Optimality Archive, http://roa.rutgers.edu, ROA-110-0000.]

McCarthy, John J. 1999. Sympathy and phonological opacity. *Phonology* 16, 331–399.

McCarthy, John J. 2002a. Comparative markedness. Ms., University of Massachusetts, Amherst. [Available on Rutgers Optimality Archive, http://roa.rutgers.edu, ROA-489-0102.]

McCarthy, John J. 2002b. *A thematic guide to Optimality Theory.* Cambridge: Cambridge University Press.

McCarthy, John J., and Alan S. Prince. 1993a. Generalized Alignment. In *Yearbook of morphology*, edited by Gert Booij and Jaap van Marle, 79–153. Dordrecht Kluwer.

McCarthy, John J., and Alan S. Prince. 1993b. Prosodic Morphology I: Constraint interaction and satisfaction. Ms., University of Massachusetts, Amherst, and Rutgers University. [To appear, MIT Press, Cambridge, Mass.]

McCarthy, John J., and Alan S. Prince. 1994. The emergence of the unmarked: Optimality in prosodic morphology. In *NELS 24*, edited by Mercè Gonzàlez, 333–379. Amherst: University of Massachusetts, GLSA.

McCarthy, John J., and Alan S. Prince. 1995. Faithfulness and reduplicative identity. In *Papers in Optimality Theory*, edited by Jill N. Beckman, Laura Walsh, and Suzanne Urban-czyk, 249–384. Amherst: University of Massachusetts, GLSA.

McCawley, James D. 1968. *The phonological component of a grammar of Japanese*. The Hague: Mouton.

McCawley, James D. 1977. Accent in Japanese. In *Studies in stress and accent*, edited by Larry Hyman, 261–302. Southern California Occasional Papers in Linguistics 4. Los Angeles: University of Southern California, Department of Linguistics.

Meade, Rocky R. 1998. Toward an OT grammar of a creole continuum. Ms., University of Amsterdam and University of the West Indies, Mona.

Mester, Armin. 1986. Studies in tier structure. Doctoral dissertation, University of Massachusetts, Amherst. [Published, New York: Garland, 1988.]

Mester, Armin. 1994. The quantitative trochee in Latin. *Natural Language and Linguistic Theory* 12, 1–61.

Mester, Armin, and Junko Ito. 1989. Feature predictability and underspecification: Palatal prosody in Japanese mimetics. *Language* 65, 258–293.

Miyake, Takerô. 1932. Dakuon kô [A study of voiced sounds]. *Onsei no kenkyû* 5, 135–192.

Mohanan, K. P. 1986. *The theory of Lexical Phonology.* Dordrecht: Reidel.

Mori, Yoko. 2001. Lengthening of Japanese monomoraic nouns. Handout of talk given at the meeting of the Phonological Association in Kansai (PAIK), Doshisha University, Kyoto, Japan, April 2001.

Myers, Scott. 1987. Tone and the structure of words in Shona. Doctoral dissertation, University of Massachusetts, Amherst. [Published, New York: Garland, 1989.]

Nasu, Akio. 1999. Onomatope-ni okeru yuuseika-to [p]-no yuuhyoosei [Voicing in onomatopoeia and the markedness of [p]]. *Journal of the Phonetic Society of Japan* 3, 52–66.

Nathan, Lance. 2001. Constraint conjunction and OTP. Ms., MIT.

Nelson, Nicole. 1998. Right anchor, aweigh. Ms., Rutgers University.

Nespor, Marina, and Irene Vogel. 1986. *Prosodic phonology.* Dordrecht: Foris.

Ní Chiosáin, Máire, and Jaye Padgett. 2001. Markedness, segment realization, and locality in spreading. In *Segmental phonology in Optimality Theory: Constraints and representations*, edited by Linda Lombardi, 118–156. Cambridge: Cambridge University Press.

Nishimura, Kohei. 2001. Lyman's Law in Japanese loanwords. Handout of talk given at the meeting of the Phonological Association in Korea (PAIK), Kobe University, October 2001.

Noske, Manuela. 2000. [ATR] harmony in Turkana: A case of Faith Suffix ≫ Faith Root. *Natural Language and Linguistic Theory* 18, 771–812.

Odden, David. 1994. Adjacency parameters in phonology. *Language* 70, 289–330.

Ohala, Manjari. 1983. *Aspects of Hindi phonology*. Delhi: Motilal Banarsidass.

Ohno, Kazutoshi. 2000. The lexical nature of *rendaku* in Japanese. In *Japanese/Korean linguistics*, vol. 9, edited by Mineharu Nakayama and Charles J. Quinn, 151–164. Stanford, Calif.: CSLI Publications.

Otsu, Yukio. 1980. Some aspects of *rendaku* in Japanese and related problems. In *Theoretical issues in Japanese linguistics*, edited by Yukio Otsu and Ann Farmer, 207–228. MIT Working Papers in Linguistics 2. Cambridge, Mass.: MIT, Department of Linguistics and Philosophy, MITWPL.

Padgett, Jaye. 1995a. Partial class behavior and nasal place assimilation. In *Proceedings of the South Western Optimality Theory Workshop 1995*, edited by Keiichiro Suzuki and Dirk Elzinga, 145–183. Tucson: University of Arizona, Department of Linguistics.

Padgett, Jaye. 1995b. *Stricture in feature geometry*. Stanford, Calif.: CSLI Publications.

Padgett, Jaye. 1997. Perceptual distance of contrast: Vowel height and nasality. In *Phonology at Santa Cruz 5*, edited by Dan Karvonen, Motoko Katayama, and Rachel Walker, 63–78. Santa Cruz: University of California, Santa Cruz, Linguistics Research Center.

Padgett, Jaye. 2002. Constraint conjunction versus grounded constraint subhierarchies in Optimality Theory. Ms., University of California, Santa Cruz.

Padgett, Jaye. 2003. Contrast and post-velar fronting in Russian. *Natural Language and Linguistic Theory* 21, 39–87.

Paradis, Carole, and Jean-François Prunet, eds. 1991. *The special status of coronals: Internal and external evidence*. San Diego, Calif.: Academic Press.

Pater, Joe. 1996. *NC. In *NELS 26*, edited by Kiyomi Kusumoto, 227–239. Amherst: University of Massachusetts, GLSA.

Pater, Joe. 2000. Nonuniformity in English secondary stress: The role of ranked and lexically specific constraints. *Phonology* 17, 237–274.

Paul, Hermann. 1880. *Prinzipien der Sprachgeschichte*. 5th ed., 1920. Tübingen: Niemeyer.

Pierrehumbert, Janet, and Mary Beckman. 1988. *Japanese tone structure*. Cambridge, Mass.: MIT Press.

Pinker, Steven. 1999. *Words and rules: The ingredients of language*. New York: Basic Books.

Port, Robert, and Penny Crawford. 1989. Incomplete neutralization and pragmatics in German. *Journal of Phonetics* 17, 257–282.

Port, Robert, and Michael O'Dell. 1985. Neutralization of syllable-final voicing in German. *Journal of Phonetics* 13, 455–471.

Poser, William J. 1984. The phonetics and phonology of tone and intonation in Japanese. Doctoral dissertation, MIT.

Poser, William J. 1990. Evidence for foot structure in Japanese. *Language* 66, 78–105.

Postal, Paul. 1968. *Aspects of phonological theory*. New York: Harper and Row.

Prince, Alan. 1987. Planes and copying. *Linguistic Inquiry* 18, 491–510.

Prince, Alan. 1990. Quantitative consequences of rhythmic organization. In *Parasession on the Syllable in Phonetics and Phonology*, edited by Michael Ziolkowski, Manuela Noske, and Karen Deaton, 355–398. Chicago: University of Chicago, Chicago Linguistic Society.

Prince, Alan. 1997. Elsewhere and otherwise. Ms., Rutgers University. [Available on Rutgers Optimality Archive, http://roa.rutgers.edu, ROA-217-0997.]

Prince, Alan. 1998. Foundations of Optimality Theory. Handout of lecture given at the Phonology Forum 1998, Kobe University, Japan, September 1998.

Prince, Alan. 2001. Invariance under re-ranking. Handout of lecture given at West Coast Conference on Formal Linguistics xx, University of Southern California, February 2001.

Prince, Alan, and Paul Smolensky. 1993. Optimality Theory: Constraint interaction in generative grammar. Ms., Rutgers University and University of Colorado, Boulder.

Prince, Alan, and Bruce Tesar. 1999. Learning phonotactic distributions. Ms., Rutgers University. [Available on Rutgers Optimality Archive, http://roa.rutgers.edu, ROA-353-1099.]

Pulleyblank, Douglas. 1986. *Tone in Lexical Phonology.* Dordrecht: Reidel.

Pullum, Geoffrey, and Arnold Zwicky. 1988. The syntax-phonology interface. In *Linguistics: The Cambridge survey*, edited by Frederic Newmeyer, 255–280. Cambridge: Cambridge University Press.

Ramsey, S. Robert, and James Marshall Unger. 1972. Evidence for a consonant shift in 7th century Japanese. *Papers in Japanese Linguistics* 1, 278–295.

Revithiadou, Anthi. 1999. Headmost accent wins: Head dominance and ideal prosodic form in lexical accent systems. Doctoral dissertation, Leiden University.

Rice, Keren. 1997. Japanese NC clusters and the redundancy of postnasal voicing. *Linguistic Inquiry* 28, 541–551.

Rose, Sharon, and Rachel Walker. 2001. A typology of consonantal agreement as correspondence. Ms., University of Southern California. [Available on Rutgers Optimality Archive, http://roa.rutgers.edu, ROA-458-0801.]

Rosen, Eric Robert. 2001. Phonological processes interacting with the lexicon: Variable and non-regular effects in Japanese phonology. Doctoral dissertation, University of British Columbia.

Sansom, George. 1928. *An historical grammar of Japanese.* Oxford: Clarendon Press.

Sato, Hirokazu. 1988. Fukugôgo ni okeru akusento kisoku to rendaku kisoku [The accent rule and the *rendaku* rule in compounds]. *Nihongo no Onsei to On'in* 2, 233–265.

Schlindwein, Deborah. 1986. Tier alignment in reduplication. In *Proceedings of NELS 16*, edited by Steve Berman, Jae-Woong Choe, and Joyce McDonough, 419–433. Amherst: University of Massachusetts, GLSA.

Sei Shōnagon. n.d. *Makura-no sōsi* [Pillow book]. Translated by Ivan Morris. New York: Columbia University Press, 1991.

Selkirk, Elisabeth. 1980. Prosodic domains in phonology: Sanskrit revisited. In *Juncture*, edited by Mark Aronoff and Mary-Louise Kean, 107–129. Saratoga, Calif.: Anma Libri.

Selkirk, Elisabeth. 1984. *Phonology and syntax: The relation between sound and structure.* Cambridge, Mass.: MIT Press.

Selkirk, Elisabeth. 1986. On derived domains in sentence phonology. *Phonology* 3, 371–405.

Selkirk, Elisabeth, and Koichi Tateishi. 1988. Constraints on minor phrase formation in Japanese. In *CLS 24*, edited by Lynn McLeod, Gary Larson, and Diane Brentari, 316–336. Chicago: University of Chicago, Chicago Linguistic Society.

Shinmura, Izuru, ed. 1983. *Koozien* [Comprehensive dictionary]. Tokyo: Iwanami.

Sihler, Andrew L. 1995. *New comparative grammar of Greek and Latin*. Oxford: Oxford University Press.

Smith, Jennifer. 1998. Noun faithfulness: Evidence from accent in Japanese dialects. In *Japanese/Korean linguistics 7*, edited by Noriko Akatsuka, Hajime Hoji, Shoichi Iwasaki, Sung-Ock Sohn, and Susan Strauss, 611–627. Stanford, Calif.: CSLI Publications.

Smith, Jennifer. 2001. Phonological augmentation in prominent positions. Doctoral dissertation, University of Massachusetts, Amherst.

Smolensky, Paul. 1993. Harmony, markedness, and phonological activity. Handout from Rutgers Optimality Workshop I, Rutgers University, October 1993.

Smolensky, Paul. 1995. On the internal structure of the constraint component Con of UG. Handout of talk given at University of Arizona, March 1995.

Smolensky, Paul. 1997. Constraint interaction in generative grammar II: Local conjunction. Handout of talk given at the Hopkins Optimality Theory Workshop/University of Maryland Mayfest, May 1997.

Smolensky, Paul, Lisa Davidson, and Peter Jusczyk. 2000. The initial and final states: Theoretical implications and experimental explorations of richness of the base. Ms., Johns Hopkins University.

Spaelti, Philip. 1994. Weak edges and final geminates in Swiss German. In *NELS 24*, edited by Mercè Gonzàlez, 573–588. Amherst: University of Massachusetts, GLSA.

Spaelti, Philip. 1997. Dimensions of variation in multi-pattern reduplication. Doctoral dissertation, University of California, Santa Cruz.

Spencer, Andrew. 1988. Bracketing paradoxes and the English lexicon. *Language* 64, 663–682.

Steriade, Donca. 1982. Greek prosodies and the nature of syllabification. Doctoral dissertation, MIT.

Steriade, Donca. 1987. Redundant values. In *CLS 23: Parasession on Autosegmental and Metrical Phonology*, edited by Anna Bosch, Barbara Need, and Eric Schiller, 339–362. Chicago: University of Chicago, Chicago Linguistic Society.

Steriade, Donca. 1988. Reduplication and syllable transfer in Sanskrit and elsewhere. *Phonology* 5, 73–155.

Steriade, Donca. 1995a. Positional neutralization. Ms., University of California, Los Angeles.

Steriade, Donca. 1995b. Underspecification and markedness. In *The handbook of phonological theory*, edited by John Goldsmith, 114–174. Oxford: Blackwell.

Steriade, Donca. 1997. Lexical conservatism and its analysis. Ms., University of California, Los Angeles.

Struijke, Caro. 2000. Reduplication, feature displacement, and existential faithfulness. Doctoral dissertation, University of Maryland, College Park.

Sugioka, Yoko. 1984. Interaction of derivational morphology and syntax in Japanese and English. Doctoral dissertation, University of Chicago. [Published, New York: Garland, 1986.]

Sugito, Miyoko. 1965. Shibata-san to Imada-san: Tango-no chookakuteki benbetsu-no ichi koosatsu [Mr. Shiba-ta and Mr. Ima-da: A study in the auditory differentiation of words]. *Gengo Seikatsu* 165, 64–72.

Suzuki, Keiichiro. 1997. NN: Rendaku and licensing paradox. In *Japanese/Korean linguistics 6*, edited by Ho-min Sohn and John Haig, 215–228. Stanford, Calif.: CSLI Publications.

Suzuki, Keiichiro. 1998. A typological investigation of dissimilation. Doctoral dissertation, University of Arizona.

Takayama, Tomoaki. 1999. Shakuyoogo-no rendaku/kooonka-ni-tsuite [On *rendaku*/strengthening in loanwords]. In *Report of the Special Research Project for the Typological Investigation of Languages and Cultures of the East and West. Part I*, 375–385. Tsukuba, Japan: Tsukuba University.

Tanaka, Shin-ichi. 2001a. Factorial typology in Japanese compound accentuation. Handout of talk presented at the meeting of the Phonological Association in Kansai (PAIK), February 2001.

Tanaka, Shin-ichi. 2001b. The emergence of the "unaccented": Possible patterns and variations in Japanese compound accentuation. In *Issues in Japanese phonology and morphology*, edited by Jeroen van de Weijer and Tetsuo Nishihara, 159–192. Berlin: Mouton de Gruyter.

Tateishi, Koichi. 1990. Phonology of Sino-Japanese morphemes. In *General linguistics*, edited by Greg Lamontagne and Alison Taub, 209–235. University of Massachusetts Occasional Papers in Linguistics 13. Amherst: University of Massachusetts, GLSA.

Tesar, Bruce. 1995. Computational Optimality Theory. Doctoral dissertation, Rutgers University.

Tesar, Bruce, and Paul Smolensky. 1998. Learnability in Optimality Theory. *Linguistic Inquiry* 29, 229–268.

Tranel, Bernard. 1998. Suppletion and OT: On the issue of the syntax/phonology interaction. In *Proceedings of the Sixteenth West Coast Conference on Formal Linguistics*, edited by Emily Curtis, James Lyle, and Gabriel Webster, 415–429. Stanford, Calif.: CSLI Publications.

Trigo, Loren. 1988. On the phonological derivation and behavior of nasal glides. Doctoral dissertation, MIT.

Trubetzkoy, Nikolai Sergeevich. 1939. *Grundzüge der Phonologie.* Göttingen: Vandenhoeck and Ruprecht.

Truckenbrodt, Hubert. 1999. On the relation between syntactic phrases and phonological phrases. *Linguistic Inquiry* 30, 219–255.

Tsuchida, Ayako. 1997. Phonetics and phonology of Japanese vowel devoicing. Doctoral dissertation, Cornell University.

Tsujimura, Natsuko. 1996. *An introduction to Japanese linguistics.* Oxford: Blackwell.

Tucker, Archibald Norman. 1969. Review of Burssens, A. (1969) *Problemen en inventarisatie van de verbale strukturen in het dho alur (Noordoost-Kongo). Journal of African Languages* 8, 125–126.

Unger, James Marshall. 1975. Studies in early Japanese morphophonemics. Doctoral dissertation, Yale University.

Unger, James Marshall. 1986. Some notes on rômazi. *JAT Bulletin* 11.

Unger, James Marshall. 2000. *Rendaku* and proto-Japanese accent classes. In *Japanese/Korean linguistics 9*, edited by Mineharu Nakayama and Charles J. Quinn, Jr., 17–30. Stanford, Calif.: CSLI Publications.

Ussishkin, Adam Panter. 2000. The emergence of fixed prosody. Doctoral dissertation, University of California, Santa Cruz.

Ussishkin, Adam Panter, and Andrew Wedel. 2002. Neighborhood density and the root-affix distinction. In *NELS 32*, edited by Masako Hirotani, 539–549. Amherst: University of Massachusetts, GLSA.

Vance, Timothy J. 1987. *An introduction to Japanese phonology*. New York: SUNY Press.

Vance, Timothy J. 2002. Sequential voicing and Lyman's Law in Old Japanese. Ms., University of Arizona, Tucson.

Vennemann, Theo. 1972. On the theory of syllabic phonology. *Linguistische Berichte* 18, 1–18.

Wade, Juliette. 1996. An examination of word borrowings into Japanese. Master's thesis, University of California, Santa Cruz.

Walker, Rachel. 1997. Faith and markedness in Esimbi transfer. In *Phonology at Santa Cruz 5*, edited by Rachel Walker, Motoko Katayama, and Daniel Karvonen, 103–115. Santa Cruz: University of California, Santa Cruz, Linguistics Research Center.

Walker, Rachel. 1998. Nasalization, neutral segments, and opacity effects. Doctoral dissertation, University of California, Santa Cruz. [Published, New York: Garland, 2001.]

Whitney, William Dwight. 1889. *Sanskrit grammar*. Cambridge, Mass.: Harvard University Press.

Yip, Moira. 1993. Cantonese loanword phonology and Optimality Theory. *Journal of East Asian Linguistics* 2, 261–292.

Yip, Moira. 1998. Identity avoidance in phonology and morphology. In *Morphology and its relation to phonology and syntax*, edited by Steven G. Lapointe, Diane K. Brentari, and Patrick Farrell, 216–246. Stanford, Calif.: CSLI Publications.

Zoll, Cheryl. 1997. Conflicting directionality. *Phonology* 14, 263–286.

Zoll, Cheryl. 1998. Positional asymmetries and licensing. Ms., MIT. [Available on Rutgers Optimality Archive, http://roa.rutgers.edu, ROA-282-0998.]

Index